Global Logistics and Supply Chain Management

Second Edition

Global Logistics and Supply Chain Management

Second Edition

John Mangan,
Chandra Lalwani, Tim Butcher and Roya Javadpour

John Wiley & Sons, Ltd

This edition first published 2012
© 2012 John Wiley & Sons Ltd

Registered office
John Wiley & Sons Ltd, The Atrium, Southern Gate, Chichester, West Sussex, PO19 8SQ, United Kingdom

For details of our global editorial offices, for customer services and for information about how to apply for permission to reuse the copyright material in this book please see our website at www.wiley.com.

The right of John Mangan, Chandra Lalwani, Tim Butcher and Roya Javadpour to be identified as the authors of this work has been asserted in accordance with the Copyright, Designs and Patents Act 1988.

Reprinted April 2012, August 2012

Library of Congress Cataloging-in-Publication Data

Global logistics and supply chain management / John Mangan . . . [et al.]. — 2nd ed.
    p. cm.
  Rev. ed. of: Global logistics and supply chain management / John Mangan, Chandra Lalwani
and Tim Butcher. c2008.
  Includes bibliographical references and index.
  ISBN 978-1-119-99884-6 (pbk.)
 1. Business logistics. I.Mangan, John, 1968- II. Mangan, John, 1968- Global logistics
and supply chain management.
  HD38.5.M3637 2011
  658.7—dc23

                                                                                    2011028966

A catalogue record for this book is available from the British Library.

Set in 10/13 Optima Roman by Thomson Digital, India
Printed in Great Britain by CPI Group (UK) Ltd, Croydon, CR0 4YY

Dedication

Maeve, Cathal, Eibhlín and Eoghan
Mohini, Nikita and Nishant
Brenda, Malcolm, Jen and Beth
Mahin and Hossein

Contents

About the authors   ix

About the contributors   xi

Foreword   xv

Preface   xvii

Acknowledgements   xxi

Map   xxiii

PART ONE – LOGISTICS AND SUPPLY CHAIN CONTEXT   1
  1. Introduction   3
    Appendix: Containers and Container Seals   20
  2. Globalisation and International Trade   23
  3. Supply Chain Relationships   36
  4. Supply Chain Strategies   59
  5. Simulation   78
    Appendix: Student *t* table   94
  Part One Case Studies   95
    Dell: High Velocity, Focused Supply Chain Management   95
    The Medical Devices Company   98
    Humanitarian Aid Supply Chains   99
    Mediaware – Turning the Supply Chain Upside Down in Packaging   107
    Collaborative Planning in an Auto Parts Supply Chain in China:
    A Tale of Two Tier-One Suppliers   112

PART TWO – LOGISTICS AND SUPPLY CHAIN OPERATIONS   121
  6. Transport in Supply Chains   123
    Appendix A: Transportation Model   134
    Appendix B: Planning Transport Infrastructure   137
  7. Transport Security   142
  8. Logistics Service Providers   153
  9. Procurement   166
  10. Inventory Management   189
  11. Warehousing and Materials Handling   210

12. Information Flows and Technology 227
13. Logistics and Financial Management 247
14. Measuring and Managing Logistics Performance 266
Part Two Case Studies **284**
  John Lewis Partnership: Semi Automated National Distribution Centre ... 284
  Deutsche Post/DHL 290
  Gate Gourmet: Success Means Getting to the Plane on Time ... 295
  Supplier Evaluation at EADS 300

PART THREE – SUPPLY CHAIN DESIGNS **305**
15. Supply Chain Vulnerability, Risk, Robustness and Resilience ... 307
16. Sustainable Logistics and Supply Chain Systems 326
17. Reverse Logistics 338
18. Service Supply Chains 355
19. Emerging Supply Chain Designs 366
Part Three Case Studies **378**
  Patient Safety and the Pharmaceutical Supply Chain 378
  Contamination in the Bulk Agri-Commodity Logistics Chain ... 386
  Why Supply Chains should be Involved in Product Design ... 393
  From Terrestrial to Extraterrestrial Supply Chain Networks ... 397

Glossary **399**
Index **411**

About the Authors

John Mangan is Professor of Marine Transport and Logistics at Newcastle University in the UK. Born in Cork, Ireland, he holds a PhD degree from Cardiff University, Masters degrees from both Cranfield and Lancaster Universities, and a BSc degree from University College Cork. He was a Fulbright Scholar at Boston College and also spent a sabbatical teaching at MIT. Initially he worked as an air freight clerk (Aer Lingus) and then as a civil servant (Irish Civil Service – Marine and Finance ministries). He subsequently held academic appointments at University College Dublin, the Irish Management Institute and the University of Hull (where he was founding Director of the University of Hull Logistics Institute). He has conducted a range of consulting assignments for both public and private sector clients and has served as an independent evaluator for the European Commission. He also regularly teaches on graduate and executive education programmes in logistics and related areas. John's teaching and research is primarily focused upon global logistics and supply chain management, maritime transport and logistics management development. He has an extensive raft of publications and is co-editor of the *International Journal of Logistics: Research and Applications*. He has supervised many PhD students and regularly sits on PhD examination committees; in addition he is external examiner at a number of universities. He has participated in a variety of funded research projects, a recent example being the multi-partner 'Low Carbon Shipping: a Systems Approach' research project (www .lowcarbonshipping.co.uk) where he is one of the principal investigators.

Chandra Lalwani is Emeritus Professor of Supply Chain Management at the University of Hull Business School. He is a Visiting Professor at Newcastle University in the UK and at RMIT University in Australia. He holds a BEng in Electrical Engineering, an MEng in Control Systems and another MEng in Systems Engineering. He obtained his PhD from the University of Wales in 1978 based on his research on the dynamic modelling of commodity flow systems. Prior to joining the University of Hull he taught at Cardiff University Business School and was responsible for doctoral research in logistics and operations management. Professor Lalwani was a Deputy Director and Co-investigator at Cardiff Business School on the Cardiff University Innovative Manufacturing Research Centre, and Principal Investigator on one of its three flagship research projects on sustainable logistics. Chandra's teaching and research focus is on supply chain management, retail logistics, logistics and transport modelling, and integration of transport in supply chains. With his research in transport in supply chains, he has worked closely with the retail and distribution industry in the UK. He is also a member of a consortium in the UK researching into low carbon shipping and is co-editor in chief of *International Journal of Logistics Management* published by Emerald.

Tim Butcher is a Senior Lecturer at RMIT University's School of Management in Melbourne, Australia. Besides his research and lecturing responsibilities, he is Deputy Head of School for Industry Engagement. Tim holds a BEng (Hons) (University of Liverpool), an MSc (Cranfield University), and EngD (Cranfield University), and previously worked in production and maintainability engineering in the aerospace sector. His last academic role was as MSc Programme Director at the University of Hull Logistics Institute. He has led various manufacturing, logistics and business improvement projects as a practitioner, a researcher and as a research supervisor. Tim researches the impact of technologies on work and society, with particular reference to logistics and supply chain management. His current research interests include inter-organisational social networks, distributed decision making and local versus global sourcing. Tim currently teaches the History of Management Thought at undergraduate level and Sustainable Practice at Masters level for RMIT, plus Operations Management on the Hull Executive MBA.

Roya Javadpour is Professor of Industrial and Manufacturing Engineering at California Polytechnic State University in San Luis Obispo, California. She holds a BS in Industrial Engineering (Isfahan University of Technology), MS in Industrial Engineering (Louisiana State University), MS in Engineering Science (Louisiana State University), and PhD in Engineering Science with Industrial Engineering emphasis (Louisiana State University). Prior to joining academia Roya worked as a supply chain management consultant at i2 Technologies, Inc. Before her appointment at Cal Poly, Roya taught at the University of San Diego as Visiting Professor of Engineering. Roya's teaching and research is mainly focused on supply chain management and project management. In addition to her teaching and research roles at Cal Poly, she is the founder of the PolyHouse Project, an annual home improvement project for local economically disadvantaged families who have one or more members challenged by a physical disability. She initially pursued this innovative approach to teaching project management skills in 2004 as part of her graduate level Technological Project Management course and was recognised as runner up for the International Innovation in Curriculum Award sponsored by the IIE Council of Industrial Engineering Academic Department Heads in 2008. Her other recent awards include: Northrop Grumman Excellence in Teaching Award, Cal Poly President's Innovation in Service Award and she was named one of the San Luis Obispo Tribune's 'Top 20 Under 40' in recognition of her professional excellence in her field and commitment to the community.

About the Contributors

Peter Baker (Chapter 11 plus the John Lewis case) is a Senior Lecturer at the Centre for Logistics and Supply Chain Management at Cranfield School of Management, lecturing on Warehousing and International Transport. He spent the early part of his career in international freight forwarding. After taking an MSc in Distribution and Technology at Cranfield, he entered supply chain consultancy, where he undertook over 70 supply chain projects across a wide range of industries and public sector organisations in many parts of the world. These projects have included supply chain strategy, procurement, international logistics, distribution centre design, inventory control, transport operations and supporting computer systems. He then joined Cranfield University as a lecturer where he successfully completed a PhD by publication, on the subject of the role, design and operation of distribution centres in agile supply chains. He is a Fellow of the Chartered Institute of Logistics and Transport (UK) and a Fellow of the Higher Education Academy. He has published regularly in quality journals namely: *International Journal of Logistics Management*, *International Journal of Logistics: Research and Applications*, *Supply Chain Management: An International Journal*, *International Journal of Production Economics* and the *European Journal of Operational Research*.

Chuda Basnet (Chapter 10) is an Associate Professor at the University of Waikato, New Zealand. He has received a Bachelor's degree in Mechanical Engineering, a Master's degree in Industrial and Management Engineering, and a PhD in Industrial Engineering and Management. He teaches in the areas of operations management and supply chain management. His research interests are in manufacturing modelling, supply chain management and decision support systems. He has published papers in *Decision Support Systems*, *Journal of the Operational Research Society* and *Annals of Operations Research*.

Paul Childerhouse (Chapter 10) is an Associate Professor at the University of Waikato. He obtained his PhD in 2002 whilst a member of the Logistics Systems Dynamics Group at Cardiff University for his research into supply chain integration and market orientation. His major research interests are in supply chain change management and the development of methods to enable supply chain integration and market orientation. He is practitioner focused and enjoys auditing and advising organisations on how to improve their supply chain practices. This focus has resulted in a great deal of first-hand industrial knowledge especially in the automotive, aerospace, dairy, construction and retail sectors. He has published over 20 articles in quality journals including: *Journal of*

Business Logistics, Journal of Operations Management, International Journal of Physical Distribution and Logistics Management, International Journal of Production Research and *OMEGA*.

Noel McGlynn (Chapter 14) is employed by Microsoft as a Senior Logistics Manager, and is currently working on a range of performance improvement initiatives within the company's European Operations Centre based in Ireland. He previously has held the role of Business Relationship Manager for Hewlett-Packard in Ireland, where he had specific responsibility for managing third-party logistics providers. He has also worked for Irish Express Cargo/Flextronics Logistics in a range of logistics related roles in Europe, the USA and Asia. He holds a Bachelor's degree in Commerce and a Master's degree in Business Studies, both from the National University of Ireland, Dublin.

Martin Murphy (Chapter 9) is the Managing Director of SCMG (Supply Chain Management Group). He has worked internationally with businesses and organisations over the last 20 years providing strategic advice and tactical support on supply chain projects. This includes oil and gas companies, chemicals and refining, pharmaceuticals, aerospace and defence, manufacturing, automotive, rail and transport through to local and central government, non-departmental public bodies and the higher education sector. He has worked on assignments all over Europe, North America, the Middle East and Far East. He has a degree in Mechanical Engineering and an MBA. Martin is a Member of the Advisory Board to CSIRN (Complex Services Innovation Research Network) at the University of Glasgow, an Industry Advisor to *Strategic Outsourcing*, an international journal, and a Member of the Institute of Directors.

Helen Peck (Chapter 15) is a Senior Lecturer in Commercial & Supply Chain Risk in the Department of Management and Security at Cranfield University. She joined the university in 1983, having previously worked for a major UK clearing bank. Initially employed within the university's library and information service, Helen transferred to the academic staff of Cranfield School of Management in 1988, working in the Marketing & Logistics Group where she completed her PhD as a first degree. Today Helen teaches on graduate programmes and short courses at the DDMSA and guest lectures at a number of other universities in the UK. She has led Cranfield University's government-funded programme of research into all aspects of supply chain related risk and resilience since its inception in May 2001. She is author of numerous academic papers and practitioner journal articles, co-editor and author of several books, and an award-winning writer of management case studies. Her research and consultancy interests span mainstream commercial, defence and other public service contexts. Helen is a regular speaker at academic, business and defence conferences around the world.

Shams Rahman (Chapter 17) is a Professor of Supply Chain Management at the School of Business IT and Logistics, RMIT University, Australia. His academic qualifications include an ME in Industrial Engineering, MSc in Mechanical Engineering and PhD in Operations Research. Shams, a former British Commonwealth scholar, has worked in various universities in Australia, the UK and Thailand. In Australia he worked for the University of Western Australia, University of Sydney, Wollongong University, prior to joining RMIT

University. He also held visiting fellowship at the Virginia Tech, USA and University of Exeter, UK. Shams has extensive consulting experience, organising and delivering workshops and training with and for multinational companies. He is frequently called upon to make presentations for professional bodies and senior executives on issues such as lean approaches, six sigma and quality management, reverse logistics, cold chain and theory of constraints. He is on the editorial board of 10 international journals and has published widely in international academic and trade journals. He is a foundation member of the International Advisory Committee of the Asia-Pacific Federation of Logistics and Supply Chain Systems.

Risto Talas (Chapter 7 and Chapter 1 Appendix) is a Research Fellow at Hull University Logistics Institute. He recently completed his PhD at Cass Business School in the field of maritime port security. Previously he worked for Maritime and Underwater Security Consultants Ltd as a port security consultant which included a secondment to UK Trade & Investment as an International Business Specialist promoting UK companies in the port security sector. Prior to his MBA at Cass Business School he worked as a marine war and terrorism underwriter for a Marine Syndicate at Lloyd's of London. He is also a visiting lecturer at the School of Engineering and Mathematical Sciences at City University lecturing in maritime security studies and at Cass Business School lecturing in supply chain security. He is the author of various book chapters, academic and newspaper articles in maritime security and piracy.

Mike Tayles (Chapter 13) is Emeritus Professor of Accounting and Finance at Hull University Business School. He is also a Visiting Professor in Barcelona, Spain and in Malaysia. He is the European editor of the *Managerial Auditing Journal* and on the editorial boards of other journals. Mike is a Chartered Management Accountant with approximately 10 years' experience in industry and commerce, some of this at a senior level. His first degree is in economics and statistics and his PhD involved a study of contemporary management accounting practices. In the last 10 years he has produced almost 100 publications in academic and professional journals, research monographs, textbook chapters and conference presentations. He has experience of and publications from both survey and case study research. Mike has worked in the food processing, light engineering and textile industries and has consulting and research experience in various manufacturing, service and not-for-profit businesses.

The following authors provided case studies: Dr Peter Baker, Mr Ciarán Brady (PLS Pharma Logistics), Professor Louis Brennan (Trinity College Dublin), Professor Marc Day (Henley Management College), Mr Tom Ferris, Mr Simon Healy (Mediaware), Dr Graham Heaslip (National University of Ireland, Maynooth), Dr Elizabeth Jackson (Newcastle University), Professor Booi Kam and Mr Jin Hao (RMIT University), Professor Roger Moser (European Business School), Ms Anne Nagle (Nagle Business Solutions), Dr Seamus O'Reilly (University College Cork) and Professor Mike Tayles (University of Hull).

Foreword

It is now almost thirty years since the phrase 'supply chain management' first appeared in print. Since then there has been a revolution in the way that organisations view their upstream supply arrangements and their downstream routes to market. The talk now is of 'end-to-end' pipelines and seamless connectivity and we think in terms of highly inter-dependent networks rather than stand-alone business entities. Of course there are still major gaps between the theory and the practice of supply chain management but there can be no doubting that it is now seen as a key priority in most companies today.

One of the major changes in the way in which logistics and supply chain management is viewed is that whilst originally the focus was primarily on cost reduction there is now a recognition that, properly managed, these ideas can deliver enhanced customer value as well as reducing costs. Hence the reason why in many businesses there is a growing emphasis on the strategic implications of supply chain design and the need for stronger relationships with key partners across the supply chain. It is probably no coincidence that those companies who are leaders in their sectors tend to have created supply chains that are closely aligned with their business goals. In particular these organisations see their supply chain as a vehicle for value-delivery and as a powerful tool for gaining competitive advantage in the marketplace.

These changes in both the philosophy and the practice of logistics and supply chain management underpin the content of this present book and have shaped its innovative structure. It is a book with appeal to both practitioners and students, recognising as it does that new skills and capabilities are needed if the full potential of all we have learned in the brief history of supply chain management is to be achieved. Reading this book and leveraging the ideas it presents will provide a strong foundation for business success.

Martin Christopher
Emeritus Professor of Marketing & Logistics,
Cranfield School of Management

Preface

This book traces its origins to the University of Hull Logistics Institute in the UK where three of the four authors (Mangan, Lalwani and Butcher) worked together between 2005 and 2008. It was during this time that we recognised the need for this textbook which we are glad to say has been very well received by students, practitioners and lecturers, and which we are now happy to present as an updated and enhanced second edition. For this second edition we are delighted that Roya Javadpour from California Polytechnic State University has joined us as a co-author. Since producing our first edition Tim Butcher has moved to Royal Melbourne Institute of Technology (RMIT) in Australia, John Mangan has moved to Newcastle University in the UK, and Chandra Lalwani now shares his time between a number of universities around the world including both Hull and Newcastle in the UK. In this second edition we have endeavoured to again produce a comprehensive book with the following key characteristics:

- *Be concise* – logistics is a very pragmatic subject and it has been our intention throughout to 'stick to the point'. We hope that you the reader will appreciate this. Notwithstanding such intended brevity, we have endeavoured to cover both practical and strategic aspects of the subject matter. The book is neither a 'how to' cook book, nor is it a high-level strategy book with little relevance to practice. The aim of the book is to convey to both advanced students and practitioners of logistics and supply chain management the diverse operational and strategic content of the subjects of logistics and supply chain management.

- *Truly global, up-to-date perspective* – the world is changing daily and the typical 'Western' worldview no longer necessarily dominates. As we will see in the book, logistics is a key driver of globalisation and a facilitator of international trade and development. We have thus endeavoured to reflect these characteristics by adopting a truly global perspective and hope that the book will appeal to students regardless of what geography they are located in. The context of logistics is constantly shaped by emerging trends and new technologies and we have tried to ensure that the book is as up to date as possible and takes cognisance of these trends and technologies. Sadly, despite much progress, today's world still contains many divisions, tensions and inequalities. We have attempted to be aware of these while fully embracing a neutral and non-political perspective.

- *Pedagogical approach* – we have endeavoured to use a variety of pedagogies in this book, which we hope will create a fertile learning platform for the reader. Both long(er) and short(er) case studies are included and are intended to highlight key issues in a focused manner. Key points are detailed in separate boxes and this should also help with revision. Italics are used within the text to emphasise specific issues. Various terms are in bold when first used to indicate that explanations are given in the glossary at the end of the book. We hope you find these various features useful. There are two other features of our pedagogical approach which we believe are especially important.

Firstly, the four authors named on the cover are not the only people to have contributed to this book. We are also very fortunate to have contributions from various experts in specific areas of logistics and supply chain management. They have written chapters and case studies based on their specific areas of expertise and which we believe add to the richness of this book over and above what we could have achieved working on our own. This multidisciplinary approach has allowed us to draw into the book not just logisticians, but also people from backgrounds as diverse as, for example, military and accounting.

The second pedagogical feature we wish to highlight is the mix of qualitative and quantitative content in this book. We are of the view that many logistics books tend to occupy one of two opposite positions, either containing a large share of quantitative material, or else none at all. We believe that a certain level of quantitative aptitude and knowledge is an important feature of most logistics and supply chain managers' jobs (for example, in the areas of logistics costs and inventory management). Many such managers, however, do not routinely engage in sophisticated mathematical analysis; this is usually the domain of operations researchers, engineers and management accountants. We thus aim to convey the necessary quantitative features of logistics and supply chain management, while at the same time not excessively burdening the reader with quantitative analysis.

These various characteristics and perspectives adopted in the book are discussed further in Chapter 1. The book is divided into three parts, again this is discussed, and the content of each part elaborated, in Chapter 1. In this second edition, we have restructured the book and updated relevant content from the first edition. For example the area of relationships in the supply chain is increasingly seen as a topic of importance and we have thus revised and added to the content on this topic which was previously spread across a number of chapters in the first edition; in this second edition this topic is afforded its own chapter (Chapter 3). In addition new chapters have been added dealing with: simulation, security, reverse logistics, and services supply chains. New chapter supplements on containerisation, modelling and transport planning have now been included, and a number of new cases have also been introduced.

BOOK COMPANION WEBSITE

Our text is also supported by additional teaching and learning resources, which are available on the companion website at www.wileyeurope.com/college/mangan. They include PowerPoint slides, suggested answers to end-of-chapter questions and case teaching notes for lecturers. Students will also find an online glossary and multiple choice quizzes.

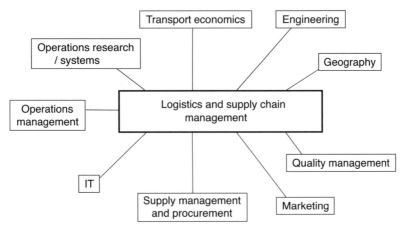

Figure 1   Links to other disciplines

RELATIONSHIP TO OTHER DISCIPLINES, ESPECIALLY OPERATIONS MANAGEMENT

Chapter 1 details the various factors that have led to the evolution of logistics and supply chain management. Figure 1 outlines the various disciplines which we believe logistics and supply chain management are closely linked to. In fact it is only in recent years that third-level courses and explicit career paths have emerged in logistics and supply chain management. It is thus often the case that many practitioners today will have backgrounds in one or other of the disciplines illustrated in Figure 1. Various issues pertaining to some of these disciplines are discussed in this book.

Perhaps the discipline to which logistics and supply chain management is most often closely linked is *operations management*. As we will see in Chapter 1, supply chains involve three interdependent flows: material, information and resources. We discuss these flows in depth throughout the book. The study of operations management is also concerned with these flows. We are in fact of the view that this book could also be effectively used for teaching more general operations management courses, and especially those with a particular emphasis on logistics and supply chain issues. It is becoming increasingly apparent that many operations managers today are engaging more and more in wider supply chain management activities. As processes become increasingly automated and simplified, the focus of many operations managers is shifting to service issues beyond core manufacturing, and to flows and interactions along the supply chain. All of these issues are discussed in this book.

Logistics and supply chain management are ever changing and demanding disciplines, but provide attractive and rewarding opportunities to people who wish to work in these areas. The purpose of this book has been to equip you, the reader, regardless of whether you are a student or a practitioner, with the necessary knowledge and skills to allow you to work more effectively in these areas. We hope you enjoy working with this book and find it of benefit.

John Mangan, Chandra Lalwani, Tim Butcher and Roya Javadpour

Acknowledgements

Many people have helped us on our journey to produce the first and now the second editions of this book. First and foremost, the book would not exist but for the continuing support and advice received from many people at John Wiley & Sons Ltd. These include Sarah Booth, Nicole Burnett, Jennifer Edgecombe, Steve Hardman, and Anneli Mockett. We thank them for their professionalism and patience. We would also like to thank the various anonymous reviewers for their helpful comments. Thanks also to the many lecturers and students who used the first edition: we thank them for their feedback which is always beneficial. Thanks too to our universities and our many colleagues who have given us the space and encouragement to complete this time-consuming, yet rewarding, project.

Special thanks are also due to our mentor and friend Professor Martin Christopher of Cranfield University who kindly again provided the foreword.

Certain specific elements of the book were generated from funded and/or collaborative research undertakings and in this regard we would like to acknowledge with much gratitude the support of the various sponsoring agencies and individuals. We are also very grateful to various copyright holders for allowing us to use certain material.

We sincerely thank the various chapter contributors whose expert inputs have added considerably to our own endeavours: Dr Chuda Basnet and Dr Paul Childerhouse (Waikato University), Dr Peter Baker (Cranfield University), Mr Noel McGlynn (Microsoft), Mr Martin Murphy (SCMG), Dr Helen Peck (Cranfield University), Professor Shams Rahman (RMIT University), Dr Risto Talas (University of Hull) and Professor Mike Tayles (University of Hull). We would like to also thank the various case contributors for agreeing to the inclusion of their insightful cases: Dr Peter Baker, Mr Ciarán Brady (PLS Pharma Logistics), Professor Louis Brennan (Trinity College Dublin), Professor Marc Day (Henley Management College), Mr Tom Ferris, Mr Simon Healy (Mediaware), Dr Graham Heaslip (National University of Ireland, Maynooth), Dr Elizabeth Jackson (Newcastle University), Professor Booi Kam and Mr Jin Hao (RMIT University), Professor Roger Moser (European Business School), Ms Anne Nagle (Nagle Business Solutions), Dr Seamus O'Reilly (University College Cork) and Professor Mike Tayles (University of Hull).

Map

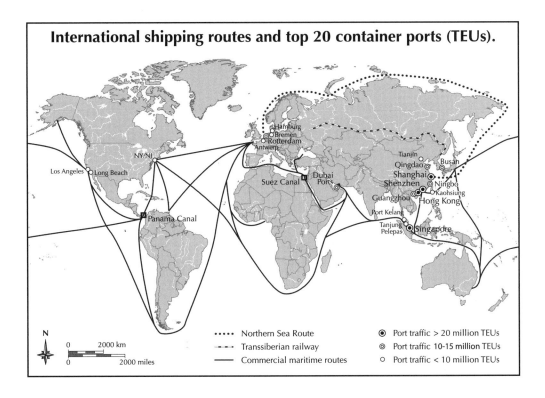

International shipping routes and top 20 container ports (TEUs).

Part One

Logistics and Supply Chain Context

1 Introduction

LEARNING OBJECTIVES

- Explain the origins of logistics and supply chain management.
- Define both terms and outline how logistics and supply chain management differ from each other.
- Highlight the importance of these areas in both manufacturing *and* services contexts.
- Identify how best practice logistics and supply chain management can yield both cost reduction *and* value addition.

INTRODUCTION

This chapter lays the foundations of the textbook and explains the origins and applications of logistics and supply chain management, as well as giving descriptions of key concepts. A framework for the textbook is developed and this illustrates where each chapter fits in the overall schema of the book, while the various perspectives adopted by the authors when writing this book are also described.

The chapter comprises six core sections:
- The evolution of logistics and supply chain management
- What is logistics?
- What is supply chain management?
- Distinguishing logistics and supply chain management
- Applications to manufacturing *and* services
- Book framework

THE EVOLUTION OF LOGISTICS AND SUPPLY CHAIN MANAGEMENT (SCM)

Both logistics and SCM are fascinating and exciting areas that touch all of our lives. Just think of the many different products that are purchased and consumed each day –

> The commonly accepted abbreviation for supply chain management is SCM, so that abbreviation will be used in the remainder of this book.

how do they reach the customer and at what cost? Although logistics and SCM are areas that have only come to widespread prominence in the last two decades or so, the reality is that they have roots which run much longer than that. Later in the chapter we will trace the word 'logistics' back to its original military application in ancient Roman and Byzantine times. One of the first references in the academic literature to the notion of taking a supply chain view (although that specific term was not used) is in what is widely regarded as a seminal paper by the MIT academic Jay Forrester published in the *Harvard Business Review* in 1958.[1] In that paper, Forrester put forward a schematic of the production–distribution system (what we would call today a supply chain) and he simulated how inventory levels can fluctuate along that chain.

Not only are logistics and SCM key aspects of today's business world, but they are also of importance in the not-for-profit and public sectors. In addition, while the origins of much logistics thinking and practice are in a manufacturing context, we are witnessing increased and highly successful application of logistics and SCM principles in a services context also (just think of the efficiencies which have been driven into many service-based activities such as banking and hospitals where the emphasis has shifted to serving more customers, better, faster, cheaper).

The terms logistics and SCM, although often used interchangeably, are distinct and will be defined later in the chapter. First, however, it is appropriate to examine how some key developments over the past couple of decades have shaped the evolution of these important areas. In fact six separate and important developments, each of which evolved largely independently, can be identified and are now detailed.

Reduced transport intensity of freight

In the past, international trade was dominated by bulky raw materials. Times have, however, changed and in-process and finished products, not raw materials, now play a much greater role in world trade. Some simple examples illustrate this clearly. Compare the value of the various consumer electronics products currently being shipped globally each day with the bulky, low-value, agricultural produce shipped around the world 100 years ago. Agricultural produce, and indeed other comparatively high-volume/low-value freight, does still of course traverse the world but, in general, the size and value of the freight which is transported today is very different to that of times past. In the case of agriculture, many food producers, rather than transporting bulky foodstuffs, now tend to try and 'add value' to the product near to the point of production: for example rather than ship live chickens, the international poultry trade generally comprises processed, ready-to-cook chicken. The same is true for many other trades, across a range of industries, whereby manufacturers try and increase the value-to-volume ratio of products being shipped. We will see in later chapters that there is also an increasing trend towards having the final value-adding stages in the production of various products as close as possible to the final customer.

Higher value freight is better able to 'absorb' transport costs than is lower value freight, with the 'transport cost penalty' imposed by having to move freight over greater distances often being somewhat offset by the fact that the freight is of higher value. Hence, we refer to a generally reducing **transport cost sensitivity** of freight.

Indeed for some products it is now not even necessary to ship physical product at all. Just think for example of the way much software is now transmitted around the world via the internet. This replacement of physical product by virtual product is referred to as **material substitution**.

> For many individual shipments: increased value/decreased volume = lower transport cost sensitivity.

Falling product prices

In many markets, increased competition and falling marketplace prices have forced numerous companies to reduce costs. Just think of the falling prices of various electronics products in recent years such as DVD players, or the fact that the prices of many automobiles have stayed flat in real terms at best, despite the fact that product specifications, performance and quality have improved dramatically. This has forced companies to focus on other areas where savings can be made, and the storage and movement of inventory is a key area in this regard. Thus companies will seek to ensure that any products (especially those with flat or declining value) being transported are configured (in terms of product design, packaging etc.) so as to reduce as much as possible their transport cost sensitivity.

Deregulation of transport

The important role played by transport in logistics will be discussed later in the book in particular in Chapters 6 and 8. There are five principal modes of transport namely air, road, water, rail and pipeline. In recent decades transport markets in many countries have been **deregulated** by various governments. The essence of effective deregulation is that by removing unnecessary barriers to competition, markets become more contestable and (in theory at least) prices should come down and service should improve. We say 'in theory' because the reality in some deregulated markets has been somewhat different (with private monopolies sometimes replacing public ones) but, in general and over the long run, deregulation has had a positive impact on many transport markets, leading to the provision of both more and cheaper services. This of course in turn makes it easier and more efficient to move freight around the world.

A good example is that of *FedEx*, a company which today has one of the world's largest air freight fleets. Constrained by burdensome government regulations in the United States in the 1970s, it was not until the late 1970s with the deregulation of the US air freight market (which relaxed the rules governing both who could participate in the market and how they would be allowed to operate) that the company was able to expand and grow.

Productivity improvements

Up to the mid-1950s most maritime freight was carried on bulk vessels. This began to change, however, when some ship owners started to carry freight containers (see Appendix at the end of this chapter on 'Containers and Container Seals' for more information on this topic). In 1956 an iconoclastic entrepreneur Malcom McLean put 58 aluminium truck bodies aboard an ageing tanker ship (called the *Ideal-X*) which set sail from Newark, NJ to Houston, TX in the United States. This marked the start of containerised transport as we know it today.[2] Containers can be stacked on top of each other onboard the ship, thus allowing very efficient space utilisation and cargo handling. Furthermore, freight could now move from origin to destination across many modes and services with greater ease of handling. The introduction and growth of containerisation led to huge changes in ports which previously were dominated by large workforces responsible for manual handling of bulk cargo. Containerisation also reduced the costs of transporting freight by maritime transport and significantly improved its efficiency. Containerisation spread to other modes and various alliances were formed between combinations of transport companies.

There were of course many other improvements in transport, for example in propulsion technologies (faster transport) and the application of various information and communications technologies. Companies such as DHL, FedEx and UPS have pioneered the use of barcoding and online tracking and tracing of freight, developments which also increase the efficiencies of logistics systems. Another technology, radio frequency identification (RFID), is now emerging and should also drive more efficiencies into logistics systems. Technology is a very important component and enabler of logistics and SCM, and Chapter 12 in particular will look in detail at information flows and technology applications.

Emphasis on inventory reduction

The penultimate trend to consider has been a shift of management and financial attention into analysing where an organisation's funds are tied up. Inventory management will be covered in detail in Chapter 10, but suffice to say for now that many organisations have become increasingly aware of the fact that often significant funds are lying tied up in unnecessary inventory. Furthermore it became obvious in the latter years of the twentieth century that often inventory was not well managed. During the decades which followed World War II the responsibility for, and management of, inventory in many firms was very fragmented. The various functions in which inventory played a key role, for example transport, warehousing, purchasing and marketing, were usually considered by managers to be separate and distinct. However, firms began to realise that cost savings and significant efficiency gains could be harnessed from more integrated and focused management of inventory. As far back as 1962 the late Peter Drucker, one of the foremost management thinkers of the twentieth century, wrote a celebrated *Fortune* magazine article entitled 'The Economy's Dark Continent'.[3] In this article he suggested that distribution represented the last frontier for significant cost reduction potential in the firm.

Increased market competition and customer requirements also led to the necessity to see improvements in the management of inventory as an essential competitive weapon. In the increasingly competitive, global marketplace firms began to realise that they could leverage marketplace advantage through superior logistics performance. Cost savings were identified through eliminating unnecessary inventory and just-in-time (JIT) deliveries became normal operating practice in many industries. Indeed many companies came to recognise the risks associated with holding too much stock which rendered them less flexible in their ability to respond to changing demand conditions.

Changes in company structure

A more recent trend concerns changes in how companies are structured and operate. In recent years many companies have become less **vertically integrated** (a concept that implies ownership or at least control of upstream suppliers and downstream customers) and more specialised. Outsourcing has become more common, with suppliers playing a more central role for many manufacturers (subsequent chapters in the book will consider in detail strategies and practices such as JIT, outsourcing, etc). Many companies have also come to realise that so-called functional or silo-based thinking (viewing the various departments within the firm as separate and non-overlapping entities) will only hinder the overall performance of the company and they have as a result endeavoured to ensure that the various functions and activities across the company are integrated more closely. In more recent years in particular, competition based on *time*, for example order to delivery time, has become a key success factor (KSF) in many markets.

All of the above six trends, while they emerged independently, have both placed an increased emphasis on the role of transport and inventory, and have led to improvements in the way freight is handled and moved around the world. They have led to what is often termed the *supply chain revolution*.

Before proceeding further it is important to highlight one small, but important, distinction. People often use the terms 'freight' and 'cargo' interchangeably, however, they are in fact distinct, at least in terms of their use within the logistics sector. In essence: *cargo = freight + mail*. Mail, also known as post, is of course still a very important component of trade and commerce, despite the many technological advances which shape today's world. It is an important and regular source of revenue for many transport companies, especially airlines. Sometimes people also use the term 'goods', usually to refer to freight (not cargo), but we will try to avoid use of this term. Another term worth defining at this juncture is **consignment** which the *Collins English Dictionary* defines as 'a shipment of goods consigned'; we could thus regard a consignment as a shipment of freight which is passed on usually to some type of logistics service provider from a manufacturer or other source.

THE ROLE OF LOGISTICS IN NATIONAL ECONOMIES

The size of the logistics sector varies from country to country. In the UK, for example, it is estimated to be worth £74 billion to the economy, with one in twelve people in the UK working in logistics, some 2.3 million people spanning approximately 196 000 companies.[4]

Economists note that a variety of factors determine the wealth and rate of growth of national economies. These factors are many and varied, and range from available energy sources to institutional factors such as a good banking system. In the late 1990s the US economy experienced a rapid rise in productivity. Closer examination of the economic data by researchers at the McKinsey and Company Global Institute revealed the impact on national productivity of developments in the retail sector, and most notably the impact of the giant retailer Wal-Mart.

According to Beinhocker (2006)[5] 'Wal-Mart's innovations in large-store formats and highly efficient logistical systems in the late 1980s and early 1990s enabled the company to be 40 percent more productive than its competitors'. Wal-Mart has been a global leader in best practice retail logistics, with many other retailers imitating some of its strategies. In the case of the US economy, the increases in Wal-Mart's productivity led to an 'innovation race' with suppliers and other retailers also seeking to enhance their productivity, in turn leading to a rise in whole-sector productivity. Wal-Mart is one of the world's largest companies and in the context of the discussion in this chapter it is interesting to observe the considerable impact and importance of how it organises its logistical systems.

WHAT IS LOGISTICS?

Now that the key developments which have shaped the evolution of logistics and SCM have been outlined, it is appropriate to attempt to describe and define these concepts. Some authors have pointed to the often confusing and overlapping 'plethora of terminology' that is used in logistics and SCM.[6] While at one level defining logistics and SCM might seem an elementary task, it is in fact critically important to define, and differentiate, these terms correctly at this juncture as this will shape your understanding and interpretation of the contents of this book. First to logistics. The *New Oxford Dictionary of English* defines logistics as:

> the detailed coordination of a complex operation involving many people, facilities, or supplies. Origin late 19th century in the sense 'movement and supplying of troops and equipment', from French *logistique*, from *loger* lodge

There are various views with regard to the linguistic origins of the word, with some pointing to the Greek adjective *logistikos* which means 'skilled in calculating' (and which most likely gave us the mathematical term *logistic*). It has also been noted that in Roman and Byzantine times there was a military official called *Logista*. In more recent times we have seen, as in the above definition, the French words *logistique* and *loger*. Most agree that the word entered the English language in the 19th century, with its application generally seen in military terms and concerned with the organisation of moving, lodging and supplying troops and equipment.

These origins suggest then that logistics has something to do with applications of mathematics and is primarily a military concern. Indeed the field of military logistics has evolved quite considerably and is now quite sophisticated.[7] Similarly there are many useful applications of mathematics to logistics. Today, however, logistics spans beyond the military and mathematical domains. It was in fact only in the latter decades of the 20th century that the term logistics entered into common non-military use. The US based Council of Supply Chain Management Professionals (www.cscmp.org) suggests the following definition of logistics and which we adopt in this book (note: we have added the underlining (of transportation and storage) to the original definition):

> **Logistics** is the process of planning, implementing, and controlling procedures for the efficient and effective <u>transportation</u> and <u>storage</u> of goods including services, and related information from the point of origin to the point of consumption for the purpose of conforming to customer requirements. This definition includes inbound, outbound, internal, and external movements.

Another way of understanding what is involved in logistics is to see it as including various (actually we can think of at least eight) 'rights': getting, in the right way, the right product, in the right quantity and right quality, in the right place at the right time, for the right customer at the right cost. Some of these 'rights' may be obvious, others perhaps less so. For example, the right customer: in many industrial locations today typically many different companies will be co-located on the one site. Even on the one production line there may be various subcontractors collaborating with the manufacturer and there will be clear demarcation lines with regard to who has ownership of what, where and when. Therefore getting the product to the right place may be only half the journey, the challenge would be to get it to the right customer at this right place. To consider briefly 'the right way': there is now a substantial and growing interest in environmental and related issues, and Chapter 16 deals in detail with sustainability. There is thus a

Logistics involves getting
- . . . the right product
- . . . in the right way
- . . . in the right quantity and right quality
- . . . in the right place at the right time
- . . . for the right customer at the right cost

necessity to get the product to the customer in the 'right way', meaning in such a way as to cause as little damage as possible to the environment.

Logistics was once described as 'just trucks and sheds'; others see it as concerned with 'just wheels and walls'. As the discussion above illustrates, and notwithstanding the fact that trucks and sheds (warehouses) are indeed important components of logistics systems, it is obvious that logistics encapsulates much more than this.

Ensuring optimum performance with regard to some of these 'rights' may be easy for many, but getting all correct together can be quite a challenge. For example in both retail distribution and in high-value manufacturing, it is now quite common to offer suppliers quite specific and narrow time windows within which to deliver freight. Not only will the suppliers be expected to execute deliveries within these strict time limits, but also they may be expected to deliver directly onto a specific retail outlet shelf or factory production cell.

WE LOVE LOGISTICS

In 2010 one of the world's leading logistics service providers (we will learn more about such companies in Chapter 8) launched an international, high-profile media campaign to boost the image of logistics (see www.thenewlogistics.com). The aim of the highly creative campaign was to get people to understand that logistics involves more than simply moving freight around the world, and that it can also be a very effective means of saving money and gaining competitive advantage.

WHAT IS SUPPLY CHAIN MANAGEMENT?

The various functions that now comprise the discipline of logistics were regarded as separate and distinct, and managed accordingly, up to the 1960s and 1970s. This began to change radically, however, in the 1980s and beyond with firms realising the benefits of integration and, more recently, collaboration.

The term supply chain management (SCM) was originally introduced by consultants in the early 1980s and, since then, has received considerable attention. The supply chain is a much wider, intercompany, boundary-spanning concept, than is the case with logistics. Figure 1.1 illustrates the evolution and structure of the integrated supply chain.

> The supply chain is the network of organisations that are involved, through upstream and downstream linkages, in the different processes and activities that produce value in the form of products and services in the hands of the ultimate consumer.

Martin Christopher, Emeritus Professor of Marketing and Logistics at Cranfield School of Management and one of the key thought leaders in logistics and SCM spanning the past several decades, suggests that the **supply chain** is the network of organisations that are involved, through **upstream** (supplier end of the supply chain) and **downstream** (customer end of the supply chain) linkages, in the different processes and activities that produce value

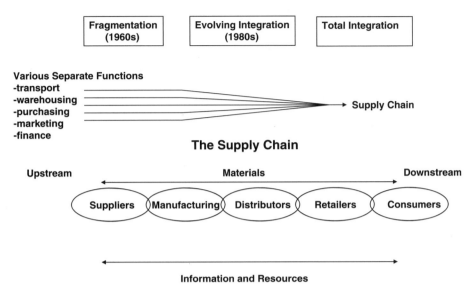

Figure 1.1   The evolution of the integrated supply chain

in the form of products and services in the hands of the ultimate consumer.[8] He distinguishes SCM from vertical integration as SCM does not necessarily imply any ownership or control of supply chain partners. In this book we appropriate Professor Christopher's description of the supply chain.

It is our view that supply chains encompass a number of key flows:

- Physical flows of materials
- Flows of information that inform the supply chain
- Resources (especially finance, but also others such as people and equipment) which help the supply chain to operate effectively. Furthermore, not all resources in the supply chain are tangible, for example good quality intercompany relationships are often cited as a highly important ingredient of effective supply chains.

The following definition is thus posited of SCM:

> Supply chain management (SCM) is the management, across and within a network of upstream and downstream organisations, of both relationships and flows of material, information and resources. The purposes of SCM are to create value, enhance efficiency, and satisfy customers.

This definition largely concurs with what can be regarded as a consensus definition of SCM. To develop such a definition, Stock and Boyer examined a total of 166 definitions of SCM that appeared in the literature, and using various analytical techniques developed the following consensus definition of SCM. It is longer than our definition above, but worth noting as it is more detailed:

> SCM is the management of a network of relationships within a firm and between inter-dependent organisations and business units consisting of material suppliers, purchasing, production facilities, logistics, marketing, and related systems that facilitate the forward and reverse flow of materials, services, finances and information from the original producer to final customer with the benefits of adding value, maximising profitability through efficiencies and achieving customer satisfaction.[9]

An important feature to note with regard to SCM is that it involves taking an 'end-to-end' perspective from the upstream to the downstream end of the supply chain. Depending upon the sector being looked at, terminology such as the following can be used to describe the end-to-end supply chain:

- Farm to fork
- Cradle to grave
- Dust to rust

A final important point to note at this juncture is that increasingly it is the case that supply chains compete more so than individual firms and products (this concept was first mooted by Professor Christopher in the early 1990s). This represents something of a paradigm shift in terms of how people usually view the global business environment; this important issue is discussed further in particular in Chapter 4 which deals with supply chain strategy.

The term 'echelon' is sometimes also used to refer to different parts of the supply chain.

Note the use of the word *network* in the definition of the supply chain above. While the supply chain is usually depicted as a linear chain (as in Figure 1.1), it is perhaps better to envisage it as a *multidimensional network of collaborating entities*. Furthermore, such networks can be more fully understood as *systems*; taking a systems view highlights the impact of the interaction that occurs between the various entities. In logistics and SCM these various entities are sometimes referred to as *links* (for example transport services) and *nodes* (for example warehouses). The various links and nodes can of course contemporaneously play different roles across multiple supply chains.

DISTINGUISHING LOGISTICS AND SCM

Now that logistics and SCM have been defined, the issue of how both terms differ needs to be considered. This is in fact a question which has led to much debate with people often coming up with their own distinctions. It has also been studied by a number of academics.[10] Larson and Halldorsson for example surveyed international logistics/SCM experts and identified four different perspectives which are illustrated in Figure 1.2.

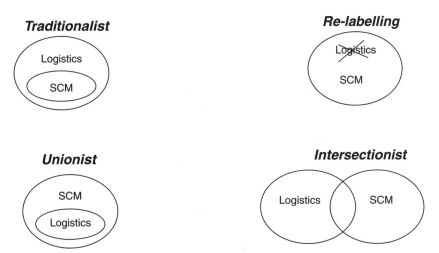

Figure 1.2 Four perspectives on logistics versus supply chain management (Source: Larson & Halldorsson, 2004)[11]

SCM in many respects evolved from logistics and the **traditionalist view** thus regards SCM as a subset of logistics, as if it were an add-on to logistics. In the **re-labelling view** it is contended that logistics has been re-labelled by the more recent term SCM. Indeed it is worth noting here that sometimes transport gets re-labelled as logistics, for example the authors have observed heavy goods vehicles (HGVs) where the word 'logistics' is painted over the word 'transport' on the side of the vehicle! Becoming a professional logistics company requires more than just a name change, however. In the **unionist view** logistics is seen as part of a wider entity, SCM. Finally the **intersectionist view** suggests that there is overlap between parts of both logistics and SCM, but also that each has parts that are separate and distinct.

In this book our approach is to adopt the *unionist view*, i.e. that logistics is part of the wider entity which is SCM.[12] To reiterate what was stated earlier, the supply chain is a much wider, intercompany, boundary-spanning concept, than is the case with logistics. We believe that

> Logistics is part of SCM; SCM is a much wider, intercompany, boundary-spanning concept, than is the case with logistics.

if you now look again at the definitions of logistics and SCM that are outlined above and the surrounding discussion in this chapter then this will be quite evident.

APPLICATIONS TO MANUFACTURING AND SERVICES

The previous sections have given an insight into the origins and forces shaping the evolution of logistics and SCM. Much of the early application of both logistics and supply chain thinking has been in a manufacturing context and this will be considered in more detail in Chapter 4. It is now generally agreed that for those who take a supply chain view, two dimensions of value often arise, namely cost savings and service enhancements. This is evident in the *Dell* case at the end of Part I of the book where the PC maker uses robust logistics strategies and competes using its entire supply chain. Not only does Dell sell relatively cheap PCs, but it also competes on the basis of certain service attributes (for example the ability for customers to purchase their products online and the fast delivery of purchased products to customers).

More and more then manufacturers are using service criteria (for example after sales service and delivery add-ons) in order to compete. Such has been their success that now many service companies are waking up to the advantages that can be gained from adopting best-in-class logistics practices and taking an end-to-end supply chain view. This is evident across a diverse range of service sectors such as retail, financial services, healthcare and tourism.

> Logistics and SCM can be used to generate both cost savings and service enhancements.

In the healthcare sector, for example, expensive increases in medical technology and increasing life expectancy are leading to greater demands on healthcare services with hospitals striving to offer better services at less cost. The average length of stay of patients within hospitals is declining, partly due to technological advances in healthcare, but partly also because increasingly hospitals take a more holistic supply chain perspective on all aspects of patient care and also increasingly apply core logistics principles to their every-day activities. By eliminating unnecessary blockages and delays (for example by ensuring that required expertise in terms of medical skills and equipment is available when needed), patients get faster access to a range of services allowing them to get better sooner and leave hospital earlier, thus leading to improvements in whole system efficiency.

IKEA (WWW.IKEA.COM)

The Scandinavian home furnishings retailer *IKEA* is a good example of a company that uses best practice logistics and SCM in the manufacturing and services aspects of its business. Many products are manufactured for self-assembly by the customer. They are 'flat packed', making them easier to ship and store. Self-assembly is generally straightforward, with many products comprising components which easily assemble together. Even the instruction leaflets often have no words, only pictures, cutting down on the need for multiple language translations. Its network of worldwide stores are usually easily accessible and have similar layouts, making the shopping experience as easy and user friendly as possible for customers.

TRIAGE[13]

The concept of triage, originally devised by the French military, is now widely applied in medical emergency situations. Triage involves rapid assessment of patient needs and thus allows those most in need of care to be attended to first. The concept has evolved considerably and has moved beyond merely deciding between those who are critically ill and those who are not, into an activity which tries to match patients with the right care stream. This may involve various downstream activities from trauma care to bypassing hospital emergency departments completely and going straight to an appropriate community care facility. Importantly, more recent applications of triage involve not just assessment once the patient reaches the hospital, but also triage at other upstream points of contact (for example via telephone or when an ambulance first arrives at an accident scene). Medical triage is an example of the application of logistics practices in a services context and is especially relevant given the pressures on many modern healthcare systems.

BOOK FRAMEWORK

A number of perspectives were adopted by the authors when writing this book and these are reflected in its content and summarised below.

Global perspective

Logistics and SCM are truly global disciplines that underpin international trade and span across international borders. Consequently, this book seeks to reflect the global nature of the subject matter and draws upon diverse examples from multiple geographies. It is not our intention to present a particular 'Western' perspective on the subject matter, but instead to present a global worldview of what is happening in logistics and SCM today.

The terms *international* and *global* are often used interchangeably in a logistics context, but this is not in fact accurate. *International* is defined by the *Collins English Dictionary* as 'of, concerning, or involving two or more nations or nationalities', while the same dictionary defines *global* as 'covering, influencing, or relating to the whole world'. This book aims then to go beyond a focus on international logistics and to take a broader, whole world, global perspective on logistics and SCM issues.

Both practical and strategic perspectives

The book aims to comprise both a *practical element*, that is to help the reader to 'do' logistics (for example select carriers, determine how much inventory to carry, select appropriate performance metrics, etc.) and a *strategic element* (understand the role of logistics and SCM in the wider business context and how it fits with the various functional areas).

In Chapter 19 the desired 'T-shaped' profile of the effective logistics manager is discussed; suffice to note for now that logistics managers, as well as needing to know how to 'do' logistics, also require good interpersonal skills and in addition need to be able to work effectively with various functions such as marketing and finance. As well as this they need to be good strategic thinkers. In this book, the aim is to present a balanced insight across all of these areas. We contend that while it is important to understand how global supply chain strategies are developed, it is also equally important to know how to, for example, calculate the cost of inventory in a warehouse or what information to put on an air waybill. For a student at any level to have knowledge of supply chain strategy is vacuous without concomitant knowledge of how to 'do' logistics.

Logistics is a part of SCM

As discussed above, the book adopts the *unionist view* of logistics, that is, that logistics is part of the wider entity which is SCM.

Focus on material, information and resource flows

The three flows across supply chains detailed above (material, information and resource) are each considered. None are regarded as more important than the other, rather the book recognises the interdependency of each.

Neutral and non-political perspective adopted

Despite the economic successes pointed to in Chapter 2, the world is not a perfect place, with too many conflicts, injustices and poverty pervading many regions. In this book we have adopted a neutral and non-political perspective; any reference to individuals, situations or countries is only done to illustrate logistics/SCM issues. Our hope is that best practice logistics and SCM, which this book hopes to advance, can help *all* regions to prosper.

The book is divided into three parts and these are now detailed.

Part One – Logistics and supply chain context

This first section sets the context for the book. The growth of logistics and SCM correlates directly with both increasing globalisation and international trade and this is the focus of Chapter 2. Pertinent issues such as trends in foreign direct investment (FDI) flows and how regional logistics performance can be measured are also developed in Chapter 2. In Chapter 3 the focus is on relationships in the supply chain. Outsourcing, offshoring and related practices are considered and the goal of supply chain integration is discussed. Chapter 1 has already given an historical perspective vis-à-vis the origins of logistics and SCM and in Chapter 4 we will see how in recent decades various strategies (e.g. leanness, agility) and trends have emerged and shaped the discipline, especially moving it from a producer–push paradigm to one of consumer–pull. The aim of Part One of the book will be to bring the reader to a position whereby they accept the now generally held maxim that it is increasingly supply chains that compete and not individual products and/or companies. The reader will be sufficiently informed to progress to Part Two, which focuses on logistics and supply chain operations. One other chapter, however, completes Part One – Chapter 5 deals with simulation, a powerful tool that can be used to better understand and improve supply chains. A number of simulation exercises related to subsequent chapters are also provided in the online material accompanying this book.

Part Two – Logistics and supply chain operations

The second section of the book focuses on logistics and supply chain operations, how to 'do' logistics. The nine chapters in Part Two focus on different aspects of 'doing' logistics. Chapter 6 deals with physical transportation, and chapter supplements are provided which consider how to plan transport infrastructure and how to generate insights from using transport modelling. Security is a topic of global importance and Chapter 7 outlines how logistics systems and supply chains are being secured. Chapter 8 details a sector of activity that is key to how supply chains function, namely the logistics service providers (LSPs) sector. Chapter 9 deals with procurement, the activity that generates the materials that flow along supply chains. Chapters 10 and 11 outline how to manage inventory, manage warehouses and handle materials. Chapter 12 illustrates how information flows along the supply chain, while Chapter 13 deals with another resource flow, finance, and its role in the supply chain. Finally, Chapter 14 discusses the area of performance management in logistics and SCM.

Part Three – Supply chain design

Having learned how 'to do' logistics, the focus of the third and final section of the book will move towards more strategic issues. In recent years a major focus in SCM concerns business continuity management and ensuring supply chains can cope with both uncertainty and the equally strong challenges which arise as a result of growing marketplace competition. This is the focus of Chapter 15 which deals with supply chain vulnerability, risk, robustness and resilience. Chapter 16 covers the increasingly important issue of sustainability in the context of logistics and SCM, while Chapter 17 deals with materials moving back upstream in the supply chain, the area of reverse logistics. Many of the insights gained from physical logistics and SCM are beginning to be applied in a services context, and this is the focus of the penultimate chapter in the book, Chapter 18, which considers services supply chains. The concluding chapter in the book (Chapter 19) brings together the key issues covered throughout the book and considers logistics system and emerging supply chain designs for the future.

Part One of the book aims to take you to the point whereby you understand that increasingly it is now supply chains that compete. The end point of the book will be to take you to the position whereby you understand that not only is it true that supply chains compete, but that, more and more, these supply chains are not simple, linear chains, but are instead complex, global, multidimensional, multipartner, networks.

LEARNING REVIEW

The chapter sought to explain the origins of logistics and SCM and to define and differentiate both terms. The importance of these areas to both manufacturing *and* services has been highlighted and the chapter showed how best practice logistics and SCM can yield cost reductions *and* value addition. A framework for the book was outlined and the particular perspectives embraced in the book were elucidated.

Now that the origins and meaning of both logistics and SCM have been described, other developments which have been closely associated with the growth of logistics and SCM can be discussed. Chapter 2 looks at both increasing globalisation and international trade. Growth in these two areas correlates closely with the growth in logistics and SCM, and indeed there is a significant level of interdependence between all of these areas.

QUESTIONS

- Are logistics and SCM only of interest to manufacturers?
- Explain the key developments behind the evolution of logistics and SCM.
- How do logistics and supply chain management differ?
- How can best practice logistics and SCM lead to both cost reduction and service enhancement?
- What are the benefits of deregulation of transport markets? Why does such deregulation sometimes not work out quite as planned?

APPLICATIONS OF LOGISTICS AND SCM IN A SERVICES CONTEXT

In this chapter we outlined key principles and concepts of logistics and SCM and how both can be applied in manufacturing and services contexts. Many application examples will be developed in the following chapters of this book (while both manufacturing and services examples are used throughout the book, Chapter 18 in particular focuses on services supply chains). At this juncture, however, it is worth pausing to consider the application of logistics and SCM in a services context, as many students regard the subjects as only of relevance in a manufacturing context. Think of examples of sectors and organisations where logistics and SCM principles and concepts can be, or are already, applied. Earlier in this chapter we illustrated the application of logistics and SCM principles and concepts to the medical context (the 'Triage' caselet). Are there other services contexts where similar application is evident?

NOTES

1. Forrester, J. (1958) Industrial dynamics: a major breakthrough for decision makers, *Harvard Business Review*, July–August.
2. For a fascinating insight into the life of McLean and the growth of containerisation see: Levinson, P (2006) *The Box*, Princeton University Press, Princeton, NJ.
3. Drucker, P. (1962) The economy's dark continent, *Fortune*, April, 103–104.
4. www.skillsforlogistics.org.

5. Beinhocker, E. (2006) *The Origin of Wealth*, Random House Business Books, London, p. 262.

6. Chen, I. & Paulraj, A. (2004) Understanding supply chain management, *International Journal of Production Research,* 42(1), 131–163.

7. The Canadian military (www.forces.gc.ca), for example, define logistics as: 'Logistics is the provision of resources to support the strategy and tactics of combat forces'.

8. Christopher, M. (2011) *Logistics and Supply Chain Management (4th Edition),* Financial Times/Prentice Hall, London, p.13.

9. Stock, J. & Boyer, S. (2009) Developing a consensus definition of supply chain management: a qualitative study, *International Journal of Physical Distribution and Logistics Management,* 39(8), 690–711.

10. See for example: Cooper, M.C., Lambert, D.M. & Pagh, J.D. (1997) Supply chain management: more than a new name for logistics, *International Journal of Logistics Management,* 8(1), 1–13; Lambert, D.M., Cooper, M.C. & Pagh, J.D. (1998) Supply chain management: implementation issues and research opportunities, *International Journal of Logistics Management,* 9(2), 1–19; and Larson, P. & Halldorsson, A. (2004) Logistics versus supply chain management: an international survey, *International Journal of Logistics: Research and Applications,* 7(1), 17–31.

11. Larson, P. & Halldorsson, A. (2004) Logistics versus supply chain management: an international survey, *International Journal of Logistics: Research and Applications,* 7(1), 17–31.

12. Recent empirical studies support this view, see for example: Larson, P., Poist, R. and Halldorsson, A. (2007), Perspectives on logistics vs SCM: a survey of SCM professionals, *Journal of Business Logistics,* 28 (1) 1–25.

13. For more on medical triage see, for example: Robertson-Steel, I. (2006) Evolution of triage systems, *Emergency Medicine Journal,* 23, 154–155.

APPENDIX: CONTAINERS AND CONTAINER SEALS

Risto Talas, *University of Hull, UK*

In this appendix we will discuss the origin and usage of the different sizes and types of shipping container, concluding with a section on container seals. The first commercial application of a container in intermodal transport took place on 26 April 1956 on a route from Newark to Houston in the United States aboard a converted tanker, the *Ideal-X*. The key figure at the time was Malcolm McLean, a well-known haulier who had the idea of converting the T-2 tanker ships to carry containers while maintaining their capability to carry oil.[1]

McLean pioneered the introduction of containers for the efficient movement of cargo compared with the old method of loading and unloading packages by hand. McLean acquired four ships belonging to the Pan-Atlantic Steamship Corporation from Waterman Steamship, a large well-established shipping company based in Mobile, Alabama, and in so doing was forced under competition law to sell his own successful road haulage company. McLean hired Keith Tantlinger, a container expert from Brown Industries, who designed and built the new 33-ft aluminium containers which would sit on the deck of the converted tankers, eight containers abreast. The length of 33 feet was chosen because the available deck space aboard the *Ideal-X* was divisible by 33.[2] Furthermore, Tantlinger also designed the spreader bar that stretched the length of the container which engaged the hooks at the corners to lift and release the container.

While McLean is credited with ushering in the age of containerisation, it was not until the late 1960s that the International Organisation for Standards (ISO) completed the task of recommending standardised container dimensions and strengthened corner fittings.[3]

The most common container dimensions are detailed and illustrated in Table A1.1 and Figure A1.1.

The most common containers in use today are welded steel or aluminium boxes constructed of corrugated metal, which gives them their strength. They are generally enclosed except for a set of double doors at one end which are held shut by two sets of vertical steel tubes that twist to lock by levers, which are themselves lockable by applying a container seal.

Table A1.1   Container dimensions

Size	Type	Dimensions (feet)			Maximum payload (kg)
		Length	Width	Height	
20 ft	Standard	20 ft	8 ft	8 ft 6 in	28 200
40 ft	Standard	40 ft	8 ft	8 ft 6 in	28 800
40 ft	High	40 ft	8 ft	9 ft 6 in	28 620
45 ft	High	45 ft	8 ft	9 ft 6 in	27 600

Source: Maersk Line (www.maerskline.com/globalfile/?path=/pdf/containerDimensions)

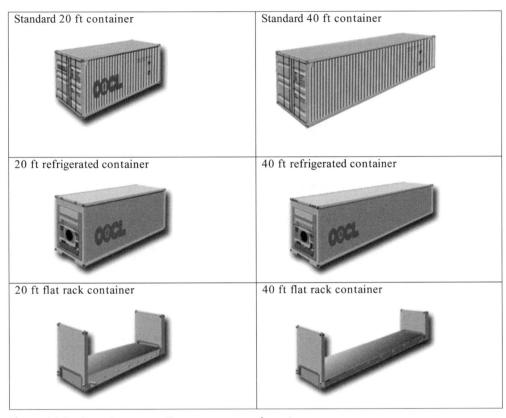

Figure A1.1   Container types (Source: www.oocl.com)

Container volumes are calculated in twenty-foot-equivalent units (TEU), which means that a 40 ft container is equivalent to 2 TEU. Containers vary not only in size and payload but also in their use. In addition to the standard dry containers, there are also refrigerated (reefer) containers, as well as open top, insulated, ventilated, flat rack, side opening and platform containers. While the standard 20 ft and 40 ft containers are used to transport all manner of commodities at ambient temperatures, refrigerated containers have revolutionised the transportation of temperature-sensitive goods such as fresh fruit and vegetables. When loaded onto a container vessel or parked in a port's container marshalling yard, a reefer container must be connected to a power supply to ensure that the correct internal temperature is maintained so that the cargo does not spoil.

Other specialised containers include those used in the fashion and wine industries. The fashion industry has developed containers which are specially fitted out with clothes rails to allow for easy loading and unloading of hanging garments. The wine industry is increasingly transporting wine in bulk in 20 ft containers, also known as flexi tank containers, which contain a single-use inflatable man-made bladder which can hold up to 24 000 litres of wine.

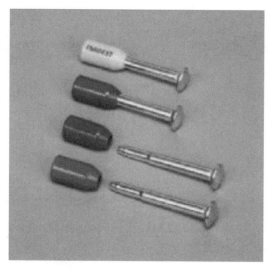

Figure A1.2   Container seals (Source: www.securityseals.com)

CONTAINER SEALS

The purpose of a container seal is to ensure the integrity of the container's contents. Depending on the level of security, a seal may provide little more than a means of a visual check that the container's doors have not been opened. However, high-security seals which comply with the international standard ISO 17712, such as those in Figure A1.2, offer more of a physical barrier to any would-be thief or smuggler. Container seals may even hold electronic data about the container on a radio frequency identification (RFID) tag, which can be read at different stages in the supply chain. Such seals are known as electronic or e-seals. Sophisticated e-seals can even communicate with sensors inside the container which can record the temperature, humidity and light levels within the container.

REFERENCES

1. Levinson, M. (2006) *The Box: How the Shipping Container Made the World Smaller and the World Economy Bigger*, Princeton University Press, Princeton, NJ.
2. Ibid.
3. Ibid.

2 Globalisation and International Trade

LEARNING OBJECTIVES

- Highlight the growth that has occurred in recent decades in international trade. Regional and country differences and relative shares will also be illustrated.
- Explain what is meant by globalisation, identify the most globalised countries in the world and explain the drivers for globalisation.
- Consider the (unequal) distribution of economic wealth among the world's countries.
- Explore the role of multinational companies and their role in global trade, together with the impact of overseas investment by companies.
- Finally, look at what happens when unequal volumes or types of freight flow in opposite directions in freight markets.

INTRODUCTION

Chapter 1 both introduced and differentiated logistics and SCM, and their application in manufacturing and services contexts. It was also noted that best practice logistics and SCM can lead to both cost reduction and value addition. This chapter now turns to areas which over the last number of decades have been closely associated with the evolution and growth of logistics and SCM, namely the growth of international trade and the emergence of the phenomenon known as globalisation.

Given the increased volumes in recent years of international trade and its related activities, many companies now have overseas facilities and supply chain partners. Regional differences in logistics performance will also be examined. Imbalances in freight volumes in opposite directions are a characteristic of many freight markets; how this arises and its consequences will also be discussed.

Chapter 2 comprises four core sections:

- Growth in international trade
- Measuring logistics performance
- Globalisation
- Directional imbalances

GROWTH IN INTERNATIONAL TRADE

> There has been considerable growth in recent decades in world trade; world exports grew from $62 billion in 1950 to a peak of $16 000 billion by 2008 before subsequently declining.

Global trade has grown considerably in recent decades and has fuelled the evolution of logistics and SCM, which was outlined in Chapter 1. Much of this growth has been facilitated by the reduction of trade barriers between countries and regions, thus making it easier for countries to trade with each other. **Regional trade agreements**, such as the EU (European Union) and ASEAN (Association of South East Asian Nations), have been and continue to be developed, and allow more open trading within regions.[1] In 1950 the value of total merchandise exports from all countries in the world was just under $62 billion.[2] By 2008 this had peaked at circa $16 000 billion (Figure 2.1) before declining with the widespread economic recession. In 1960 the share of world merchandise exports in world gross domestic product was 10%. By 2000 it had climbed to 20%. So today, more than ever, more freight is moving all around the world, with logistics systems thus having to play an increasingly important role in the global economy.

The value of total exports of world services is much less than that of merchandise exports, but it is still quite significant. In 2002 the value of total exports of services was $1611 billion. Almost three-quarters of these were from developed countries. The share of services in world output was 3% in 1960 and this grew to almost 5% by 2000.

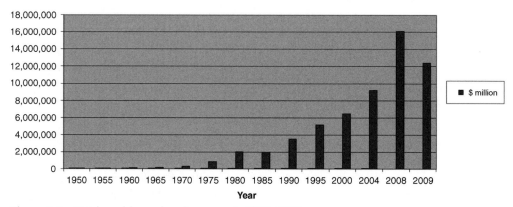

Figure 2.1 Total world merchandise exports 1950–2009

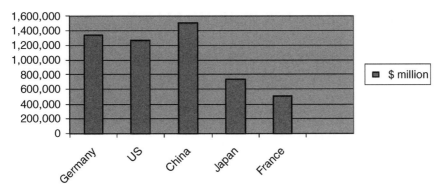

Figure 2.2   Exports by country (2010 estimates) (Source: www.cia.gov)[3]

Approximately two-thirds of the merchandise exports in 2004 were from developed counties. After a slow start, the participation in world trade by developing countries is growing. According to the United Nations Conference on Trade and Development (UNCTAD) developing countries' merchandise exports grew on average 12% a year in the period 1960 to 2002, while the corresponding figure for developed countries was 11%. Figure 2.2 ranks the world's largest exporting countries.[4]

There are of course regional variations with regard to the performance of individual developing economies with some countries demonstrating outstanding growth. China, for example, has been a very strong performer with regard to growth in its merchandise exports: in 1980 its annual merchandise exports were valued at $18 billion but by 2004 this had grown to $574 billion. According to the World Trade Organisation (WTO), China's trade grew three times faster than that of the global economy in the 1990s, and while world trade stagnated between 2000 and 2002, China's imports and exports rose by 30%.[5] In fact China is sometimes described as 'the factory to the world'. In contrast to all of this, Liberia's merchandise exports for example, dropped from $600 million in 1980 to $220 million in 2004 as a result of political and other difficulties in that country.

There are considerable differences in terms of economic wealth among many countries across the world. One way to measure and compare the wealth of economies is to compare them in terms of their GNI (gross national income) per capita; analysis of such data highlights the considerable inter-country differences in economic wealth that exist today. It is usually the case that more wealthy countries will have good quality transport systems, sometimes a measure known as *transport mobility* (an aggregate measure which comprises an assessment of the available services, quality of the transport infrastructure, ease with which people and freight can move into, around and out of a country, etc.) is used in this regard and is correlated quite closely with measures of a country's gross domestic product (GDP). The supplement to Chapter 6 will consider issues concerning the planning of transport infrastructure.

MEASURING LOGISTICS PERFORMANCE

The World Bank has developed a tool to measure logistics performance by country. The *global logistics performance index* (LPI) (available via the World Bank website) ranks 155 different countries in terms of their logistics performance; six key dimensions are used in the index:

- Customs
- Infrastructure
- International shipments
- Logistics competence
- Tracking and tracing
- Timeliness

The aim of the index is to benchmark countries' overall performance on these dimensions and to assess the quality of a country's connections to the global market. Table 2.1 lists the top 10 countries in the index as reported in 2010.

Another measure that looks at logistics performance is UNCTAD's liner shipping connectivity index (LSCI), which measures 162 coastal countries' access to container shipping services. The LSCI is generated from five components:[6]

- The largest vessel deployed on services to a country's ports. Larger vessels require deeper ports and investments in specialised container cranes.
- The number of companies that provide services to a country's ports. A higher number of competing companies implies more choices and often lower freight costs for shippers.
- The number of services offered by the liner companies. A higher number of services gives more options to shippers to connect to overseas markets.
- The number of ships deployed on services to a country's ports. More ships are correlated with higher frequencies.
- The twenty-foot-equivalent unit (TEU) capacity on the deployed ships. This is correlated with economies of scale and lower freight costs.

Table 2.1   Top 10 countries in the global logistics performance index (LPI)[7]

1	Germany
2	Singapore
3	Sweden
4	Netherlands
5	Luxembourg
6	Switzerland
7	Japan
8	United Kingdom
9	Belgium
10	Norway

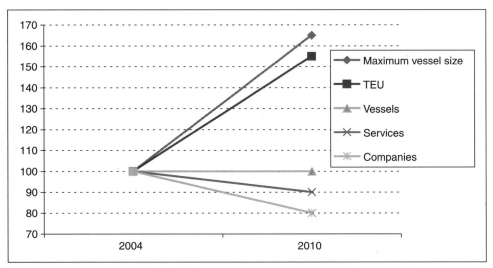

Figure 2.3   Trends within the 2010 LSCI

The top ranked country in the 2010 LSCI was China while the bottom ranked country was Paraguay.[8] Analysis of data within the index since 2004 highlights some interesting trends (Figure 2.3). The key underlying trend is consolidation, with fewer companies (perhaps indicative of mergers and alliances in the sector) offering fewer services and using larger vessels.

One of the goals of logistics is to facilitate the process of trade, and this in turn can aid the economic well-being of all counties. Ensuring good logistics systems are in place is thus a key component in efforts to help developing countries in particular.

GLOBALISATION

The term **globalisation** has been in use for a number of decades and is generally regarded as an umbrella term for a complex series of economic, social, technological, cultural and political changes, which continue to take place throughout the world. Some argue that it is a force for good, allowing people and companies throughout the world to be inter-connected. Others oppose it, some vehemently, and see it largely as a proxy for global capital flows exploiting especially the poor. You can make up your own mind. Perhaps in truth globalisation is a mix of both extreme viewpoints. Regardless, it looks as if globalisation is here to stay.

Commercial shipping activity is a good example of globalisation. Kumar and Hoffmann[9] give the following example: 'a Greek owned vessel, built in Korea, may be chartered to a Danish operator, who employs Philippine seafarers via a Cypriot crewing agent, is registered in Panama, insured in the UK, and transports German made cargo in the name of a Swiss freight forwarder from a Dutch port to Argentina, through terminals that are concessioned to port operators from Hong Kong and Australia.' Surely an example of globalisation in action!

BARBIE: THE ALL-AMERICAN GIRL[10]

Conceived in 1959 as the all-American toy doll, Barbie today is a true global citizen! Originally made in Japan (and not the USA), today different parts of Barbie are made in various different countries: for example her hair is still made in Japan, the plastic in her body comes from Taiwan, her cotton clothing from China, and the moulds and pigments used in production come from the USA.

One writer credited with bringing the term globalisation into mainstream use is the American academic Theodore Levitt. In a now famous 1983 article in the *Harvard Business Review*,[11] Levitt suggested that companies must learn to operate as if the world were one large market – ignoring superficial regional and national differences.

'GLOCALISATION' – THINK GLOBAL, ACT LOCAL

Much of what Levitt asserted in his famous 1983 *Harvard Business Review* article has stood the test of time and no doubt one can think of many global companies with global products. Conscious though of subtle, yet often important, regional and local differences, many companies now adopt a policy which some refer to as **glocalisation** – thinking on a *global*, world-market scale, but adapting to *local* wants as appropriate. Just think, for example, of how McDonald's has both globally recognised and desired products (burgers, Coca-Cola, etc.) side by side with locally desired products in its many different restaurants across the world. We will also see in later chapters how companies can employ modern manufacturing and distribution strategies that allow them to tailor, often at little extra cost, global products to satisfy local wants.

Figure 2.1 illustrated the growth in the value of total merchandise exports from all countries in the world and thus highlighted the growth in international trade. Using this and other data, the extent of increased globalisation in the world economy can be illustrated; this could be done by adding, for each year in a time series, world exports and world imports, and dividing the total by annual world GDP.

All of this is not to deny that cultural and other differences exist between countries. Such differences do exist and can impact on how effectively logistics systems work in practice. We will return to some of these issues later in the book when dealing with sourcing and procurement, areas where understanding cultural differences is a matter of considerable importance as companies negotiate and manage across cultures.[12]

In terms of trading relationships, a number of different stages can be identified in the path towards globalisation. First, countries begin to trade with each other, importing and exporting goods. As trade develops, sometimes companies will establish a presence in an overseas market. Such companies are usually referred to as **multinational companies (MNCs)** when they have operations in areas beyond their home country. In turn, entities sometimes referred to as **transnational corporations (TNCs)** emerge, these are companies that trade across many borders, with operations in multiple countries. Often it can be difficult to identify the 'home' country of a TNC, as they will typically portray a truly global identity. Three other terms are also worth noting and these relate to how companies think and behave as they internationalise:

- **Ethnocentricity**: where the company when doing business abroad thinks only in terms of the home country environment (thinks and acts as if it were still operating in for example the USA, where the company may be headquartered, notwithstanding the fact that many business environments outside of the USA can be quite dissimilar to that country).

- **Polycentricity**: where the company adopts the host country perspective (to coin the old phrase: 'when in Rome, do as the Romans do').

- **Geocentricity**: where the company acts completely independent of geography and adopts a global perspective, and will tailor to the local environment as appropriate (see the box on 'glocalisation').

As companies internationalise they set up operations in overseas locations. This can range from relatively simple activities, such as having a sales presence in an overseas market, to setting up production facilities, and even (in the case of TNCs) having core company functions located in countries other than where the company was originally established. Behind such developments lie what are referred to as **foreign direct investment (FDI)** flows. FDI flows are financial flows from a company in one country to invest (for example in a factory) in another country. Such flows are very significant in the overall global economy and in some cases can be key to dictating a country's success. Indeed many countries, and regions, compete quite strongly to attract FDI, and some will put in place certain conditions (for example low rates of corporate taxation) in order to attract more FDI.[13]

Table 2.2 outlines some of the many factors that have to be considered when deciding on an optimum location for an overseas facility. Indeed many of the factors listed for consideration arise regardless of the type or location of facility being considered, and in addition to their relevance in the context of the discussion here on FDI, they are also relevant in the context of issues considered in subsequent chapters of this book (for example those dealing with outsourcing and with warehousing).

Table 2.3 lists the world's top 10 non-financial TNCs in 2008 ranked by foreign assets. This is not a listing of the world's 'biggest' companies, which could be assembled based on, for example, total revenue or market capitalisation. Our interest here is in companies with extensive global activities, as they are the companies generating large global logistics flows. Regardless of measure of company size, it is also important to note

Table 2.2 Site selection factors

Labour costs	Political stability
Employment regulations	Environmental regulations
Available skills	Taxation rates
Land costs and availability of suitable sites	Government supports
Energy costs	Currency stability
Availability of suitable suppliers	Benefits of being part of a cluster of similar companies
Transport and logistics costs	Preferred locations of competitors
Transport linkages	Access to markets
Communications infrastructure and costs	Community issues and quality of life

that many individual large companies (whether measured by foreign assets, revenue or market capitalisation) play a very significant role in the global economy and their power should not be underestimated. In fact it is estimated that some of the largest companies have annual turnover greater than the annual GDP of some smaller European countries.[14] How such large companies arrange their logistics activities is thus highly relevant for various stakeholders.

Financial TNCs have been excluded from Table 2.3 as their global capital flows are very significant and thus would distort the list away from other types of companies; from a logistics perspective our interest is in those TNCs who move physical product around the world. Obviously this would exclude many of the activities of the utilities companies in the list (telecommunications, water, etc.), although they too often move product internationally, albeit virtually over telecommunications networks or via proprietary gas pipelines for example.

DIRECTIONAL IMBALANCES

As Figure 2.1 illustrated, world trade has grown considerably over the past 50 years. This has been driven by various developments discussed above such as the growth

Table 2.3 World's top 10 non-financial TNCs in 2008 ranked by foreign assets[15]

Rank	Name	Home	Sector
1	General Electric	USA	Electrical and electronic
2	Royal Dutch/Shell	UK	Petroleum
3	Vodafone	UK	Telecommunications
4	BP	UK	Petroleum
5	Toyota	Japan	Motor vehicles
6	ExxonMobil	USA	Petroleum
7	Total SA	France	Petroleum
8	E.On	Germany	Utilities
9	Electricite De France (EDF)	France	Utilities
10	ArcelorMittal	Luxembourg	Metal and metal products

of globalisation, and more recent trends such as the growth of **offshoring**. One particular characteristic of freight markets, which distinguishes them from passenger markets, is what are commonly referred to as **directional imbalances**. A simple analogy explains. Most people who make a journey today aim to make a return trip at some point. This, however, is not the case with freight, which usually moves to either be consumed at the destination point or have further value added to it before making another journey. In other words most freight makes one-way, and not return, journeys. Figure 2.4 illustrates the traffic volumes on the main global freight corridors.

This of course would be fine if the same volume and type of freight (certain types of freight have particular handling and equipment characteristics, e.g. refrigerated containers for perishable freight) went in both directions on all routes. But of course it doesn't, and in some cases the differences can be quite pronounced. This in turn raises interesting challenges for the transport companies who are faced with variable directional utilisation of their equipment.

> Directional imbalances arise in freight markets when there are mismatches in the volumes or types of freight moving in opposite directions in a freight market.

DIRECTIONAL IMBALANCES: THE CHINA–EU ROUTE

- It can cost the same amount to transport a container unit by road between Munich and Hamburg in Germany as it does to ship the same container by sea from Shanghai in China to Hamburg in Germany.
- It can cost twice as much to ship a typical 20-ft container between Hong Kong and the EU when compared with the opposite direction (EU–Hong Kong). This is because of the huge volume of exports from China into European markets.

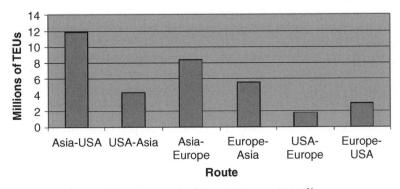

Figure 2.4   Major trade corridors (Source: Rodrigue & Hesse, 2007)[16]

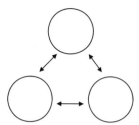

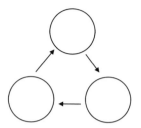

In the **traditional** system vessels move in both directions on each route. If imbalances exist on any of the routes then these will not be avoided.

In the **circular** system vessels move in one direction only, preferably in the direction of greatest traffic volume. Of course in reality different combinations and mixes of frequencies will be used (for example where an imbalance exists one in four vessels may ply in the opposite direction where there are lower traffic volumes).

*Sometimes circular routeings are referred to as liner routeings as this is a pattern that was in the pas and to an extent still is, adopted by many passenger liner vessels.

Figure 2.5   Traditional versus circular routeings*

Sometimes directional imbalances can exist in opposite directions on the same route for different commodities. This can arise with, for example, perishable products such as foodstuffs and flowers, which usually require refrigerated containers. There could be a surplus of empty containers in one direction, thus allowing low rates to be charged for freight in that direction. Perishable products might not, however, be able to use this available equipment and special refrigerated containers would have to be imported to carry such products.

The challenge for carriers is obviously to match as much inbound freight capacity with outbound freight capacity as possible.[17] When, however, there are gross imbalances in import and export volumes and cargo types this is not always possible. As a result empty containers may need to be repositioned to where they are required. Furthermore this can lead to problems for ports, which sometimes have to store such empty containers. Shipping companies have also endeavoured to come up with solutions such as developing new routeing patterns which minimise empty container movements and seek to maximise operations on routes with higher traffic densities (Figure 2.5). New container designs are also emerging (such as collapsible and foldable containers) making the movement of empty containers less expensive.

LEARNING REVIEW

The chapter sought to introduce the concept of globalisation and the nature of international trade in the global economy, and in turn the interrelationship of both with logistics systems. Issues such as the role played by multinational companies and the impact of directional imbalances in freight markets were also explored. The global economy today is increasingly interconnected with logistics playing an essential *lubricating* role – just as oil lubricates a car engine (without oil the engine would quickly seize up), so too the global economy relies on efficient and effective logistics systems in order to function (just look for example at what happens when transport services are delayed or there is industrial action at a port or airport). As the data and trends outlined in this chapter have attempted to illustrate, the global economy has evolved and grown quite considerably, especially in the latter decades of the twentieth century and into the current century. To facilitate this, the logistics sector has also had to evolve and grow.

Chapters 1 and 2 have sought to give an understanding of both the drivers for the evolution of logistics and SCM, and the global context within which both operate. The next chapter will now turn to look at relationships in the supply chain and the importance of supply chain integration.

QUESTIONS

- Is your country among the world's most globalised countries? If not, what could it do to improve its position?
- Identify examples of companies/products which attempt to think global and act local ('glocalisation').
- Differentiate ethnocentricity, polycentricity and geocentricity, and give examples of companies from your own country that you believe fit into each category.
- Taking your own country as an example, identify freight routes where you believe directional imbalances exist.

LARGE COMPANIES AND THEIR LOGISTICS ACTIVITIES

It was noted above that some very large companies can be bigger than some small countries (for example in terms of company revenue when compared to country GDP). How such large companies arrange their logistics activities is thus highly relevant for various stakeholders.

Take a large company with which you are familiar and attempt to evaluate its logistics activities. Examining company annual reports, company websites, and other information sources should generate information of interest. Detailed investigation may highlight specific issues of interest from a logistics perspective: for example it is not uncommon for some sea ports to be highly dependent on individual large manufacturers in their hinterland. Try to identify linkages such as these and their implications. For example what would happen to such a port if the manufacturer decided to relocate production to another factory in its global network?

NOTES

1. Many of these have evolved from being just trading agreements into wider social, political and economic entities (a good example being the EU, which started life originally as an agreement for trading coal and steel between a small number of countries).

2. Merchandise exports are goods leaving the statistical territory of a country. Data are in current US dollars. A lot of detailed statistics on world trade can be accessed via the website of the United Nations Conference on Trade and Development (www.unctad.org) and which is the source of many of the statistics quoted in this chapter.

3. Country export data sourced from the CIA World Factbook, available at www.cia.gov.

4. Sometimes people are surprised to see Germany ranked ahead of the United States as the world's second largest exporter. Two points are worth noting in this regard: (i) some of Germany's exports are to other (nearby) EU countries; (ii) the United States consumes, rather than exports, a lot of what it produces, thus reducing its export performance (it also imports a lot of freight and runs a trade deficit). In any event Germany is a powerful economy and home to some of the world's leading companies.

5. Quoted in Christopher, M., Peck, H. & Towill, D. (2006) A taxonomy for selecting global supply chain strategies, *International Journal of Logistics Management*, 17(2), 276.

6. UNCTAD *Transport Newsletter #47*, p. 5.

7. The full index and background material is available via the World Bank at: http://info.worldbank.org/etools/tradesurvey/mode1b.asp. The lowest ranked country in the index is Somalia with a score of 1.34.

8. The full LSCI is detailed in Annex 4 of UNCTAD's *Review of Maritime Transport 2010*.

9. Kumar, S. & Hoffmann, J. (2002) Globalization – the Maritime Nexus, in *The Handbook of Maritime Economics and Business*, LLP Professional Publishing, London.

10. Adapted from Levinson, P. (2006) *The Box*, Princeton University Press, Princeton, NJ, p. 265.

11. Levitt, T. (1983) The globalization of markets, *Harvard Business Review*, May–June, 92–102.

12. For further reading on the issue of cultural differences we recommend you look at some of the many writings of the Dutch academic Geert Hofstede who has pioneered research in this area.

13. For more on this topic see for example: Ferdows, K. (1997) Making the most of foreign factories, *Harvard Business Review*, March–April; Mangan, J., Hannigan, K. & Cullen, J. (2006) Behind the cost-savings advantage, *Sloan Management Review*, 47(2).

14. Wal-Mart, for example, is apparently the world's largest retailer and was one of the world's largest corporations when measured in revenue terms in 2007 with revenues of some $351 billion. Recall the discussion in Chapter 1 on the role of logistics in national economies and in particular the role of Wal-Mart in the US economy.

15. UNCTAD *World Investment Report 2010*, Annex Table 26.

16. Rodrigue, J. & Hesse, M. (2007) Globalized trade and logistics: North American perspectives. In Leinbach, T. & Capineri, C. (eds), *Globalized Freight Transport*, Edward Elgar, Chichester.

17. Olivo, A., Zuddas, P., Di Francesco, M. & Manca, A. (2005) An operational model for empty container management, *Maritime Economics and Logistics*, 7, 199–222.

3 Supply Chain Relationships

LEARNING OBJECTIVES

- Highlight the growth in international trade.
- Explain factors affecting outsourcing decisions.
- Highlight the need for outsourcing in view of both globalisation and the growth of international trade.
- Identify the problems faced by outsourcing companies that can result in failure.
- Outline how outsourcees are selected.
- Examine how outsourcer–outsourcee relationships develop.
- Define the terms integration and collaboration in the global SCM context.
- Explain how internal and external integration can be achieved to benefit supply chain performance.
- Elaborate on specific methods used to enable collaboration.
- Offer a holistic perspective of SCM to provide an understanding of how supply chains can gain greater integration and collaboration in the future.

INTRODUCTION

In Chapters 1 and 2 we discussed the critical role of contemporary global supply chains. This chapter discusses the importance of relationships across those chains, and offers insights into how such relationships can be established, maintained and enhanced. In today's world of international trade and global competition, where increasingly supply chains compete rather than individual firms and products, effective relationships between suppliers and customers have become differentiators of high-performing supply chains. In this chapter, we will learn about key concepts from research and practice to understand how this critical area is evolving.

Chapter 3 comprises nine core sections:

- Growth in international trade
- Outsourcing
- Offshoring
- Failures in outsourcing
- Evaluating and selecting outsourcees

- Outsourcer and outsourcee relationship development
- Supply chain integration
- Supply chain collaboration principles
- Supply chain collaboration methods

GROWTH IN INTERNATIONAL TRADE

In the manufacturing and service sectors new sourcing patterns have emerged due to the growth in international trade and global competition, which has already been detailed in Chapter 2. In the manufacturing sector international networks of production are increasingly being established. Within this scenario the development of supply networks is a critical issue for multinational enterprises in order to achieve efficiency and quality of the final product. Multinational enterprises have the tendency to implement their own supply chain operations and management practices across countries within their global networks of subsidiaries and operational units.

Globalisation of the manufacturing sector has resulted in the following trends:[1]

- Global competition
- Competitors, partners and customers from around the world
- Global sourcing
- Global presence
- Global value chains resulting in increasing complexity and competition
- Global access to knowledge and new technologies
- High levels of customer awareness and expectation
- Rapid pace of technological change
- Fast rate of product commoditisation
- SCM expertise and innovation are preconditions for business success

In Asia, China and India have become global centres for a large number of sectors such as manufacturing, software development, retailing and financial services, and in recent years there has been an unprecedented increase in companies outsourcing and/or offshoring processes to Asia. Rates of pay, when compared to those in Europe and North America, are much lower, although we will see later in the chapter in the context of the *total cost of outsourcing* that these are not the only factors to be considered.[2] In a 2006 count, it was found that 400 of the Fortune 500 listed companies have research bases in China, while 125 were in India.[3] Inward foreign direct investment (FDI) in the manufacturing sector in China and India in 2006 totalled US$42 trillion and US$33.6 trillion, respectively.[4]

This approach, however, of transferring operations and activities from Europe and North America to Asia has caused a number of difficulties leading to failure for some, as many firms are unable to contextualise to factors such as infrastructure (energy, materials, transport and communication), education, training, local and national regulations, culture and organisational networks.

VOLVO TRUCKS (INDIA)

Volvo Trucks India, a wholly owned subsidiary of a Swedish firm, is the world's second largest producer of heavy trucks. Volvo has approximately 72 000 employees and production in 25 countries. It commenced operations in 1998 in India, based near Bangalore. The vendor development department at Volvo India plays a major role in selection and development of Indian vendors for global supplies. Their responsibility ranges from verification of parts against specification to training of suppliers on Volvo specifications and metrology. The exports from Indian suppliers amount to €26 million from a total of 10 suppliers. Two to three of these suppliers are strategic suppliers, i.e. they are 100% suppliers to Volvo.

In the manufacturing sector there have been a number of changes in recent years. Manufacturing organisations now give greater importance to relationships with partners in their supply chains.

OUTSOURCING

Sometimes companies, for various reasons, decide to outsource certain activities to other companies, commonly referred to as 'third parties'. Some companies outsource for *cost* reasons, as the outsource partner may be able to provide the service more cheaply than the outsourcing company can itself provide it for. Increased *flexibility* is another reason to outsource, as the outsource partner may be more readily able to provide more or less of the service as required by the outsourcing company, and thus save it having to commit its own resources. A third reason often cited for outsourcing is more of a strategic one whereby a company decides to focus upon its *core competences* – that is, the tasks it is good at or has advantages in – and outsource all other activities. Finally, given the rapid advances everywhere in *technology*, companies may no longer always necessarily have the most up-to-date technology available to them and thus will outsource to partners who do have such technology.

Obviously these four reasons are not mutually exclusive and a company may decide to outsource for any combination of the four reasons.

There are a number of issues to be considered in outsourcing: first how to go about selecting an outsource partner, and then how to effectively manage the chosen partner.

In order to effectively manage the outsource arrangement, companies generally put in place a service level agreement (SLA) and performance metrics.

Outsourcing can be defined as the transfer to a third party of the management and delivery of a process previously performed by the company itself.

An SLA is a key part of a contractual agreement between a customer and a supplier to identify upfront the performance (i.e. service) levels expected. This is a legally binding contract. Potential suppliers will have to first qualify by meeting those criteria and/or performance expectations defined in the SLA before they are given proper consideration. We refer to these minimum requirements as **order qualifiers**, while the criteria that allow the supplier to actually be selected we refer to as **order winners**. We will discuss both of these terms in more detail later in this chapter.

Ongoing monitoring of suppliers and managing the buyer–supplier relationship are also critical. Sometimes the relationship can extend to **supplier development** where, in both parties' interests, improvement efforts are made leading to, for example, new and better products and solutions being provided by suppliers. Such an approach 'inverts' the traditional approach that sought to squeeze suppliers as much as possible on price. Of course price is still regarded as important, but it is now not the only criterion to be considered.

Many studies have shown that good supplier relationship management leads to better results and added benefits, especially when it is over an extended period of time, sharing risks and benefits.[5] Such collaborative partnerships help in improving quality, product development and logistics efficiency, as both parties are able to share information on forecasts, sales, supply requirements, production schedules and problem alerts in advance. Additional benefits such as higher quality, lower inventories and better planning can also be achieved. We discuss collaboration further later in this chapter.

Later chapters will return to these issues: Chapter 8 will look in particular at the selection of logistics service providers, Chapter 9 will look at procurement and Chapter 14 will look at performance management.

Another important issue for any organisation to consider is exactly which activities to outsource and which activities to do itself, the classic 'do versus buy decision'. In fact some organisations, especially many in the e-business sector, outsource almost everything. These organisations are referred to as **virtual organisations**. In contrast other organisations, more so in the past than today, outsource little or nothing. For example the Ford Motor Company was reputed in the first half of the twentieth century to even own farm animals in order to guarantee a source of supply of fabric for its cars (it was noted in Chapter 1 that the technical term for this is vertical integration: that is, how much of the upstream and downstream activities the company actually owns or controls itself).

In the last decade or so there has also been a shift in the way suppliers are arranged. Previously, many companies, especially in the manufacturing sector, had multiple suppliers. Indeed it was not unknown for some large multinational companies to have thousands of suppliers, and this is still the case today for some companies. Managing so many suppliers can of course bring its own problems; similarly with large numbers of suppliers it can be difficult to leverage other advantages from them such as, for example, sharing research and development and new product development (generally speaking better done with few, rather than many, suppliers). The response to much of this has been the organisation of suppliers into tiers.

If you think of a pyramid, the top tier is the manufacturer or client organisation. Below this are what are referred to as first-tier suppliers, below these the second-tier suppliers and so forth. Sometimes the term **original equipment manufacturer** (OEM) is used to describe the top-tier organisation, i.e. the manufacturer/ultimate client organisation. Such OEMs are the producers of the final product that carries their brand. In some cases such OEMs make little (for example they may just assemble the various supplied components) or no (as such they are virtual organisations as described above) physical modifications to the product, with the first and lower tier suppliers doing most of the manufacturing (sometimes the term **contract manufacturer** is used to refer to such suppliers).

DESIGNING PRODUCTS THAT ARE EASY TO MAKE: DESIGN FOR MANUFACTURE (DFM)

Simchi-Levi et al.[6] describe the advent in the 1980s of **design for manufacture** where designers and engineers moved from focusing solely on designing products to a focus on including consideration of the actual manufacturing process when designing products, i.e. not only to design good products, but also ones that can be manufactured cheaply and efficiently. Mass customisation, for example, can be enabled by designing postponement into the production process—this can be something straightforward such as delayed product differentiation enabled by downstream supply chain partners (we will discuss these practices further in Chapter 4). Having suppliers organised into tiers is also a key enabler of DFM as it allows components to be produced by suppliers, which can in turn be assembled by the higher tiers. The OEMs then just need to combine the various 'modules' supplied by the first-tier suppliers.

Research on a number of manufacturing companies in the UK and India has shown that companies are outsourcing mostly due to the following reasons:[7]

- Reduce direct and indirect costs
- Reduce capital costs
- Reduce taxes
- Reduce logistics costs
- Overcome tariff barriers

- Provide better customer service
- Spread foreign exchange risks
- Share risk
- Build alternative supply sources
- Pre-empt potential competitors
- Learn from local suppliers, foreign customers or competitors
- Gain access to world-class capabilities or attract talent globally

OFFSHORING

With increased competition in many markets, combined in some instances with falling prices, many companies are looking at ways in which to reduce their costs. It was noted in Chapter 1 that effective management of logistics can lead to cost savings and value advantages for companies. **Offshoring** is another, and increasingly popular, approach companies are using to reduce costs.

Offshoring and outsourcing are often confused, so first the term offshoring will be defined and then both terms will be differentiated.

Offshoring is not the same as outsourcing because outsourcing involves handing process ownership over to a third party, whereas with offshoring the company may still own and control the process itself in the lower cost location. Of course one can both outsource and offshore a process at the same time in that the outsource partner can also decide to offshore and transfer the newly acquired outsourced process to a lower cost location in another country.

> Offshoring is the transfer of specific processes to lower cost locations in other countries.

Some leading authors have noted that the lure of cost savings, largely due to fewer regulatory controls and significantly lower wages, has prompted the mass migration of manufacturing from the developed world to emergent economies in other regions.[8] They note that geopolitical events moving in step with technological developments and the deregulation of trade have made global sourcing and supply a reality. It is important to note that it is not just manufacturing processes that are offshored, but many service-based processes are often also offshored. Examples include call centres, transaction processing (e.g. typical accounts functions such as invoicing) and even aspects of human resource management. Table 3.1 outlines some of the reasons behind companies' decisions to offshore.

One of the questions which sometimes emerges with regard to offshoring is: can the cost savings enjoyed by offshoring be offset by other unforeseen costs? Examples of such costs include extra monitoring costs incurred as a result of the location of the offshore activities. The other main set of costs are extra transaction costs as a result of for example moving materials over greater distances. Ultimately the challenge is to ensure that these extra

Table 3.1   Some of the reasons why companies offshore

Lower costs in offshore regions
Less stringent regulatory controls in offshore regions
Deregulation of trade facilitates offshoring
Lower communication and IT costs
Improving capabilities in many offshore regions
Clusters of specific activities (e.g. call centres) emerging in certain regions

monitoring and transaction costs are less than the savings enjoyed as a result of offshoring. As a result of the potential risks and delays associated with moving products from a distant location, some companies are moving their offshored activities to countries closer to their home market, a practice called **nearshoring**. In some cases companies will abandon offshoring and move the activities back to the original home market, a practice called **backshoring**.

FAILURES IN OUTSOURCING

Finally, it is important to note that just because outsourcing can at times be the right thing to do, it does not always follow that all outsourcing arrangements always run smoothly. In fact the opposite can often be the case. Research shows that four out of five business process outsourcing (BPO) contracts signed today will need to be renegotiated within two years and that 20% of such contracts will collapse.[9] Similarly, in a recent survey it was found that 50% of outsourcing relationships worldwide fail within five years and the most reported reasons for failure are summarised in Figure 3.1. Some of the various problems illustrated in this figure are now discussed.

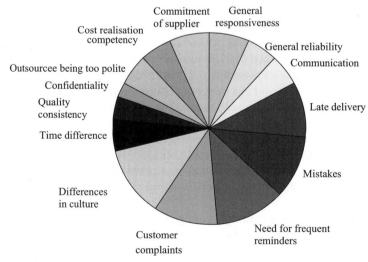

Figure 3.1   Most frequently reported problems leading to failure in outsourcing (Source: Pandit 2005)[10]

Late delivery is one of the most common causes of failure in outsourcing relationships and this in turn leads to outsourcers not being able to meet their own customer expectations. 'Delivery on time' in the evaluation of potential outsourcees is usually considered as an order-winning factor and failure to provide this service can cause serious problems in relationships. In the manufacturing sector this can also lead to outsourcees incurring additional costs using for example more expensive, faster modes of transport in order to compensate for late delivery. In an article on the importance of time in the supply chain, it was noted that high-speed transportation can be used to compensate for manufacturing delays where the penalty for failure might cost as much as £1 million an hour.[11] Because of the risk of late delivery, outsourcers sometimes insist that the supplier holds safety stock (we will discuss this in more detail in the next chapter) nearby so as to mitigate against the problems that late delivery can cause.

Consistency of quality with regard to products or services delivered by the outsourcee is one of the problems frequently faced by outsourcers. This relates to the outsourcee delivering high quality at the start of the operation but not maintaining it over time. This leads to rejects and returns by outsourcers and in additional costs for outsourcees. This also leads to poor customer service levels for both outsourcer and outsourcee.

General reliability problems can lead to the necessity for excessive checks by outsourcers and this could raise mistrust between outsourcer and outsourcee. Reliability on quality, delivery, cost and service are the expectations that have to be met by the outsourcee.

General responsiveness problems could mean that the outsourcee is not being flexible to make changes to specifications, outsourcees not responding to queries made by the outsourcer, and also relates to being in regular contact to adapt to the changing circumstances beyond the control of both parties.

Cost realisation relates to the outsourcee not working out the costs properly when quoting to the outsourcer at the evaluation/negotiating stage. This could lead to the outsourcee asking for a subsequent increase in the quoted price.

Confidentiality is a serious issue relating to intellectual property (IP) rights and confidential information being passed over to competitors.

One of the reported problems shown in Figure 3.1 is the outsourcee being overly polite in negotiations. This relates to the problem that could develop due to an outsourcee agreeing to everything the outsourcer asks for but then fails to deliver. This could be due to the culture of the country where saying 'no' to a request is considered rude and saying 'yes' is being polite.

In view of the issues that commonly lead to the failure of outsourcing, it is important to evaluate potential outsourcees before selection and agreement. In addition, a good outsourcer–outsourcee relationship development strategy can help to overcome a number of factors causing failure in outsourcing and we consider these in a later section.

EVALUATING AND SELECTING OUTSOURCEES

Once the outsourcing decision has been made, the first step is to evaluate potential outsourcees. As shown in Figure 3.2, the first stage of the evaluation comprises ascertaining if the outsourcee meets the qualifier parameters determined for the process under consideration. These parameters will vary depending on the product or service to be outsourced.

As we noted above, order qualifiers are those criteria and/or performance expectations that a company must meet for a customer to even consider it as a possible supplier. In Asia, the vendors in the manufacturing sector need to get certification under the ISO 9000 series as in most cases it allows them to bid or be considered for an order as potential supplier.

Some criteria that could be included as order qualifiers include:

- Reliability of delivery
- Quality certifications
- Conformance to agreed specifications
- Delivery lead time
- Financial capability
- Performance track record
- Price or cost reduction
- Senior management attitude
- Responsiveness to demand uncertainty
- Record of corporate social responsibility

The issue of **corporate social responsibility (CSR)** is growing in importance in business. CSR covers a multitude of activities and issues, and in essence concerns how 'ethical' a company's activities are. In this regard, the external image of a company is very critical. In recent years many companies have become embarrassed by revelations that they outsource upstream activities to suppliers with poor labour and safety records for example. More recently CSR issues have arisen downstream in the marketplace with concerns among consumers that some toys, largely produced by suppliers in low-cost locations, might comprise harmful components (see the Mattel case in Chapter 9). This in turn raises the issue of how closely outsourcers need to monitor outsourcees.

It is usual that some order qualifiers will be more critical than others in terms of the outsourcer's requirements and these are distinguished by labelling them as **order-losing sensitive qualifiers**. For example it may be the case that if a supplier does not perform to a delivery reliability of at least 95%, then it would cease to be an outsourcee for that particular line of business. In this case the delivery reliability forms an order-losing sensitive qualifier.

If the qualifier parameters are not met, then the outsourcer starts looking at alternative outsourcees. If the qualifier conditions are satisfied, but the outsourcer has no prior working experience with the outsourcee, then it is important to look at the level of difference between the working environments (the **environmental separation index**) of the outsourcer and outsourcee companies (or perhaps between the two countries). In addition, the outsourcer should consider how critical the outsourced product/process or service is to their core business. This will determine the management approach the outsourcer should use for supplier development, monitoring and supervision.

THE ENVIRONMENTAL SEPARATION INDEX (ESI)[12]

The environmental separation index (ESI) is used to assess the level of difference between the working environments of the outsourcer and outsourcee companies. A higher value of ESI indicates large differences in work practices, culture and perceptions. Once the outsourcee gains experience in working closely with the outsourcer and performs as per the expectation of each other, the ESI could reduce to a lower value.

In addition to qualifying for orders, some criteria may also act as order winners for a particular outsourced process. Depending on the situation, one or more of the qualifying criteria may give a cost–benefit advantage to become order-winning criteria for the supplier. The cost–benefit trade-off for implementing and managing an outsourcing arrangement has to be positive to constitute an order winner for the outsourcee.

We noted above that in a supplier development context, price is not the only criterion to be considered. The outsourcer needs to consider the total cost of outsourcing and this should include, as well as the basic cost of the product or service, the cost incurred by the outsourcer to manage the outsourcing arrangement. This is the cost of monitoring the outsourcee and the cost of setting up the relationship right from initiation through to operations and to termination. This cost should also reflect the risks involved in terms of transfer of technologies and intellectual property for example. In addition to the cost of coordination, there is also the cost of contingency planning to ensure delivery on time, for example by keeping higher inventory levels in the outsourcer country, or the need at times to deliver by air at premium costs due to not being able to meet the agreed schedule when using cheaper forms of transport. Related to the total cost of outsourcing is the concept of 'landed costs', which we will discuss further in Chapter 14.

Figure 3.2 outlines a framework for evaluating potential outsourcees.

OUTSOURCER AND OUTSOURCEE RELATIONSHIP DEVELOPMENT

The relationship between the outsourcer and the outsourcee evolves over time. It is possible that the initial outsourcing arrangement could change as the outsourcer starts to have more confidence in the capability of the outsourcee. This could also mean that the level of monitoring carried out by the outsourcer with respect to the outsourcee's operations is likely to reduce. It may be that that the outsourcer was involved in day-to-day operations management of the outsourced activity in the initial phases of the arrangement, however, as the relationship evolves the outsourcer

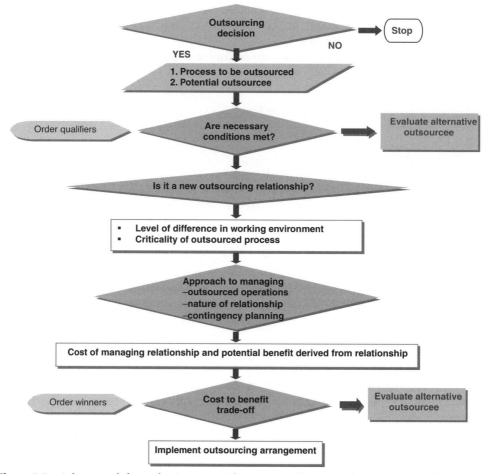

Figure 3.2   A framework for evaluating potential outsources (Source: Lalwani, Pawar & Shah, 2007)

would gradually reduce involvement in the outsourced activity. In fact research has shown that outsourcer–outsourcee relationships can move across four stages:[13]

- *Master–servant stage*: in this conventional relationship the outsourcer sets the expectations and the rules and the outsourcee delivers as per the stipulated norms. Low cost is the main driver of the outsourcing arrangement.

- *Consultative stage*: this stage is a type of a 'consultant–client' relationship. The outsourcer consults with the outsourcee on a regular basis. In addition to the cost, other factors such as quality, reliability and responsiveness are also important for sustaining the outsourcing arrangement.

- *Peer-to-peer relationship stage*: this is considered to be the ideal stage where the outsourcer and the outsourcee share a peer-to-peer relationship. This stage of collaboration results in a more synergistic long-term relationship creating 'win–win' situations for both the parties.

- *Competitive stage*: in this stage the original outsourcee company takes the lead role and starts to compete with the outsourcing company in global markets.

We have already noted that sometimes the relationship between both parties can involve supplier development, a topic we will return to again later in this chapter.

SUPPLY CHAIN INTEGRATION

Supply chain integration is a term that embodies various communication channels and linkages within a supply network. However, it should not be confused with **collaboration**. While supply chain integration is the alignment and interlinking of business processes, collaboration is a relationship between supply chain partners developed over a period of time. Integration is possible without collaboration. For example, order processing via electronic data interchange (EDI) (as discussed in Chapter 12) or the Scala system in the Gate Gourmet case are integrated transactions, but do not require the customer and supplier to operate collaboratively. Conversely, integration is an enabler of collaboration. This is discussed further in this chapter. Hence the terms integration and collaboration should not be confused.

There are four primary modes of integration within a supply chain (also illustrated in Figure 3.3):

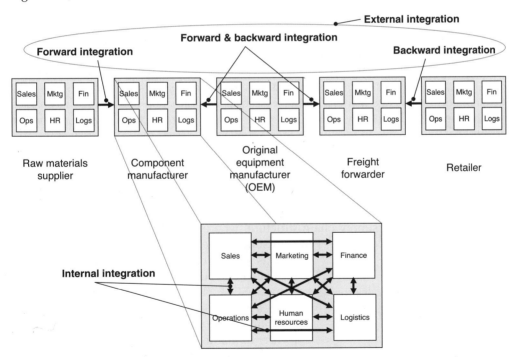

Note: arrows do not represent material flows

Figure 3.3   Distinctions between the primary modes of integration (Source: Fawcett & Magnan 2002)[14]

- *Internal integration*: cross-functional integration within a selected organisation.
- *Backward integration*: integration with selected first-tier and increasingly second-tier suppliers.
- *Forward integration*: integration with selected first-tier customers or service providers (e.g. logistics service providers). Forward integration with second-tier customers is uncommon.
- *Forward and backward integration*: integration with suppliers and customers. This 'total' integration is rare but theoretically ideal.

The latter three modes listed above can be classified as **external integration** (i.e. extending beyond the confines of a single organisation) as opposed to **internal integration**, which limits integration to within a particular organisation.

Focusing firstly on internal integration, the aim is to integrate communications and information systems so as to optimise their effectiveness and efficiency within the organisation. This can be achieved by structuring the organisation and the design and/or implementation of information systems for improved communication and information sharing. In doing so, non-value adding activity is minimised (e.g. duplication of effort), costs are reduced (e.g. reduced error rectification), lead times are reduced (e.g. order processing) and service quality is improved (e.g. improved order tracking).

External integration can take one of three forms: backward, forward or a combination of the two. EDI, as discussed later in Chapter 12, is a key enabler of supply chain integration. The automated transfer of order data between supply chain partners streamlines information sharing and processing. However, effective and efficient organisational design is a prerequisite. Leading automotive manufacturers, for example, work closely with their first-tier suppliers to integrate manufacturing, logistics and information processes. This enables just-in-time line-side delivery at their assembly plants. Typically, the OEMs (e.g. Ford or Toyota) use consultants to work with their suppliers to design their work structures and processes to fit with their own. By adopting the same practices, a seamless lean supply chain is created. That is, the processes up to line-side delivery at the assembly plant are part of one extended operation.

To filter these same principles further upstream, the Japanese automotive OEMs typically adopt a *keiretsu* supply chain structure, where the OEMs support their first-tier suppliers, their first-tier suppliers in turn support the second tier, and so on. *Keiretsu* was pioneered in Japanese banking and has since been adopted with great success in Japanese SCM. Thus, while information technologies are enablers of supply chain integration, optimal and uniform organisational structures are fundamental to integrating various parties across the supply chain. Nevertheless, the scale and complexity of global supply chains remains the key constraint to integration across multiple echelons.

> Whilst information technologies are enablers of supply chain integration, optimal and uniform organisational structures are fundamental to integrating actors in a supply chain.

SUPPLY CHAIN COLLABORATION PRINCIPLES

As discussed at the beginning of this chapter, supply chain integration is an enabler of collaboration. Whilst integration is product and process oriented, collaboration is focused on relationships. Information sharing can be achieved by implementing integrated processes and applications, but may not be of benefit to all supply chain partners, possibly exposing suppliers to their competitors. For example, supermarket retail is intensely competitive, as are automotive sales. This drives down consumer prices at the supermarket shelves and car dealers' forecourts, which in turn causes them to 'squeeze' their suppliers to operate with lower profit margins and tighter delivery schedules whilst maintaining service quality. Consequently, suppliers are forced by these market conditions to behave competitively rather than collaboratively. Collaboration is dependent on the provision of mutual benefit. Clearly in such supply chains, mutual benefit between suppliers is difficult to achieve. Hence trust becomes an issue.

The dynamics of trust and collaboration can be explained via the prisoner's dilemma, an example of Nash equilibrium game theory. Here is the analogy:

You and a partner are suspected of committing a crime and arrested. The police interview each of you separately. The police detective offers you a deal: your sentence will be reduced if you confess! Here are your options:

- If you confess but your partner doesn't: your partner gets the full 10-year sentence for committing the crime, whilst you get a 2-year sentence for collaborating.
- If you don't confess but you partner does: the tables are turned! You get the full 10-year sentence, whilst your partner gets the 2-year sentence.
- If both of you confess: you each get a reduced sentence of 5 years.
- If neither of you confess: you are both free people.

The dilemma you face is 'do you trust your partner to make the same decision as you?'

As we can see in Figure 3.4, the best strategy is based on trust, and results in a win–win situation. Yet, if neither partner trusts each other, it is most likely that both will confess and spend time in prison.

		You	
		Confess	Don't confess
Your partner	Confess	5,5	2,10
	Don't confess	10,2	0,0

Figure 3.4   The prisoner's dilemma

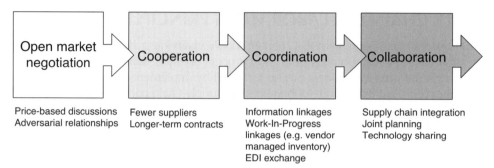

Figure 3.5   The journey from open market negotiations to collaboration (Source: Adapted from Spekman, Kamauff & Myhr 1998)[17]

Traditionally, business relationships have been built upon open market negotiations (i.e. gaining the lowest priced products and or services). From this common 'competitive' starting point, a trust-based win–win situation in a supply chain partnership takes time. Trust needs to be built up step by step. The journey towards a collaborative supply chain can be long and arduous. This is illustrated in Figure 3.5.

Collaboration has two dimensions: **vertical collaboration** between suppliers and customers, and **horizontal collaboration** between competitors and other supply chain actors. This is illustrated in Figure 3.6. As per our discussion thus far, vertical collaboration is more common and easier to implement than horizontal collaboration. However, supply networks that achieve both will gain significant business benefit. In the context for example of transport management, the combination of vertical and horizontal collaboration can achieve reduced inventory-carrying costs, reduce unproductive waiting time, reduce overall transport costs, improve integration of the transportation network, reduce empty running times and improve lead-time performance by adopting collaborative methods such as joint planning and technology sharing.[18] Imagine the benefits of two major high-street

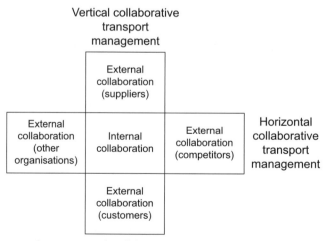

Figure 3.6   The two dimensions of collaboration applied to transport management (Source: Mason, Lalwani & Boughton, 2007)[19]

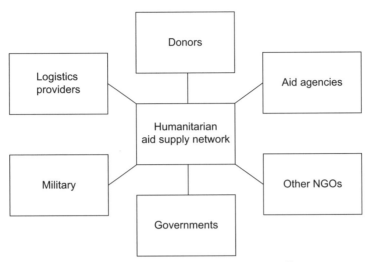

Figure 3.7   Actors in humanitarian logistics (Source: Kovács, 2007)[18]

retailers sharing transport capability in and out of London for their stores. This reiterates the prisoner's dilemma. Both retailers would benefit from improved logistics performance, but the fact that they compete directly for consumers' business is a significant barrier. Indeed we will see in Chapter 16, which deals with sustainability, that retailers are in fact adopting solutions such as this.

So far, the focus of our discussion has been in the business context. But what for example of the **humanitarian logistics** context? In a humanitarian disaster, competition between supply chain actors could have potentially devastating consequences. For example, two or more non-government organisations (NGOs) attempting to deliver the same aid to a particular location could overstock one area and understock another. Figure 3.7 identifies the actors in humanitarian logistics.

In humanitarian logistics, vertical coordination and collaboration between representatives/ governors of a disaster-struck region and actors from outside of that region, such as the national government or United Nations, is essential for preparation, immediate response and reconstruction – as illustrated in Figure 3.8. Nevertheless, horizontal collaboration is uncommon. Whilst some NGOs may share warehouse facilities, this is not usual.[19] Yet, if achievable, it is arguable that significant benefits could be gained. For further insights into the important and growing area of humanitarian logistics, see the case study on this topic (Humanitarian Aid Supply Chains) at the end of Part One of the book.

SUPPLY CHAIN COLLABORATION METHODS

As discussed above, global supply network complexity is a major constraint of both integration and collaboration. In networks such as those of the major retailers and manufacturers, there are multiple echelons with many suppliers competing for the same business.

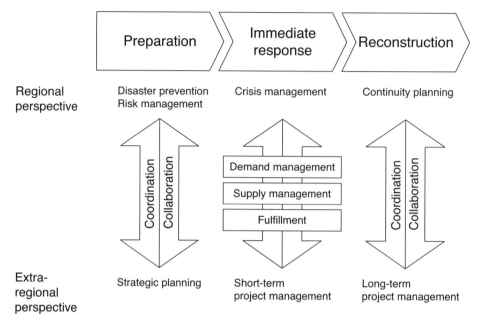

Figure 3.8 A framework for humanitarian logistics (Source: Kovács, 2007)[20]

Hence **supply base rationalisation** is periodically a key focus of such organisations. For example, Sony aimed to cut its supply base from 2500 to 1200 suppliers by March 2011 to reduce complexity and therefore costs as part of a strategic response to significant losses in 2009; more recently, however, the company's supply chain has been severely disrupted by the March 2011 Japanese earthquake.[21] This is a response to market pressures. However, upstream in such a supply chain it is not uncommon to find two companies with the same capabilities (e.g. engineering SMEs manufacturing cylindrical engine components) competing for the same orders handed down from their first-tier customer. This traditional competitive behaviour creates supply chain inefficiencies. If small-scale suppliers with limited resources are continually competing for business, they will inevitably drive down their prices, promise unrealistic lead times and lose their focus on product and service quality. Whilst we are conventionally led to believe that competition in business is good, in this case it is destructive. From our discussion of *keiretsu* above, it is far easier for a company such as Nissan to work with a few selected suppliers than to work with many suppliers. Furthermore, from our discussion of horizontal collaboration, suppliers who are not directly competing against each other for individual orders are more likely to collaborate. Supply chain rationalisation and horizontal collaboration are also discussed in the SupplyAero caselet below.

Coupled with the inevitable periodic supply base rationalisation should be supplier development activity (see earlier in this chapter on our discussion of outsourcing). As discussed in the context of *keiretsu* above, supplier development can enable improved integration and also collaboration. In the SupplyAero caselet example the company employs supplier development to shift its suppliers' mindsets from thinking competitively to collaboratively. This enables them to utilise their integrated order-processing application for

aggregated procurement. That is to say, rather than individual suppliers tendering for particular orders, specific suppliers are selected by a supplier selection software package based on their capabilities. In the previous *competitive* environment some suppliers would win orders whilst others would not. In the new *collaborative environment* each supplier gains a share of

> Supply chain collaboration cannot be achieved through IT solutions alone. Substantial investment in building resilient, long-term relationships is a prerequisite.

the total orders based on their ability to deliver the order on time and to specification. Consequently, the overall supply base incrementally improves, reducing the likelihood of future rationalisation.

SUPPLYAERO HOLDINGS LTD

The UK has a strong aerospace industry with a number of market-leading original equipment manufacturers (OEMs). Hence a number of UK-based manufacturers exist to supply aerospace components to these OEMs. Meanwhile these suppliers also supply to maintenance, repair and overhaul companies (MROs) who maintain in-service aircraft. A typical existing UK aerospace supply chain is illustrated in Figure 3.9.

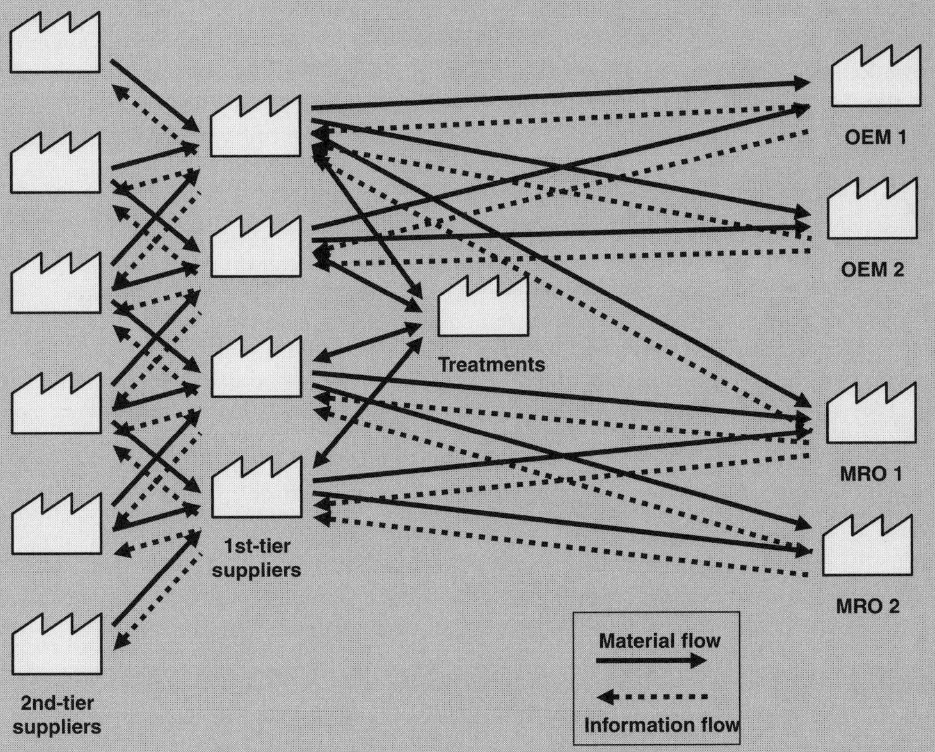

Figure 3.9   An existing UK aerospace supply chain

A significant issue in this existing supply chain is the late delivery of components to OEMs and MROs. Late delivery is caused by demand fluctuations from a mixture of three types of order: steady state production orders (i.e. components required to build new aircraft, which can be forecast from OEM production order data); spares orders (i.e. components required for scheduled maintenance of in-service aircraft, which can be forecast from MRO maintenance schedule data); AoG (Aircraft on Ground) orders (i.e. components urgently required for unscheduled maintenance of in-service aircraft that cannot be used until repaired, which cannot be forecast).

Upstream suppliers are typically SMEs (small and medium sized enterprises) operating with low profit margins. Hence, these suppliers bid for any orders that are offered, regardless of whether they have sufficient capability to fulfil those orders to the customers' requirements. Furthermore, they neither have the time nor the finances to implement best practice processes and information systems to improve their responsiveness to this complex and difficult-to-forecast overall market demand. These suppliers are therefore locked into a vicious cycle of competing for orders that they cannot effectively fulfil. Likewise, OEMs and MROs have the burden of chasing unfulfilled and late orders, and typically receive individual components (e.g. an undercarriage axle shaft) at irregular intervals from each supplier rather than consolidated kits of parts from a single source (e.g. a complete kit of undercarriage axle parts for assembly/replacement).

SupplyAero Holdings Ltd specialises in integrating aerospace supply chains, and has developed a solution to this problem. It has purchased the treatments plant[22] in the supply chain represented above. The treatments plant is both positioned close to the downstream end of the supply chain and is conventionally viewed as a 'bottleneck' where a number of component batches from various suppliers converge simultaneously. It is therefore in a key position to gain visibility and control of both upstream and downstream processes. Yet this alone is not enough to improve the supply chain. The company has also developed three new businesses to improve supply chain agility, namely:

1. *An order-processing business:* using a bespoke suite of software, order-processing operatives (i) receive orders from OEMs and MROs; (ii) select suppliers based upon their capabilities (e.g. experience of producing that component, lead time, dependability); and (iii) forward orders to the selected suppliers. Orders are then tracked via software through to fulfilment. OEMs and MROs therefore benefit from aggregated procurement and order processing by a third party. Suppliers receive less (but more focused) orders, enabling them to no longer waste resources on competing for orders that they could not fulfil, and focus on their core competencies.

2. *A supplier development consultancy:* supplier development consultants work with suppliers to improve their capability via initiatives aimed at lead-time reduction, product and service quality improvement, delivery reliability and cost reduction.

3. *A kitting warehouse:* when orders have completed all manufacturing and treatment operations they are consolidated and packaged (i.e. kitted) before being shipped to the OEM or MRO as a complete order.

This supply chain redesign is represented in Figure 3.10.

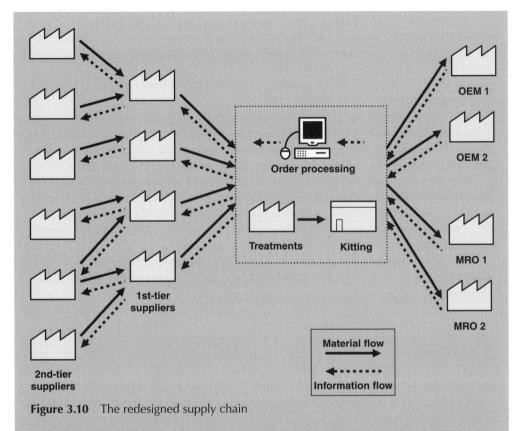

Figure 3.10 The redesigned supply chain

Thus SupplyAero has integrated the supply chain and enabled supplier collaboration by: aggregating procurement and offering single-source supply to OEMs and MROs; matching orders to suppliers' capabilities to rationalise the number of transactions; supporting suppliers in improving their internal processes.

LEARNING REVIEW

In this chapter we have explored, and differentiated, the areas of outsourcing, offshoring, integration and collaboration. We discussed the need for outsourcing and have explained the most frequently reported problems leading to failure in outsourcing arrangements. We identified and differentiated order-qualifying and order-winning criteria in terms of what outsourcers look at when deciding who to outsource to, and we detailed the process typically followed for evaluating and selecting suppliers. Outsourcer–outsourcee relationship development is generally regarded to evolve through phases of development and we also examined these phases.

It is apparent that for outsourcing companies, a range of possibilities exist with regard to how they interact with their outsourcees. In our discussion around CSR we noted that for some outsourcing companies, the outsourcee can end up being a source of embarrassment. At the other end of the spectrum some leading companies engage in supplier development programmes with their outsource partners, leading to mutual benefit for both parties.

We then extended our discussion to supply chain integration and collaboration. In discussing integration, we introduced different modes of integration, illustrating that it extends beyond the integration of computer systems to the integration of business processes, both within a single organisation and between supply chain partners.

We discussed both the principles and practices of supply chain collaboration. The prisoner's dilemma illustrates how collaborative behaviour can be more beneficial than competitive behaviour. This is further illustrated by the SupplyAero caselet, enabling the whole supply chain to improve. In practice, collaboration between supply chain partners takes a great deal of time and effort.

The next chapter will now turn to identifying the various strategies that companies employ in order to survive and compete within this complex and dynamic environment.

QUESTIONS

- Cost pressures are driving manufacturers to increasingly go offshore to low-cost economies. This in turn is increasing international trade and freight movements. Referring to the world map in this book, how does this impact the major logistics hubs in the world, and will there be a need for more hubs?
- Explain the distinction between outsourcing and offshoring.
- What are the most frequently reported problems in outsourcing?
- Explain what factors would typically be considered in contingency planning in outsourcing arrangements.
- Explain the distinction between integration and outsourcing.
- How might a response to a humanitarian disaster be improved through vertical and horizontal collaboration between the various actors?

NORTH EUROPEAN SHOE COMPANY (OUTSOURCER)–BX SHOES (OUTSOURCEE)

BX Shoes is a subsidiary of one of the leading brands in India. It has a completely export-oriented partnership with an Italian shoe company. The supplier selection parameters for the Italian firm as outsourcer were that the outsourcee should be financially strong – since it is a cash-intensive, high-working capital business. BX Shoes were a good fit to the outsourcer's requirements. There are inherent problems in procurement of leather such as long lead times, it is a very cash-intensive activity and the quality can only be judged at the final product stage. Due to these risks, a supplier partnership approach was preferred by the outsourcer to reduce the uncertainties. The entire manufacturing activity is outsourced, including the procurement of raw material, with a lot of ongoing close cooperation between the management of the outsourcer and the management of the outsourcee.

Let us look at the partnership evolution of BX Shoes with its Italian outsourcer:

- In 1997 the Italian partner was looking at extending its manufacturing operations to India and BX was looking at getting into a new business. The two companies signed a memorandum of understanding specifying broadly the roles and responsibilities of both parties. BX was looking for somebody who knew the business and the Italian partner was looking for someone who was an established group in India.

- The arrangement was not exclusive initially. The Italian outsourcer was working multiple outsourcees in India. The arrangement started on a small scale initially. The business model essentially at the beginning was pure finished goods outsourcing. However, down the line BX decided that procurement of some key raw material would be done by them – essentially material contributing 70–80% of material costs.

- Revenues in year 2 went up by 50%, but fell by 20% in year 3. This was a period of trial. They were establishing the business but not making headway. Then in 1999–2000 an 'exclusive marriage' between the Italian partner and BX took place and growth began again.

- The partnership effectively works like a joint venture – it is a collaboration. Their involvement does not stop at the design stage. Other players feel that the collaboration is an innovative way of doing things. The normal practice is to have a model with less involvement and operate through agents. In the BX case the participation by both the partners is complete. For example, if improper material is procured both partners will work together to resolve the issue there and then. The material either needs to be sent back or repaired. The trust between BX and the Italian partner has been built up over time – at the top management level. At the trade fairs both the names BX as well as the Italian partner are displayed.

NOTES

1. Lalwani, C.S., Pawar, K.S. & Shah, J. (2007) Contextualisation framework for the manufacturing supply chain, published by the Centre for Concurrent Enterprise, University of Nottingham Business School, Nottingham, UK.

2. Rates of pay in, for example, China and India are much lower than in Europe and North America. This varies significantly both by sector and also by geographical region (in effect basic laws of supply and demand at work with employees in more industrialised regions commanding higher pay).

3. *India Today* (2006) India in numbers, 21 August, The India Today Group, New Delhi.

4. *China Statistical Yearbook, 2007,* Ministry of Commerce and Industry of India, and the *World Investment Report, 2007,* cited in Lo, C.P. & Liu, B.J. (2009) Why is India mainly

engaged in offshore service activities, while China is disproportionately engaged in manufacturing?, *China Economic Review*, 20(2), 236–245.

5. Van Weele, A.J. (2005) *Purchasing Supply Chain Management: Analysis, Strategy, Planning and Practice*, Thomson Learning, London.

6. Simchi-Levi, D., Kaminsky, P. & Simchi-Levi, E. (2003) *Designing and Managing the Supply Chain (2nd Edition)*, McGraw-Hill, New York, p. 214.

7. Lalwani *et al.* (see note 1).

8. Christopher, M., Peck, H. & Towill, D. (2006) A taxonomy for selecting global supply chain strategies, *International Journal of Logistics Management*, 17(2), 276.

9. SAP INFO Solutions, quoted in *Sloan Management Review*, Winter, 2006.

10. Pandit, P. (2005) Quality of customer service in outsourcing, unpublished dissertation, Nottingham University Business School: Operations Management Division, Nottingham, UK.

11. Whittle, G. (2007) Critical limits, *Logistics and Transport Focus*, 9(2), March.

12. USER-MIND (2006) Understanding Potential Synergies in Manufacturing Supply Chains between Europe and India, EU Asia IT & C project, www.usermind.org (investigators: C.S. Lalwani, K.S. Pawar, J. Shah & K.-D. Thoben).

13. Pawar, K.S., Gupta, A., Lalwani, C.S., Shah, J., Ghosh, D. & Eschenbacher, J. (2005) Outsourcing to India: exploring the management implications for the outsourcer and outsourcee, *Proceedings of the 37th Annual Convention of OR Society of India*, IIM, Ahmedabad, India.

14. Fawcett, S. & Magnan, G. (2002) The rhetoric and reality of supply chain integration, *International Journal of Physical Distribution and Logistics Management*, 32(5), 339–361.

15. Spekman, R., Kamauff, J. & Myhr, N. (1998) An empirical investigation into supply chain management: a perspective on partnerships, *Supply Chain Management*, 3(2), 53–67.

16. Mason, R., Lalwani, C. & Boughton, R. (2007) Combining horizontal and vertical collaboration for transport optimisation, *Supply Chain Management: An International Journal*, 12(3), 187–199.

17. Ibid.

18. Kovács, G. (2007) The humanitarian supply chain: challenge or role model? *Centre for Logistics Research Inaugural Seminar*, Hull University Business School, Hull, 4th July.

19. Ibid.

20. Ibid.

21. Reuters (2010) Sony nears goal of cutting suppliers, accessed 8th November 2010.

22. Many of the components are metal. Metal components require protection from corrosion, hardening and non-destructive testing. These specialist processes are commonly known as treatments.

4 Supply Chain Strategies

LEARNING OBJECTIVES

- Highlight the role of logistics and supply chain strategy in the context of firm strategy, and see how logistics and supply chain strategy can actually sometimes drive firm strategy.
- Outline the evolution of manufacturing, from which various logistics and supply chain strategies have emerged.
- Look at both lean and agile logistics strategies, and the role of mass customisation in the latter.
- Develop a taxonomy of supply chain strategies.

INTRODUCTION

The preceding three chapters gave us an understanding of the drivers for the evolution of logistics and SCM, the global context within which both operate, the role of outsourcing in supply chains, the importance of relationships, and the need for integration across the supply chain. This chapter now turns to introducing the various logistics and supply chain strategies that companies employ in order to survive and compete within this complex and dynamic environment. Logistics and supply chain strategy is not, however, divorced from a firm's strategy, and so we first have to look at firm strategy and examine its relationship to logistics and supply chain strategy. We will also see in this chapter that not only is logistics and supply chain strategy part of a firm's strategy, but also in many instances logistics and supply chain strategy can be the key component within, and driver of, a firm's strategy.

Chapter 4 comprises six core sections:

- Strategy
- The evolution of manufacturing
- Lean production
- Agile supply chains and mass customisation
- Combined logistics strategies
- Critical factors to consider in supply chain planning

STRATEGY

The field of business strategy is a wide, fascinating and varied subject. It is also of crucial importance because an organisation without a strategy is, in our view, like a ship without a compass! Strategy can be generally described as being concerned with planning and configuring the organisation for the future in accordance with certain stakeholder expectations. More simply, the *Collins English Dictionary* defines strategy as 'a particular long term plan for success'. Our specific purpose in this chapter is not, however, to explore the whole field of strategy, but instead to examine the link between strategy and both logistics and SCM, and to consider specific logistics and supply chain strategies. In fact we will view logistics strategy and supply chain strategy together – as we already noted above in Chapter 1, in this book we adopt the *unionist view*, i.e., that logistics is part of the wider entity which is SCM. It follows then that logistics strategy and supply chain strategy will be closely connected and for the purposes of this book we consider both conjointly.

A usual starting point when considering a firm's strategy is to work from the 'top down'. Thus people will often first consider the wider whole organisation or *corporate strategy* and its objectives. For example, what are the overall financial and growth targets for the organisation? Similarly, organisations need to decide what technologies and markets they want to focus upon. Increasingly of late, organisations are also turning to consider the impact of their operations on the environment. We will return to this issue of sustainability, and its link to global logistics, in Chapter 16.

Below the whole organisation level is what is often referred to as the *business unit* level. Many large organisations are divided into such business units, which focus on specific products and markets. For example some large logistics service providers may have separate warehousing, transport and other business units, and may develop separate strategies for each of these areas.

The final level is often referred to as *functional strategy* and refers to the development of strategies for specific areas of activity within a business unit (e.g. marketing, IT and logistics). Figure 4.1 depicts this top–down structure.

Not everyone agrees, however, that this is the best way to formulate strategy. Two questions which arise are: (i) it doesn't allow for a 'bottom–up' perspective and (ii) in the case of logistics and to a lesser extent SCM, it assumes that these are functions just like other functions within the organisation. Furthermore, there is an increasingly held view that much of what constitutes strategy is *emergent*, that is, that companies need to evolve their strategies to meet the challenges of the dynamic, ever-changing business environment. More and more then the view that a strategy can be dictated from the 'top' of an organisation and not revised for a number of years is becoming redundant.

Taking a 'bottom–up' perspective of strategy allows us to see how logistics can contribute to the wider business unit and firm strategies. Some argue that logistics can in

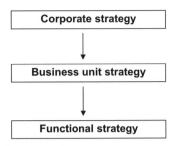

Figure 4.1 Top–down perspective on strategy

fact be the foundation for overall strategic action.[1] In this context it would seem to be inappropriate to reduce the formulation of logistics and supply chain strategy to the same level as that which pertains to most other functions. Furthermore SCM is an activity which is truly cross-functional and not limited to one functional area. Many firms are organised into what are sometimes referred to as functional **silos**, for example marketing and production, and often the various functions do not integrate sufficiently with each other. Such a structure, however, is often not sufficiently responsive to meeting customer demands, which typically do not (and should not) respect internal organisational barriers.

SCM in contrast seeks a take a cross-functional, process-based perspective. To quote Fabbe-Costes and Colin,[2] there is a mature perception of logistics as a cross-functional and deliberately open-ended management domain in the firm, and as a proactive interface with external partners in the supply chain. Figure 4.2 attempts to capture a more holistic view of strategy formulation as it applies to logistics and SCM.

We started out this section by highlighting the importance of strategy, and this is indeed the case. We must not lose sight, however, of the fact that what is also very important is

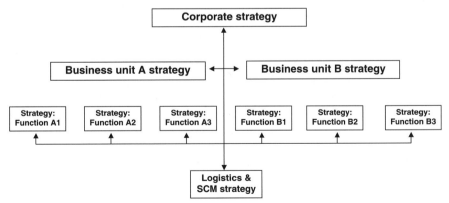

Figure 4.2 A holistic view of logistics and SCM strategy formulation

> Formulating a strategy for logistics and SCM should not be restricted to the logistics function: instead it should involve taking a cross-functional, process-based perspective.

that organisations effectively implement their strategies (some call this strategy execution), as many elaborate strategy planning exercises no doubt just remain sitting on office shelves. To quote the famous management thinker Henry Mintzberg, 90% of strategy is implementation. What is important then is that the organisation monitors the implementation of its strategy, and makes whatever changes are necessary and appropriate in the following weeks, months and indeed years, without being bound to a plan which may not be working out in practice.

Two principal logistics and supply chain strategies (although there are others, and indeed combinations of strategies are also used – more on this later) have emerged in recent decades, namely *lean* and *agile*. We will review these in turn in subsequent sections. We will then progress on to an understanding that a 'one-size-fits-all' approach to logistics strategy increasingly makes less sense, and thus we will consider combined logistics strategies.

Before we start to look specifically at lean and agile logistics and supply chain strategies, it is useful to first briefly look at how different models of manufacturing have evolved over the last 100 years or so. In the evolution of manufacturing two key output criteria, namely output volume and output variety, have been separate goals that firms have worked towards. It is, however, only in recent years that the goal of simultaneously achieving both has really been accomplished.

THE EVOLUTION OF MANUFACTURING

Other things being equal, most production units will endeavour to produce goods and services which satisfy high levels of customer demand (via a high level of output variety), while at the same time producing large volumes so as to enjoy economies of scale in production. It was not always like this. Prior to the industrial revolution, and indeed for many years during and after it in some industries, skilled artisans produced goods customised for individual customer needs. This was called *craft production*. Just think of the history of shoe production, for example. While this undoubtedly satisfied customer needs, it was a costly form of production. Craft production still of course exists in certain specialist, high-value industries.

If we fast forward to the early twentieth century, one of the most exciting advancements was the widespread development of *mass production*. A notable example is that of car manufacturing by Henry Ford. His company certainly exploited economies of scale in manufacturing and enjoyed tremendous success for many years. The choice of products was, however, quite limited – just think of his famous maxim concerning the *Model T* motor car that customers could have any colour as long as it was black! We had yet to

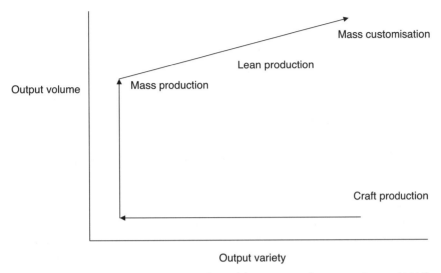

Figure 4.3 Production strategies (Source: Adapted from Womack, Roos & Jones, 1991)[3]

arrive at a situation where both volume and variety of output could be maximised. We will consider the remaining elements in Figure 4.3, the emergence of lean production and mass customisation, via the sections that follow.

LEAN PRODUCTION

The origins of **lean** production and logistics can be traced back in particular to the car company Toyota and its ingenious Toyota Production System, pioneered by people such as Kiichiro Toyoda (son of the company's founder), Taiichi Ohno and others during the 1930s and especially after World War II. In developing the Toyota Production System they drew heavily on the work of Ford and identified areas in the Ford model that could be improved. They also drew on the work of the American quality guru, W. Edwards Deming. In fact much of Deming's early work received a richer response in Japan than it did in the USA, and the Japanese were to enjoy significant competitive advantage as a result of their embracing of what came to be called total quality management (TQM).

Toyota sought to develop a production system where the emphasis was not on the efficiency of individual machines, but on total flows through a system. Significant emphasis was placed on quick machine turnovers, elimination of waste (known in Japanese as *muda*), even production flows, low levels of inventory, faster total process time and achieving total quality. Where many production systems are '**push**' based, Toyota sought to develop a system where inventory is '**pulled**' downstream through the system. This prevents stockpiling and inefficiency and is known as **just-in-time (JIT)** inventory replenishment (discussed further in Chapter 10), where inventory is kept to a minimum and replenished only as it is used. The **Toyota Production System (TPS)** was born and in particular it sought to eliminate waste (in the form of unnecessary inventory and inefficient processes) in seven key areas (discussing these areas gives us insights into much of the thinking behind lean production):

1. Overproduction – basically producing too much. In this instance some inventory ends up being held in a warehouse or other holding area. This is referred to as **make-to-stock (MTS)**, as opposed to the more efficient **make-to-order (MTO)**.

2. Waiting – poor process design and/or poor planning may result in work-in-progress inventory waiting until a machine or operator becomes available so that it can go through the next stage of production. Many aspects of the TPS philosophy also find application outside of manufacturing contexts. In the case of 'waiting' think, for example, of the inefficiencies that arise in some healthcare systems where patients have to wait in hospital, sometimes for days, for the appropriate doctor to examine them or read their test results.

3. Transportation – except in the case of products such as software, invariably most products have to be physically transported to the marketplace. In a sense this is non-value adding time with the freight just sitting on the truck. Again, adopting the TPS philosophy, one might try to think of ways in which value could be added to the product during this idle time. Just think, for example, of bananas ripening in transit. Another example concerns certain medical devices which have to be sterilised after production but before use. Some manufacturers have developed special packaging which allows chemicals to dissipate from the post-production sterilised product within the package over a fixed period of time. During this fixed period the devices can of course still be transported to the market, the only caveat is that the product is not opened until the due date.

4. Inappropriate processing – in some production systems sometimes all products may enjoy the same level of processing, even though this might only be required for some of the products. An example might be using a certain advanced type of packaging on all products, even though this might only be required in certain markets.

5. Unnecessary inventory – inventory has various costs associated with it which we will study in detail in Chapter 10. Suffice to note for now that holding unnecessary inventory *just-in-case* it may be required is costly and may also actually hide problems.

6. Unnecessary motion – in a poorly designed production system it may be the case that work-in-progress inventory moves in an erratic route between stages around the factory. In a retail distribution example in Chapter 6 a similar scenario (albeit on a larger scale) is illustrated whereby a supplier delivers product from region X to a consolidation centre in region Y, only for the product to then be moved back to a regional distribution centre operated by the retailer near region X.

7. Defects – product that is defective invariably can cause production delays as it may be necessary to see what caused the defect. Furthermore, if the defect is only observed at the end stage of production, it may take time to discover where exactly the problem arose. This is all wasteful downtime which total quality systems, by their emphasis on zero defects, seek to minimise.

A key aspect of lean is ensuring that value is added at each stage of the process ('the value stream') and steps in the process that do not add value are eliminated.

In recent years an eighth area, underutilisation of resources, has been added to the list. Toyota became one of the world's most successful manufacturers and while companies in the West were initially sceptical of Toyota's ideas, they quickly began to embrace them. A key study of the worldwide auto industry, the International Motor Vehicle Programme, by Womack, Roos and Jones in 1990 brought the world of lean to a wide audience. The study was published in a highly influential book called *The Machine that Changed the World*[4] and resulted from a five-year, $5 million, 14-country study conducted by MIT, apparently the largest and most thorough study ever undertaken in any industry.

> Traditionally, many production systems worked on a *push* mentality, that is materials are produced according to a planned forecast (which may or may not be accurate) and moved to the next stage of the supply chain; in *pull*-based systems inventory is only produced and moved when it is required, and thus is more closely aligned with actual demand. (In essence, push systems relate to MTS, while pull systems relate to MTO – see point 1 in the TPS.)

Such has been the success of lean production and logistics that in recent years many of their ideas have been translated to the services sector. Two of the authors of the book, *The Machine that Changed the World*, Womack and Jones, wrote that 'lean production transformed manufacturing. Now it's time to apply lean thinking to the processes of consumption. By minimising customers' time and effort and delivering exactly what they want when and where they want it, companies can reap huge benefits'.[5] Womack and Jones developed their own principles of lean consumption:[6]

- Solve the customer's problem completely.
- Don't waste the customer's time.
- Provide exactly what the customer wants.
- Provide what's wanted exactly where it's wanted.
- Provide what's wanted where it's wanted exactly when it's wanted.
- Continually aggregate solutions to reduce the customer's time and hassle.

> Lean production and logistics is concerned with eliminating waste in a pull-based value stream of activities with level production (i.e. even production runs with neither idle time nor surges in demand) and just-in-time inventory management.

AGILE SUPPLY CHAINS AND MASS CUSTOMISATION

Managing supply chains effectively is a complex and challenging task, due to the current business trends of expanding product variety, short product life cycles, increased outsourcing, globalisation of businesses and continuous advances in information technology.[7] Indeed we can add more factors to this list such as hyper competition in markets and increasing demands from customers. In recent years the area of risk in supply chains, whether from natural sources (for example disease in the food supply chain) or manmade sources (for example terrorism), is adding to the challenges in SCM (we will return to this growing and important area in Chapter 15). All of these disparate factors have led to a high level of volatility in demand for products.

To mitigate such volatility another supply chain model has emerged, the **agile** supply chain. Pioneered by Professor Martin Christopher and colleagues at Cranfield University, and others, the agile supply chain is designed so as to cope with such volatility. According to Professor Christopher, 'to a truly agile business volatility of demand is not a problem; its processes and organisational structure as well as its supply chain relationships enable it to cope with whatever demands are placed upon it'.[8] A particular characteristic of the agile supply chain is that it in effect seeks to act as a 'demand chain' with all movement upstream in the supply chain as a result of customer demand.

One of the key enablers of agile supply chains is the use of a technique known as **mass customisation**. This involves *customisation* into various different finished products of what are often largely *mass*-produced products. Even when different product configurations contain a majority of shared components and features, the customer will usually concentrate upon the dissimilar features among the similar products.

Mass customisation makes use of a production philosophy known as the **principle of postponement** (Figure 4.4). Think of the black circles in the diagrams as work-in-progress inventory with the black squares on the right of each diagram as the (8) finished products. Both of the production processes depicted thus comprise three intermediate

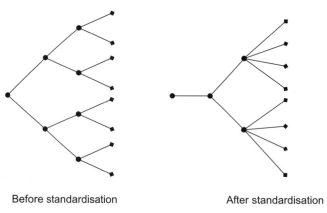

Before standardisation   After standardisation

Figure 4.4 The principle of postponement

production stages prior to production of the finished products. Production processes with many different parallel production lines can be very inefficient (left-hand side of Figure 4.4), especially if demand reduces for the output of one line and increases for that of another. However, by reconfiguring processes and standardising certain inputs and steps, the impact of variability in demand for finished products can be reduced. We can see on the right-hand side of Figure 4.4 that if it is discovered during the production process that demand for certain finished products reduces, semi-processed product can easily be 'diverted' into the production of other finished products.

Many manufacturers are now realising the benefits of producing products on what have come to be known as common or shared platforms. Various labels have been given to these shared platforms in different industries, for example the base product, the core product, the vanilla product (using the ice cream analogy of undyed plain ice cream), the generic product and the grey product (a term used in garment manufacturing to refer to undyed fabric). In a postponed production system, ideally the final value-adding activities in the supply chain are delayed until customer orders are received.

The point at which we move from the base product to customised products is called the **decoupling point**. If you look to the case study on Dell at the end of Part One of the book, the decoupling point is the point in the production process where the core PC platforms are configured into final products demanded by customers.

The automobile manufacturing industry has been a keen user of mass customisation (see the box: Small Car Manufacturing: Cooperation between Toyota, Peugeot and Citroën). Indeed Toyota, Peugeot and Citroën were not the first to do so. Other advocates of the approach include the Volkswagen Group which comprises among others the brands Volkswagen, Audi, Skoda and Seat. Many of the product offerings in the different car models across these brands share similar platforms and components. Apart from making sense from production and financial perspectives, consolidation in the automobile manufacturing sector, where once many companies were keen competitors but are now working together and sometimes even merging, is now driving increased application of mass customisation in the industry.

Mass customisation is enabled by a production philosophy known as postponement, which involves the reconfiguration of product and process design so as to allow postponement of final product customisation as far downstream as possible. Other names for this approach are simply 'delayed product configuration', 'delayed product differentiation' and 'late stage customisation'.

The postponement approach doesn't just apply to manufacturing. *Packaging postponement* for example is merely delaying final packaging of products until customer orders are received (different packaging may be required for different customers, and rather than make different packaged product lines to stock, product could be quickly packaged as required once specific orders are received).

Toyota, Citroën and Peugeot decided to adopt a different approach for the manufacture of a new range of cars

All three are produced in the new, purpose-built joint TPCA factory in the Czech Republic.

All three share 92% of the same components.

Peugeot/Citroën are responsible for sourcing and procurement and Toyota for production.

Small Car Manufacturing: Cooperation between Toyota, Peugeot and Citroën

BUYING PAINT

It's not just the automobile manufacturing industry that employs mass customisation, many other industries have also adopted the technique. Just think of the way in which the purchase of paint has changed. Because of developments in both production technology and the marketing of paint, the range of different paint colours it is now possible to purchase has increased dramatically. In addition, it is usually possible to buy paint in various different can sizes (e.g. 1 litre, 5 litres). The range of potential stock-keeping units (SKUs) in paint distribution is thus huge.

Rather than keeping all possible SKUs in each store, mass customisation has become very popular in paint distribution. Each store holds the primary colours of paint and a machine then mixes these to a specific formula to produce the exact required colour of paint from a range of possible colours. All that is otherwise required are paint cans in the different sizes and a simple printing machine that can produce labels with the name of the paint.

Note: A **stock-keeping unit** is a unique version in terms of size, packaging etc. of a particular product type, e.g. 2-litre cans of white paint would be one unique SKU, 2-litre cans of harvest yellow paint would be another unique SKU, while 1-litre cartons of harvest yellow paint would be yet another unique SKU, and so forth.

Now back to agility. Professor Christopher describes agility as 'the ability to respond rapidly to unpredictable changes in demand'.[9] In his view 'agility is not a single company concept, it extends from one end of the supply chain to the other'.

Christopher points out that 'agility is concerned primarily with responsiveness. It is about the ability to match supply and demand in turbulent and unpredictable markets'.[10]

The questions which now arise are: which approach is better, lean or agile? And are the lean and agile supply chain approaches mutu-

> The agile supply chain is a demand-pull chain designed to cope with volatile demand. It is structured so as to allow maximum flexibility and will often incorporate postponed production.

ally exclusive, i.e. can we have both together? These are questions of much debate in the academic literature and which we attempt to answer in the next section.

COMBINED LOGISTICS STRATEGIES

So which is better, a lean or agile supply chain strategy? And can we have both together? Certainly it is now becoming apparent that there is no one generic supply chain typology that works in all situations. A simple scenario is to use lean strategies to manage base demand (a forecast-driven approach) and to use agile strategies to manage surge demand (a demand-driven approach). We can build further upon this as we consider the variable nature of product lead times, life cycles, marketplace demand, etc.

In an often quoted paper from the *Harvard Business Review* in 1997, Professor Marshall Fisher from the University of Pennsylvania put forward a framework for supply chain selection based upon the nature of product demand.[11] He distinguished functional products, which have predictable demand, long product life cycles, low variety and long lead times, from innovative products, which have unpredictable demand, short product life cycles, high variety and short lead times. Fisher suggested that two different types of supply chains are required for these two different types of products, which he termed efficient supply chains for functional products and responsive supply chains for innovative products.

Christopher *et al.*, building upon the work of Fisher and others, have put forward a taxonomy (Figure 4.5) for selecting global supply chain strategies and which uses both predictability of demand for products and replenishment lead times.[12] It also incorporates lean and agile philosophies as appropriate. They again argue that a 'one-size-fits-all' approach will not work and that companies need to continually assess their product range and market characteristics so that changing scenarios may be identified and appropriate supply chain designs configured. This is the approach also taken by other authors, such as Professor John Gattorna whom we will discuss in the next section. He argues for a dynamic capability in supply chain designs so that they can respond to any changes and he argues against designing supply chains for specific products because, as he argues, different types of demand can in fact exist for the same product, even among the same customer depending on when and why he/she wants to buy the product.

	Lean Plan and execute	**Leagile** Postponement
Long lead time		
Short lead time	**Lean** Continuous replenishment	**Agile** Quick response

Predictable demand   Unpredictable demand

Supply demand characteristics	Resulting pipelines
Short lead time + predictable demand	Lean, continuous replenishment
Short lead time + unpredictable demand	Agile, quick response
Long lead time + predictable demand	Lean, planning and execution
Long lead time + unpredictable demand	Leagile production / logistics postponement

Figure 4.5   A taxonomy for selecting global supply chain strategies (Source: Christopher, Peck, & Towill, 2006)[13]

Lean, continuous replenishment: this applies in situations where demand is predictable and replenishment lead times are relatively short. This would apply for example in the case of a supplier making regular deliveries to a retailer. Over time a steady demand pattern will likely be apparent, allowing the supplier to 'lean' the supply chain with a high level of certainty. In such situations it is often the case that the supplier will take total responsibility for stock replenishment (we refer to this as vendor managed inventory – it will be discussed further in Chapter 12), sometimes even directly onto retailers' shelves. Predictability in the supply chain can be enhanced by retailers facilitating full visibility in the supply by allowing suppliers direct access to **electronic point of sale** (EPOS) data.

Agile, quick response: this applies in situations where replenishment lead times are still short but where demand is now unpredictable. In such situations suppliers need to respond rapidly to changes in demand. An excellent example is that of the Spanish clothing manufacturer and retailer Zara (see the case study below) who have designed a highly responsive supply chain which can translate the latest fashion trends into new products and deliver them to stores within a very short space of time. Because of the unpredictability in demand, manufacturers such as Zara can make use of postponed production/ delayed configuration so that they can quickly configure the base product (referred to in the case of clothing manufacturers as the *grey* garment) into the required final product.

Lean, planning and execution: this applies in situations where demand is predictable and replenishment lead times are long. It is a similar scenario to 'lean, continuous replenishment' described above, except here lead times are longer so more planning is required at a point well ahead of when demand will actually be realised. Lean principles can be applied in such supply chains once any uncertainty caused by long lead times can be managed. A classic example cited by Christopher *et al.* is that of artificial Christmas trees sourced into Europe each year from Asia.

Leagile: this applies in situations where replenishment lead times are still long, but now to add to the complexity demand is unpredictable. In this scenario we can combine both lean and agile logistics philosophies to create what is termed the **leagile supply chain** (this is sometimes referred to as a 'hybrid strategy'). Using postponed production/delayed configuration as described above, the base product can be manufactured at a remote location and shipped to locations nearer the final market (with both manufacturing and distribution using lean principles), where it is then configured into the required final product (using agile principles). The final postponement could range from something as simple as using different types of packaging for different markets to manufacturing postponement where different components are added to the base product downstream as required.

If we now consider the concept of the decoupling point which was described in the previous section, in the leagile supply chain lean principles can apply up to the decoupling point, and agile principles can apply downstream beyond the decoupling point (Figure 4.6).

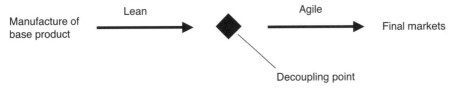

Figure 4.6   The leagile supply chain

ZARA

Based in La Coruna in North Western Spain, Zara is one of the fastest growing apparel companies in the world. Its supply chain is key to its success, in particular in terms of speed and lower inventory levels than its peers. As a result it is not hindered by product obsolescence, a key difficulty for many apparel manufacturers who are often stuck with fashion lines that the market does not want and which they cannot get rid of.

Zara's designers stay close to the latest fashion trends and design and manufacture new products within a short time frame. All of this is done within the same facility to minimise delays and ensure maximum interaction among colleagues. Industry observers describe the Zara model as 'fast fashion' where buyers don't have to wait months for the latest fashions. After manufacture, product is shipped to Zara's various stores according to a fixed distribution schedule. Most store managers use handheld electronic devices to post real-time orders from the distribution centre, which organises twice weekly deliveries according to a fixed schedule. Products contain multi-country labels so if a line is not selling, the store manager simply puts it back on the truck and it is redistributed to another store via Zara's hub and spoke network where it may fare better.

From the store managers with their handheld ordering devices all the way back upstream to the single design and manufacturing site, Zara has full visibility of its supply chain. Another key feature of Zara's supply chain is that it has spare capacity on hand (in terms of trucks, warehousing and production not always being full) and it can facilitate fast response when needed. Professor Kasra Ferdows of Georgetown University and co-writers labelled this 'rapid fire fulfilment'.[14] Many other companies in the retail sector have closely examined Zara so see where they themselves can apply some of its key success factors.

CRITICAL FACTORS TO CONSIDER IN SUPPLY CHAIN PLANNING

THE SEVEN PRINCIPLES OF SUPPLY CHAIN MANAGEMENT

In 2007 the journal *Supply Chain Management Review* republished its most requested article in the preceding 10 years since the journal's first edition appeared in 1997. That article, 'The Seven Principles of Supply Chain Management'[15] outlined seven key actions for successful SCM:

1. Segment customers based on the service needs of distinct groups and adapt the supply chain to serve these segments profitably.
2. Customise the logistics network to the service requirements and profitability of customer segments.
3. Listen to market signals and align demand planning accordingly across the supply chain, ensuring consistent forecasts and optimal resource allocation.
4. Differentiate product closer to the customer and speed conversion across the supply chain.
5. Manage sources of supply strategically to reduce the total cost of owning materials and services.
6. Develop a supply chain-wide technology strategy that supports multiple levels of decision making and gives a clear view of the flow of products, services and information.
7. Adopt channel-spanning performance measures to gauge collective success in reaching the end-user effectively and efficiently.

Now that we have looked in detail at various aspects of different supply chain strategies, it is useful to look at some guidelines that help managers develop their supply chain strategies and facilitate best fit with overall firm strategy. Hopefully the preceding section has shown that a one-size-fits-all approach to supply chain design will not work. There is just too much variability in terms of lead times, product life cycles, marketplace demand, etc. to allow this to be the case.

Focus on processes and flows

Many companies get stuck in what we call a functional or silo mentality where they focus individually on separate areas, instead of configuring according to customer needs (a demand-driven supply chain approach). This is one of the advantages of taking a supply chain approach in that it allows a full end-to-end perspective to be taken.

Some authors argue that the functional (or silo) nature of many organisations at an operational level acts as a barrier to aligning supply chains effectively with the markets they serve, thus working against a customer responsive supply chain strategy being pursued.[16]

Another way to understand supply chain strategy is to observe some of the many strategic activities that take place along typical supply chains. Tang,[17] for example, identified nine areas which facilitate more robust supply chain strategies: postponement, strategic stock, flexible supply base, make-and-buy, economic supply incentives, flexible transportation, revenue management, assortment planning, and silent product rollover. While Tang's focus was on robust strategies to mitigate supply chain disruptions (we will return to this topic in Chapter 15), the list of nine areas is useful because it gives an insight into the many strategies and activities that can be pursued along supply chains. Indeed there are a number of other strategies that can also be pursued such as factory gate pricing and cross-docking. We will look at many of these in various parts of the book. It is also important to note that companies can adopt different roles in different supply chains, for example lead one supply chain and be a participating member of another.

Focus on high-level objectives

Some writers argue that supply chains need to meet certain high-level objectives. Professor Hau Lee from Stanford for example argued that the best supply chains are *agile, adaptable* and have *aligned* interests among the firms in the supply chain.[18] He calls this the 'Triple A Supply Chain'. It is also important to note of course that the supply chain cannot, and is not, the solution to all ills. Professor Christopher and colleagues highlight this when they state that 'responsive supply chains . . . cannot overcome poor design and buying decisions which fail to introduce attractive products in the first place'.[19]

The importance of people

It is obvious that SCM has grown in significance in recent years. As we will also see in Chapter 12 in particular, SCM is benefiting from the application of some powerful technologies. But often overlooked is the role played by people in the supply chain. Professor John Gattorna notes that 'In fact it's people who really drive the dynamic supply chains that are at the heart of your business'.[20] Similarly James Quinn notes that to achieve any measure of supply chain success, three critical elements (people, process and technology) need to be kept in balance.[21] He adds that there is no single answer as to which of these three is the most important to supply chain success, although he does add that 'you can't do *anything* without the right people'.

It's supply chains that compete

You will see in the Dell case study at the end of Part One of the book that the PC maker uses robust logistics strategies and competes using its entire supply chain. The idea of supply chains competing was put forward by Professor Martin Christopher in his seminal book *Logistics and Supply Chain Management*, the first edition of which appeared in 1992. It is a powerful concept, and one that is becoming more and more relevant as we see the way

> Increasingly it is supply chains that compete more so than individual firms and products.

companies structure their supply chains often being a key determinant of success. A company can have the best and most sophisticated product in the world, but if it doesn't have a good supply chain it will likely not be able to compete, especially in terms of cost and speed, and indeed many other attributes also. Christopher notes that when supply chain excellence is achieved, often two key shifts are apparent:

- Relative customer value increases.
- Relative delivered cost decreases.

'SUPPLY CHAIN 2.0': MANAGING SUPPLY CHAINS IN THE ERA OF TURBULENCE*

We noted above, when introducing the concept of agility, the impact of risk on SCM. We will return to this important topic in Chapter 15. Christopher and Holweg argue that in the light of increasing turbulence a different approach to SCM is needed. They emphasise the impact of growing volatility on supply chains and point out that many of our current supply chain designs are predicated on stability and control. They suggest that we need to embrace volatility and revisit the management accounting assumptions and procedures that we currently use to evaluate different supply chain decisions. They argue that what is needed to master the era of turbulence is structural flexibility which builds flexible options into the design of supply chains.

* Christopher, M. & Holweg, M. (2011) '"Supply Chain 2.0": managing supply chains in the era of turbulence', *International Journal of Physical Distribution and Logistics Management,* 41(1), 63–82.

LEARNING REVIEW

The chapter sought to identify the various different logistics and supply chain strategies, and their origins and evolution. This culminates in particular in strategies based around lean and agile principles, and varying combinations of both. We saw a useful taxonomy which helps choose strategies appropriate to various demand and lead-time characteristics. The importance of logistics and supply chain strategy in the context of overall firm strategy was also highlighted. To again quote Fabbe-Costes and Colin, at the least logistics offers new ways of thinking about strategy.[22] In their view, because it motivates and supports organisational change, it also offers new frames for piloting managerial action in a strategic way. And in their view this is why logistics and SCM are now of such strategic importance.

Before moving into the second part of the book which deals with logistics and supply chain operations, Chapter 5 will describe one of the most useful tools in helping with the analysis of supply chains, namely simulation, a tool that can then be applied when considering some of the material in subsequent chapters.

QUESTIONS

- What are the three typical levels of firm strategy?
- Outline the various stages in the evolution of manufacturing.
- Explain how mass customisation works.
- Outline the various scenarios in which we can use combined logistics strategies.
- Outline how some of the principles outlined in the Toyota Production System could be applied in a services context.

THE 'BULLWHIP EFFECT'

In Chapter 1 we briefly mentioned the work of Jay Forrester who showed how inventory levels can fluctuate along the supply chain. Today we call this the **bullwhip effect**. This is the distortion of orders along the supply chain, where small fluctuations in end customer demand result in amplification of demand upstream (**demand amplification**). Hence the term 'bullwhip', where just a small flick of the wrist at the handle will create a large crack of the whip at its tip.

Bullwhip is a serious problem for any supply chain. Demand amplification creates excess inventory, which in turn consumes warehouse capacity, has serious cost implications, and may indeed never be used. Bullwhip has one or more of five causes: non-zero lead times and demand signal processing, order batching, price variations, and rationing and gaming.[23] Each is now discussed in turn.

Non-zero lead times and *demand signal processing* are each causes of the *Forrester effect*. By developing the DYNAMO simulation, Jay Forrester demonstrated that the time lag between orders along the supply chain and a lack of downstream visibility of orders causes inaccurate decisions about upstream orders.[24] If decision makers at upstream operations have limited visibility of actual end customer demand and/or the order processing lead time is greater than zero, they will have to make assumptions about how many to manufacture and/or deliver. Such assumptions will commonly be based on knowledge of previous order quantities and frequencies or forecasts of demand. This is reasonable if demand trends are constant, but this is rarely the case.

Order batching, or the *Burbidge effect*, refers to the impact of ordering in batches.[25] Conventional materials management employs a calculation of economic order quantities (EOQ) (discussed later in Chapter 10). This benefits supply, but not demand. That is to say that, by manufacturing and delivering in batches of a certain quantity the cost-effective use of supply-side resources will be ensured, but this will not necessarily fit demand. Hence, order batching is not conducive to supply chains with end customer demand fluctuations. The just-in-time principle of 'a batch size of one', for example, overcomes order batching, but must be implemented as part of a complete JIT philosophy to guarantee success.

Price variation, such as three items for the price of two promotions, is increasingly common to stimulate demand.[26] Consequently, customers will buy more than they need at that point in time and 'stock up' for the future. While this generates sales, it causes ever-greater peaks and troughs in demand, which are in turn amplified upstream. Such sales and marketing campaigns should therefore be entered into with due consideration of their operational consequences.

Rationing and gaming, such as customers over-ordering due to stock shortages causes the *Houlihan effect*. That is to say that customers who experience missed orders from their suppliers or stock-outs will typically over-order in future to prevent those situations reoccurring. Consequently demand is distorted upstream, with suppliers reacting by overproducing to compensate.[27] Thus materials management decisions should consider their consequences across the supply chain. Management of actual end customer demand will minimise demand fluctuations and thereby enable supply to better meet demand. This is difficult to achieve, however, particularly in consumer markets. Hence, stratagems must be employed to cope with demand amplification and limit the bullwhip effects discussed.

LOGISTICS AND THE WIDER STRATEGY OF THE FIRM

In this chapter we illustrated examples of companies such as Zara where a good logistics and supply strategy is at the core of the company's wider strategy. Can you think of other examples of companies where their logistics and supply chain strategies are central both to the company's wider strategy and in turn to their success?

NOTES

1. See, for example, Fabbe-Costes, N. & Colin, J. (2001) Formulating logistics strategy, in D. Waters (ed.), *Global Logistics: New Directions in Supply Chain Management*, Kogan Page, London.

2. Ibid., p. 37.

3. The ideas in this figure are based on a diagram originally contained in a book entitled *The Machine that Changed the World: The Story of Lean Production* (J. Womack, D. Roos & D. Jones, Harper Perennial, 1991).

4. Womack, J., Roos, D. & Jones, D. (1991) *The Machine that Changed the World: The Story of Lean Production*, Harper Perennial, New York.

5. Womack, J. & Jones, D. (2005) Lean consumption, *Harvard Business* Review, March, 5–68.

6. Ibid.

7. Lee, H. (2002) Aligning supply chain strategies with product uncertainties, *California Management Review*, 44(3), 105–119.

8. Christopher, M. *Creating the Agile Supply Chain*, available at www.martin-christopher. info; for a wider elucidation of Professor Christopher's work see his seminal textbook, now in its fourth edition, *Logistics and Supply Chain Management* (2011), Financial Times/Prentice Hall, London.

9. Christopher, M. (2006) Keynote address to the Humber International Logistics Convention, Hull, June.

10. Christopher, M., Peck, H. & Towill, D. (2006) A taxonomy for selecting global supply chain strategies, *International Journal of Logistics Management*, 17(2), 277–287.

11. Fisher, M. (1997) What is the right supply chain for your product? *Harvard Business Review*, March/April.
12. Christopher *et al.* (see note 10).
13. Ibid.
14. Ferdows, K., Lewis, M. & Machuna, J. (2004) Rapid fire fulfilment, *Harvard Business Review*, November.
15. Anderson, D., Britt, F. & Favre, D. (2007) The seven principles of supply chain management, *Supply Chain Management Review*, April.
16. Godsell, J., Harrison, A., Emberson, C. & Storey, J. (2006) Customer responsive supply chain strategy: an unnatural act? *International Journal of Logistics: Research and Applications*, 9(1), 47–56.
17. Tang, C. (2006) Robust strategies for mitigating supply chain disruptions, *International Journal of Logistics: Research and Applications*, 9(1), 33–45.
18. Lee, H. (2004) The triple-A supply chain, *Harvard Business Review*, October.
19. Christopher *et al.* (see note 10).
20. Gattorna, J. (2010) *Dynamic Supply Chains* (2nd edition), Financial Times/Prentice Hall, London.
21. Quinn, F. (2004) People, process, technology, *Supply Chain Management Review*, January/February, 3.
22. Fabbe-Costes & Colin, p. 53 (see note 1).
23. Lee, H., Padmanaghan, P. & Whang, S. (1997) The bullwhip effect in supply chains, *Sloan Management Review*, Spring, 93–102.
24. Forrester, J. (1958) Industrial dynamics: a major breakthrough for decision makers, *Harvard Business Review*, July–August, 37–66.
25. Disney, S. & Towill, D. (2003) Vendor-managed inventory and bullwhip reduction in a two level supply chain, *International Journal of Operations and Production Management*, 23(6), 625–651.
26. Ibid.
27. Ibid.

5 Simulation

LEARNING OBJECTIVES

- Differentiate between the different types of simulation.
- Explain the steps involved in a simulation process.
- Understand how random behaviour is simulated.
- Understand how discrete event simulation works.
- Discuss the potential role of simulation in supply chain management decisions.

INTRODUCTION

Simulation represents one of the tools most frequently utilised as a decision support system to observe the behaviour of supply chains in order to assess the effects of different supply chain configurations and decisions on the resulting supply chain costs and performance. This chapter focuses on introducing the concepts required to understand and carry out a simulation study. We will discuss the different types of simulation and how random behaviour is simulated as well as outlining the potential applications of simulation in supply chain management.

Chapter 5 comprises seven core sections:

- Why and when to simulate
- Different types of simulation
- Simulation process
- Simulation methodology
- Discrete event simulation
- Simulation replications and output analysis
- Supply chain management simulation

WHY AND WHEN TO SIMULATE?

Simulation is the process of building a model and experimenting with it in order to develop insight into a system's behaviour based on a specific set of inputs and assist in decision-making processes.

Simulation models can estimate a measure of performance or evaluate the behaviour of a system for a specific set of inputs. Therefore a major focus of simulation is to conduct experiments with the model and analyse the results in order to evaluate and improve system perform-

> A simulation is the imitation of the operation of a real-world process or system over time.[1]

ance. By using simulation models it is possible to reproduce and test different decision-making alternatives in a controlled setting, in order to both determine the robustness of a given strategy and see the impact it may have prior to implementation.

There are several reasons why a simulation study can support supply chain management decision making:

- The actual exercise of building a simulation model facilitates the understanding and analysis of the operational details, system behaviour and supply chain interdependencies.
- It captures the supply chain dynamics and variations and shows system behaviour over time.
- It allows the evaluation of proposed strategies without implementation providing a way to validate whether or not desirable decisions are being made.
- What-if analysis can be carried out allowing management to test the effects of various design or operation alternatives without having to make changes and interruptions in the real system.
- Insight can be obtained about the importance of variables to the performance of the system: which inputs significantly affect which outputs?

However, it is important to keep in mind that simulation models do not automatically generate optimal solutions. Instead, the models allow the decision makers to experiment with different input values and see the effects on the outputs and performance metrics. In addition, simulation is useful in characterising the performance of a particular configuration and is appropriate only when:[2]

- an operational decision is being made
- the process being analysed is well defined and repetitive
- activities and events are interdependent and variable
- the cost impact of the decision is greater than the cost of doing the simulation
- the cost to experiment on the actual system is greater than the cost of simulation

DIFFERENT TYPES OF SIMULATION

The type of simulation model to be used depends on the characteristics of the system, input data that is available and type of managerial question to be answered. Some of the most common classifications include:

- stochastic or deterministic
- static or dynamic
- discrete event and/or continuous

Stochastic models have at least one input variable that is random, while **deterministic models** have no random input variables.

Static models do not include the passage of time and represent the system at a particular point of time, while **dynamic models** include the passage of time and represent systems as they change over time. Examples of dynamic systems include inventory, production and transportation systems.

Dynamic models are further divided into discrete event and continuous simulations. In **discrete event simulation**, state changes occur at discrete points in time as triggered by events, observations are then gathered at these points in time when changes occur. An inventory model for medical devices is an example of discrete event simulation since the amount of inventory on hand or the number of orders pending are discrete state change variables (Figure 5.1a). In **continuous simulation** the state variables change continuously with respect to time and therefore observations are collected continuously. Examples of continuous state change variables include temperature or pressure of a liquid or gas in a tank (Figure 5.1b).

Simulation models can require both discrete and continuous modelling capability at the same time, such as models of the petroleum, beverage and food industries. In a soup-making facility, the number of pending orders is a discrete state change variable while the temperature under which the soup is being cooked is a continuous state

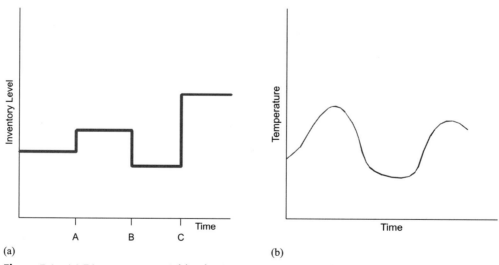

(a)   (b)

Figure 5.1   (a) Discrete state variable; (b) Continuous state variable

change variable. However, most supply chain simulation models are classified as stochastic, dynamic and discrete event simulation, meaning a simulation model can have all three features.

SIMULATION PROCESS

Simulation models are generally developed using a process map flowchart of the system based on events and activities. For model development, historical time-based data and statistical distributions for actual data sets and estimates are required. The simulation process itself consists of (Figure 5.2):

1. Developing a conceptual model of the supply chain system under study. It is essential to understand the problem and identify the goals and objectives of the study. Input variables and system performance metrics are determined as well as the operating policies and interdependencies in the supply chain.

2. Building the simulation model by using a spreadsheet or simulation software package such as ProModel or Arena.[3] Each of the random elements of the

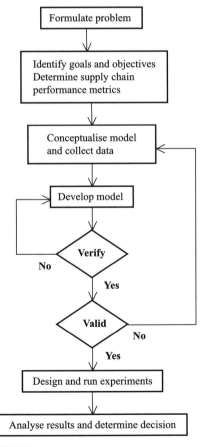

Figure 5.2 The simulation process

model (e.g. demand, travel time, lead time) is specified with a probability distribution (discrete or continuous) based on historical data.

3. Verification and validation of the model. Verification refers to the process of ensuring that the model does not contain any logical errors and is built correctly. Validation is the process of ensuring that the right model has been built, making sure that the performance measures from the model match those of the real system. Once developed and validated the model can be used to investigate a variety of what-if scenarios about the real-world system.

4. Design and run the experiments. Plan out the combination and number of input variables to be changed and determine the number of independent replications needed to observe performance characteristics of a system over time and get the results in an efficient way.

5. Analyse the results. Outputs are averaged and confidence intervals are determined as well as what kind of statistical analysis to run to increase the accuracy of the decisions.

SIMULATION METHODOLOGY

Simulation modelling places considerable demands on operational data. In addition, its development, validation and application require good understanding of simulation methodology and the software to be used for this purpose. In order for the simulation model to be meaningful we need to understand the logic and process behind the model development. There are many books that provide detailed explanations, analysis and discussions of the simulation process.[4] The following sections provide an overview and summary of the knowledge required to understand the supply chain simulation applications presented in the remainder of the book and online supplements.

Random number generation

A random number generator creates a stream of random numbers that are independent and uniformly distributed numbers between 0 and 1. These numbers are then used in simulation models to simulate the events that take place in the real system such as breakdown of machines, lead time for delivery, and number of orders placed by the customer.

There are various methods for creating random numbers. However, generating random numbers from a known method that can be duplicated contradicts the concept that the numbers being generated are truly random. Therefore the random number generators are referred to as "pseudo" random number generators, where pseudo means false. This "falseness" is necessary for simulation applications. Using a known method for generating the random numbers allows the user to duplicate the input values for debugging purposes in addition to comparing the alternatives of the system models. It should be noted that even though the numbers generated are not truly random they do appear to be random, because the next number being generated is not easily predicted by just looking at the previous number. The stream of random numbers also usually has a long cycle and will most likely not be repeated within a simulation experiment. Among the various random number generation methods, the linear congruential generator (LCG) method is the most widely used.[5] Simulation software has random number generators built within them and if using a spreadsheet the RAND( ) function in Excel can be used to generate random numbers.

The random numbers are then used to produce *random variates,* which are the outputs generated from a probability distribution function and variables used by the simulation model.

Random variate generation

The use of simulation in supply chain applications allows the incorporation of various uncertainties, for example, customer orders arriving at random points in time, machine breakdowns at random points in time and repair times. However, in order to generate and simulate this randomness into the model the underlying distribution in the real system needs to first be identified. The inverse transform method can then be used to generate random variates from continuous distributions. This is done by transforming a random number into a value that conforms to a given distribution. The process is straightforward:

1. Identify the probability distribution function *f(x)*
2. Find the cumulative distribution $F(x) = P(X \leq x)$
3. Set $R = F(x)$ where R is the random number generated by a random number generator.
4. Solve for *x*.

Let's say we want to generate variates from the exponential distribution with mean β.

$$f(x) = \begin{cases} \dfrac{1}{\beta}\, e^{\frac{-x}{\beta}} & \text{For } x > 0 \\ & \text{elsewhere} \end{cases}$$

$$F(x) = \begin{cases} 0 \\ 1 - e^{\frac{-x}{\beta}} & \text{For } x > 0 \\ 0 & \text{elsewhere} \end{cases}$$

Set $R = F(x)$ and solve for x

$$R = 1 - e^{-x/\beta}$$

$$e^{-x/\beta} = 1 - R$$

$$\ln(e^{-x/\beta}) = \ln(1 - R)$$

$$-x/\beta = \ln(1 - R)$$

$$x = -\beta \ln(1 - R)$$

Example: Suppose we would like to simulate the arrival of customers to a retailer at an exponentially distributed inter-arrival time with a mean of 3.0 minutes.

Assuming that our random number generator has produced the following random numbers:

$$R_1 = 0.633 \qquad R_2 = 0.313 \qquad R_3 = 0.586 \qquad R_4 = 0.328 \qquad R_5 = 0.914$$

Our customer inter-arrival times would be calculated as follows:

$$X_1 = 3 \ln(1 - R_1) = 3.01$$
$$X_2 = 3 \ln(1 - R_2) = 1.13$$
$$X_3 = 3 \ln(1 - R_3) = 2.65$$
$$X_4 = 3 \ln(1 - R_4) = 1.19$$
$$X_5 = 3 \ln(1 - R_5) = 7.36$$

The same application can be applied for discrete distributions. Once the discrete distribution associated with a random input has been identified, the cumulative probability distribution function $F(x)$ is constructed. The cumulative probability distribution function is then used to divide the interval between 0 and 1 into subintervals whose sizes are proportional to the probabilities of the associated outcomes. To generate a random variate from this distribution, we then take the random number generated and determine which interval it falls into and then identify the corresponding discrete value.

Suppose that the number of items purchased by each customer arriving at the retailer in the above example is represented by the discrete distribution shown in Table 5.1.

Assuming that our random number generator has produced the following random numbers:

$$R_1 = 0.273 \qquad R_2 = 0.766 \qquad R_3 = 0.102 \qquad R_4 = 0.156 \qquad R_5 = 0.305$$

The first customer will purchase two items and customers 2, 3, 4, and 5 will purchase four, one, two, and two items respectively.

Given that accurate probability density functions are identified, the random variates generated mimic what happens in the real system creating the foundation for simulation models.

Simulation example

A classical inventory problem concerns the purchase and sale of newspapers.[6] Each morning the newspaper vendor buys the same fixed number of papers for $0.65 and

Table 5.1 Distribution and random number range for demand

Demand	Probability	Cumulative probability	Random number range
1	0.15	0.15	0.00–0.15
2	0.20	0.35	0.15–0.35
3	0.25	0.60	0.35–0.60
4	0.40	1.00	0.60–1.00

Table 5.2   Distribution of newspapers demanded

Demand	Demand probability distribution
50	0.10
60	0.15
70	0.20
80	0.35
90	0.15
100	0.05

sells them for $1.50 each. Newspapers not sold at the end of the day are sold as scrap for $0.10 each. The newspapers can be purchased in bundles of 10 by the newspaper seller. Demands from day to day are independent of each other and the distribution of papers demanded each day is given in Table 5.2. The problem is to determine the number of newspapers the newspaper seller should purchase to maximise his expected profit.

To solve this problem we will simulate the demands for 15 days and calculate profits from the sales of each day. The system's performance metric, which is the daily profit, is determined by defining the following variables:

R Retail price per unit for the newspapers

C Cost per unit for the newspapers

S Salvage value per unit for the newspapers

D Daily demand

Q Number of newspapers ordered by the newspaper seller

$$\text{Daily profit} = (\text{revenue from sales}) + (\text{salvage from sale of scrap}) - (\text{cost of newspaper}) \tag{5.1}$$

$$\text{Revenue from sales} = \text{Min}\,(D, Q) \times R \tag{5.2}$$

$$\text{Salvage from sale of scrap} = \begin{cases} (D - Q) \times S & \text{if } D > Q \\ 0 & \text{if } D \leq Q \end{cases} \tag{5.3}$$

$$\text{Cost of newspaper} = Q \times C \tag{5.4}$$

$$\text{Lost profit} = \begin{cases} (D - Q) \times (R - C) & \text{if } D > Q \\ 0 & \text{if } D \leq Q \end{cases} \tag{5.5}$$

Inputs to the simulation model are the order quantity (decision variable determined by the newspaper seller), the daily demand which is uncontrollable and stochastic, and the cost and revenue factors which are set values and do not change. Since it does not matter when the customers show up during the day, the problem can be simulated through a static and stochastic model.

We first need to choose a value for the decision variable Q and then set up the simulation where the demand is generated from the probability distribution in Table 5.2.

Figure 5.3 shows the logic for the simulation, Table 5.3 provides the random digit assignments for the daily demand, and Table 5.4 shows the simulation table for the decision to purchase 80 newspapers.

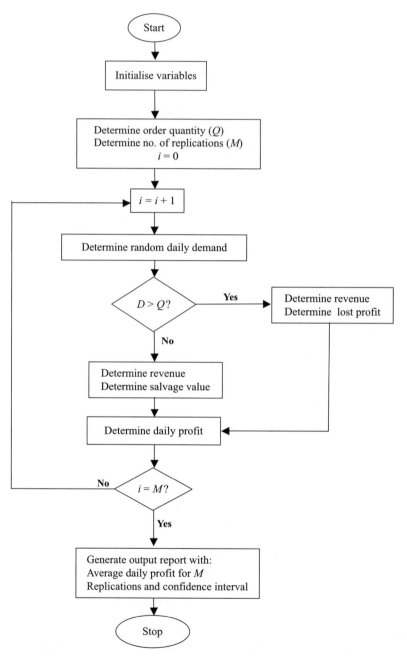

Figure 5.3 Logic for newspaper vendor simulation model

Table 5.3 Random number range for daily demand

Demand	Probability	Cumulative probability	Random number range
50	0.10	0.10	0.00–0.10
60	0.15	0.25	0.10–0.25
70	0.20	0.45	0.25–0.45
80	0.35	0.80	0.45–0.80
90	0.15	0.95	0.80–0.95
100	0.05	1.00	0.95–1.00

Since the input value of demand is stochastic the average profit determined in Table 5.4 is only an expected estimate and not a precise value. In addition interval estimates can be calculated to determine how far off the calculated profit average may be from the true profit mean. This is done through confidence interval estimation. A *confidence interval* is a range which we can have a certain level of confidence that the true mean falls within. Assuming that the average profit and standard deviation calculated are independent and normally distributed the following equation can be used to calculate the half width of a confidence interval for a given level of confidence.

$$hw = \frac{(t_{n-1,\,\alpha/2})s}{\sqrt{n}} \tag{5.6}$$

where n is the number of replications, s is the standard deviation, α is the probability that the mean will fall outside the confidence interval and $t_{n-1,\,\alpha/2}$ is a factor that can be

Table 5.4 Simulation table for purchase of 80 newspapers

Day	Random numbers for demand	Demand	Revenue from sales	Salvage from sale of scrap	Daily profit	Lost profit from excess demand
1	0.149	60	90	2	40	—
2	0.447	70	105	1	54	—
3	0.931	90	135	—	83	8.5
4	0.407	70	105	1	54	—
5	0.140	60	90	2	40	—
6	0.313	70	105	1	54	—
7	0.563	80	120	0	68	—
8	0.424	70	105	1	54	—
9	0.763	80	120	0	68	—
10	0.264	70	105	1	54	—
11	0.300	70	105	1	54	—
12	0.185	60	90	2	40	—
13	0.368	70	105	1	54	—
14	0.546	80	120	0	68	—
15	0.518	80	120	0	68	—
Average					$56.87	

	A	B	C	D	E	F	G	H
1	Newspaper Seller Simulation							
2								
3	Demand	Probability						
4	50	0.10		Selling price	$ 1.50			
5	60	0.15		Cost	$ 0.65			
6	70	0.20		Salvage Value	$ 0.10			
7	80	0.35						
8	90	0.15						
9	100	0.05						
10								
11								
12	Random Number Range		Demand	Quantity to Buy	80			
13	0.00	0.10	40	Average net profit	47.64		Upper Limit (95% confidence)	50.66
14	0.10	0.25	50	Standard deviation	16.79		Lower Limit (95% confidence)	44.61
15	0.25	0.45	60					
16	0.45	0.80	70					
17	0.80	0.95	80					
18	0.95	1.00	90					
19								
20	Simulation Results							
21								
22	Day	Random Demand	Revenue	Salvage Value	Daily Profit	Lost profit		
23	1	50	$ 75.00	3	$ 26.00	0		
24	2	70	$ 105.00	1	$ 54.00	0		
25	3	80	$ 120.00	0	$ 68.00	0		
26	4	80	$ 120.00	0	$ 68.00	0		
27	5	40	$ 60.00	4	$ 12.00	0		

Sheet1 / Sheet2 / Sheet3

Figure 5.4 Spreadsheet simulation model for newspaper vendor problem

obtained from the *Student t* table in the appendix to this chapter. The upper and lower limits of the confidence interval are then determined as follows:

$$\text{Upper limit} = \text{Average} + hw \tag{5.7}$$

$$\text{Lower limit} = \text{Average} - hw \tag{5.8}$$

The more replications we run the closer we get to the true expected output. This can be done by developing a spreadsheet simulation model in Excel.

Figure 5.4 shows an Excel spreadsheet model for simulating 121 replications of the newspaper vendor problem.

To create this spreadsheet we first enter the probability distribution of the newspapers demanded, as well as the numerical inputs that are needed to calculate the profit, and the random number range for daily demand (Figure 5.5).

The number of newspapers the vendor intends to buy is entered in cell E12. We then use Excel's VLOOKUP function to create daily demand values based on the given probabilities and calculate the revenue, salvage value, daily profit and lost profit for a predetermined number of newspapers that the vendor intends to buy (Figure 5.6).

Based on the simulation performed we can conclude with 95% confidence that if the newspaper vendor purchases 80 newspapers at the beginning of the day, his average

⊿	A	B	C	D	E
1	Newspaper Seller Simulation				
2					
3	Demand	Probability			
4	50	0.10		Selling price	$ 1.50
5	60	0.15		Cost	$ 0.65
6	70	0.20		Salvage Value	$ 0.10
7	80	0.35			
8	90	0.15			
9	100	0.05			
10					
11					
12	Random Number Range		Demand		
13	0.00	0.10	40		
14	0.10	0.25	50		
15	0.25	0.45	60		
16	0.45	0.80	70		
17	0.80	0.95	80		
18	0.95	1.00	90		
19					

Figure 5.5 Known variables for the simulation model

daily profit will be between $44.61 and $50.66. If we wish to narrow the confidence interval for daily profit, we will need to increase the number of replications.

In order to determine the optimal number of newspapers, the simulation needs to be repeated for different values of quantities purchased and the expected profit from the different alternatives compared. For the complete spreadsheet analysis for the comparison of alternatives please refer to the online supplemental material.

DISCRETE EVENT SIMULATION

As the name implies, discrete event simulation (DES) operates based on simulation events. A simulation event is triggered by a lapse of time, a condition, or some other event: examples include the arrival of an order, the start of a downtime and the completion of an operation. Observations are gathered only at points in time when the changes take place in the system. For example, changes in the status of the system take place when a customer arrives and places an order. At these points of time, performance measures such as amount of inventory on hand, number of orders unfilled, number of customers in queue and the waiting time in facility may be affected. These measures (response variables) will then remain unchanged until another simulation event takes place.

During a simulation run an internal clock tracks the passage of time. After the completion of all possible actions at a simulated event time, the clock is then advanced to the time of the next earliest event. This process is repeated until the simulation duration ends or a predetermined condition is met.

	A	B	C	D	E	F	G	H
10								
11								
12	*Random Number Range*		*Demand*	*Quantity to Buy*	80			
13	0.00	0.10	40	*Average net profit*	47.64		Upper Limit (95% confidence)	50.66
14	0.10	0.25	50	*Standard deviation*	16.79		Lower Limit (95% confidence)	44.61
15	0.25	0.45	60					
16	0.45	0.80	70					
17	0.80	0.95	80					
18	0.95	1.00	90					
19								
20	Simulation Results							
21								
22	Day	Random Demand	Revenue	Salvage Value	Daily Profit	Lost profit		
23	1	50	$ 75.00	3	$ 26.00	0		
24	2	70	$ 105.00	1	$ 54.00	0		
25	3	80	$ 120.00	0	$ 68.00	0		
26	4	80	$ 120.00	0	$ 68.00	0		
27	5	40	$ 60.00	4	$ 12.00	0		
28	6	90	$ 120.00	0	$ 68.00	8.5		
29	7	40	$ 60.00	4	$ 12.00	0		
30	8	50	$ 75.00	3	$ 26.00	0		
31	9	70	$ 105.00	1	$ 54.00	0		
32	10	70	$ 105.00	1	$ 54.00	0		
33	11	90	$ 120.00	0	$ 68.00	8.5		
34	12	40	$ 60.00	4	$ 12.00	0		
35	13	60	$ 90.00	2	$ 40.00	0		
36	14	50	$ 75.00	3	$ 26.00	0		

Sheet1 / Sheet2 / Sheet3

Cell	Cell Formula	Equation	Copied to
B23	=VLOOKUP(RAND(), $A$13:$C$18,3)		B24:B143
C23	=IF(B23<$E$12,B23,$E$12)*$E$4	5.2	C24:C143
D23	=IF($E$12>=B23,($E$12-B23)*$E$6,0)	5.3	D24:D143
E23	=C23+D23-($E$12*$E$5)	5.1	E24:E143
F23	=IF(B23>$E$12,(B23-$E$12)*($E$4-$E$5),0)	5.5	F24:F143
E13	=AVERAGEA(E23:E143)		
E14	=STDEVPA(E23:E143)		
H13	=$E$13+((1.98*$E$14)/SQRT(121))	5.7	
H14	=$E$13-((1.98*$E$14)/SQRT(121))	5.8	

Figure 5.6   Simulation results for newspaper vendor problem

In the case of the newspaper seller example, if instead of the probability distribution of demand, the probability distribution of the inter-arrival times of customers was known, we would then model the simulation as a dynamic, stochastic and discrete event simulation, with the customer arrivals being the simulation events. Figure 5.7 shows the logic for the discrete event simulation.

It should be emphasized again that the simulation model by itself does not determine an optimal solution. It can, however, address decisions where the number of alternatives is limited and the model has various interdependencies and complexities that make the development of a mathematical model infeasible. Running the simulation also allows the decision maker to observe the behaviour of the supply chain system over time, and identify bottlenecks that would be missed by utilising mathematical optimisation techniques.

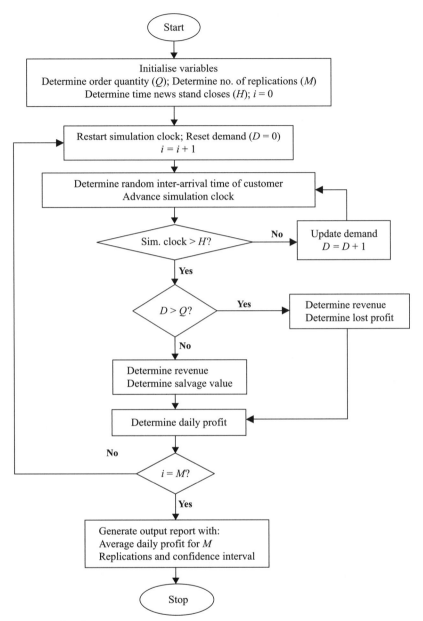

Figure 5.7 Logic for discrete event simulation

SIMULATION REPLICATIONS AND OUTPUT ANALYSIS

A simulation study comprises experiments that are differentiated by the use of alternatives in a model's logic and/or change of the decision variables. For example, an alternate transportation mode and route might be tried, or the quantity of various machines or operators can be changed. Each experiment consists of a number of trials referred to as replications. A replication involves initialising the model, resetting all statistical variables for the output measures, running the simulation until a predetermined condition or time is met, and reporting results. The model parameter settings remain the same for all replications.

The simulation runs need to be long enough and repeated to ensure that a precise estimate of the system performance is produced. The goal of experimentation is to run enough replications to get a sufficiently accurate estimate of the true population parameters while staying within the time and cost constraints of the study. Each replication uses a different stream of random numbers, and therefore produces different statistical results that can then be averaged and analysed in detail with statistically based procedures across a set of replications. Further analysis such as paired-t confidence intervals or analysis of variance (ANOVA) can be carried out to compare the different alternatives under study to ensure that the differences being observed are because of the actual differences in the system and not because of the statistical variations.

SUPPLY CHAIN MANAGEMENT SIMULATION

The successful management of any supply chain requires careful decisions being made about the flow of products and information. Because of the uncertainties and complexities within the supply chain, in most cases analysing the different alternatives through mathematical models is not straightforward and in some cases infeasible. Therefore, because of its ability to model uncertainty, simulation has become a widely used tool for supply chain decision analysis. The simulation models attempt to create a real-world process simulating the operating characteristics of the supply chain being modelled and can include the decision-making mechanism. Simulation models can replicate existing supply chain systems and assist a decision maker in determining how performance will be affected if the system is modified. Using a simulation model reduces the time and cost of the analysis and avoids any disruption from experimenting on the actual system.

At the strategic level, simulation models can be used to study the design (or redesign) of supply chain systems. This will allow the analysts to predict the performance of the new system while taking the uncertainty of the future market conditions as well as other uncontrollable factors into consideration. Decisions can include facility expansion and location, choice of transportation modes and technology selection (for example whether to roll out radio frequency identification (RFID) technology).

At the planning level, simulation models can be used for predicting the effects of policy decisions and changes in a variety of supply chain functions such as demand and sales planning, inventory planning, distribution and transportation planning, and production planning and scheduling.

Throughout the remainder of this book as we discuss logistics and supply chain operations as designs we will provide examples of simulation applications with corresponding models and discussions included in the online supplemental materials.

LEARNING REVIEW

This chapter discussed how simulation modelling can be an effective tool in decision making, especially for supply chain applications. Supply chain simulation requires real-life, accurate data on the supply chain system operations and seeks the estimated data on the proposed operations. With the use of simulation we can analyse the impact of interdependencies and variation over time, so rather than providing a solution it provides information that is used to make a decision.

In summary, a well-designed supply chain simulation model can evaluate the impact of a wide range of strategic and operational decisions on the supply chain performance in a risk-free environment with minimal costs. Once a simulation model has been validated, it is a valuable tool for a decision maker to apply, experiment with and compare performance of a supply chain over a range of alternative designs. It allows for the proactive management of supply chains by analysing the supply chain structural and policy changes under consideration.

We are now ready to move into the second part of the book. We have laid the foundations for logistics and SCM, explained where they have come from and defined key terms. The link with globalisation and international trade has been discussed in detail and we have worked through various logistics strategies. The importance of supply chain integration has been highlighted and we have also introduced the very valuable tool of simulation. Part Two of the book now moves into logistics and supply chain operations, how supply chains actually work in operational detail.

QUESTIONS

- What is simulation?
- What are some of the advantages of using simulation?
- What is the main difference between a static simulation model and a discrete event simulation model?
- Provide an example of a discrete state change variable and a continuous state change variable
- What kind of supply chain decisions can a simulation model be beneficial for?

NOTES

1. Banks, J., Carson, J.S., Nelson, B.L. & Nicol, D.M. (2001) *Discrete Event System Simulation*, 3rd Edition, Prentice Hall.
2. Harrell, C., Ghosh, B.K. & Bowden, R.O. (2003) *Simulation Using ProModel*, 2nd Edition, McGraw-Hill.
3. See Harrell *et al.* ibid.; Kelton, W.D., Sadowski, R.P. & Sturrock, D.T. (2007) *Simulation with Arena*, 4th Edition, McGraw-Hill.
4. See for example Banks *et al.* (see note 1); Law, A.M. & Kelton, W.D. (2000) *Simulation Modeling and Analysis*, 3rd Edition, Prentice Hall; Harrell *et al.* (see note 2).
5. For details see Law & Kelton, ibid.
6. Adapted from Banks *et al.* (see note 1).

APPENDIX: STUDENT T TABLE

CRITICAL VALUES FOR STUDENT'S *t* DISTRIBUTION AND STANDARD NORMAL DISTRIBUTION

(Critical values for the standard normal distribution (z_α) appear in the last row with df $= \infty$, $z_\alpha = t_{\infty,\alpha}$.)

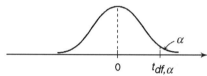

	$\alpha = 0.40$	$\alpha = 0.30$	$\alpha = 0.20$	$\alpha = 0.10$	$\alpha = 0.05$	$\alpha = 0.025$	$\alpha = 0.01$	$\alpha = 0.005$
1	0.325	0.727	1.367	3.078	6.314	12.706	31.827	63.657
2	0.289	0.617	1.061	1.886	2.920	4.303	6.965	9.925
3	0.277	0.584	0.978	1.638	2.353	3.182	4.541	5.841
4	0.271	0.569	0.941	1.533	2.132	2.776	3.747	4.604
5	0.267	0.559	0.920	1.476	2.015	2.571	3.365	4.032
6	0.265	0.553	0.906	1.440	1.943	2.447	3.143	3.707
7	0.263	0.549	0.896	1.415	1.895	2.365	2.998	3.499
8	0.262	0.546	0.889	1.397	1.860	2.306	2.896	3.355
9	0.261	0.543	0.883	1.383	1.833	2.262	2.821	3.250
10	0.260	0.542	0.879	1.372	1.812	2.228	2.764	3.169
11	0.260	0.540	0.876	1.363	1.796	2.201	2.718	3.106
12	0.259	0.539	0.873	1.356	1.782	2.179	2.681	3.055
13	0.259	0.538	0.870	1.350	1.771	2.160	2.650	3.012
14	0.258	0.537	0.868	1.345	1.761	2.145	2.624	2.977
15	0.258	0.536	0.866	1.341	1.753	2.131	2.602	2.947
16	0.258	0.535	0.865	1.337	1.746	2.120	2.583	2.921
17	0.257	0.534	0.863	1.333	1.740	2.110	2.567	2.898
18	0.257	0.534	0.862	1.330	1.734	2.101	2.552	2.878
19	0.257	0.533	0.861	1.328	1.729	2.093	2.539	2.861
20	0.257	0.533	0.860	1.325	1.725	2.086	2.528	2.845
21	0.257	0.532	0.859	1.323	1.721	2.080	2.518	2.831
22	0.256	0.532	0.858	1.321	1.717	2.074	2.508	2.819
23	0.256	0.532	0.858	1.319	1.714	2.069	2.500	2.807
24	0.256	0.531	0.857	1.316	1.708	2.060	2.485	2.797
25	0.256	0.531	0.856	1.316	1.708	2.060	2.485	2.787
26	0.256	0.531	0.856	1.315	1.706	2.056	2.479	2.779
27	0.256	0.531	0.855	1.314	1.703	2.052	2.473	2.771
28	0.256	0.530	0.855	1.313	1.701	2.048	2.467	2.763
29	0.256	0.530	0.854	1.310	1.697	2.042	2.457	2.756
30	0.256	0.530	0.854	1.310	1.697	2.042	2.457	2.750
40	0.255	0.529	0.851	1.303	1.684	2.021	2.423	2.704
60	0.254	0.527	0.848	1.296	1.671	2.000	2.390	2.660
120	0.254	0.526	0.845	1.289	1.658	1.980	2.358	2.617
∞	0.253	0.524	0.842	1.282	1.645	1.960	2.326	2.576

Degrees of Freedom (df)

Source: Harrell, C., Ghosh, B.K. & Bowden, R.O. (2003) *Simulation Using ProModel*, 2nd Edition, McGraw-Hill.

Dell: High Velocity, Focused Supply Chain Management

Dell (www.dell.com) has grown phenomenally since its establishment in 1983 by Michael Dell, then a medical student, now a multi-millionaire. The company's mission is simply 'to be the most successful computer company in the world at delivering the best customer experience in the markets we serve'. It was ranked 38 on the *Fortune 500* listing of America's largest corporations with revenues of over $52 billion. Dell ascribes much of its success to its expertise in supply chain management and the velocity with which it is able to process and deliver orders – where competitors take weeks to build and ship product, Dell's metrics are hours and days.

DIRECT TO CUSTOMER

Central to Dell's phenomenal success is its distribution strategy: since it started to build its own machines in 1985 (prior to this the company had focused on upgrading old IBM machines) it has sold direct to the customer, disintermediating any middlemen and getting product faster to the customer. The computers themselves were viewed by some as not particularly remarkable from a technological perspective, so much so that in 1996 *The Economist* magazine described Dell as 'selling PCs like bananas'. The business market segment is highly important to Dell and the company has invested in customer relationship management (CRM) systems in order to stay close to key customers, while similarly evaluating the cost-to-serve different customer segments and designing product offerings accordingly. Finished products are delivered by third-party logistics partners direct from the manufacturing plants to customers, often merging-in-transit with peripherals.

FULL VISIBILITY AND PARTNERSHIPS WITH SUPPLIERS

The internet is key to Dell's strategy, allowing direct communication with customers and real-time visibility of purchasing patterns. Indeed a key attribute of the Dell supply chain is full visibility along the chain with sales and production systems linked to suppliers who supply components just-in-time, usually direct to the production line and often with very short lead times (sometimes just one hour!). Consequently, Dell needs limited warehouse space for inbound raw materials. These preferred suppliers play a key role in Dell's success according to their senior VP for worldwide procurement: 'our suppliers play an essential role in helping us provide customers with the quality and value they come to expect from Dell'. Each year Dell conducts an awards programme to acknowledge the eight suppliers who stand out in terms of quality, technology, service, continuity of supply and cost.

FOCUSED MANUFACTURING AND BUILDING TO ORDER

Dell pioneered the adoption of standardisation and postponed manufacturing (also known as mass customisation) in the electronics industry (Figure C1.1). This involves producing a small number of common platforms, which are then customised according to customer demands (the customer generally recognises more so what is different among products, not what is the same!). Before standardisation (left side of Figure C1.1) there are multiple product lines at both the upstream and downstream ends, whereas after standardisation (right side of Figure C1.1) the number of different product lines upstream reduces drastically and products are only customised (i.e. configured into different products) at the downstream end (once customer orders are visible).

The benefits of this strategy are many and include sharing of common components across product lines, thus reducing the number of stock keeping units (SKUs) that have to be carried. This strategy is also adopted in a number of other sectors where demand is volatile and margins are tight, such as the automobile industry (Volkswagen, Audi, Seat and Skoda) and the fashion industry (Benetton and Zara).

Dell's 'manufacturing associates' can assemble desktops at a rate of 16–17 per day using 'single person build' rather than traditional assembly line techniques. This leads to both increased job satisfaction and product quality. In early 2000 the company introduced business process improvement in order to change and improve work practices right

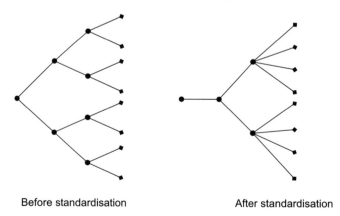

Before standardisation   After standardisation

Figure C1.1 The principle of postponement

across the business and eliminate non-value-adding work. Modular manufacturing using standardised components is employed to build the 'vanilla products', which are then customised for market.

Increasingly, Dell is moving into higher value offerings and markets. In its view, it sells solutions, not products. The company has not, however, been immune to problems. Difficulties associated with faulty laptop batteries, which attracted a lot of negative publicity about the company, led to the recall of four million laptop batteries in 2006 (BBC News, January 2007). A weakening market position has led to the founder Michael Dell stepping back into an executive role as CEO again. Strong competition in the marketplace combined with downward price pressure on sales present Dell with a challenging environment.

QUESTIONS

- What are the fundamental reasons for Dell's success?
- What should Dell do next to maintain its competitive advantage? Is its business model still viable?
- Will the Dell formula work elsewhere? If not, why not?

The Medical Devices Company

MDC is a successful and innovative multinational company which manufactures and distributes a range of sophisticated medical devices used by surgeons in the operating room. Individual unit value for MDC's product range is high and begins at €2000 for some standard, widely used devices. Products for the European market are manufactured at two plants, one in Ireland and one in Poland. Other products and peripherals are also sold under the MDC brand and these are shipped in the first instance to both of the European manufacturing plants, before being moved downstream in the MDC supply chain. From both manufacturing plants the entire product range is then shipped to some 15 warehouses located across Europe. These 15 warehouses act as hubs and feed a further 40 warehouses, located mostly near the large urban centres across Europe. It is from these latter 40 warehouses that MDC's sales representatives and distribution agents draw their inventory.

MDC faces a range of challenges. Advances in medical technology and an expanded product range are driving business growth. Many customers (i.e. hospitals) want improved service solutions centred around increased product availability combined (paradoxically) with lower levels of stock holding. Indeed many users are demanding a solution whereby a number of different variants of a particular device are readily available for immediate use, but whereby payment is only made for the particular variant actually used during the operation. Competition in the marketplace is increasing with some competitors beginning to offer such solutions. Inventory turnover is, however, problematic for MDC's European operation and has steadily fallen to five turns per year (the industry norm is around 10) resulting in increased inventory in the system, while issues with product obsolescence have also arisen on a number of occasions. Stock-outs at various stages along the chain are also becoming common (especially in the case of patients ready for surgery and requiring a specific device immediately in order for the surgery to go ahead) with the resulting need to expedite inventory direct to users from either manufacturing plant.

QUESTIONS

- Recommend a logistics strategy that could enable MDC in Europe to improve service to its customers and simultaneously reduce the total inventory in its European network.

Humanitarian Aid Supply Chains

Graham Heaslip

School of Business, NUI Maynooth, Ireland

When disasters strike, relief organisations respond by delivering aid to those in need. Their supply chains must be both fast and agile, responding to sudden-onset disasters, which may occur in places as far apart as New Orleans and rural Pakistan. Since 2004, five large-scale natural disasters have captured the attention of the international media: the 2004 tsunami in Asia, the 2005 earthquake in Pakistan, the 2010 earthquake in Haiti, the 2010 floods in Pakistan, and the 2011 earthquakes in Japan. Disasters of this magnitude cause donors, beneficiaries and the media to closely monitor how quickly and efficiently relief organisations are able to respond.

Humanitarian logistics, the function that is charged with ensuring the efficient and cost-effective flow and storage of goods and materials for the purpose of alleviating the suffering of vulnerable people, came of age during the tsunami relief effort.[1] There are clear parallels between business logistics and relief logistics, but the transfer of knowledge between the two has been limited and the latter remains relatively unsophisticated, although, more recently, greater effort has been put into understanding and developing systems that can improve the relief supply chain.[2] Outside the world of business, logisticians in many other fields face the challenge of successfully managing the transition between steady-state and surge situations.[3] This is particularly true for humanitarian logisticians preparing and executing their organisations' response to a rapid onset disaster where the price of failure can be counted in lives rather than lost profits.[4]

Humanitarian organisations have come under increasing pressure to prove to donors who are pledging millions in aid and goods that they are reaching those most in need. Such organisations are under greater scrutiny to monitor the impact of the aid that they deliver, not just the input and output but the whole operation. This means humanitarian organisations have to become more results orientated as they become ever more accountable and therefore their operations must be more transparent. Since disaster relief is about

80% logistics[5] it would follow then that the only way to achieve this is through slick, efficient and effective logistics operations and more precisely, supply chain management.

IMPORTANCE OF COORDINATION IN HUMANITARIAN SUPPLY CHAINS

Coordination is central to a successful humanitarian supply chain. To stage a response, humanitarian organisations need to coordinate their activities with other humanitarian organisations and key stakeholders with a view to manage fit, flow and sharing resource dependencies.[6] As time is crucial during an emergency response, the humanitarian community needs to avoid parallel efforts and duplications along the supply chain by combining their efforts and activities with other stakeholders. Joint contingency planning helps reduce lead times and avoids reliance on expensive transport options (e.g. airlifting) or last-minute sourcing.[7] This planning further helps in the development of alternative plans and ensures the mobilisation of the right range of relief items. During joint contingency planning sessions, implementation strategies such as prepositioning – strategic placement of food or non-food items (NFIs) throughout a country/area accessible for distribution to recipients – act as key coordination mechanisms.

Humanitarian logisticians often have little or no advance notice of when and where they have to move and store what type of material and in what quantities. To come to terms with unpredictable disasters, the evolving logistics challenges and the specificity of each operation and country, humanitarian organisations (e.g. World Food Programme (WFP)) formulate flexible plans that can accommodate frequent and numerous last-minute changes. Where possible, they build redundant capacity into their operations.[8] In terms of transport modes, the humanitarian community calls upon a diverse and combined transportation portfolio to reach remote areas. This includes trucks, motorcycles, boats and helicopters as well as unconventional modes such as donkeys, elephants and airdrops. In WFP operations, trucking often replaces airlifts after the initial emergency phase.[9] Ocean transportation is used to move significant quantities of cargo (e.g. food) at low cost.

During a relief operation an influx of aid workers, military and others enter the fray often having differing objectives. Cooperation, coordination and collaboration among the organisations taking part in the response are therefore paramount. In a disaster of the scale which occurred in Haiti, the United Nations (UN) activates the cluster group system (which was developed after Hurricane Katrina and the Asian tsunami in order to improve coordination) which includes:[10]

- Water, sanitation and hygiene (Wash) cluster: chaired by UNICEF (United Nations Children's Fund).
- Camp coordination and management cluster: chaired by IOM (International Organisation for Migration) for natural disasters.
- Emergency shelter cluster: chaired by IFRC (International Federation of Red Cross and Red Crescent Societies) for natural disasters.

- Logistics cluster: chaired by WFP (World Food Programme).
- Emergency telecoms and IT (information technology) cluster: chaired by UNICEF/WFP Health cluster: chaired by WHO (World Health Organisation).
- Nutrition cluster: chaired by UNICEF.
- Early recovery cluster: chaired by UNDP (United Nations Development Programme).
- Protection cluster: chaired by UNHCR (United Nations High Commissioner for Refugees)/UNICEF.

Relief items differ in terms of their urgency (water), life-saving contribution (medicine), volumes required (food), complementary (kitchen kits) or simple (clothing) function, continuous (food) or one-at-a-time (vaccines) usage, degree of substitutability and need for specialised input (medical personnel for medicines and medical care). The different value and characteristics of relief items together with the mismatch between available transport and handling capacity and the volume of cargo moving into a region call for the coordination and prioritisation of relief item movements into the disaster theatre.[11]

REDUCING UNCERTAINTY IN HUMANITARIAN SUPPLY CHAINS

The first challenge facing a humanitarian organisation immediately after an emergency is declared is how to bridge the relief resource and capability gap, in other words uncertainty, which is often significant. To stage a response and overcome this gap, military and humanitarian organisations depend on their supply network composed of a number of loose partnerships with a range of actors.[12] Uncertainty can stem from many elements relating to the mission, the organisation itself, or nature of the demand. For example, uncertainty may arise from inherent characteristics such as what and how much material is demanded, product traits, process fluctuations and supply problems.[13] Van der Vorst and Beulens also recognise how decision complexity, supply chain configuration and control structures, long forecast horizons, poor information reliability and agency culture may create uncertainty.[14] Regarding uncertainty, Sowinski[15] quotes Lynn Fritz, founder of the Fritz Institute:

> . . . disasters are the embodiment of randomness. You don't know when they're going to happen, where it's going to happen, and who's going to be affected.[16]

The Asian tsunami highlighted another element of uncertainty. Aid agencies receive many unsolicited and sometimes even unwanted donations. Well-intentioned donors generate supplies and manpower support for the relief effort that are of the wrong type or condition. This places an added burden on the relief effort as variability in quantity, quality and suitability of products as well as overloading the process of sorting, storing and distribution become an unnecessary headache for the relief community. Unsolicited supplies clog airports and warehouses and create redundancies.

THE ROLE OF HUMAN RESOURCES IN HUMANITARIAN SUPPLY CHAINS

Poor or non-existent training ultimately affects the quality of any operation, particularly a relief operation. The unpredictable nature of emergencies makes it difficult to retain well-trained employees, and those who have been trained are often volunteers who can only work for short periods before they must return to their 'real-world' jobs. Organisations may experience as high as 80% annual turnover in field logistics personnel,[17] further compounding personnel issues. This results in a constant influx of untrained personnel, inexperienced in the particulars of logistics within the organisation and relief as a whole.

Thomas points out that there may be problems with employee reliability[18] stemming from lack of training. There is a notable lack of employees who are knowledgeable in supply chain or logistics management. In the logistics area, the challenges facing humanitarian organisations are the formal qualification of logistics staff,[19] optimisation of their logistics activities and the integration of activities across business functions. Long notes that 'most people from development agencies . . . have backgrounds in public policy or third world development, and professional logisticians are rare'.[20] Recently, however, the setting of standards and framework agreements to the training and education of staff has improved.[21]

As in business logistics the quality of people is critical in the delivery of humanitarian aid, particularly those that have the skill set to operate complex logistical systems. The implications for training and the costs of solutions are important in this regard. Innovation in problem solving is needed, along with the importance of understanding the sources of uncertainty in the humanitarian supply chain.

HUMANITARIAN SUPPLY CHAINS IN PRACTICE

Central to any relief operation is the establishment and management of an emergency supply chain, which is often fragile and volatile.[22] Provision of humanitarian aid generally, although not exclusively, takes place in locations where sophisticated logistics techniques are difficult to implement (such as Haiti) and which therefore require some form of coordination between NGOs or between the host nation and NGOs.[23] The speed of delivery of humanitarian aid after a disaster depends on the ability of logisticians to procure, transport and receive supplies at the site of a humanitarian relief effort. But disaster relief operations struggle with very special circumstances. They often have to be carried out in an environment with destabilised infrastructures ranging from a lack of electricity supplies to limited transport infrastructure. Furthermore, since most natural disasters are unpredictable, the demand for goods in these disasters is also unpredictable.

Even before a crisis situation has arisen, the quality of the infrastructure of a potential host country, its topography and its political situation are all factors that often conspire against efficient logistical operations. Inadequate transportation, housing, shelter and communications are further barriers to effective delivery of aid. System-wide, humanitarian managers could encounter delivery options ranging through ships, aircraft, rail and trucks. At the same time, those routes may be closed or clogged,[24] thus limiting distribution.

A major barrier to delivery of aid is poor communication. Not only are there obvious difficulties associated with speaking to someone using a different language, but as in Haiti the communications infrastructure may be crippled. Relief agencies may not be able to communicate upstream with headquarters or donors during a disaster. With the priority being the completion of an accurate assessment in the immediate aftermath of a humanitarian crisis, a fully functional communications and information systems network plays an important role in delivering the right information regarding the right amount of aid to be delivered to the right people.[25] In the humanitarian community the United Nations Office for the Coordination of Humanitarian Affairs (UNOCHA) is tasked with the role of coordinating the assessments, the dissemination of information regarding the affected areas and the appeals process; however, sometimes it is not in a position to provide the communications infrastructure to deliver the necessary information (e.g. Haiti) and in these situations the military has a key role in filling the communications gap.

Complex documentation requirements for customs and port clearance can also be a problem. Aid must sometimes travel through several countries using several modes of transportation. Each time the goods change hands, an inventory must also be completed for accountability purposes.

Something often forgotten about delivering aid is packaging. Special packaging requirements dictate what type of food can be brought into a country. The standard transport container for grain products is a 50-kg bag. This is the largest parcel that one person can carry, and is more practical than bulk issue. In addition, bags can easily be loaded and unloaded from many different transportation modes, but they are not impervious to moisture or pests. Medical goods such as pharmaceuticals, blood and equipment often have temperature and moisture sensitivities, as well as an associated manpower burden thanks to a variety of wrappings and markings that complicate sorting and storage.

THE ROLE OF BUSINESS – HUMANITARIAN PARTNERSHIPS

Lack of funding for back-office infrastructure and processes and the need to upgrade the logistics function including its information and knowledge management aspect[26] have attracted the first wave of structured business–humanitarian partnerships. Both NGOs and corporations are pursuing these partnerships suggesting potential benefits are perceived by organisations in both sectors.[27] Business contributions range from ad hoc donations to donations provided through a partnership structure.[28] Businesses can contribute to a humanitarian organisation's relief operation with their specialised resources and expertise in a number of ways: sharing of physical logistics resources (e.g. airplanes, trucks, warehouses), donation of company products (e.g. food and NFIs), secondment or allocation of personnel, access to organisational capability and resources (e.g. tracking and routeing systems).[29]

In terms of HR resources and development, a business can contribute to the professionlisation of the humanitarian sector in general (e.g. TNT's partnership with WFP, see box)[30] and the logistics function in particular by supporting research on disaster management, delivering formal training, and establishing networking initiatives, for example. Business can facilitate the transfer of sound and relevant supply chain practices from the commercial sector to the humanitarian community. By using, for example, IT solutions that generate, store, manage and transfer information along the supply chain, humanitarian organisations can improve the management of their dynamic supply chains and their preparedness capabilities.[31]

TNT–WFP PARTNERSHIP

One of the most successful logistical partnerships in the humanitarian sector is that of TNT and WFP. The partnership was driven by the two principals leading each organisation, namely, Peter Bakker, CEO of TNT, and James Morris, executive director of WFP.

To ensure that TNT would partner with the right organisation, a detailed candidate selection process was established. The selection process initially focused on the reputation and neutrality of potential humanitarian organisations. Another key component in the selection process involved matching TNT's core competencies with potential humanitarian organisations. After four months of searching, TNT was able to rank finalists and confirm an organisational fit with a small group of agencies, which included WFP. Before committing to the partnership, TNT invested even more time in confirming the emotional fit (commitment, shared vision, enthusiasm) and organisational readiness of WFP. This included senior management of TNT participating in a WFP field mission. The outcome of the field mission enabled both parties to develop possible areas for cooperation, such as the WFP school-feeding support, private-sector fundraising, emergency response, joint logistics supply chain (JLSC) and transparency and accountability.

Two months later TNT partnered with WFP and on 19 December 2002 the TNT–WFP partnership was officially launched with the signing of a Memorandum of Understanding that committed TNT to a yearly contribution of €5 million in services and cash for the next five years. At the beginning of 2008, TNT's CEO Peter Bakker pledged TNT's "never-ending" commitment to continue to support WFP's activities – a pledge that was gratefully received by WFP's new Executive Director Josette Sheeran who commented: "I am a true believer in the difference TNT continues to make in the fight against hunger."

CONCLUSION

Commercial supply chains focus on the final customer as the source of income for the entire chain. However, in humanitarian supply chains the end user (the recipient or consumer of aid) seldom enters into a commercial transaction and has little control over supplies. Instead, 'customer service' or 'marketing' of the humanitarian service may need to target the supplier/donor, who has to be convinced that humanitarian action is taking place. For example, there may be greater 'humanitarian visibility' in providing food or medicine before basic logistical equipment such as forklifts, although the latter may be necessary for effective delivery of the former.

The graphic images broadcast to the living rooms of the West opened the wallets of individuals and governments. Emergency funding became big business and the number of NGOs grew. Unfortunately, disaster relief is, and will continue to be, a growth market. Both natural and manmade disasters are expected to increase another five-fold over the next 50 years[32] due to environmental degradation, rapid urbanisation and the spread of HIV/AIDS in the developing world. According to the Munich Reinsurance group, the real annual economic losses have been growing steadily, averaging US$75.5 billion in the 1960s, US$138.4 billion in the 1970s, US$213.9 billion in the 1980s and US$659.9 billion in the 1990s.

Business logistics usually deals with a predetermined set of suppliers, manufacturing sites and stable or at least predictable demand – all of which factors are unknown in humanitarian logistics.[33] Humanitarian logistics is characterised by large-scale activities, irregular demand and unusual constraints in large-scale emergencies.[34] In terms of the end result strived for, business logistics aims at increasing profits whereas humanitarian logistics aims at alleviating the suffering of vulnerable people.[35] The importance of logistics to humanitarian response cannot be ignored; without the rapid establishment of supply and distribution channels for aid resources, the disaster will certainly be more protracted and damaging for the affected population.

As a European Ambassador at a post-tsunami donor conference said, 'We don't need a donor's conference, we need a logistics conference'.[36]

NOTES

1. Thomas, A. & Kopczak L.R. (2005) *From Logistics to Supply Chain Management – The Path Forward in the Humanitarian Sector*, Fritz Institute.

2. Thomas, A. (2004) *Humanitarian Logistics: Enabling Disaster Response*, Fritz Institute; Heaslip, G., Mangan, J. & Lalwani, C. (2007) Integrating military and non-governmental organisation (NGO) objectives in the humanitarian supply chain: a proposed framework, *Proceedings of the Logistics Research Network Conference*, ILT, Hull, 5–7 September.

3. Tatham, P. & Kovács, G. (2007) An initial investigation into the application of the military sea-basing concept to the provision of immediate relief in a rapid onset disaster, *Proceedings of the POMS 18th Annual Conference*, Texas, 4–7 May.

4. Ibid.

5. Van Wassenhove, L.N. (2006) Humanitarian aid logistics: supply chain management in high gear. *Journal of the Operational Research Society*, 57(5), 475–589.

6. Kovács, G. & Tatham, P. (2009) Responding to disruption in the supply network – from dormant to action, *Journal of Business Logistics*, 30(2), 215–228.

7. Heaslip, Mangan & Lalwani (see note 2).

8. Tomasini, R.M. & Van Wassenhove, L.N. (2004) The TPG-WFP partnership: looking for a Partner, INSEAD case study 06/2004-5187.

9. Ibid.

10. UNJLC (2008) UNJLC Training Material, Copenhagen.

11. Heaslip, G. (2010) Civil military coordination, *Irish Times*, 19 January, p. 13.

12. Kovács, G. & Spens, K. (2007) Humanitarian logistics in disaster relief operations, *International Journal of Physical Distribution and Logistics Management*, 37(2), 99–114.

13. Van der Vorst, J.G.A.J. & Beulens, A.J.M. (2002) Identifying sources of uncertainty to generate supply chain redesign strategies, *International Journal of Physical Distribution and Logistics Management*, 32(6), 409–430.

14. Ibid.

15. Sowinski, L.L. (2003) The lean, mean supply chain and its human counterpart, *World Trade*, 16(6), 18.

16. Ibid.

17. Thomas, A. (2003) Why logistics?, *Forced Migration Review*, 18, 4.

18. Ibid.

19. Oloruntoba, R. & Gray, R. (2006) Humanitarian aid: an agile supply chain?, *Supply Chain Management – An International Journal,* 11(2), 115–120.

20. Long, D. (1997) Logistics for disaster relief: engineering on the run, *IIE Solutions*, 29(6), 26–29.

21. Kovács & Tatham (see note 6).

22. Byman D., Lesser, I., Pirnie, B., Bernard, C. & Wazman, M. (2000) *Strengthening the Partnership: Improving Military Coordination Relief Agencies and Allies in Humanitarian Operations,* Rand, Washington DC.

23. Pettit, S. & Beresford, A. (2005) Emergency Relief Logistics: an evaluation of military, non military and composite response models, *International Journal of Logistics: Research and Applications,* 8(4), 313–332.

24. Moody, F. (2001) Emergency relief logistics: a faster way across the global divide, *Logistics Quarterly*, 7(2). www.lq.ca/issues/summer2001/articles/article07.html (accessed 9 March 2007).

25. Kovács & Spens (see note 12).

26. Van der Laan, E., de Brito, M.P. & Vermaesen, S. (2007) Logistics information and knowledge management issues in humanitarian aid organisations, *Proceedings of the SIMPOI/POMS Conference*, Brazil, 8–10 August.

27. Yamamoto, T. (1999) *Corporate–NGO Partnership: Learning from Case Studies.* In T. Yamamoto & K. Gould (Eds), *Corporate–NGO Partnership in Asia-Pacific*, Japan Centre for International Exchange.

28. Binder, A. & Witte, J.M. (2007), Business engagement in humanitarian relief: key trends and policy implications, *Humanitarian Policy Group*, Overseas Development Institute, London.

29. Thomas & Kopczak (2005) (note 1).

30. Tomasini & Van Wassenhove (2004) (note 8).

31. Ibid.

32. Thomas & Kopczak (2005) (note 1).

33. Cassidy, W.B. (2003) A logistics lifeline, *Traffic World*, 27 October, p. 1.

34. Beamon, B.M. & Kotleba, S.A. (2006) Inventory modelling for complex emergencies in humanitarian relief operations, *International Journal of Logistics: Research and Applications*, 9(1), 1–18.

35. Thomas & Kopczak (2005) (note 1).

36. *New York Times* (2005) 6 January.

Mediaware – Turning the Supply Chain Upside Down in Packaging[1]

Simon Healy

Mediaware, Ireland

Seamus O'Reilly

University College Cork, Ireland

INTRODUCTION

While digital printing, or print on demand (POD), has been used for some time in office environments, it has only recently started to impact in industrial printing. In an industrial setting this technology has the potential to transform packaging design, inventory management and, most significantly, the ability to respond rapidly to changing design, brand management and regulatory requirements. In late 2008 a number of entrepreneurs from various backgrounds (including printing, packaging, marketing, financing, retailing and management consultancy) came together with a view to exploring this potential. They established Mediaware Digital Ltd. This company set out to establish itself as a provider of 'business solutions that provide brand owners with a unique opportunity to reconfigure their supply chain and marketing functions to enhance both efficiency and responsiveness through new and dynamic innovative approaches'.

THE MEDIAWARE BUSINESS MODEL

Mediaware viewed packaging on demand as a process where instead of a warehouse full of boxes, users could access a virtual packaging warehouse through a unique IT interface. Digital technology eliminates surplus inventory and overruns. It also eliminates

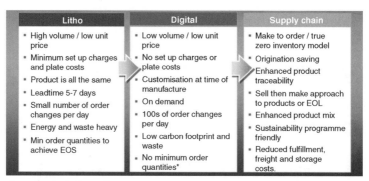

Litho	Digital	Supply chain
• High volume / low unit price	• Low volume / low unit price	• Make to order / true zero inventory model
• Minimum set up charges and plate costs	• No set up charges or plate costs	• Origination saving
• Product is all the same	• Customisation at time of manufacture	• Enhanced product traceability
• Leadtime 5-7 days	• On demand	• Sell then make approach to products or EOL
• Small number of order changes per day	• 100s of order changes per day	• Enhanced product mix
• Energy and waste heavy	• Low carbon footprint and waste	• Sustainability programme friendly
• Min order quantities to achieve EOS	• No minimum order quantities*	• Reduced fulfillment, freight and storage costs.

Figure C4.1   Supply chain benefits

plate production and many other pre-press processes, reduces waste, improves budget, reduces headcount and saves on space. Mediaware also saw it as a sustainable process. The environmental advantages of digital printing for folding carton packages include a zero inventory manufacturing model, thereby eliminating packaging obsolescence. This is in sharp contrast to the traditional mode (litho) where waste is expected as minimum order runs and buffer stocks are built into the operation and inevitably create waste. Figure C4.1 summarises the benefits of digital over litho and lists supply chain improvements.

COLLABORATIVE APPROACH

Mediaware looked to leading equipment providers for the hardware. It identified Xerox as a leading original equipment manufacturer (OEM) in colour digital printing and has worked with the company to integrate the Xerox Gallop Digital Packaging Line with customised work flows. This integrated, inline, cut-sheet digital packaging system enables print providers and packaging converters to cost effectively deliver personalised folding cartons and other packaging applications in short runs. Using its own unique customised proprietary software (Arc-Link), Xerox's PrintCise software, and the Xerox Automated Packaging solution, Mediaware created a system that could accept orders via a range of automated interfaces, print in multiple languages, quickly switch from one language to the next and produce small batches with relevant consumer information. This digital packaging solution significantly reduced minimum order quantities. The inline finishing meant that Mediaware could produce customised packaging cost effectively, without having to stop production and manage offline equipment.

The Mediaware process integrates with the client's workflow and supply chain to deliver what is needed, when it is needed and in the exact quantity required. Its proprietary software allows Mediaware to receive electronic orders (including detailed packaging specifications), segregate jobs into queues and print the carton without any human interaction until it is ready for insertion into the folder and glue machine. Figure C4.2 compares the efficiencies achieved with the traditional litho print process.

The electronic transfer of data from the customer facilitates a virtual supply chain where the physical printing takes place in Dublin, Ireland in response to an order signal from

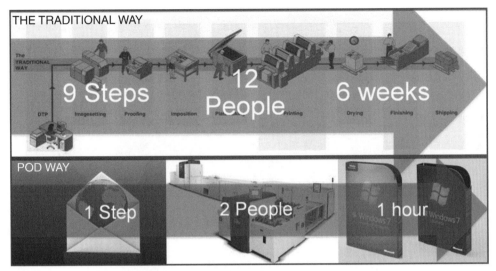

Figure C4.2 Traditional process versus POD process

elsewhere. The finished goods logistics solution (e.g. next-day delivery) depends on customer requirements. Furthermore, this approach also facilitates the establishment of Mediaware as a tier zero supplier – i.e. the supplier is physically located in the customer's plant. It has the capability to set up one of its machines on the customer's line and to interface seamlessly with the production flow producing packages on demand. In addition to the working capital benefits to the customer (derived from reduction in inventory and obsolescence) this also reduces capital expenditure (whether through leasing or purchase) as the supplier not only provides the equipment but also the entire packaging solution.

FIRST MAJOR CUSTOMER

In early 2009, Microsoft engaged with Mediaware for the production of folding cartons to support its soon-to-be-launched Windows 7 software and other products (Figure C4.3). The specifications were demanding, requiring printing a stream of short runs of glossy, full-colour folding cartons to hold software products, in dozens of languages, for distribution throughout the EMEA (Europe, Middle East, Africa) region on a daily demand basis. Production had to begin in time for the launch of Windows 7 in October 2009, and it needed to satisfy Microsoft in terms of price, quality, environmental footprint and security.

Mediaware also needed to integrate with the client's workflow and supply chain to deliver what was needed, when it was needed and in the exact quantity required. As we noted above, using its customised workflow process, Mediaware could accept orders via a range of automated interfaces, print in multiple languages, quickly switch from one language to the next and produce small batches with relevant consumer information. This digital packaging solution significantly reduced minimum order quantities.

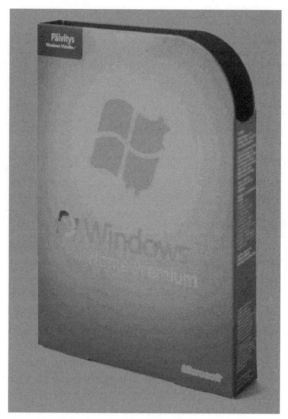

Figure C4.3   Microsoft's folding carton

The competing bids for the Microsoft contract offered solutions bound by old rules of conventional analogue offset print technology. Competitors relied on the old business model, printing short runs in analogue for the best unit price they could offer and storing excess prints for possible use with later orders. In contrast, the process developed by Mediaware in collaboration with Xerox provided close coordination between production and consumption, as well as the ability to operate with lean and agile supply chain manufacturing principles.

Mediaware won the contract as its solution enabled lower minimum orders (in this case as few as five cartons), less waste, less storage, quicker time to market and more secure printing. The workflow process, integrated with Microsoft's order entry, manufacturing and delivery operations, was critical to meeting and exceeding expectations and requirements.

FUTURE DEVELOPMENTS

With the Microsoft agreement well underway, Mediaware is exploring different markets, applications and opportunities for digital folding cartons. The company is currently working with a number of companies on providing short-run packaging solutions across the IT, pharmaceutical and FMCG (fast moving consumer goods) sectors. Mediaware's business model is equipped to handle the folding carton needs of manufacturers ranging from multinationals to local enterprises. In addition to software companies, pharmaceutical companies are another top prospect. They have some of the same business needs that top software companies have. They have a regular use of small format cartons, they sell internationally and they have a high need for secure print. Mediaware prints a unique code on each carton, allowing item-level tracking worldwide. The total solution also prints a precise number of cartons per job, lessening the risk of counterfeiters gaining access to legitimate packaging.

QUESTIONS

- List and discuss the opportunities that POD technology offers supply chain managers, brand managers and operations managers.
- Discuss the impact of this on supply chain strategy and configuration and on marketing strategies.

NOTE

1. This case draws (with permission) on Mediaware case history published by InfoTrends, 24 March, 2010 (available at www.infotrends.com) and the authors are grateful for input from Nichole Jones, Bob Leahey and Barb Pellow (InfoTrends, US). The authors are also grateful to Xerox for the information provided.

Collaborative Planning in an Auto Parts Supply Chain in China: A Tale of Two Tier-One Suppliers

Booi H Kam and Jin Hao

RMIT University, Melbourne, Australia

In China, auto manufacturers usually assign one supplier to provide the same range of parts for different car models. The 'one supplier' strategy avoids excessive investment in expensive dyes and fixtures. Suppliers, in turn, can achieve scale economy. The strategy also helps cement the relationship between customer and supplier.

T2S, T1SA and T1SB are three companies that formed a section of an auto parts supply chain, servicing two major vehicle assembly plants, OEMA and OEMB, in China. Both T1SA and T1SB are tier-one car seat suppliers, which engage the same power track manufacturer, T2S, the tier-two supplier. Both also have very similar organisational structures and employ over 200 staff. T1SA is the largest car-seat supplier to OEMA, manufacturing over 95% of OEMA's car seats. Because of the need to provide just-in-time (JIT) delivery and vendor managed inventory (VMI) service to OEMA, T1SA is located very close to OEMA, which is its sole customer. T1SB, OEMB's largest car-seat supplier, also provides JIT deliveries to OEMB. Supplying over 85% of OEMB's car seats, T1SB also chooses to locate close to OEMB.

T2S employs the same design concept, product structure and production process for both T1SA's and T1SB's car-seat tracks. The products for the two tier-one suppliers are assembled in the same production line, with similar production lead time. Likewise, the component supply base for both T1SA's and T1SB's car-seat tracks from tier-three (T3) suppliers is the same, which means purchasing lead time is equivalent. T2S also

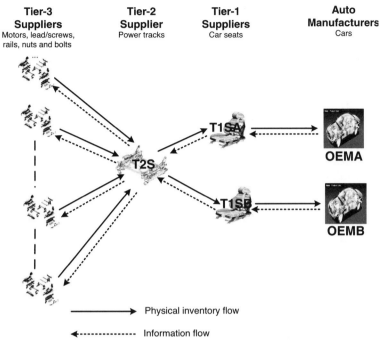

Figure C5.1   The auto parts supply chains of OEMA and OEMB

keeps the same level of inbound inventory and stores the same level of WIP (work in process) for both T1SA and T1SB. The delivery terms from T2S to both T1SA and T1SB are also similar, i.e. T2S holds the same level of finished goods inventory and warehouse inventory for both T1SA and T1SB. In almost all instances, the components used for manufacturing the car-seat tracks for both T1SA and T1SB are comparable. To reduce capital investment, and operating cost, T2S maximises its production capacity by using a common production platform for different vehicle models, but a flexible assembly line to suit multiple products. T2S adopts a push system in its operation to keep cost down, while the two tier-one suppliers adopt a pull system and set high service level as their first priority. Figure C5.1 shows the auto parts supply chains of OEMA and OEMB.

OPERATIONAL ARRANGEMENTS

T2S has an operational contract with both T1SA and T1SB. The scope of the contract includes how T2S and its tier-one supplier client would collaborate to develop new product design, to provide quality assurance, to establish engineering capability requirements, delivery requirements, logistics solutions and payment terms as well as the collaboration duties and obligations of the contracting parties. The contract, though formal, has no expiry date. Either party, however, could exit the contractual arrangement by giving the other a 90-day advance notice.

Both OEMA and OEMB share their production schedule and forecast with their tier-one suppliers. OEMA established an EDI system with T1SA to facilitate quick information transfer. To facilitate their JIT operations, the two OEMs release their delivery order at a pre-agreed time. OEMA transmits its order to T1SA every two hours. As this would not leave enough time for T1SA to assemble the complete seats after order release, T1SA setup a Kanban system to help it maintain a safety stock to meet the high service requirement imposed by OEMA. In other words, T1SA's production department will assemble car seats continuously to fill its inventory pool. The order cycle time given by OEMB to T1SB is longer than that of T1SA and allows T1SB to start production after it receives a delivery order. Final goods delivery performance was of the essence. Both OEMs ask for a 100% on-time delivery rate. Significant penalties are imposed if their tier-one suppliers miss a delivery target.

T2S PRODUCT FLOW AND INVENTORY MANAGEMENT

Figure C5.2 shows the inventory management profile of the tier-three, tier-two and tier-one suppliers of this auto parts supply chain. On average, the tier-three suppliers keep a 3–10-day safety stock to meet T2S's delivery requirements. Inventory within T2S comprises inbound inventory, warehouse inventory, WIP and finished goods inventory. To its local suppliers, T2S would issue a purchase order one week before actual production. Also, T2S would provide a three-month forecast for its suppliers to procure their raw material. To its overseas suppliers, T2S would release a six-week firm order and a three-month forecast.

T2S typically keeps a two-week (based on supplier delivery lead time by air in case of emergency) safety inventory for imported materials. For local materials, T2S would ask suppliers to deliver one day before actual production.

T2S employs a pull system to manage its WIP, using a Kanban system to indicate production line inventory. Warehouse inventory is fed to assembly line according to actual production consumption. T2S programmes the work flow of its assembly line according to tier-one suppliers' requirements. Typically, finished goods would be ready half a day before actual delivery. T2S also maintains a safety finished goods inventory (20% of daily requirement) to cater for unexpected increase in demand.

INFORMATION TRANSFER AND SHARING PRACTICES

The two OEMs use a different method to release forecast and delivery orders to their tier-one suppliers. OEMA issues in total three types of material planning information. The first is a weekly rolling forecast that covers the entire year, which would be updated within the week if major changes occur. When T1SA receives the rolling forecast, it inputs the information into its intranet to enable all concerned departments to know what is forthcoming. At the same time, it will transmit the information to T2S via email, fax and telephone to request the latter to review the forecast and comment on material availability in the next few months. If T2S could not fulfil 100% of the requirement,

	Tier-three suppliers	Tier-two supplier (T2S)				Tier-one suppliers (T1SA and T1SB)
Roles in supply chain	Component suppliers providing parts (e.g. motors, rails, lead screw, bolts and nuts)	Plant assembling components to build power tracks				T1SA and T1SB assemble tracks with other parts (e.g. foam and trim) to form complete seats and deliver to OEMA and OEMB
Material handled	Components	Components	Components	Semi-finished products	Finished goods	Finished goods
Inventory status	Outbound inventory of suppliers	Inbound inventory	Warehouse inventory	WIP	Finished goods inventory	Inbound inventory of tier-one suppliers (T1SA and T1SB)
Inventory management strategy	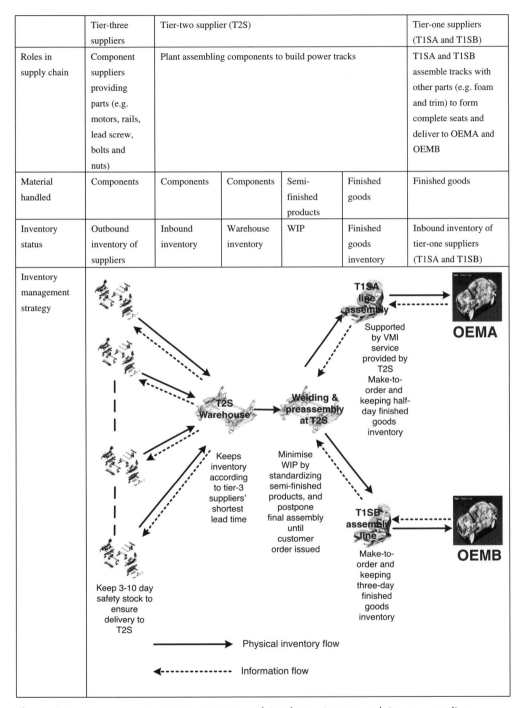					

Figure C5.2   Inventory management strategy of tier-three, tier-two and tier-one suppliers

which could be due to an unplanned increase in production volume by OEMA, the power track manufacturer would ask T1SA to discuss with OEMA to find a mutually agreeable solution.

The second type of information released by OEMA is its daily production volume, which is issued to T1SA a day before actual production. Again, T1SA would upload the data onto its intranet for its staff and relay the information to T2S to review and to organise production according to the required volume. The third set of information is the delivery plan, which OEMA would issue on the production day every two hours through its EDI system. T1SA would pack the seats according to OEMA's sequence number and arrange JIT delivery.

Apart from sharing production information and forecast released by OEMA, T1SA also sends advanced alert, its inventory status and new project launch information to T2S. Again, transmission is via three modes: email, fax and telephone. This is to ensure that T2S is aware that the requisite information has been transferred.

OEMB, by contrast, releases a rolling forecast covering its whole year's requirement only two to three times a year. Every month, however, OEMB would announce the requirement for the next three to six months. Normally, production planning for the first three months would be announced on a weekly basis, and the balance for the year would be on a monthly basis. OEMB would release its weekly production schedule one week in advance, with data split into daily requirement. T1SB would carry out JIT delivery to OEMB on the production day. Though T1SB would distribute the annual forecast to T2S, it would not release the monthly updated planning data (3–6-month period) to the latter, despite their pre-agreement. Instead, T1SB would only issue weekly production figures for the current month and the total order volume for the following month to T2S. T1SB justifies its reluctance to provide such information on the grounds that the forecast is for information only. T1SB is concerned that T2S may use the forecast as a basis to claim for loss or additional cost resulting from volume change. T1SB top management's attitude is: 'the less information is provided to T2S, the fewer headaches the company would face'. T1SB's deliberate move to conceal partial information from T2S has far-reaching implications on the latter's performance. To ensure that it would not be caught off-guard, T2S has to take a gamble on the volume of future requirements based on past experience. Should OEMB cancel an order, T2S would suffer significant stock obsolesces.

COLLABORATIVE PLANNING AND PRODUCTION

T1SA and T2S

T1SA and T2S have rather dissimilar operational objectives. T1SA sets on-time delivery to OEMA as a top priority, while T2S regards cost and inventory control as most important. Yet, both companies recognise that fulfilling OEMA's production needs should form the basis upon which their operations, processes and inventory levels should be set. The senior management of the two companies view their business relationship as mutually interdependent. Whenever an exceptional incident occurs or is looming,

T1SA will convey the information to T2S in real time or notify T2S in advance of an impending change that has direct implications on their joint operations. A commonly agreed solution will be sought in consultation with OEMA before implementation. For example, when OEMA decides to stop production for a particular model, OEMA will inform T1SA, seeking information on inventory status. T1SA will compile the requisite data with help from T2S and other suppliers and present them to OEMA. The three supply chain partners – OEMA, T1SA and T2S – would meet to jointly establish an optimal phase-out schedule to minimise inventory obsolescence. OEMA will decide how best to minimise losses and what compensation to give to T1SA and T2S, if inventory obsolescence were to occur. Likewise, whenever OEMA signals its intention to increase its order quantity, T1SA and T2S would work together to ensure OEMA's requirements are fulfilled at the lowest possible cost, with little regard to protect their interest. When an OEMA new project is behind schedule, T1SA would inform T2S to postpone its production to enable OEMA to catch up with the schedule. The practice of giving advanced notice and holding joint discussions to solve problems has obviated unnecessary inventory build-up and potential conflict within the T2S–T1SA–OEMA supply chain.

Senior management of T2S and T1SA meet not only under exceptional circumstances, but also regularly to explore ideas for new collaborative initiatives, formulate plans for continuous improvement and obtain feedback on operational performance. Communication between the two companies, which is always cordial and constructive, is also not confined to senior management. Middle level managers of their corresponding departments, such as between the quality departments or between the procurement departments of the two companies, also have frequent direct contact with each other to discuss operational matters and issues of mutual benefit. T1SA and T2S managers also make it a point to educate their staff about the benefits and necessities of collaborative planning. In some instances, operational meetings between T1SA and T2S even extend to tier-three suppliers or OEMA. These collaborative meetings provide a platform for information exchange and sharing of experience, enabling both companies to verify each other's requirements, identify gaps in information transfer, and set up mutually agreed operating objectives, processes and measurement systems. They also help employees of the two companies to understand and appreciate each other's responsibility and obligations, knowing what to do, when to do, how to do and with whom to do. Typically, mutually beneficial solutions for the entire supply chain emerge in these meetings. Because of their close and mutually supportive relationships, T2S agrees to second an onsite service person at the premises of T1SA to support the latter's operations as an integral part of a VMI system to ensure on-time replenishment of power tracks at T1SA.

T1SB and T2S

In sharp contrast to the frequent and regular meetings held between T2S and T1SA, managers of T1SB and T2S meet only under exceptional situations. The agenda is also primarily confined to discussing specific problem situations, such as potential delivery failures or sudden OEM production volume increase. Though these meetings are intended to resolve problems or explore mutually beneficial solutions for changed circumstances, T1SB typically retreats to an 'arm's-length position' under pressure, especially when the issue has cost implications. As a consequence, rather than focusing on exploring solutions to resolve issues, many meetings between T1SB and T2S end up as debates on operational accountability and negotiation sessions for loss appropriation.

T1SB does not regard T2S an equal partner in their supply chain operations and likes to flex its power as a major client of T2S, coercing the latter to bear the losses whenever a project phases out. Additionally, should OEMB alter its production volume, T1SB would insist that T2S meet the increase without claiming for any extra cost, including cost of premium freight (such as via air freight) to ensure product delivery. In most instances, T2S does comply as it does not want to get into any unproductive confrontation with T1SB due to the large volume of business that it gets from T1SB. When T1SB cancels its order, it also shuns responsibility, leaving T2S to bear all the losses. Worse still is T1SB's habit of engaging in forward buying activities by enlarging inventory requirement at the product launch stage to secure availability. This causes excessive inventory build-up at T2S, when T1SB cancels its orders after production begins to stabilise. T1SB has cancelled its purchase orders many times without giving T2S forewarning and refuses to compensate T2S according to their agreement. Occasionally, T1SB would attempt to soften its hard-line attitude towards T2S by dispatching some of its employees to T2S to work with their counterparts for short periods. T1SB claims that this arrangement helps staff from both companies to understand each other's processes and establishes personal friendship. T2S, however, does not see it as a sincere gesture, branding it as a 'mechanistic relationship building' behaviour.

Because of the opportunistic and exploitative behaviours of T1SB, T2S declines to offer a parallel VMI scheme to support T1SB's production, despite repeated requests from the latter. Without VMI support from T2S, T1SB has to keep three days' inventory on hand, which is six times that of the half-day inventory carried by T1SA. T1SB also has a lower inventory turn. Further, T2S also takes the opportunity to retaliate at times by not agreeing to step up production when T1SB has to meet a sudden order increase from OEMB. This forces T1SB to seek expensive alternatives, such as using air shipment to import car seats from overseas to fulfil OEMB's order requirement.

COLLABORATIVE OUTCOMES

All three plants subscribe to on-time delivery as their top priority. They measure the cost of achieving this objective by inventory turn. Inventory turn measures how fast raw materials could be transformed into finish goods. It is an indication of the speed of inventory flow: the higher the inventory turn rate, the quicker the transformation. High inventory turn reduces material holding cost, implying more efficient inventory utilisation. The higher the inventory turn, the lower would be the risk of inventory

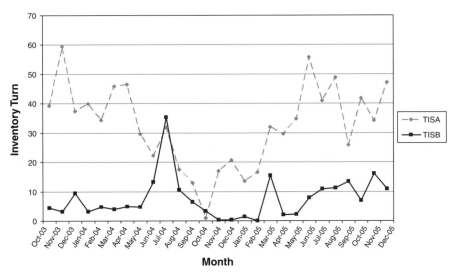

Figure C5.3   Inventory turn report

obsolescence and capital cost of inventory acquisition, which contribute to bigger profit margin. T2S utilises inventory turn to monitor its inventory performance, calculated as follows:

$$Inventory\ Turn = \frac{Cost\ of\ Goods\ Sold\ (COGS)}{Inventory}$$

where Inventory = Inbound inventory + Warehouse inventory + WIP + Finished goods inventory.

The inventory turn performance of T2S from 2003 to 2005 shows that the inventory turn of T1SA's products is much higher than that of T1SB's products (Figure C5.3). This means that the material flow speed of T1SA products is quicker, and the inventory holding cost of T1SA's products is less. It suggests that T2S was able to benefit more by servicing T1SA than T1SB. T2S attributes its ability to secure a higher inventory turn for T1SA's products to the close collaboration that it has with the latter. T1SA's willingness to share information openly and its understanding and supportive attitudes are instrumental in helping T2S to manage its inventory efficiently, including optimising the volume of raw material purchase from tier-three suppliers. Due to more efficient use of inventory, T2S's return of sales for T1SA's products averaged 11.4% between 2003 and 2005, which is 2.3% higher than that for T1SB's products (9.1%). During this period, T2S's inventory obsolescence rate and excessive material for T1SB's products amount to 0.9% of sales, compared with close to 0% for T1SA's products.

T1SA has also benefited from the close relationship it has with T2S. Because of the availability of updated forecast and production information provided by T1SA, T2S is able to continuously improve the efficiency of its VMI service to T1SA. T2S's VMI service gives T1SA the confidence to hold no more than half a day of inventory compared with T1SB's holding of a three-day inventory. T1SA also has a higher inventory turn and lower material management cost compared with T1SB.

QUESTIONS

- From the collaboration experience of T2S with T1SA and T1SB, what would be the key enablers and inhibitors of collaborative planning and forecasting?
- Do you think that collaborative planning success is a question of promoting the 'enablers' and containing the 'inhibitors'?
- What are the fundamental ingredients to ensure collaborative planning and forecasting success?

Part Two

Logistics and Supply Chain Operations

Part Two

Logistics and Supply Chain Operations

6 Transport in Supply Chains

LEARNING OBJECTIVES

- Understand the cost structures and operating characteristics of the different transport modes, and the relationships between freight rates and consignment weight, dimensions and distance to be travelled.
- Highlight key terms used in transport.
- Discuss the roles of distribution centres and highlight the concept of factory gate pricing.
- Identify some of the many issues (including the effect of supply chain strategies) that can impact the efficiency of transport services.
- Identify the range of issues to be considered in planning transport infrastructure.
- Explain the application of a technique known as the transportation model.

INTRODUCTION

Freight transport is an integral part of SCM, but traditionally it has been treated as a service that is easily available when required by suppliers and distributors. Also, transport is typically regarded as a non-value-adding activity in the supply chain, although we challenge this assumption on the basis that it plays an essential role in the supply chain and when managed properly can allow supply chains to work more efficiently and effectively.

There are essentially five modes of transport:

- air
- road
- water

- rail
- pipeline

The 'information superhighway' can also be regarded as a possible sixth mode of transport.

Chapter 6 comprises three core sections:
- Characteristics of the different transport modes
- Transport operations, distribution centres and the role of factory gate pricing
- Efficiency of transport services

Two chapter appendices are also provided, on transport modelling and on planning transport infrastructure.

CHARACTERISTICS OF THE DIFFERENT TRANSPORT MODES

Choosing which mode(s) to use for freight transportation will usually be a function of the volume and value of the freight, the distance to be travelled, the availability of different services, freight rates to be charged and so forth. Once the appropriate mode of transport has been chosen, it is usually the case that there is not a simple linear relationship between the freight rate charged and both the weight of the freight and the distance to be travelled (Figures 6.1 and 6.2). Regardless of how short the distance to be travelled, the logistics service provider (LSP) will still have to recover certain fixed costs for transporting a consignment (Figure 6.1). For heavier shipments, the rate per kilo will typically decrease as the fixed costs can be spread over a larger weight (Figure 6.2). For bulky or difficult to handle shipments, LSPs will typically apply what is known as **volumetric charging** based on the dimensions of the consignment. This is to compensate for lost capacity as a result of carrying the bulky shipment where applying a rate per kilo would not sufficiently cover the costs incurred of carrying the shipment. Think for example of a roll of carpet in an aircraft hold, by weight this shipment may be quite light, but because of its dimensions there may be a lot of lost space in the aircraft hold which cannot now be utilised.

An interesting feature of logistics systems is that sometimes consignors do not know exactly which transport mode their freight travels on,

The term **intermodal transport** is often used in transport. This is where freight moves within a loading unit (known as an ITU – intermodal transport unit). This unit may move upon a number of different transport modes, but the freight remains within the unit at all times. There are various types of ITUs, the most common being the standard sized containers (typically 20 and 40 feet in length) seen on ships, trains and trucks. Other types of ITUs include the 'igloo' containers used in air freight.

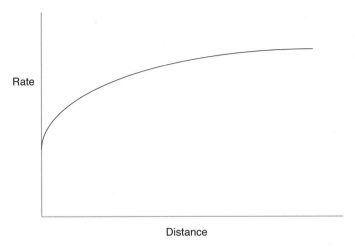

Figure 6.1   Relationship between rate and distance

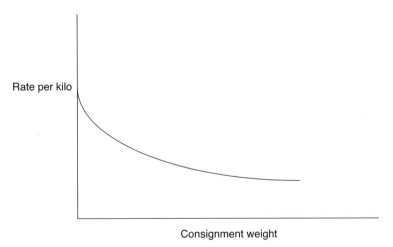

Figure 6.2   Relationship between rate per kilo and consignment weight

leaving this decision to the LSP. For the LSP it is not a simple matter of trading off one mode against another; sometimes multiple transport modes are used in combination. Table 6.1 illustrates the cost structures and operating characteristics of the different transport modes.

The split of freight among different modes varies by region and type of freight. Figure 6.3 for example shows the modal split within the European Union. Total goods transported within the 27 Member States of the EU in 2008 are estimated to be 4091 billion tonne kilometres. This does not include transport activities between the EU and the rest of the world.

Table 6.1   A summary of costs and relative operating characteristics of the different transport modes

Mode	Relative costs and operating characteristics by mode
Road	Fixed cost is low as the physical transport infrastructure such as motorways are in place through public funding; variable cost is medium in terms of rising fuel costs, maintenance and increasing use of road and congestion charges. In terms of operating characteristics, road as a mode of transport scores favourably on speed, availability, dependability and frequency, but not so good on capability due to limited capacity on weight and volume. Uniquely among transport modes, it can allow direct access to consignor and consignee sites
Rail	Fixed cost is high and the variable cost is relatively low. Fixed costs are high due to expensive equipment requirements such as locomotives, wagons, tracks and facilities such as freight terminals. On relative operating characteristics, rail is considered good on speed, dependability and especially capability to move larger quantities of freight
Air	Fixed cost is on the lower side but high variable cost that includes fuel, maintenance, security requirements, etc. The main advantage of air is speed; it is however limited in uplift capacity, similarly other modes of transport are required to take freight to and from airports, thus air cannot directly link individual consignors and consignees
Water	Fixed cost is on the medium side including vessels, handling equipment and terminals. Variable cost is low due to the economies of scale that can be enjoyed from carrying large volumes of freight – this is the main advantage of the water mode, together with its capability to uplift large volumes of freight. Like air, it cannot offer direct consignor-to-consignee connectivity, and vessels are sometimes limited in terms of what ports they can use. It is also quite a slow mode
Pipeline	Fixed cost is high due to rights of way, construction and installation, but the variable cost is relatively low and generally just encompasses routine maintenance and ongoing inspection/security. On operational characteristics, the dependability is excellent but this mode can only be used in very limited situations

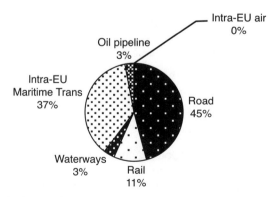

Figure 6.3   Modal split for goods transport in the EU 27 in 2008 (% tonne kilometres) (Source: EU Mobility and Transport, 2010)[1]

Maritime transport is the dominant mode of transport for international transport movements. According to the United Nations Conference on Trade and Development (UNCTAD), the volume of international seaborne trade in 2008 was estimated at 8.17 billion tonnes (of which 34% was oil).[2] Road transport is the dominant mode of transport for inland transport. Due mainly to the flexibility, directness and speed that the movement of freight by road offers, when compared to rail, inland waterway or sea transport, it has become the principal freight transport mode, carrying the majority of inland freight.[3] It is, however, also the most environmentally damaging mode of transport, an issue we will return to in Chapter 16 which deals with sustainability. Policy makers are thus endeavouring to shift freight from road to more environmentally friendly transport modes, in particular to rail and inland waterway. This is not an easy task, however, as many transport systems are predicated on extensive use of road transport.

> Macro volumes of freight are usually measured in **freight tonne kilometres** (FTKs), that is volume of freight measured in tonnes multiplied by the distance the freight travels measured in kilometres. Macro volumes of passengers are usually measured in revenue passenger kilometres (RPKs), the *revenue* denotes that the passengers are fare paying (as opposed to positioning crew, staff travelling on concession, etc.).

TRANSPORT OPERATIONS, DISTRIBUTION CENTRES AND THE ROLE OF FACTORY GATE PRICING

Chapter 10 will illustrate how inventory is stored at multiple points in supply chains. In this section we will consider the role of distribution centres and in particular a concept known as 'factory gate pricing'. Over the past 30 years, supply chain configurations have been changing to achieve higher levels of logistics performance and customer service. In the 1970s and 1980s **distribution centres (DCs)** were introduced in the retail sector, with retailers taking over responsibility for deliveries to their stores (sometimes DCs are referred to as **RDCs – regional distribution centres**, and **NDCs – national distribution centres**). A distribution centre is a type of warehouse where a large number of products are delivered by different suppliers, preferably in full truck loads. Each distribution centre services a number of retail stores in the regional area. In the 1990s, **consolidation centres (CCs)** were added and served to consolidate deliveries from multiple suppliers into full loads, which could be delivered onwards to the DCs (see Figure 6.4). A recent development has been for the retailers to take control of the delivery of goods into their DCs and this is known as **factory gate pricing – FGP**. This gives a single point of control for the inbound logistics network and can be defined as:

> Factory Gate Pricing (FGP) is the use of an ex-works price for a product plus the organisation and optimisation of transport by the purchaser to the point of delivery.[4]

The case below on FGP highlights the savings for the retailer due to increased supply chain visibility and better management of transport leading to reduction in delays in their inbound logistics.

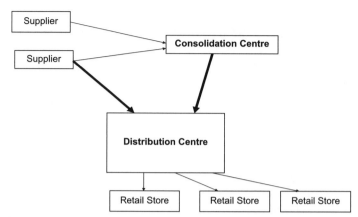

Figure 6.4 Inbound logistics in the retail sector

Figure 6.5 illustrates the evolution of grocery distribution over the past half century.

In addition to the control of their inbound logistics using FGP, retailers are also looking at further improving their efficiency by increasing the backloading of store delivery vehicles and the consolidation of smaller loads into consolidation centres. In the grocery sector in the UK, Tesco was the first to move towards FGP in 2001, and subsequently other retailers applied the concept. In addition to the retail sector, FGP has also been used in a number of other industry sectors.

The application of FGP within the grocery sector has complexities due to the large number of suppliers, huge number of products and the scale of distribution. With regard to the impact of FGP on transport, LSPs could feel that the retailers can use it as a lever to reduce haulage rates and reduce their profit margins. Research by the ITeLS research team at Cardiff University suggests that there are numerous operational benefits that arise for the retailer from implementing FGP.[5] These include increased supply chain vis-

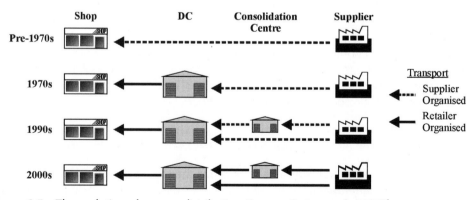

Figure 6.5 The evolution of grocery distribution (Source: Potter *et al.*, 2003)[6]

ibility provided to the retailer giving management greater insight into the behaviour of its replenishment processes in response to changes in demand; in addition the research showed that the retailer benefits from higher delivery service levels. For the suppliers, FGP enables them to focus on their core competencies. In the grocery industry, this is pertinent as the retailers do not add value to the product through manufacturing, but do so through the efficient delivery of products. Therefore, distribution is one of their key strengths. Conversely, many suppliers outsource their distribution in order to focus upon the core competency of manufacturing.[7]

For FGP implementation a single point of control is required in the supply chain. With no overall single point of control, there will be additional costs such as in achieving collaboration between all parties for transport movements. In the grocery sector, the power of the retailers makes FGP suitable for managing the single point of control. However, this may not apply in all cases. The implementation of FGP heavily depends on the use of ICT, particularly for transport planning but also for communication with the LSPs.

The next section turns to the issue of minimising total transport cost within a transport network. Minimum total transport cost solutions could be arrived at by balancing the distribution centre demands with suppliers' capacities in an existing transport network. In addition, where there is a possibility of redesigning the network, the total transport cost could be further minimised by optimising the location of consolidation centres and/ or distribution centres in relation to the supplier network. One of the methods to do this is using what is known as the **transportation model** and this is discussed in detail in the end-of-chapter Appendix A.

AN EXAMPLE OF THE APPLICATION OF FACTORY GATE PRICING (FGP)[8]

This example illustrates that implementation of FGP could generate savings to justify the investment for its adoption in the retail sector. The case company is a leading UK grocery retailer with over 1750 stores in the UK and nearly 2000 own-brand primary suppliers in 98 countries. The example discussed here is based on the UK suppliers, UK distribution centres and UK consolidation centres only.

The suppliers to the case company retailer could deliver products in full or less than full truck loads. Less than truckload suppliers are defined by the retailer as those supplying less than 18 pallets per day to a DC (a full vehicle can hold 24 to 26 pallets).

With less than truckload suppliers, the decision was taken by the retailer to consolidate these shipments through a new network of consolidation centres (CCs) so as to make deliveries to the DC in full vehicle loads.

In analysing the data collected from the retailer on flows of existing consolidated products, it was found in some cases that a supplier was transporting products across the UK to a CC, only for them to then be moved back along almost the same route for delivery to a DC. This obviously increased transport costs. Under FGP, products are routed more rationally, going from suppliers to the local CC for onward movement to the DCs. Where the supplier is close to the DC, direct deliveries to the DC continue to be the most cost-effective approach. With full truckload suppliers, the ability of the retailer to have visibility of its whole inbound distribution network also created opportunities for transport cost reduction.

While the application of FGP delivers reductions in transport miles and costs, the implementation has required the use of the latest developments in ICT. If the technology was not available, the efficiency of the process would be significantly reduced due to the number of people required to plan and manage the inbound distribution process. Through the acquisition of an effective transport management system, the retailer can control the whole inbound distribution network with a limited number of people working at any one time.

In 2004, the ITeLS research team at Cardiff University carried out a mini-project with the case company and made an attempt to quantify the transport benefits. In the context of the retailer's business, less than full truck load deliveries accounted for 18% of the total ambient volume, 57% of composite volume and 35% of total grocery volume. Composite distribution networks are the centres used for distributing multi-temperature controlled products (fresh, chilled and frozen). The data from the retailer was modelled in a network planning software package to determine the transport distance and cost benefits.[9] The results for both ambient and composite networks are detailed in Table 6.2. There are a number of assumptions that should be kept in mind in interpreting the results. It is assumed that the demand is spread evenly over time, with 100% availability at the supplier. The decision on less than truckload suppliers was made strategically at the retailer, rather than incorporating all suppliers into the model. Costs were based on current charges incurred by the retailer and levied on a per mile basis for transport and per pallet basis for handling charges at the CCs. Finally, the figures only represent the movement of products from the supplier to the DC and do not take into account any costs in positioning the vehicle at the supplier. Because the retailer uses third-party logistics providers for the majority of their requirements, it has been assumed that any cost associated with this is included in the haulage cost.

By controlling the consolidation network from a single point through FGP, it is possible to reduce the total distance products travel between suppliers and stores by 23–25% (see Table 6.2). This results from reducing the number of suppliers that deliver directly to the DC, particularly for ambient products. The relative reduction in transport costs is less, being 13.9% and 17.2% for ambient and composite products, respectively. This is because there is cost associated with handling the pallets at the consolidation centre. The researchers estimate that, given the volume of products these savings are achieved on, it can be extrapolated that FGP will reduce the retailer's total distribution cost by

Table 6.2   The impact of the primary consolidation network with FGP[9]

Product type	Scenario	Weekly transport miles (normalised)	Total weekly cost (normalised)	Volume	
				Direct	Consolidated
Ambient	As is	100	100	88.7%	11.3%
	FGP design	74.7	86.1	16.7%	83.3%
Composite	As is	100	100	39.0%	61.0%
	FGP design	77.0	82.8	12.8%	87.2%

approximately 5.7%. However, this value does not consider any gains from implementing the strategies for full vehicle loads or the potential for the retailer, as a large user of transport, to realise economies of scale for freight rates.

In this example, the benefits of FGP in the retail sector have been highlighted, but it is important to comment upon potential issues that arise through its implementation. First of all it is likely that there will be additional costs for achieving collaboration between all parties for the transport movements if is implemented using the consolidation centres. Second, there is the question of who manages the point of control. In the grocery sector, the power of the retailers makes FGP suitable. However, this may not apply in all instances. Finally, the implementation of FGP has been heavily dependent upon ICT, particularly for transport planning but also for communication with hauliers.

EFFICIENCY OF TRANSPORT SERVICES

A variety of issues impact the efficiency and effectiveness of transport services. These include congestion problems, waste including empty running of vehicles, carbon emissions, regulatory directives on maximum permitted working time, road user charges and skill shortages. These problems cause inefficiencies and waste such as excessive waiting time, poor turnaround time, low vehicle fill rates, poor asset utilisation, unnecessary administration and excessive inventory holding.

Poor asset utilisation for example is illustrated in Figure 6.6 that uses real-life data from the steel sector. It can be seen that the demand placed by corporate customers on the transport operator per day during a week can vary from 83 vehicles to 170 vehicles.

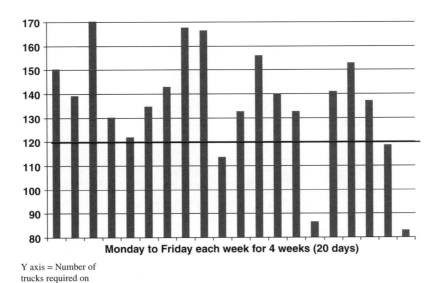

Monday to Friday each week for 4 weeks (20 days)

Y axis = Number of trucks required on each day

Figure 6.6   Poor asset utilisation in transport (Source: Mason, Lalwani & Boughton, 2006)[10]

The term **FCL** is used in transport to refer to *full container loads* while the term **LCL** is used to refer to *less than full container loads*. When carriers have a consignment that will not fill an entire loading unit they will usually try to build a consolidated shipment to make up a FCL.

The strategies pursued in a supply chain impact the efficiency of the transport services demanded. Pursuing a JIT strategy for example has many advantages, but one of its downsides is that it can lead to inefficient transport utilisation with frequent small loads. In fact from the LSP's perspective JIT can lead to: inconsistent fleet utilisation, reduced payload optimisation, reduced ability to effectively plan fleet operations, an image of expendable and infinitely flexible resource in the eyes of customers, etc.

In Chapter 14 we will return to this issue of the efficiency and effectiveness of transport and look in particular at the various solutions that LSPs can pursue.

LEARNING REVIEW

This chapter focused on physical flows using transport in supply chains. The characteristics of the five principal transport modes were described and issues in determining freight rates were reviewed. The role of distribution centres and in particular the concept of factory gate pricing were described. This led us to a discussion around the efficiency and effectiveness of transport services, an issue we will return to later in the book in Chapter 16, which deals with sustainability and logistics.

We noted at the outset to this chapter that transport is typically regarded as a non-value-adding activity in the supply chain. In conjunction with the understanding that will be gained from studying Chapter 8 on the key roles played by LSPs, and the contributions we will see in Chapter 16 that transport can make around issues concerning sustainability, it is evident that transport plays a vital role in ensuring that supply chains operate both efficiently and effectively.

The next chapter will continue the discussion on transport in the supply chain and will focus upon the critically important topic of security. Chapter 8 will describe and distinguish the various types of logistics service providers and clarify the terminology commonly used.

QUESTIONS

- In your view does transport add value in the supply chain?
- What is volumetric charging?
- What are the key characteristics of the five principal modes of transport?
- Why do we say that transport is a derived demand?
- What is factory gate pricing?

MODAL SPLIT BY COUNTRY

Try to determine what the modal split is for freight in your country. You will usually be able to find this in government transport statistics. What are the reasons for this modal split and how does it compare with other countries and regions?

In view of increased awareness of environmental and related issues, is this modal split sustainable going forward? If it is not, what future changes in transport industry structure in your country do you envisage?

NOTES

1. EU Mobility and Transport (2010) *Transport Statistics: Statistical Pocket Book 2010*, http://ec.europa.eu/transport/publications/statistics/statistics_en.htm.
2. UNCTAD Review of Maritime Transport 2009.
3. Davies, I., Mason, R.J. & Lalwani, C.S. (2006) Assessing the impact of ICT on UK general haulage companies, *International Journal of Production Economics*, 106(1), 12–27.
4. Potter, A.T., Lalwani, C.S., Disney, S.M. & Velho, H. (2003) Modelling the impact of factory gate pricing on transport and logistics, *Proceedings of the 7th International Symposium on Logistics*, Seville, 6–8 July, pp. 625–630.
5. Lalwani, C.S., Mason, R.J., Potter, A.T. & Yang, B. (Eds) (2004) *Transport in Supply Chains*, Logistics and Operations Management Section, Cardiff Business School, UK.
6. Potter *et al.* (see note 4).
7. Rushton, A., Oxley, J. & Croucher, P. (2000) *Handbook of Logistics and Distribution Management*, 2nd Edition, Kogan Page, London.
8. Potter, A., Mason, R. & Lalwani, C. (2007) Analysis of factory gate pricing in the UK grocery supply chain, *International Journal of Retail and Distribution Management*, 35(10), 821–834.
9. Potter *et al.* (see note 4).
10. Mason, R.J., Lalwani, C.S. & Boughton, R. (2006) Alternative models for collaboration in transport optimisation management, *Supply Chain Management: An International Journal*, 12(3), 187–199.

APPENDIX A: TRANSPORTATION MODEL

One of the most commonly used models that seeks to work out a minimum total transport cost solution for the number of units of a single commodity that should be transported from given suppliers to a number of destinations is the **transportation model**. The input data required for this model include the number of units of the product required by the destination store/warehouse/distribution centre (destination) and the number of units available with each supplier (origin). In addition, the unit transport cost of the product from each origin to each destination is also required. When it is not possible to have the data on unit transport costs, it is common practice to use the actual travelling distance between each origin and each destination. The model application aims to determine the number of units that should be transported from each supplier to each destination such that total transport cost or total distance travelled is minimised.

There are a number of assumptions made in the application of the model (see any of the standard texts, for example: Taha, H.A. (2008) *Operations Research: An Introduction*, Prentice Hall). The main assumption is that there is a linear relationship between the transport cost and the number of units being transported. It is important that the units of supply and the demand (requirement) from destinations are consistent.

Let us assume that the amount of supply at origin i is s_i and demand at destination j is d_j and the unit cost between i and j is c_{ij}. Let x_{ij} be the amount or the number of units transported from origin i to destination j. The transportation problem using linear programming can be defined as follows:

Minimise total transport cost $\mathbf{C} = \sum_{i=1}^{m} \sum_{j=1}^{n} c_{ij} x_{ij}$ (6.1)

subject to

$$\sum_{j=1}^{n} x_{ij} \leq s_i \ \text{ for } i = 1,2,...,m \tag{6.2}$$

$$\sum_{i=1}^{m} x_{ij} \leq d_j \ \text{ for } j = 1,2,...,n \tag{6.3}$$

$$x_{ij} \geq 0 \text{ for all } i \text{ and } j \tag{6.4}$$

Equation (6.2) suggests that the total of supply shipments from a supplier should be less than or equal to the available supply. Equation (6.3) means that the sum of shipments to a destination should be less than or equal to the demand or the requirement by that destination. These constraints have to be satisfied with the objective of minimising total transport cost $\mathbf{C}$ given in equation (6.1). In addition to these constraints, the transport problem formulation must also satisfy equation (6.4) implying that the goods are only shipped from origins to the destinations which means from suppliers to purchasers but not in the reverse direction. There is a special requirement of the transportation allocation problem that *the total plant capacity (origins) must equal the total warehouse (destinations) demand*. This helps in finding the solution of the problem.

Table A6.1   Cost table

	Doncaster (1)	Newcastle (2)
Birmingham (1)	£25	£35
Manchester (2)	£15	£20
Glasgow (3)	£40	£30

Standard transportation model: a simple exercise

Alpha Limited manufactures washing machines in the UK with factories in Birmingham, Manchester and Glasgow. Its main UK distribution centres are located in Doncaster and Newcastle. The capacities of the three factories in the next month are respectively 300, 200 and 150 washing machines. The monthly demand for the washing machines from distribution centres are 400 (Doncaster) and 250 (Newcastle) washing machines. The transport cost per washing machine from factories to distribution centres are shown in Table A6.1.

Calculate the least total transport cost solution for delivery of the required washing machines by the two distribution centres.

The solution is worked out using the equations (6.1) to (6.4) as follows:

Minimise transport cost $C = 25x_{11} + 35x_{12} + 15x_{21} + 20x_{22} + 40x_{31} + 30x_{32}$

Subject to

$x_{11} + x_{12} = 300$

$x_{21} + x_{22} = 200$

$x_{31} + x_{32} = 150$

and

$x_{11} + x_{21} + x_{31} = 400$

$x_{12} + x_{22} + x_{32} = 250$

The final solution for this simple exercise is worked out solving the above equations for x_{ij} for $i = 1, 2$ and 3 and for $j = 1$ and 2. The exact solution is given in Table A6.2.

Total cost for this solution is $= 300 \times 25 + 100 \times 15 + 100 \times 20 + 150 \times 30$

$$= £15,500$$

The above solution allocates the number of washing machines that should be transported from a specific factory to a specific warehouse to achieve minimum total transport cost

Table A6.2

	Doncaster (1)	Newcastle (2)	Factory capacity
Birmingham (1)	300	0	300
Manchester (2)	100	100	200
Glasgow (3)	0	150	150
Distribution centre demand	400	250	

which is £15,500. Any variation in the allocation given in the above solution will increase the total transport cost.

NB: It should be noted in the above example that the total of plant capacity is exactly the same as the total of the distribution centre demand which is 650 as shown below:

300 + 200 + 150 = 400 + 250

This is required for solving the transportation problem for allocation using the transportation model algorithm. In most practical applications this will not be the case and this would require setting up a **dummy** plant or a dummy distribution centre as needed to make the two totals exactly match.

Both specialist and off-the-shelf software packages are available for solving the transportation problem. In fact the 'Solver' function in Excel can easily be employed to solve many such problems. The 'screen grabs' illustrate the solution to the above example using this function. Note that it is important in this case to click the Solver options 'assume linear model' and 'assume non-negative'.

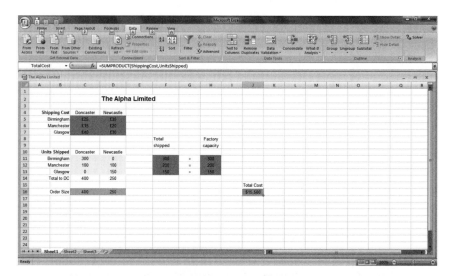

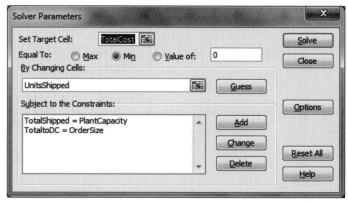

APPENDIX B: PLANNING TRANSPORT INFRASTRUCTURE

Improving Efficiency in Planning Large-Scale Transport Infrastructure Projects

Tom Ferris
Transport Economist and former President of Chartered Institute of Transport, Ireland

Planning what public transport infrastructure is to provide, and where, is a complex task for policy makers. A key feature of transport is that it is a **derived demand**; that is, people or freight do not travel for the sake of making a journey, they travel for some other reason (for example, in the case of people to go on holidays or to go on a business trip; in the case of freight to go to a market or another factory for further processing). The case study below illustrates the range of issues to be considered in planning transport infrastructure, including the requirement of taxpayers (who largely provide the funding of such projects), in order to provide evidence that they are getting value for money.

Transport demand

Economists like to point out that transport is a derived demand. Transport infrastructure and facilities have to be planned to accommodate economic requirements and social needs. They don't just happen. Transport is needed to get goods from A to B, either as raw materials or as finished products. Equally, transport is needed to get people from Y to Z, either for work or for social activities. Getting the balance right, throughout an economy, means avoiding overinvestment while not suffering underinvestment. As taxpayers pay more tax, they want to see evidence that they are getting value for money from such investment.

It is clear that large-scale transport infrastructure projects need to be well designed, fully evaluated and effectively implemented to ensure that there is value for money.[1] There is also the need to assemble the outputs and outcomes of what such projects actually deliver. Such information needs to be shared with the public to demonstrate the extent to which such projects do in fact generate benefits and contribute to economic growth and social development. And better projects can be delivered over time where countries enhance their national procedures and practices which will, in turn, sustain and strengthen effective and efficient management of public transport infrastructure.

The effective planning and management of public transport infrastructure projects is a challenge for most countries. The World Bank, as an international organisation, is well placed to provide assistance in the planning, evaluation and monitoring of projects worldwide. It does so while discharging its main functions of providing financial and technical assistance. It also publishes the results of much of its work. It does so in order to communicate the results of its ongoing research and to stimulate public discussion.

This case study is built around the results of two published World Bank research papers which focus on different dimensions of investment. First, in 'A Diagnostic Framework for Assessing Public Investment Management', the 'must-have' features of a well-functioning public investment system were published.[2] Second, in 'Public Investment Management in the New EU Member States', the World Bank has published the results of an examination of public investment management (PIM) in seven EU countries as it applies to a single sector: transport infrastructure.[3]

The first World Bank paper provides good practical guidance for practitioners so that they can undertake objective assessment of the quality of public investment proposals. The emphasis is placed on the basic processes and controls that are likely to produce the greatest assurance of efficiency in public investment decisions. The approach does not seek to identify best practice, but rather to identify the 'must-have' institutional features that address major risks and provide an effective systemic process for managing public investments. The framework is also intended to motivate governments to undertake periodic self-assessments of their public investment systems and design reforms to enhance the productivity of public investment. An earlier version of the World Bank's paper was discussed at an international conference in Seoul in November 2008.[4]

Efficient delivery

While planning public infrastructure projects systems is important, executing the delivery of such projects is equally important. In this regard, the second World Bank paper looks at public investment management in seven EU countries as it applies to a single sector: transport infrastructure. An earlier version of this report was discussed at an international conference in Istanbul in February 2008.[5] The paper highlights some of the common challenges that four relatively new EU member states – Poland, Slovakia, Slovenia and Latvia – face as they plan and execute their transport infrastructure projects. It recognises the importance that EU-mandated processes and procedures have in shaping national systems in the new member states. The paper found that actual practices often fell short of EU goals due to capacity constraints, weak institutional structures and other factors.

The paper examines the experiences of the new EU member states compared with those of more developed economies, namely Spain, the UK and Ireland. Where countries have limited experience of undertaking significant transport infrastructure investment projects, it is necessary for them to build up technical, financial and managerial capacity in order to have the capability to successfully deliver infrastructure projects in the future. This is not to suggest that all of the experiences of the older member states are transferable. It is a matter of ensuring that the key principles of sound public finance management are adopted and implemented and that a better planning and evaluation culture is promoted.

There is not sufficient space to discuss all of the suggested changes that the new EU member states might consider introducing. Instead, nine key features, of more advanced public investment management systems, are reproduced, as follows:

1. Sector strategies that are closely linked to and consistent with projected budgetary commitments.
2. Significant investment in cost–benefit analysis methodologies, supplemented by business cases analysis and aggressive risk management strategies.

3. Procedures to evaluate projects against value-for-money criteria both *ex-ante* and *ex-post*.

4. Systematic procedures to involve external experts in the review of sector strategies and project business cases.

5. Multi-year budget commitments to facilitate efficient management of project planning.

6. Formal and informal checks and balances to assure that procedures are being complied with in terms of project appraisal and project management.

7. Public procurement strategies designed to manage risks between the government and the contractor.

8. Investment in staff training and the employment of specialist experts.

9. Effective audit and reporting processes that facilitate transparency and encourage feedback to improve the quality of the decision-making and management process.

Role of cost–benefit analysis

The technique of cost–benefit analysis is highlighted in both of the World Bank papers discussed in this case study. As the name implies, a cost–benefit analysis identifies, quantifies and adds all the possible positive factors associated with an investment project; these are the *benefits*. Then it identifies, quantifies and subtracts all the negative factors; the *costs*. The difference between *discounted costs* and *discounted benefits* (achieved by the application of, what economists call, a test discount rate) determines whether a planned public sector project is worth while over the life of the project. The real achievement in doing a cost–benefit analysis well is making sure that all the costs and all the benefits are included and properly quantified.

The first World Bank paper discusses cost–benefit analysis, when it argues that governments: '. . . should have formal and well publicized guidance on the technical aspects of project appraisal appropriate to the technical capacity of ministries and departments. The guidance should describe techniques of economic evaluation that are appropriate to the scale and scope of the project – with larger projects requiring more rigorous tests of financial and economic feasibility and sustainability.'

The application of cost–benefit analysis is also discussed in the second World Bank paper. Specifically it concludes that one of the most significant differences among the seven countries studied from the EU was the role and investment in cost–benefit analysis for guiding project selection. Though cost–benefit analysis is a standard component of project appraisal in all the EU member states examined, especially for EU-funded projects, the quality of the analysis in the new member states is not independently reviewed and the resulting analysis is not necessarily a significant factor in the project selection. By contrast, the systems in the UK and Ireland are helped by the strong coordinating role played by central government, including the comprehensive and regularly updated guidance given to line ministries as well as measures to assure their use (as is evidenced by the extension in 2009 of official guidelines for the evaluation of public investment projects in Ireland[6]). It should also be noted that these UK/Irish systems are also characterised by institutional arrangements that check up on progress at the different stages of the project cycle, from pre-planning to final project. The checking is done using both internal and external resources.

It is important to recognise that cost–benefit analysis is not a panacea for transport infrastructure projects. Individual cost–benefit analyses do not guarantee that projects will be delivered on time and within budget. In this regard, it is very interesting to see the results of a study of cost escalation in transport infrastructure projects published by Flyvbjerg *et al.* in 2002.[7] They found with overwhelming statistical significance that the cost estimates used to decide whether such projects should be built are highly and systematically misleading (based on a sample of 258 transport infrastructure projects worth US$90 billion and representing different project types, geographical regions and historical periods). In their view underestimation cannot be explained by error and is best explained by strategic misrepresentation. Clearly for cost–benefit analysis to be effective, it must be accompanied by good corporate governance arrangements that ensure openness and transparency in the manner in which public transport infrastructure projects are planned, evaluated and delivered.

Lessons to be learned

The main lesson from this case study is the importance of having a sound framework for public transport infrastructure investment, with ongoing vigilant monitoring arrangements. In addition there must be good corporate governance arrangements that ensure openness and transparency in the manner in which projects are planned, evaluated and delivered. This is easier said than done. However, there is help at hand. The World Bank provides excellent advice on how to plan and implement public transport infrastructure projects. The papers discussed herein provide very practical advice on how to plan and deliver effective public transport infrastructure projects. The practitioners of public transport infrastructure management should always be ready to listen to external advice. There is always scope to enhance the quality of project appraisals and ensure that the projects that are delivered do in fact generate benefits and contribute to economic growth and social development.

REFERENCES

1. Ferris, T. (2009) Getting better value for money, *Public Affairs Ireland Journal*, Issue 59, Dublin, June.
2. World Bank (2010) *A Diagnostic Framework for Assessing Public Investment Management*, Editors: A.D. Rajaram, T.M. Le, N. Biletska & J. Brumby, World Bank Policy Research Working Paper 5397, Washington, August.
3. World Bank (2009) *Public Investment Management in the New EU Member States*, Editors: T. Laursen & B. Myers, World Bank Working Paper Number 161, Washington, February.

4. World Bank/KDI Conference (2008) *Efficiency Enhancement in Public Investment Management*, Seoul, Korea, 20–21 November. The case-study author made a presentation to the Conference entitled 'Delivering Better Public Investment Projects – The Irish Experience'.

5. World Bank/World Bank Conference (2008) *Experiences in Public Investment Management (PIM),* Istanbul, Turkey, 28–29 February. The case-study author made a presentation to the Conference entitled 'Overview of Ireland's Experience of Public Investment Management – With Particular Emphasis on Transport Projects'.

6. Ferris, T. (2009) Wider cost benefit analysis, *Public Affairs Ireland Journal*, Issue 63, Dublin, November.

7. Flyvbjerg, B., Holm, M.S. & Buhl, S. (2002) Underestimating costs in public works projects: error or lie?, *American Planning Association Journal*, 68(3).

7 Transport Security

Risto Talas
The University of Hull

LEARNING OBJECTIVES

- Identify the need for transport security.
- Understand the application of contemporary transport security initiatives.
- Discuss the nature of security threats in transport, including terrorism and piracy.
- Acquire knowledge of security technology.

INTRODUCTION

This chapter is intended to introduce the reader to the contemporary transport security initiatives which have been introduced since the 11 September 2001 attacks (9/11) on New York and Washington. In the aftermath of 9/11, the US authorities deemed that the security of maritime transport into US ports was at risk particularly from a terrorist placing a weapon of mass destruction in a container and setting it to detonate on US soil. Consequently, the United States Congress and the International Maritime Organisation (IMO) began to work in tandem on introducing new security legislation which culminated in late 2002 in the US Maritime Transportation Security Act and the IMO's International Ship and Port Facility Security (ISPS) Code. Since then, other governmental and non-governmental agencies have also developed transport security initiatives and these key initiatives are addressed below.

In this chapter we will first examine the need for transport security. Next, we will consider the key global transport security initiatives that have come into force, and gain an overview of who is affected by them and how.

They include:

- IMO International Ship and Port Facility Security Code
- US Customs-Trade Partnership Against Terrorism
- US Container Security Initiative
- European Union Authorised Economic Operator
- ISO 28000, the new security standard for supply chain security

We will also examine some of the technology involved in transport security including access control systems, biometrics and detection systems.

THE NEED FOR TRANSPORT SECURITY

Not long after the events of 9/11, in October 2002 the French tanker *Limburg* was waiting for the harbour pilot from the port of Aden to come on board when the ship was attacked by a suicide bomber who drove a small boat packed with explosives into the starboard side. The explosion caused a major fire and pollution from the oil, which leaked from the ruptured tanks. In addition, one of the 12 crewmen who jumped overboard to escape the fire and smoke drowned. These two events, while they may be considered extreme, nevertheless underline the need for transport security.

Subsequently, in 2003 Booz Allen Hamilton carried out a simulation of the disruption to US seaborne trade on the West Coast following a series of hoax and actual bomb discoveries in the ports. The three-day 'war game' involved ports, port authorities, local businesses and local and federal officials. The outcome of the simulation was a potential loss to the US economy of $58 billion with a container backlog that would take 60 days to clear.[1] While the threat from terrorism is real, there are, however, more common security threats to the supply chain. They include piracy, theft, smuggling and other organised criminal activity.

PIRACY

Piracy is a threat to maritime transport, which has grown steadily since the breakup of the Soviet Union. The scaling back of Cold War Soviet and NATO naval activity resulted in a security vacuum in certain shipping lanes and coastal regions which, when combined with under-funded local law enforcement and lax legal regimes, has permitted a growth in modern day piracy.[2]

> Piracy is defined under article 101 of the 1982 United Nations Convention on the Law of the Sea as: 'any illegal act of violence or detention, or any act of depredation committed by individuals for private ends against a private ship'.

At the beginning of the 21st century, the key piracy areas included the Straits of Malacca and waters around Indonesia, West Africa, the South China Seas and certain ports in South America. Since 2005, a new form of piracy has grown steadily in and around the Gulf of Aden where Somali pirates have taken to hijacking ships for ransom. The world's media was first alerted

Table 7.1 Piracy attacks on shipping worldwide, 2009[3]

2009 piracy attacks worldwide	Vessels boarded	Vessels hijacked	Attempted attacks	Vessels fired upon
406	153	49	84	120

A long range acoustic device (LRAD) is a disc-shaped device about a metre in diameter which produces sonic waves that can be focused into a narrow 'beam' of sound and directed at a human target. At close range, an LRAD can cause permanent hearing loss.

to the growing problem with the attempted hijack of the cruise ship *Seabourn Spirit* on 5 November 2005. The vessel was attacked around 70 miles off the coast of Somalia by pirates in two small boats who fired rocket-propelled grenades (RPGs) at the vessel accompanied by machine gun fire. The cruise ship responded by deploying a long range acoustic device (LRAD) which repelled the pirates in the boats by convincing them they were under fire and the *Seabourn Spirit* was able to make good her escape.[4]

The largest vessel to have been attacked in the first decade of the 21st century by Somali pirates was the Saudi-owned oil tanker *Sirius Star*, which was hijacked on 17 November 2008 while sailing 450 miles east of Mombasa, Kenya. The vessel was fully laden with crude oil valued at around $100 million and an initial ransom demand of $25 million was made by the pirates for the release of the vessel and crew. However, following the payment of a $3million ransom to the pirates, which was dropped in a canister by parachute onto the deck of the vessel, the *Sirius Star* and her crew were reported released unharmed on 9 January 2009.[5]

In 2009 there were 406 pirate attacks on ships worldwide, of which 49 were vessels that were hijacked (see Table 7.1). To put the Somali piracy problem into perspective, of the 49 vessels hijacked worldwide, 47 vessels were hijacked by Somali pirates with a total of 867 crew held hostage.

The international community's response to the piracy problem has been to send an international flotilla of warships, fast patrol craft and surveillance aircraft to the Gulf of Aden and Indian Ocean in order to try to protect shipping and to deter pirate attacks. One key part of the response has been the European Union's Atalanta naval force. However, with over a million square miles of ocean to patrol and only limited resources, the job of combating Somali piracy by naval power alone seems impossible.

GLOBAL TRANSPORT SECURITY INITIATIVES

Figure 7.1 shows the relationship of the main contemporary transport security initiatives to a supply chain which includes a maritime element.

IMO International Ship and Port Facility Security (ISPS) Code[6]

The **ISPS Code** is a mandatory security initiative which came into force on 1 July 2004 and applies to all countries that are members of the International Maritime Organisation.

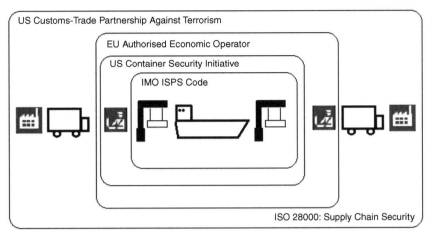

Figure 7.1 An overview of contemporary transport security initiatives (Source: Amended from OECD, 2003)[7]

The objectives of the ISPS Code are to enable the prevention and detection of security threats and the Code applies to ships engaged in international trade, including passenger vessels with 12 or more berths, cargo vessels of 500 gross tonnes and over, mobile offshore drilling units and all port facilities serving such vessels engaged in international trade. As Figure 7.1 shows, the ISPS Code addresses only the port facility–ship–port facility part of maritime transport.

For port facilities, the purpose of the ISPS Code is to:

- Ensure satisfactory performance of all port facility security duties
- Control access to the port facility
- Monitor the port facility, including anchoring and berthing areas
- Monitor restricted areas to ensure only authorised persons have access
- Supervise the handling of cargo
- Supervise the handling of ship's stores
- Ensure that security communication is readily available

Both ships and port facilities must undergo security assessments by trained security personnel from which ship and port facility security plans are prepared.

For vessels, the ship security assessment includes:

- Identifying key shipboard operations
- Identifying existing security measures
- Identifying threats and vulnerabilities
- Developing and performing a ship security survey
- Identifying weaknesses in security measures and processes

Once the ship security assessment has been conducted, the ship security plan can be drawn up. The ship security planning process comprises the following actions:

- Decide on corrective security measures
- Prepare the ship security plan, based on the ship security assessment
- Review, and if necessary amend, the ship security plan
- Approval of the ship security plan by a competent authority

Once the ship security plan has been implemented and independently verified, the International Ship Security Certificate is issued.

For ports, the Port Facility Security Assessment (PFSA) process includes:

- Identification and evaluation of important assets and infrastructure
- Identification of possible threats to the assets and infrastructure and the likelihood of occurrence
- Identification, selection and prioritisation of countermeasures and procedural changes and their level of effectiveness in reducing vulnerability
- Identification of weaknesses, including human factors, in the infrastructure, policies and procedures
- Summary report of how PFSA was conducted, a description of each vulnerability found during the assessment and a description of countermeasures that could be used to address each vulnerability

The Port Facility Security Plan will include the following:

- Measures designed to prevent carriage of unauthorised weapons or any other dangerous substances entering the port facility or on board a ship
- Measures designed to prevent unauthorised access to the port facility, to ships moored at the facility, and to restricted areas of the facility
- Procedures for responding to security threats or breaches of security
- Procedures for responding to any security instructions at an enhanced security level
- Procedures for evacuation in case of serious threats or breaches of security
- Duties of port facility personnel assigned security responsibilities
- Procedures for interfacing with ship security activities
- Procedures for the periodic review of the plan and updating same
- Procedures for the reporting of security incidents
- Identification of the port facility security officer
- Measures to ensure the security of the plan

- Measures designed to ensure effective security of cargo and cargo handling equipment
- Procedures for auditing the PFSP
- Procedures for responding to a Ship Security Alert System activation
- Procedures for facilitating shore leave for ships' personnel

US Customs-Trade Partnership Against Terrorism (C-TPAT)[8]

C-TPAT is a voluntary government–business initiative to build cooperative relationships that strengthen and improve overall international supply chain and US border security. Through this initiative, the US Customs and Border Protection Agency (CBP) asks trade-related businesses to ensure the integrity of their security practices and communicate and verify the security guidelines of their business partners within the supply chain. CBP offers benefits to certain certified C-TPAT member categories, including:

- A reduced number of CBP inspections, which results in reduced border delay times
- Priority processing for CBP inspections
- Assignment of a C-TPAT Supply Chain Security Specialist (SCSS) who will work with the company to validate and enhance security throughout the company's international supply chain
- Potential eligibility for CBP Importer Self-Assessment (ISA) program with an emphasis on self-policing, not CBP audits
- Eligibility to attend C-TPAT supply chain security training seminars

US Container Security Initiative (CSI)[9]

The Container Security Initiative was launched in 2002 with 20 of the world's largest container terminals and forms part of the US Maritime Transportation Security Act. By September 2007 there were 55 CSI ports worldwide and in 2009 there were 58 ports that were part of the scheme. The way in which CSI works is that shippers must send to US Customs and Border Protection details about the container's cargo and its origins at least 24 hours before the container is loaded onto the vessel in the foreign port. This gives the US Customs time to apply their security algorithm to the cargo manifest data to determine whether their customs officers stationed in the foreign port should investigate the contents of the container or allow it to be loaded onto the US bound ship.

The 58 CSI ports in 2009 were:

In the Americas:

- Montreal, Vancouver and Halifax (Canada)
- Santos (Brazil)
- Buenos Aires (Argentina)
- Puerto Cortes (Honduras)

- Caucedo (Dominican Republic)
- Kingston (Jamaica)
- Freeport (The Bahamas)
- Balboa, Colon and Manzanillo (Panama)
- Cartagena (Colombia)

In Europe:

- Rotterdam (The Netherlands)
- Bremerhaven and Hamburg (Germany)
- Antwerp and Zeebrugge (Belgium)
- Le Havre and Marseille (France)
- Gothenburg (Sweden)
- La Spezia, Genoa, Naples, Gioia Tauro and Livorno (Italy)
- Felixstowe, Liverpool, Thamesport, Tilbury and Southampton (United Kingdom)
- Piraeus (Greece)
- Algeciras, Barcelona and Valencia (Spain)
- Lisbon (Portugal)

In Asia and the Middle East:

- Singapore
- Yokohama, Tokyo, Nagoya and Kobe (Japan)
- Hong Kong
- Pusan (South Korea)
- Port Klang and Tanjung Pelepas (Malaysia)
- Laem Chabang (Thailand)
- Dubai (United Arab Emirates)
- Shenzhen and Shanghai (China)
- Kaohsiung and Chi-Lung (Taiwan)
- Colombo (Sri Lanka)
- Port Salalah (Oman)
- Port Qasim (Pakistan)
- Ashdod and Haifa (Israel)

In Africa:

- Alexandria (Egypt)
- Durban (South Africa)

European Union Authorized Economic Operator[10]

The EU's **Authorised Economic Operator** (**AEO**) is a voluntary security initiative which is designed to reflect the US C-TPAT security initiative. Those eligible to apply for AEO membership include manufacturers, importers, exporters, brokers, carriers, consolidators, intermediaries, ports, airports, terminal operators, integrated operators, warehouses and distributors within the EU. AEOs will be able to benefit from facilitations for customs controls or simplifications for customs rules or both, depending on the type of AEO certificate. There are three certificate types:

- Customs Simplifications: AEOs will be entitled to benefit from simplifications provided for under the customs rules.

- Security and Safety: AEOs will be entitled to benefit from facilitations of customs controls relating to security and safety at the entry of the goods into the customs territory of the Community, or when the goods leave the customs territory of the Community.

- Customs Simplifications/Security and Safety: AEOs will be entitled to benefit from both simplifications provided for under the customs rules and from facilitations of customs controls relating to security and safety.

ISO 28000 – Supply chain security[11]

The International Standards Organisation has developed security standards aimed at becoming the global supply chain security standard programme. It is intended to act in concert with and complement other contemporary transport and supply chain security initiatives. ISO 28000 is applicable to all sizes and types of organisations at any stage of production or anywhere in the supply chain. It is a voluntary Standard, which may be certified by third-party auditing companies to demonstrate that a company has taken a proactive and responsible approach to security by establishing a security management system that assures compliance with a documented security management policy.

ISO 28000 is based on the format adopted by ISO 14000 owing to its risk-based approach to management systems and is based on the methodology known as plan–do–check–act:

- Plan: establish the objectives and processes necessary to deliver results in accordance with the organisation's security policy.
- Do: implement the processes.
- Check: monitor and measure processes against security policy, objectives, targets, legal and other requirements, and report results.
- Act: take actions to continually improve performance of the security management system.

ISO 28000 requires an organisation to assess the security environment in which it operates to determine if adequate security measures are in place and to identify and comply with relevant regulatory requirements. If security needs are identified by this process, the organisation should implement mechanisms and processes to meet these needs. The security management system clearly defines the strategic security objectives of the organisation and puts into effect constant monitoring with a focus on continual improvement.

The purpose of the Standard is to provide a documented security management system which identifies security threats, assesses the risks and controls and mitigates their consequences. This process is continual so that the system can be effectively maintained and improved. The scope of the security management system needs to be defined by detailing the physical area covered by the system and the operations that are undertaken within this area. Any outsourced processes should be considered and controlled where necessary.

TRANSPORT SECURITY TECHNOLOGY

In this section we will examine three areas of security technology: access control, biometric systems and detection systems.

Access control

Access control measures essentially do as the name suggests: they permit access to authorised persons and they control access by non-authorised persons to restricted areas. Examples of everyday restricted areas include: bank vaults; aircraft cockpits; the bridge of a ship; even the stage during a pop concert. There are various forms of physical access control and they include gates, fences, bollards and security netting. Manual gates that are locked using mechanical locks or padlocks are an effective form of access control and are generally inexpensive, easy to use and will not stop functioning during a power failure. They are mainly suited to access points that are used infrequently, although they can be effectively used for main access points where they are controlled by security guards. Manual gates and locks do not identify who, when and how many times a room, building or site has been accessed. Where manual gates are used for general access points manned by security guards, a suitable system for identifying authorised persons and vehicles will need to be in place e.g. photo identification card. In order for a fence to have any protective value it must be in good repair. This means it should be intact, the fabric taut and well secured to its upright supports and the supports well anchored into the ground.[12]

A bar code is an optical machine-readable representation of data that can be read by optical scanners (bar code readers), or scanned from an image by special software. RFID (radio frequency identification) is a generic term that is used to describe a system that transmits the identity (in the form of a unique serial number) of an object or person wirelessly, using radio waves.

Biometrics

Biometric security systems fall into two groups. The majority of biometric security systems are identification card systems, including some modern passports, which hold a certain amount of data about the card or passport holder. These data can simply be a name and a photograph, which can be read using a bar code reader or a radio frequency identification (RFID) tag within the card.

Access to a restricted area can be gained by the holder of the biometric ID card when the bar code or RFID tag has been read by the reader and the data on the card have been both validated and verified to ensure that the person may enter the restricted area at that time. Biometric systems also refer to readers that conduct fingerprint or retinal scans to allow access to restricted areas. Here, the biometric data are not carried by the person on a pre-issued card but are the unique pattern of a person's retina or a fingerprint.

Detection systems

There are various types of detection systems in use in security today. The commonest types include:

- Closed circuit television (CCTV)
- Motion detector systems
- X-ray and gamma-ray detection systems

At its simplest CCTV provides a means of viewing a large area from a single location and recording it for later review. Motion detector systems can be placed along fences or in restricted areas to sense movement, which can be used together with a CCTV system to raise an alarm in the security control room while recording any unauthorised activity.

X-ray and gamma-ray detection systems are used in airports and ports to scan baggage and containers. They are known as non-intrusive inspection equipment as they use x-rays or gamma-rays to penetrate baggage containers and produce an image of the contents. Officials review images for the presence of anomalies, which may indicate contraband, weapons or illicit material. Ports also use radiation portal monitors to scan containers as they enter the port area. Containers are driven through a radiation portal monitor where the presence of any radiation emissions is detected. The equipment is passive in that it absorbs radiation from the container or its contents as it passes through the portal. The resulting graphic profile of the radiation reading is automatically assessed and the presence of any radioactive material will trigger an alarm. False positive alarms may result from cargo which is naturally radioactive, such as ceramic tiles, granite, cat litter, or food products such as bananas and avocados which contain potassium.[13]

LEARNING REVIEW

This chapter has focused on the key global contemporary transport security initiatives. These initiatives were addressed in turn and an explanation was made as to how they operate and which stakeholders are involved. The need for transport security was addressed, covering not only terrorism but other security threats to supply chains such as piracy, theft, pilferage and smuggling.

Finally, some of the technology associated with transport security was discussed, including access control, biometrics and detection systems.

QUESTIONS

- Is the ISPS Code a voluntary or a mandatory security initiative?
- Which types of internationally trading vessels are affected by the ISPS Code?
- Is there a limit on the type of company which can implement ISO 28000?
- What is an LRAD?
- When the Container Security Initiative was originally set up, how many ports were part of the scheme?
- Which types of food products can set off a radiation alarm at a port?

NOTES

1. Gerencser, M., Weinberg, J. & Vincent, D. (2003) *Port Security War Game*, Booz Allen Hamilton.
2. Murphy, M. (2007) Contemporary piracy and maritime terrorism, Adelphi Paper 388, International Institute for Strategic Studies.
3. ICC Commercial Crime Services (2010) 2009 worldwide piracy figures surpass 400, 14 January.
4. Lloyd's List (2005) IMO seeks Security Council action on pirates, 8 November.
5. Lloyd's List (2009) *Sirius Star* freed, 9 January.
6. www.imo.org.
7. Amended from OECD (2003) Security in maritime transport: risk factors and economic impact, Maritime Transport Facility Committee, Directorate for Science, Technology and Industry.
8. www.cbp.gov/xp/cgov/trade/cargo_security/ctpat/.
9. www.cbp.gov/xp/cgov/trade/cargo_security/csi/.
10. http://ec.europa.eu/taxation_customs/customs/policy_issues/customs_security/aeo/index_en.htm.
11. Talas, R., Dixon, C. & McCarthy, P. (2010) Supply chain security, TT Club.
12. Ibid.
13. Ibid.

8 Logistics Service Providers

LEARNING OBJECTIVES

- Describe, and differentiate, the various types of companies that provide logistics services.
- Discuss the role of fourth-party logistics.
- Illustrate the use of incoterms and bills of lading to show how responsibility along the supply chain is clarified and managed.
- Examine the range of issues in, and the process employed for, selecting logistics service providers.
- Also illustrate a number of other pertinent concepts and terms often used in logistics systems.

INTRODUCTION

In recent years providers of logistics services have grown both in scale and in terms of the services that they provide. Increasingly many companies no longer perform many of their own logistics activities. This chapter looks at the range of such logistics providers, and the various services that they provide, and in particular how organisations go about selecting such companies. Traditionally the only services provided were transport, warehousing and customs clearance. This, however, has expanded to encompass a raft of other activities, which we will explore later in the chapter.

At the outset it is important to clarify two important terms: the **consignor** is the company or individual who sends the consignment, and the **consignee** is the company or individual who actually receives the consignment.

Chapter 8 comprises four core sections:
- Classifying logistics companies
- Carrier responsibilities
- Fourth-party logistics
- Selecting logistics service providers and services

CLASSIFYING LOGISTICS COMPANIES

Traditionally, companies evolved to provide services within the individual transport modes (for example trucking companies, airlines, and so forth). Generally speaking this worked quite well for people who wanted to have their freight moved. In fact one of the world's largest and most successful logistics companies (UPS) is reputed to have started life delivering parcels by bicycle in North America (indeed this mode of transport is now popular again for distributing very light parcels in congested urban areas). As we saw in Chapter 1, in recent decades the fields of logistics and SCM grew both in popularity and complexity, spurred on by developments such as the proliferation of containerisation and advances in tracking technologies. For freight transport companies there was both a need and an opportunity to do more than just simply move freight using a single mode of transport from A to B.

We also saw in Part One of the book the increasing tendency, for a variety of reasons, of companies to outsource various activities, many of which they may regard as non-core, and focus on their core competencies. In recent years many companies have sought in particular to move away from **own-account transportation** to third-party transportation, and this has provided many opportunities for transport and logistics companies.

> Own-account transportation is when a company provides its own transport services.

A dynamic and profitable new sector of activity has emerged in recent decades, and we can use the generic label of **logistics service providers (LSPs)** to describe companies that operate in this sector. In fact, myriad different types of companies operate in this sector, which we can broadly categorise as follows:

- *Hauliers or trucking companies* do just that: carry freight on trucks. Similarly, operators in the other modes also carry freight – train companies, airlines (with the exception in particular of many of the 'low-cost airlines' who do not generally carry freight), and shipping companies.

- *Freight forwarders* are just like high-street travel agents, except that they arrange transportation for freight, not people. Different types of freight forwarders have evolved in recent years.

  A big area of activity for many freight forwarders is in arranging customs clearance for freight that moves internationally (this is sometimes referred to as brokerage and encompasses not just dealing with customs agencies, but also managing all documentation that should accompany freight). With the development of regional trade agreements (which we discussed in Chapter 2), increasingly freight can move freely within regions, thus obviating the need for customs clearance for that freight (customs clearance will of course still be required for freight moving *into* the region).

  Freight forwarders have thus broadened out their product portfolio to encompass many other activities. For example, some act as ships' agents for vessels that arrive into a port. Many other freight forwarders have evolved to a stage where they now operate their own vehicles and warehouses. Sometimes freight forwarders are called *freight agents* or *brokers*. Again there are minor distinctions between all of these terms, which there is no need to go into here.

- The term **NVOCC (non-vessel-owning common carrier)** has come into use in logistics and refers to companies who consolidate smaller shipments from various consignees into full container loads which the NVOCC then takes responsibility for. The terms **groupage** and **consolidated shipment** (a shipment that comprises a number of unique, individual shipments all placed together in the one loading unit) are also used in the logistics sector to refer to aspects of this activity. Many freight forwarders offer such groupage services, some quite extensively. In this case, then, the freight forwarder acts not just as an *agent* but also as a *principal*.

- *Couriers* grew significantly, especially in the 1980s and 1990s, in response to a growing demand for immediate delivery of products. Many operate within and between large urban areas and service organisations, such as banks who wish to move valuable documents quickly. In fact some people predicted that the proliferation of fax machines would eliminate the need for couriers. However, this has not been the case with consignees still demanding in many cases 'hard copies' of documents.

- A final group of companies are those that have become known as *integrators*. Examples of integrators include FedEx, United Parcels Service (UPS) and DHL. These companies' unique sales proposition is that they offer a seamless (i.e. integrated) end-to-end service from consignor to consignee (i.e. responsibility for the consignment doesn't move from, for example, a haulier to a freight forwarder to an airline, and so forth). They have evolved into very substantial companies who provide a range of logistics services (see the case examples below). One of the difficulties which often arises in supply chains is that when freight gets lost or damaged it is usually at what are known as the 'touch points' (these are where freight is handled or transferred from one carrier to another). Integrators argue that the service they provide often circumvents these problems as they retain sole responsibility for freight from origin to destination, and they will usually 'track and trace' freight as it moves along their transport chains and thus have enhanced visibility of the product and any problems which may arise.

A final organisation type, which doesn't fit easily into any of the above categories although is close to the NVOCC concept, is where individual companies come together to form an agency to arrange their freight movements and use their combined buying power to get capacity at reduced rates from carriers.

It may sound trite but the term 'shipping' has in fact two common meanings in logistics: firstly to refer to the act of sending freight from a consignor to a consignee (for example to *ship* something by air), and secondly (the more common meaning) to move freight using the maritime mode.

Distinguishing LSPs and 3PLs: as has already been noted, there is considerable overlap between the pertinent terminology used to describe the various companies that provide logistics services. We regard all such companies as *logistics service providers (LSPs)*. Those LSPs that provide multiple logistics services, often in an integrated fashion, we refer to as *third-party logistics companies (3PLs)*.

There is considerable overlap between these categories. For example, a company that operates ships can also have its own freight forwarding operations. The classification above is given then purely to illustrate the various activities and types of companies that operate across the sector. As freight companies provide a broader and more integrated range of services, many have come to be known as **third-party logistics companies (3PLs)**. The evolution of 3PLs is evident in the 'FedEx and the Hub and Spoke System' case below. DHL (which can be described as an integrator and as a 3PL; in fact it also provides 4PL® services, an area discussed in the next section) started life as an air courier company, while Kuehne + Nagel's origins, for example, were more so as a traditional freight forwarder, but it is now a full service 3PL.

Some of the many different services provided by 3PLs are given below. As the list illustrates, transportation/delivery is just one of the many services that 3PLs provide. The 3PL sector has now become quite sophisticated. In some instances consignors forge quite close links with their 3PLs who often will have people working within the consignors' logistics department.

- Transportation – often using multiple modes.
- Warehousing – including providing capacity for seasonal and other fluctuations.
- Pick and pack – for example picking multiple different SKUs and packing these into single units.
- Light manufacturing – acting as contract manufacturers for OEMs, this is quite prevalent in for example the electronics sector.
- Vendor managed inventory – see Chapters 3 and 12.
- Customs clearance – and associated regulatory requirements, such as, for example, hazardous goods clearances and food safety certificates.
- Trade financing – for example mitigating currency exposure.
- Managing reverse logistics – in some instances 3PLs manage the entire reverse logistics process for a client and manage all repairs and returns.
- Parts distribution – with their extensive networks of warehouses, it is sometimes more economical and effective for 3PLs to take over the management of critical spare parts inventories. This is quite prevalent in sectors such as electronics, automotive spares and medical technologies.
- Inventory management – management of inventory has considerable financial implications and we will explore these issues in detail in Chapter 10.

Professor Robert Lieb from Northeastern University in the USA conducts annual surveys[1] of the US 3PL industry and he has noted that since the mid-1990s the industry has undergone significant changes in areas such as industry size and make-up (growth and consolidation are evident), services offered, geographical reach and IT support. He also notes that during that time the customers for 3PL services have grown bigger and have given a greater share of their logistics operating budget to 3PLs through larger contracts. He notes that the percentage of *Fortune* 500 manufacturers using 3PL services has increased from 38% to more than 80%. In Lieb's 2009 survey, various trends evident in the sector were highlighted including reduced revenue and growth projections, intensified price competition, shortening of supply chains and, despite the global downturn, continued attention to green and environmental sustainability issues. The largest player in the global contract logistics market during 2008 was DHL Supply Chain generating revenues of more than €12 billion. Next largest in the ranking was Ceva, while Kuehne + Nagel was in third place, leaving the top three biggest contract logistics operators unchanged from 2007 (www.ciltuk.org.uk).

FEDEX AND THE HUB AND SPOKE SYSTEM

FedEx (www.fedex.com) started life in the early 1970s and was founded by Frederick Smith. As a student at Yale, Smith had pondered the economics of the route systems then dominant in US air freight markets. His deliberations were to lead to the pioneering introduction by FedEx of hub and spoke networks into air freight markets.

Rather than offer point-to-point services between all city pairs, hub and spoke networks operate on the simple, but highly effective, principle whereby freight is shipped from all origin points to a central hub, re-sorted, and then shipped out to destination. Customers were initially sceptical of this concept in that if they were sending a parcel from for example Boston to Chicago, they got confused as to why its routeing would take it to Memphis (the location of FedEx's central hub, and a place some distance away from both Boston and Chicago). The logic and economics of Smith's hub and spoke model, however, quickly won out and today all of the integrators have large hubs and associated networks across most continents.

FedEx itself has also grown considerably. Today it has one of the world's largest air freight fleets, employs some 285 000 people and enjoys revenues of approximately $35 billion. The company also operates a diverse range of logistics-related FedEx branded companies under the core FedEx brand.

EXAMPLES OF LEADING LOGISTICS SERVICE PROVIDERS

DHL (www.dhl.com)

DHL (standing for the initial letters of the surnames of the three company founders) started life in 1969. In fact it was one of the first air courier companies in that its original product was the delivery by air of ships' papers from San Francisco to Honolulu (allowing customs clearance of a ship in Honolulu before the ship actually arrived, thus dramatically reducing time spent waiting in the harbour). Today the company is 100% owned by Deutsche Post World Net, a global organisation with a workforce of about 500 000 employees present in more than 220 countries and territories. Along the way it has acquired a number of logistics companies including Danzas and Exel, making DHL today one of the world's largest logistics companies.

Kuehne + Nagel (www.kn-portal.com)

Kuehne + Nagel is one of the world's oldest logistics companies. It was founded in 1890 in Bremen, Germany and today has more than 900 locations in over 100 countries with 56 000 employees. It has evolved to become a full service 3PL, active across all modes of transport. Today it is estimated to be the number one global sea freight forwarder and in the top five global air cargo forwarders. It also moves freight by road and rail and is engaged in contract logistics with a variety of companies, being now ranked as one of the top three global contract logistics providers.

A.P. Moller – Maersk Group (www.maersk.com)

The company is probably best known today for its deep-sea container vessels that traverse the world. It is, however, much more than a shipping company. Established in Denmark in 1904, today the group employs over 115 000 people in some 130 countries. In the shipping sector, the group's subsidiaries operate more than 500 vessels (including some of the world's largest container vessels) and 50 container facilities. As well as being involved in unitised (i.e. containerised) shipping, the group is also active in other shipping areas, such as crude oil transportation and supporting offshore oil and gas activities. It has also diversified extensively into other transport and non-transport areas such as shipyards, air freight, and even the retail supermarket sector.

FOURTH-PARTY LOGISTICS

In the preceding section we noted the shift from own-account transportation towards increased use of LSPs, with more companies outsourcing more logistics activity to 3PLs. Some companies of course still perform their own logistics activities, although the share of companies doing this is declining. The topic of outsourcing was already discussed in Chapter 3. When companies do outsource, in many cases they will use more than one 3PL, either to ensure competitive rates are secured or because different 3PLs will have strengths in different markets or trades. In addition, the outsourcing company will still have to have a logistics department (even though all freight handling may be done by the 3PLs) in order to manage the 3PLs which it retains.

In recent years a new concept known as **fourth-party logistics (4PL®)** has emerged. It sought to offer a radical solution that would offer companies total outsource supply chain solutions. It was invented and trademarked by Accenture in 1996, who originally defined it 'as a supply chain integrator that assembles and manages the resources, capabilities and technology of its own organisation, with those of complementary service providers, to deliver a comprehensive supply chain solution'.[2]

The concept has evolved since then with the Australian author John Gattorna in his insightful book *Living Supply Chains* noting that 'some of the essential elements that differentiate

3PL and 4PL® business models have been lost'.[3] While a number of genuine 4PL® solutions have emerged, in practice it is now more common for some 3PLs to offer 4PL® type solutions. This involves 3PLs in turn outsourcing, where it makes most sense for the final customer, certain activities to other 3PLs. We can thus envisage a 4PL® type concept today where individual 3PLs offer an overarching solution for an individual customer and which encompasses offerings from different (competitor) 3PLs. Some people user the description '4PL control towers' to refer to the role played by such 4PLs.

CARRIER RESPONSIBILITIES

Once freight leaves a consignor, it is up to responsible LSPs to ensure that it reaches the consignee in the right condition, at the right time, etc. (recall eight 'rights' description of logistics in Chapter 1). Unlike passengers, freight cannot, of course, speak for itself (although we will see in Chapter 12, which deals with technology in the supply chain, that advances are being made in intelligent tracking systems at the individual item level). Documentation (either in physical or soft format) will need to accompany the freight so as to ensure that anyone who comes into contact with the freight will know where it comes from, what it comprises, where it is going, and how it is going to get there. Customs and security agencies, who do not have time to physically check each consignment, will also want to know the various details about individual consignments that are moving over international borders.

The document that typically contains all of this requisite information is known as a **bill of lading**, or in air freight the more common term is an air waybill, or AWB for short. In the case of consolidated shipments, the entire shipment will be covered by a master air waybill, with the individual shipments covered by documents known as house air waybills.

When freight moves from consignors to consignees, it is important to understand who has responsibility for it at various stages. If something happens to the freight, for example it becomes damaged, who will be held responsible? Similarly, if charges for customs clearance are to be paid before the freight can be collected, then who should pay such charges, the consignor or the consignee?

Issues such as these are resolved by using what are called **incoterms**, an abbreviation for international commercial terms, which were first published in 1936 by the International Chamber of Commerce (www.iccwbo.org) and are now commonly accepted standards in global trade. While incoterms are very useful with regard to various cost and risk issues, they are not intended to replace legal agreements such as contracts of sale. There are, in fact, 11 incoterms, divided into four groups, as illustrated in Figure 8.1.

SELECTING LOGISTICS SERVICE PROVIDERS AND SERVICES

Decision making is an ongoing and important part of many logistics managers' jobs: for example, trying to decide which routeing to use for a particular shipment, which carriers

Group E Departure	The seller minimises his risk by only making the goods available at his own premises
EXW (Ex-Works)	(… named place)
Group F Main carriage not paid by seller	Seller usually arranges and pays for the pre-carriage in the country of export
FCA (Free CArrier)	(… named place)
FAS (Free Alongside Ship)	(… named port of shipment)
FOB (Free On Board)	(… named port of shipment)
Group C Main carriage paid by seller	The seller arranges and pays for the main carriage but without assuming the risk of the main carriage
CFR (Cost and Freight)	(… named port of destination)
CIF (Cost, Insurance and Freight)	(… named port of destination)
CPT (Carriage Paid To)	(… named place of destination)
CIP (Carriage and Insurance Paid to)	(… named place of destination)
Group D Arrival	The seller's cost/risk is maximised because he must make the goods available upon arrival at the agreed destination
DAT (Delivered At Terminal)	(… named place of destination)
DAP (Delivered At Place)	(… named place of destination)
DDP (Delivered Duty Paid)	(… named place of destination)

Figure 8.1 Incoterms (Source: derived from International Chamber of Commerce)[4]

to use, and how much inventory to hold. Different people, depending on their role in the supply chain, will have varying views on what the optimum decision is, and it is the job of the logistics manager to reconcile these conflicting views.

With regard to using LSPs, a strategy that is often used by logistics managers is to give a large share of their business to one carrier, and the remaining smaller share to a competitor carrier. This has two advantages: firstly if there are any problems (for example delays) with the preferred carrier, then they can, if necessary, switch traffic to the alternative carrier; secondly this dual approach has the advantage of keeping both carriers 'on their toes', because they know there is an alternative available if their performance starts to weaken.

More generally, companies also need to decide which 3PL(s) to use. The list below gives some of the many factors that have to be considered when selecting LSPs.[5] Contracts with LSPs can often be worth large amounts of money and obviously cover an important area of a company's activities, therefore it is essential to choose the right partner(s).

- Services to be provided (geographical areas, volumes including fluctuations, time frame, etc.)
- Costs and costing approach (open book, gain share, penalties, inflation/ cost increases, etc.)
- Terms of carriage, applicable incoterms, insurance (responsibility for damage and shrinkage)
- Speed/transit time
- Performance metrics and service levels, reliability
- Information systems (especially with regard to systems integration), other technology issues (e.g. capability to 'track and trace' freight and requirement to use advanced technologies such as RFID), and documentation requirements
- Core versus value-adding services required
- Staffing issues (e.g. transfer of undertakings with respect to previous employees, legal responsibilities, image and responsibility, union recognition, disruptions)
- Reverse logistics issues (packaging, returns – damaged and faulty goods, failed deliveries, etc.)
- Implementation/termination/ability to alter conditions
- Details on the logistics service provider's history, client references, etc.

In the next chapter we will look more generally at the various stages in procuring products and services; the various steps applied there can be and are applied in the procurement of logistics services also.

Chapter 14, which deals with performance management, will discuss the role of service level agreements in the ongoing management of LSPs. Obviously once the appropriate providers are selected the next and important stage is to manage them effectively.

As well as deciding which LSP(s) to use, logistics managers also often need to decide which transport mode(s) to use. We say *often,* not *always,* because sometimes consignors do not know exactly which transport mode their freight travels on; they leave this decision to the 3PL. Furthermore, it is often not a simple matter of trading off one mode against another. Sometimes multiple transport modes are used in combination – in air transport, for example, the concept of **air trucking** is quite prevalent whereby freight is transported by road (sometimes over a relatively long distance) to a hub airport from where it travels onwards by air. Direct cost comparisons between alternative modes and services can be complex – this is the concept of **generalised costs** discussed in the box.

Much work has been done by academics and others to investigate the various criteria involved in logistics decision making and how such decisions are actually made in practice.[6] We do not have time to investigate the actual mechanics of logistics decision making here. Suffice to note for now that as well as identifying the relevant variables (such as those considered in the list above), it is important to understand how these variables interrelate in logistics decision making. In a paper in 1983, academics Davies and Gunton put forward a hierarchy of needs for freight purchasing, which is illustrated in Figure 8.2. They based it on Maslow's hierarchy of human needs and it gives a good insight into the relevant positioning of the criteria that transport and logistics decision makers regard as being important. Although we would like to think that logistics decision makers always engage in objective analysis and decision making, the reality is often

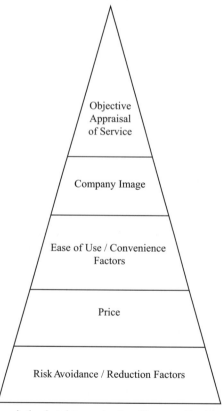

Figure 8.2 Hierarchy of needs for freight purchasing (Source: Davies & Gunton, 1983)[7]

THE CONCEPT OF GENERALISED COSTS

At this juncture it is opportune to introduce a common concept in transport economics, namely the concept of generalised costs. Button[8] noted that consignors are concerned not simply with the financial costs of carriage, but also the speed, reliability and timetabling of the service. According to Button, the demand for transport is not, therefore, simply dependent on financial costs but rather on the overall opportunity costs involved. The generalised cost of a trip can thus be expressed as a single, usually monetary, measure combining, generally in linear form, most of the important but disparate costs that form the overall opportunity costs of the trip:

$$G = g(C_1, C_2, C_3, \ldots C_n)$$

where G is generalised cost and $C_1, C_2, C_3 \ldots$ are the various time, money and other costs of travel.

Lalwani et al.[9] noted that the three main components of the generalised cost of freight transport are the money costs, the time taken, and the effects of loss, damage and delay because, in their view, it is the total effect of these, in any particular set of circumstances, which determines the choice of transport mode.

The concept of generalised transport costs is important in logistics because it helps us to understand the importance of trade-offs in decision making and how optimum decisions can be made. People engaged in marketing logistics services, for example, make use of the concept of generalised transport costs. Rates to ship freight by air are usually higher than by alternative surface modes. If, however, we factor in other costs/savings, such as the fact that because the freight is in transit for a shorter period when transported by air and as a result the opportunity cost of capital is lower, then the overall cost of air freight compared with surface freight may for some shipments actually be lower. Even though air freight rates are usually higher, air freight benefits then by usually having lower other costs associated with it over other modes such as, for example, insurance and the aforementioned opportunity cost of capital.

different. In fact many logistics decision makers often engage in what is known as *satisficing* (as opposed to *maximising*) decision-making behaviour; that is, they select routes and services which they know are not optimum, but with which they will nonetheless be largely content.

LEARNING REVIEW

This chapter described the important role played in supply chains by logistics service providers (LSPs). We discussed the various, and overlapping, types of LSPs and noted in particular the growth of a category of LSPs called 3PLs; the latter we described as LSPs who generally offer multiple logistics services, often in an integrated fashion. We then considered the raft of different services which such 3PLs actually provide, with transportation/delivery being just one of the many services offered. The concept of fourth-party logistics was then explored and we noted the reality that in many instances it is actually 3PLs that offer 4PL® type solutions.

The issue of LSP responsibilities was next explored and we looked at the important role played by the bill of lading in international transportation. The issue of who has responsibility for what at different stages in the supply chain is an important one and we considered the role that incoterms can play in clarifying this.

How consignors go about selecting LSPs and services was explored, and we saw the application of the concept of generalised costs, which helps explain trade-offs between different sets of costs in supply chains. We noted that many variables need to be considered when selecting LSPs and that a hierarchy of decision makers' needs can be identified in logistics purchasing.

The next chapter will continue the journey along the supply chain and will deal with procurement of raw materials and also the topic of outsourcing, already discussed briefly in Chapter 2.

QUESTIONS

- What is 'own-account' transportation?
- Describe the different types of logistics service providers.
- Describe the various factors that have to be considered when selecting logistics service providers. How in practice do you think consignors make decisions concerning choosing logistics services?
- What is fourth-party logistics (4PL®) and how has the concept evolved in recent years?
- How might we distinguish 3PLs from other LSPs?

'ASSET UNENCUMBERED' 3PLS

In recent years many3PLs have grown in scale and become quite sophisticated. In this chapter we also saw how some 3PLs are in practice offering 4PL® type solutions. In fact some 3PLs have advanced to the point where they believe that their knowledge and systems, and not the physical capital which they own and operate (warehouses, transport, etc.), are what gives them critical, competitive advantage. Some commentators refer to such 3 PLs as 'asset unencumbered' in that they increasingly divest themselves of physical assets, yet concomitantly grow their business via more effective use of people, knowledge and systems.

Search the web for examples of 3PLs becoming 'asset unencumbered'. Is such a strategy sustainable in the long term, in your view?

NOTES

1. Lieb, R. (2005) The 3PL industry: where it's been, where it's going, *Supply Chain Management Review,* 9(6), 20–27; Lieb, R. & Lieb, K. (2009) 2009 3PL CEO Survey, available at www.gopenske.com/newsroom/2009_9_21_executive_summary.html (accessed 2 May 2010).

2. Quoted in Gattorna, J. (2006) *Living Supply Chains,* Pearson Education, Harlow, p. 204.

3. Ibid., p. 208.

4. International Chamber of Commerce (ICC), Paris, France.

5. Adapted from: Mangan, J., Lalwani, C. & Gardner, B. (2001) Identifying relevant variables and modelling the choice process in freight transportation, *International Journal of Maritime Economics,* 3, 278–297.

6. See for example Mangan *et al.,* ibid., which includes a summary of the literature on relevant variables and transport choice decision making.

7. Davies, G. J. & Gunton, C. E. (1983) The buying of freight services: the implications for marketers, *Quarterly Review of Marketing,* Spring, 1–10.

8. Button, K. (1993) *Transport Economics*, 2nd edition, Edward Elgar Publishing, Aldershot.

9. Lalwani, C., Goss, R., Gardner, B. & Beresford, A. (1991) Modelling freight traffic, in J. Rickard & J. Larkinson (eds), *Longer Term Issues in Transport,* Avebury, Aldershot.

9

Procurement

Martin Murphy
SCMG

LEARNING OBJECTIVES

- Procurement's potential to improve business and organisational performance.
- Understand how risk and value might impact sourcing and procurement strategy and tactics in relation to markets.
- Understand the different dynamics of public and private sector procurement and how this impacts on procurement procedures and decision making.
- The distinct stages of sourcing, selecting, procuring and managing contracts.
- How consumer demand and expectations drive governance and accountability in sourcing and procurement.
- Sustainability and environmental issues as non-price factors in procurement decision making.
- The pivotal role that procurement plays in relation to wider supply chain issues.

INTRODUCTION

This chapter considers contemporary procurement as a strategic activity within a business or organisation with the potential to improve profit but also in terms of the wider social, economic and environmental issues related to sourcing and procuring goods and services for many organisations.

Chapter 9 comprises 10 core sections:

- Procurement as a strategic activity
- The difference between public and private sector procurement
- Procurement and markets
- Managing value and risk
- The role of the 'buyer'
- The procurement process
- Procurement performance
- Ethical sourcing
- Sustainability
- Procurement and supply chain management

PROCUREMENT AS A STRATEGIC ACTIVITY

Procurement as a strategic and tactical activity has become increasingly important for many organisations and businesses. This is driven by the complexity of supply issues and the fact that many supply chains are now global in terms of where products and services are procured from.

Procurement has also become more significant in response to governance issues that companies face in terms of having a clear picture of how, why and with whom they spend money and having the management processes and controls in place to ensure that this is done in a way that is consistent with legislation, regulations and the values and objectives that the organisation aspires to.

A traditional view of procurement is about spend management and at one level this is important and significant but is a rather narrow view of what procurement is all about.

A manufacturing business for example may spend as much as 70% or more of its sales on goods and services. Service companies may spend less as a percentage of sales but may be more exposed to the risk of the goods or services they acquire that are necessary in delivering their own services. In these circumstances it might be wise to ensure that both the value and risk are managed when external resources are procured. It is also important to understand the financial contribution that procurement makes. A 10%, or any reduction in procurement costs, goes straight to the bottom line versus other activities like improving sales by 10%, which is also important but will not deliver the same benefit in profit terms. The profit potential argument is a valid idea, if rather dated, as to why procurement is important. Contemporary procurement also includes many of the wider issues that organisations need to address, like corporate social responsibility, governance and environmental issues as part of the wider supply chain or ecosystems that businesses belong to.

Procurement should be considered in terms of the motivation of the buyer and the seller. The motivation and incentive for a customer in a procurement exercise is different from the supplier's perspective.

It is interesting to consider the different motivations of buyer and seller. The different motivations in Table 9.1 for buyer and seller can be considered as extremes at the opposite

Table 9.1   The difference between buying and selling

Buyer motivation	Supplier motivation
• Wants the lowest price?	• Wants the highest price?
• Increase scope?	• Decrease scope?
• Buyer power?	• Supplier power?
• Best service?	• Fit for purpose?
• Wants to limit risk?	• Limit liabilities?

> **Procurement** is about specifying requirements, identifying sources, evaluating options and acquiring resources that are fit for purpose, cost effective and sustainable.

ends of a spectrum. This tension between buying and selling is the essence of competition in terms of achieving the desired outcome that can *best* satisfy both the customer and supplier.

Rather than being about a few, or traditionally only one parameter – price, contemporary procurement reflects a wide range of criteria that includes cost or more importantly value rather than price. This would also include sustainability, for example, and in the public sector, social and environmental issues as a matter of course.

THE DIFFERENCE BETWEEN PUBLIC AND PRIVATE SECTOR PROCUREMENT

It is worth while spending some time to consider the differences between private sector and public sector procurement (see also Table 9.2). Public sector procurement in developed markets, notably the European Union, is subject to Directives, which drive levels of objectivity and transparency that are designed to support better procurement decision making. The European Union (EU) Directives[1] have provided the basis for a transformation in how public procurement has been managed in member states over the past decade and longer. In many respects the Directives provide a best practice basis to manage procurement. The private sector meanwhile is free to make decisions that are more discretionary to meet its own specific objectives and not necessarily subject to the openness and transparency that the EU procurement Directives require.

This provides an interesting basis to consider what might be the most useful elements of a procurement exercise in terms of achieving the 'best' outcome regarding the specified requirements of a contract, how suitable suppliers and contractors might be identified and how a successful candidate is selected and a contract awarded.

> In Nigeria an alternative view to a regulated public procurement marketplace is emerging. The Nigerian government commissioned the World Bank to review financial regulations and procurement procedures resulting in the Country Procurement Assessment Report (CPAR) based on UNCITRAL (United Nations Commission for International Trade Model)

and introduced public procurement regulations in the year 2000 to improve the efficiency, reliability and transparency of public procurement. This was designed to counter the very poor reputation that the country had for inefficient, including corrupt, procurement practices that were considered to be detrimental to Nigeria in terms of reforming and developing the economy. Interestingly in 2010 there were calls for the same laws to be scrapped[2] to allow the economy to develop because the regulations have added bureaucracy and time to procurement exercises and they do not support or improve procurement outcomes when trying to develop and improve the nation's infrastructure. In a rapidly developing country like Nigeria it is claimed that the procurement regulations are a luxury it cannot afford versus other mature and developed markets with established infrastructure and regulated public procurement like the European Union and the United States.

Procurement and the maturity of markets are connected in terms of considering what regulation, legislation and procedures might be most appropriate to ensure that suitable levels of competition are achieved but that sustainable results can also be delivered.

PROCUREMENT AND MARKETS

The key driver for any business or organisation is to understand how much they actually spend. The answer to this is surprisingly in many cases not as obvious as it appears or readily available. Complex organisations or multinational enterprises will operate from different global locations with different suppliers working locally with different parts of the same business.

Procurement theory and strategies are grounded in the relationships that businesses and organisations have with markets. This is a fundamental issue in terms of supply and

Table 9.2   Public sector versus private sector procurement characteristics

Characteristic	Public sector	Private sector
Obligation to publish contracts	Subject to appropriate financial thresholds for goods, works and service contracts	No obligation to publish contracts
Information generally available	Information about tender process must be generally available	Subject to internal policy but not generally available
Criteria	Established at outset and applied consistently throughout the process	Can evolve and change as process develops
Objectivity	Objective criteria must be applied and used as basis for decision making	Customer has discretion about level of objectivity to be applied
Transparency	Required for all aspects of tender process	Level of transparency in decision making is discretionary
Repeatability	Due process is legislated and applied consistently by public bodies across the EU	Reflects individual customers' own processes and requirements
Challenge	Unsuccessful candidates can challenge outcome	No right to appeal or challenge

demand and how a business secures assets and resources on favourable terms in the marketplace. Many items follow commodity markets, which makes it more straightforward to understand how price might be influenced or behave in those markets. However, many items do not depend on commodity prices, but have other cost drivers like intellectual property content, which provide a different basis to determine the price or value. In these circumstances it is important to consider what sourcing strategy is most appropriate for that category of spend.

Sourcing strategies

Sourcing strategies provide a basis on which to consider a category of spend, defining the characteristics of that category and how the marketplace determines how and sometimes when an organisation should procure items within that category to secure the best deal and continuity of supply. Strategic purchases for many organisations may include contracts looking forward for 5–10 years. A small to medium-size enterprise may have a wide range of requirements but perhaps sourced from one regional location in a local market. Consider the same issues for a large multinational enterprise with the same requirement across different locations, countries and continents. This becomes a more complex and dynamic task to organise and manage.

Sourcing strategies are the first step for any organisation to consider in how they will secure supply either on a local, national, regional or global basis and interact with the marketplace and suppliers.

As a minimum a sourcing strategy for a clearly defined requirement should include:

- Level (amount) of spend being considered
- Risk
- One-off (project) or recurring procurement
- Market maturity
- Technology lifecycle of market
- Number of sources and potential suppliers
- Contract duration
- Potential for performance improvement and cost reduction

A sourcing strategy is essentially a business case for an organisation to decide on the best way to procure resources.

Aggregation and consolidation

The most basic procurement principle to consider is leverage, that is to realise economies of scope or scale when spend can be aggregated into larger contracts that can be procured centrally as opposed to locally.

The tendency to aggregate spend also highlights the requirement to manage the procurement process properly or in a compliant fashion recognising any required legislation, regulations and internal policies and procedures. As spend is aggregated the level of risk also increases as the level of dependency on a particular supplier or groups of suppliers increases.

MANAGING VALUE AND RISK

The **Kraljik matrix**, named after Peter Kraljik,[3] provides a simple but powerful tool to understand and quantify relative value and procurement risk issues for any business or organisation (see Figure 9.1). This provides a basis to develop portfolios of spend that can be categorised, assessed in terms of impact (or risk) and value and managed.

> Goods or services that were previously procured locally are more likely now to be procured centrally or at a regional level.

> The role of procurement is to manage value and risk on behalf of the organisation.

Different strategies are appropriate in each portfolio that exists within each quadrant of the matrix. High value and risk should be managed differently from low value and low risk. The different categories are commonly described as shown in Table 9.3.

The other interesting point highlighted by Kraljik's portfolio approach is that the Pareto rule will also apply to spend within a business and organisation, i.e. 80% of spend will be with 20% of the suppliers, which raises the issue, alongside risk, about the importance and significance of some suppliers versus others.

All suppliers are not equal and the level of dependency can be high to the extent that this becomes a risk unless the relationships are also managed appropriately. It is not possible to manage every relationship on a one-to-one basis so in many cases businesses and organisations also

> A common and continuing trend is for businesses to reduce the number of suppliers and contractors they do business with directly or on a one-to-one basis.

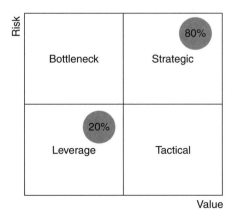

Figure 9.1 The Kraljik matrix

Table 9.3   Managing procurement portfolios

Risk/Value	Description	Strategy
High/High	Strategic	Work strategically and collaborate. High risk and value usually represents a high dependency relationship with a supplier with high exit costs. Source and manage strategically
High/Low	Bottleneck	Needs to be managed carefully. The bottleneck may be technical or commercial but to reduce the risk, buyers have to design the bottleneck out of their portfolio or ensure an appropriate relationship with the supplier is maintained – to ensure continuity of supply
Low/High	Tactical	Tactical procurement required to ensure value for money is achieved from the most appropriate source or sources. Increase sources and maintain competition between suppliers
Low/Low	Leverage	Aggregate and consolidate spend. Low-risk/low-value items are like commodities where source is less important than continuity of supply and assuming all other performance requirements are met – source on price

consider their procurement portfolio in terms of the number of suppliers and contractors that they deal with and the nature of the relationships that they have.

One of the main procurement risks for organisations is ensuring continuity of supply. Risk assessments usually consider 'what will we do if our supplier's factory burns down?'. This happens more often that you might imagine. Dell and Hewlett-Packard were both affected by a fire at the LG Chem factory in South Korea in 2008. This was a main source for both PC manufacturers of batteries for laptop computers. This meant a 50% reduction in output for LG Chem and subsequent shortages or no availability of batteries for PC manufacturers and others. The fire drove some manufacturers to alternative and competing sources of batteries including Sony and Panasonic. The shortages lasted for a three-month period.

The Kraljik matrix is used almost universally in terms of identifying portfolios or categories of spend and quantifying them by risk and value. Having quantified the level of value and risk, purchasing managers can then develop an appropriate sourcing strategy to manage the risk and value for that portfolio and category.

The implications for how portfolios of spend are managed in terms of an appropriate process, organisation and technology are more straightforward for an autonomous business in one geographical location, but the level of complexity is increased significantly when portfolios are considered across businesses operating from multiple locations.

It is easy to understand that process, organisation and technology issues are different when procuring paper clips (low risk, low value) versus a mission critical enterprise resource planning software tool (high risk, high value). These issues vary considerably between organisations of different sizes, complexity and footprint.

> Small to medium-size enterprises versus large multinational enterprises have to manage a different procurement dynamic within their business and organisation in terms of where specifiers, buyers and end users may be located throughout the business.

THE ROLE OF THE BUYER

In parallel with the improvement in procurement knowledge and practice across most private and public sector organisations the role of the 'buyer' has also developed from managing or dealing with transactions, largely through the efforts of the various professional bodies, notably the Chartered Institute of Purchasing and Supply[4] (CIPS) in the UK and the Institute of Supply Management[5] (ISM) based in North America, where the idea of procurement as a profession has been promoted vigorously. This includes the development of vocational qualifications and competence standards, which have become highly desirable in terms of employability and career progression.

Many businesses, although some would argue not enough, will also appoint a chief procurement officer (CPO), who represents procurement issues at senior or executive levels within a business or organisation. This is important when procurement decisions can be complex and high value and relate either to the bottom line or fundamental success of a business in terms of procuring assets or resources and services required or used to deliver the business's own products or services. This is also significant in terms of the governance process for an organisation, where visibility and transparency relating to the procurement of goods and services can benefit from the skills and expertise of an experienced procurement colleague rather than a more traditional financial view.

Competition can be generated in a number of ways. The Kraljik matrix again is helpful in thinking what tactics or strategy we might employ to manage the level of risk and value in a suitable way. If the risk and value are high then a rigorous and formal procurement exercise would be appropriate. Conversely a low-risk and low-value procurement does not necessarily require the same level of rigour or formality. Table 9.4 shows

> The role of a procurement manager is to create an appropriate level of competition to manage the level of risk and value that the business faces when sourcing or procuring goods, services or works.

some typical methods that can be used to achieve an appropriate level of competition.

THE PROCUREMENT PROCESS

Procurement should be considered as a process or lifecycle. This process is repeated within a business as different contracts mature, expire and are renewed on a continual basis. In addition to developing the sourcing strategy there are basically four stages to be considered as illustrated in Table 9.5.

Table 9.4   Procurement techniques and tools

Method	Description	Benefits
Request for quotation (RFQ)	Appropriate when the specification is clear and unambiguous and when risk and value are low and there is no real requirement to create unnecessary competition	High levels of discretion are possible by informed and experienced buyers
Negotiation	Appropriate to negotiate directly with a supplier or contractor when the specification, either/or both technical and commercial, requires some clarification or discussion with a supplier who has more knowledge or information than the customer	Customers can have some confidence that they have defined and agreed the specification and scope with suppliers
Formal tender process	When the risk and value is high the tendency is for organisations to revert to a formal tender process where a number of suitably qualified candidates will be invited to tender (ITT). The level of formality increases with value and risk	Tender processes create formal competitions that will deliver performance and cost reductions based on the customer's ability to properly define its requirements. Prices can be reduced by 5–20% or higher typically using a tender process
eAuction	More 'sophisticated' approaches would involve electronic auctions (eAuctions), which are appropriate if the category or commodity marketplace is properly researched and understood and there are a number of alternative suppliers who can bid against the defined requirement. eAuctions are appropriate when all other required criteria have been satisfied by suppliers who then bid in the final stages of the auction process	eAuctions require the pre-selection of suppliers who can meet the requirements or specifications. They present higher levels of risk for buyers and suppliers but are credited with delivering up to 30% or more price reductions

Procurement organisation

A key question facing a business is about how to organise procurement resources and the level of authority that procurement managers and (perhaps) executives have within the organisation. This should reflect key policies and procedures or processes. This may include a single location, legal jurisdiction or local economic factors versus more complex national, regional or global organisations, which have to consider sourcing and procurement decisions in a wider and more diverse context.

The issue of how to organise procurement depends on the level of spend and procurement skills across the business. Procurement teams can be centralised or decentralised by location and organised by business unit or by spend category and in terms of strategic or tactical roles. Traditionally and in too many cases the procurement organisation would

Table 9.5   The procurement process

Stage	Description	Key issues
Specify	Specify the requirements that the contract must deliver	• Requirements should be defined from a technical, commercial and end-user perspective • In many cases organisations do not understand the market better than suppliers • Sometimes the specification is unclear or ambiguous
Identify	Identify suitable potential suppliers who are able to meet the defined requirements or specification	• Advertising and promoting the contract opportunity • Determing an appropriate level of competition to reflect the risk and value being procured • Attracting new or more interesting suppliers who may be able to add more value to your business versus incumbents • Choosing which suppliers have the capability and capacity to deliver the required service
Select	Select a suitable supplier or suppliers to deliver the contract	• Picking a winner from suppliers who have sufficient capability and capacity to deliver the contract • The evaluation criteria in terms of quality and price • The balance needed between quality and price
Manage	Manage the contract to ensure that the key deliverables are fully met	• Success criteria or key performance indicators are required to ensure that the contract requirements are being met • Lessons learned are applied to subsequent contracts

be grouped with or be a sub-set of the finance and administration activities of a business. More typically and reflecting the more strategic nature of contemporary procurement the organisation or team would be a standalone activity with specific objectives, targets and

goals to deliver as part of the strategy or business plan. There is an overwhelming tendency to centralise procurement organisations to create a centre of gravity within the business where activities can be standardised and areas of common spend across different business units aggregated and consolidated into larger central contracts.

Category managers provide the leadership and focal point for a business to source and manage the risk and value related to a category or portfolio on behalf of the business.

Category managers[6] manage a portfolio of contracts or category of spend with similar characteristics that can be grouped and considered in strategic terms in relationship to supplying across different business units or parts of an organisation.

In larger businesses with more complex requirements and footprint a category manager would have responsibility for developing the sourcing strategy across the business taking into account local requirements and overall requirements in aggregate terms. This invariably means that the value associated with that category increases and that the risk may have to be re-evaluated versus a model where the spend is disaggregated and managed locally with local suppliers providing services to local business units and spread across a number of suppliers or sites.

Local or tactical activity is still required where a call-off against a contract or framework established by the category manager takes place to satisfy local demand but on the terms defined by the main contract with a supplier or number of different suppliers for that category. In larger organisations with multiple sites there will be a local or site buyer dealing with local supply issues and category managers dealing with common or specialist requirements across multiple sites.

The role of technology

Procurement systems have developed dramatically from early packages that were bolted on to financial management systems and accounts payable packages to reflect the procurement lifecycle from sourcing to contract management. Larger enterprise resource planning (ERP) systems like SAP[7] and Oracle[8] tend to dominate the corporate marketplace, and support complex organisations with multiple activities in different locations. There are also many standalone packages that can be integrated with ERP systems or are available as different modules, which provide a joined-up approach to sourcing, tendering, procurement and contract management.

Packages now are web or cloud based and this not only enables sharing of information within a business and across different locations but also with suppliers in terms of providing information about contract opportunities using electronic portals and/or catalogue management systems where suppliers' products are available online to any user who has the access, authority and budget to procure those items. This includes tender management software, thus allowing tenders to be submitted online ensuring secure delivery mechanisms and predetermined process parameters such as deadlines. This streamlines the process and eliminates many of the administrative tasks associated with traditional procurement.

eAuctions are common place and this has been enabled by the level of technology now available where pre-selected suppliers bid for a contract over a number of rounds or defined time period and at the same time have the visibility of competing bids. This is very popular with some buyers but is not so popular with suppliers, who may have a very different view from the customer. The perception is that eAuctions can be very impersonal and a rather blunt tool but it is hard to argue with the results that have been achieved in terms of reducing prices. eAuction software is best utilised alongside a service provider who will do the market research, develop a sourcing strategy for your particular items or services and prequalify candidates prior to the auction process.

The various tools and technology now available provide rich data and information that buyers never previously had access to. This enables them to review and analyse demand patterns and service levels from suppliers to inform future decision making and category strategy for related items.

Price, cost and value

Traditionally procurement has focused on price. Price is still an important part of the mix and, in a perfect market with multiple buyers and suppliers, it is an effective mechanism to differentiate items that can be treated as a commodity. However, many goods and services are complex and even the most basic commodity item perhaps has an element of service associated with the procurement and delivery of it.

The cost of procuring a particular item may relate to operating an asset or using a service, which in turn can drive other higher costs. This is referred to as the total cost or whole lifecycle cost. A simple example might include buying an item with a lower purchase price but higher service or maintenance and repair costs.

> It is important not to confuse price with cost, terms which are sometimes used interchangeably but mean very different things.

Value for money (VfM) also provides a different perspective or another dimension to procurement decision making. VfM is often quoted but is more difficult to define. It is like trust – in some respects we know when we trust someone or something, but it is difficult to articulate what that means. We also know when we don't trust someone or something. Similarly we describe goods or services as representing VfM but struggle to define that beyond a feeling or perception. However, the UK Treasury[9] provides a very helpful model to explain VfM as being three different components of acquiring, operating and disposing, and the 'optimum combination of whole lifecycle costs and quality (fitness for purpose) to meet the end users' requirements'. This is explained further in Figure 9.2.

A simple illustration of whole lifecycle costs is the UK programme to acquire nuclear power stations over 40 years ago. The operating costs over the life of these power stations

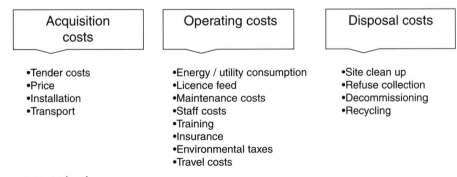

Figure 9.2   Value for money

dwarfs the original acquisition cost. However, the unquantified (at the time), unanticipated and largest cost in procuring a NUCLEAR POWER STATION is not the acquisition or operating cost but the related disposal cost. If these costs had been considered at the acquisition stage the economics would have looked quite different and the business case almost impossible to justify.

Low-cost country sourcing

Technology and improved infrastructure have also increased the options available to many organisations to source and procure goods from low-cost country sources, a trend we noted in Chapter 2. This is evident in the huge increase in global trade alongside the internationalisation of businesses and the acquisition of commodities. This was initially to manufacture products but has grown to include outsourced manufacturing or very sophisticated services provided by businesses operating on different continents and in different time zones.

China has emerged as an economic superpower due in no small part to the demand from businesses and consumers in the West. Western demand has driven its economy through manufactured products and goods and of course services exported to the West, which is a catalyst to support and create indigenous demand. Many Western companies now increasingly see China not as a cheap source of labour but as one of their key markets.

India is another low-cost country source where goods and services can be sourced at fractions of Western equivalent prices. This is complemented by improved infrastructure and East to West logistics supply routes, which provide competitive lead times for product sourced in the Far East or China.

The unanswered question regarding low-cost country sourcing is about sustainability. If we apply the VfM or whole lifecycle cost argument many of the costs, for example environmental costs, are not fully considered in the selection of a supplier and products on the basis of price. If the wider factors were fully considered like environmental costs or more working capital tied up in the supply chain or pipeline from East to West many of the sourcing decisions could not be justified.

Any reduction in prices of course delivers straight to the bottom line and when price reductions of 40% or more can be achieved then it is difficult for a business to resist the advantage that this may give them.

With labour costs in low-cost country sources of between approximately 3% and 10% of Western and US rates it is easy to see why this would be attractive to any CEO, particularly in lower margin businesses or when competitors can or already use these sources.

Price, though, as we have discussed is not necessarily a good indicator of VfM, as some businesses have found to their detriment. However, if a business can manage the relationship, logistics and related customs issues this can be a highly successful strategy. Consumers are now much more aware of sources of origin so this can be an important factor or a public relations disaster if not managed properly.

MATTEL

Mattel is one of the most successful toy manufacturers, whose range includes Barbie amongst other much loved toys like Doggie Day Care, Batman and Polly Pocket. Its policy of manufacturing two-thirds of its toy range in China backfired badly when paint on some of its children's toys were found to be lead based as reported in the media. This resulted in over 21 million toys being recalled or returned in the busy run up period to Christmas 2007. Another scare involved products with small magnets being recalled due to the risk of children swallowing small component parts. The initial reaction was to blame poor manufacturing practices in Chinese sub-contractors; however, later it was realised that more products were recalled for Mattel's design mistakes than for lead paint. One of the factory managers in China hanged himself in his factory when his export licence was revoked. China protested to Mattel who apologised in a prepared statement acknowledging that the design mistake for the magnets was its own rather than as a result of poor manufacturing practices in China.

Low-cost country sourcing is not straightforward as the Mattel example suggests. If managed properly it can be and is a highly successful strategy for many businesses. When it goes wrong the recovery costs and business disruption can be very high.

PROCUREMENT PERFORMANCE

A traditional procurement measurement is purchase price variance (PPV). PPV is a measure of the variance between the actual price paid versus the standard cost of the item. The standard cost of an item would be included in a bill of material (BoM) for a particular product and is used to calculate the product cost. The performance of the buyer would then be measured as a variance around the standard cost or original purchase price. Of course assumptions have to be made about the quantity, frequency and number of different setup activities required by the supplier to produce the particular items. In many cases these assumptions do not hold true and can be less accurate in practice. However, the performance of a buyer is measured against the standard cost in terms of a positive or negative variance. A positive variance might suggest that the buyer is performing well and a negative variance might suggest the buyer is not performing.

Inappropriate measures can have unintended consequences and Emiliani[10] *et al.* have identified different tactics that buyers can use to manipulate the PPV ranging from underestimating demand when seeking prices or sourcing from suppliers who charge high prices which in practice can be easily beaten in terms of securing a lower price when a product moves from the development stage to mass production. This is perhaps a rather cynical view but again highlights the difference between price and cost that we have discussed earlier. Another example might be where a minimum order quantity (MOQ) is specified and the buyer only wants to procure an amount less than the MOQ. In a case like this the supplier may also be entitled to a setup cost, which is not captured in the price of the parts procured or is accounted for in a different way to how the product was intended to be costed.

> Procurement performance and metrics reflect a wider range of different key performance indicators and although price is a vital component many now consider the wider aspects of performance and measure them on a regular basis.

At the opposite end of the scale from a narrow PPV perspective the University of Pennsylvania's Purchasing Services[11] has identified a top–down approach to managing procurement and contract management performance. This is driven by a strategic plan, which defines business strategies and a wide range of other issues including governance and collaborative buying with clear definitions, targets and performance measures. This provides a very transparent view of procurement for end users within the university but also for suppliers who do business with the university and those aspiring to do business in the future.

The business or 'supply chain strategies' include:

- Spend analysis
- Strategic sourcing
- Contract management
- Collaborative buying
- Compliance

This includes a comprehensive suite of performance metrics that are defined and fully described including performance targets and results achieved for the particular performance element of the strategy. This includes:

- Cost containment, from strategic sourcing activities for schools and centres within the university.
- Strategic sourcing, includes improved prices and cost reductions achieved from contracts that have been resourced.
- Spend management, includes collaborative contracts and preferred contractor agreements.
- Economic inclusion, includes spend with local suppliers and diversity targets for spend with minority groups.
- Supplier enablement, includes suppliers 'enabled' who participate in the university's own private supplier exchange.

- Purchase to pay (P2P), includes targets to conduct business electronically including invoicing and eliminating paperwork and administration as well as payment within terms of agreements with suppliers.
- Operations, includes measuring customer (end-user) satisfaction and compliance.

By using this approach, 'Penn Purchasing Services' can leverage its buying power and impact the institution's bottom line. This of course makes purchasing activity a strategic resource and the department is able to justify and demonstrate the value it adds to the business. This has resulted in a RoI of approximately 20:1 of documented cost containment versus the department's operating budget.

'Penn Purchasing Services' approach provides a more informed basis for making decisions, which reflects a value for money or total cost approach rather than a narrow focus on price.

> This focus on performance from a strategic and top–down perspective highlights the true nature and the real driver for procurement activity, which is to create a return on investment (RoI) through improved procurement and contract management.

ETHICAL SOURCING

Consumers are increasingly more interested in sources of supply. This has led many businesses to consider their procurement practices, particularly in light of the 'opportunities' created by sourcing from low-cost countries.

Ethical sourcing is a complex subject and can sometimes be difficult to manage when low-cost country sources are involved. Fashion retailers often use low-cost manufacturers in developing countries and food producers are now challenged to justify using certain products on the basis of food miles or the impact that sourcing products from low-cost sources has in terms of environmental impact and the real cost of the product. Complex logistics networks now make it possible to order and deliver products from any source to any location in relatively short lead times and in a cost-effective manner. There are of course environmental issues to be considered, which consumers are becoming more interested in as they become more aware and educated about the subject. In many cases this is contradictory when we consider global markets or competition policy, which suggests that free trade should be allowed to develop unhindered. However, the pressure from consumers and business to include environmental factors in sourcing decisions means a local supplier or solution might cost more in terms of a higher price versus a low-cost country source, but be the lowest total cost or a more ethical choice when environmental factors and costs are considered. Sourcing decisions increasingly reflect a wider range of environmental and social issues and not just price and cost.

A series of TV programmes and documentaries produced by the BBC[12] and others in the early 2000s exposed working conditions of child labourers employed in sweat shop factories for big brand Western businesses. Nike hit the headlines for all the wrong reasons for using sub-contractors employing child labour to stitch leather footballs in Cambodia. Chocolate makers Cadbury and Nestlé among others were named in an investigation that alleged that 90% of the Ivory Coast's (the world's biggest producer of cocoa) plantations used slaves. Clothes retailers Primark and Gap were also identified as indirectly using sub-contractors who used child labour. Gap suspended orders but never cancelled contracts for sub-contractors who implemented improvements. In 2008 Primark terminated contracts with three Indian suppliers when they were alerted to children being used to finish goods in sub-contracted firms. Child labour and falsifying documents are considered to be endemic in many low-cost countries. More recently Nike has responded to consumer concerns about ethical standards in retail sourcing by providing information about all of its suppliers.

The range of ethical issues to consider is increasing as consumers become more aware of certain practices that they do not consider to be ethical. Many businesses have responded with ethical reporting or sections on ethics as part of their annual report. The range of issues is complicated and growing but may include:

- Green products
- Carbon emissions
- Transport
- Environmental performance
- Health and safety
- Diversity and equality
- Standards at work including suppliers
- Role of the business as a employer, customer and corporate citizen
- Sustainability

SUSTAINABILITY

ADIDAS

In its annual Sustainability Report[13] Adidas, the sportswear firm, describes sustainability as a marathon and not a sprint concerning the 'significant challenges we face in the future to address our social, material and environmental issues'. No mean feat for a business that sells products in virtually every country in the world and with 170 subsidiaries and approximately 40 000 employees.

The contradiction for procurement managers and suppliers is how to reconcile the fact that in defining requirements and high expectations for suppliers in terms of products and services that they do more with less. This means less resources, less energy, less damage to the environment, less of everything basically, but they must still deliver to the original specification. This requires an enlightened customer and a switched-on supplier, but also wider and deeper evaluation criteria than might be associated with traditional procurement exercises.

For Adidas in 2009 this meant working with more than 1100 suppliers around the globe, monitoring environmental issues, for example reducing solvent emissions by as much as 80% per pair of shoes, monitoring suppliers and rejecting unsuitable factories as well as building capacity across the supply chain by involving suppliers, licensees, workers and employees. This also includes targets for 2015 to reduce energy consumption and carbon emissions, water saving and waste reduction by double digit percentage figures and the use of management tools like its Sustainability Compliance Initiative (SCI) audit.

The concept of 'food miles',[14] where products are transported around the globe, raises interesting issues about sustainability, sourcing and procurement decisions.

Large supermarkets can source high-quality cheap products anywhere in the world depending on the growing season. In some cases sources can be on opposite sides of the world from their final destination and consumer. This can be overcome by very efficient logistics that does not significantly impact the cost of buying and transporting products over such a long distance to the extent that they can be sold cost effectively.

However, in some cases the benefits of the lower priced products can be eroded by the increased logistics or return logistics costs for defective products. The lower price may be achieved by the increased working capital costs related to holding inventory and buffers for both safety stock at the source and delivery point as well as the product that is in the supply chain in transit between the supplier and the customer. In some cases the working capital requirements and costs to finance the supply chain or pipeline can be as much as 30% or more of the price of the product. If these costs are not considered in the initial sourcing decision or if unrealistic assumptions about quality and delivery are made then the business case may not stack up.

This has implications for how businesses and organisations account for non-price factors in their financial reporting. The profit potential argument is based on lower input costs that can be easily measured and tracked in the profit and loss account. This can create an unrealistic view if the costs are not properly recorded, if they can be calculated or accounted for or indirectly paid for by someone else.

In terms of food for example there are now many initiatives like the Fife Diet,[15] which encourage people to prepare and cook local food based on a seasonal menu throughout the year. This is an attempt to promote local sourcing and reduce food miles and is an example where consumer behaviour can have an impact on sourcing decisions and sustainability.

PROCUREMENT AND SUPPLY CHAIN MANAGEMENT

The business focus in the late 1980s and early 1990s on quality and performance combined with emerging thoughts on value not cost, service not just delivery, and the increasing complexity of product and service delivery becoming a function of different supply chain partners rather than a single entity, brought the links between customers and suppliers upstream and downstream into sharp focus. This meant that links in the supply chain became an area where business improvement could be defined in wider terms of relationships with suppliers and customers, rather than within the four walls of a business.

> A key differentiator and perhaps a still not fully understood part of a business or organisation's strategy is relationship management.

The popularity of quality improvement and lean approaches with an internal focus provided an additional successful level of improvement but was limited in terms of their momentum and sustainability when compared to working across the supply chain.

Relationship management links back to Kraljik's early ideas about portfolios. Businesses prioritise relationships with preferred customers but the same is not always true, or to the same extent, when customers consider their upstream relationships with suppliers. This increases risk and cost, and compromises the performance of the component part and the chain itself.

Many business inefficiencies are inadvertently designed into the supply chain, driven in part by sourcing decisions. The effectiveness and efficiency of the enterprise is determined by the business model, supply chain architecture and links to suppliers and with customers.

> The cost structure can be hard wired and very difficult to change once established or unable to adapt quickly enough if the inertia is too high when faced with competitive threats, new entrants or game-changing products and/or services in the marketplace.

Perhaps this relationship strategy approach beyond segmenting markets and suppliers as portfolios is worthy of more consideration in terms of defining core processes and relationships with customers and suppliers as part of the definition and management of any supply chain or business model. Table 9.6 shows how procurement and relationship strategies have evolved.

CONCLUSION

The quality of relationships and communications are key elements in defining the interactions between individuals and organisations. Procurement is at the forefront of these developments in terms of addressing the wider issues relating to sourcing and contract management and renewal.

The idea of a company operating in isolation is outdated and the development of chains or clusters as part of an ecosystem becomes more apparent and relevant when multiple partners are engaged in the delivery of a product or a service.

The coordination of activities is essential when sourcing, procuring, planning and/or delivering products and services. The quality and measurement of the relationship in

Table 9.6 Procurement and relationship strategies

Period	Stage	Relationship strategy	Communications
Late 1980s	Supplier management	Suppliers need to be managed and developed by sometimes less sophisticated customers to manage quality and delivery	Command and control
Early 1990s	Supply chain	One-to-one approach (diadic) where a customer and supplier(s) would focus on business improvement activities – customer prerogative and driven	Discussion
Millennium	Business to Business (B2B)	B2B relationship and the dot-com boom removed geography and logistics as limiting factors in defining the scope and scale of a business	Dialogue
Noughties	Networks	Improving technology infrastructure supported the development of chains into networks and an increasing focus on horizontal as well as vertical relationships resulting in informal collaboration and more formal joint ventures and alliances	'Open'
Today	Social networking	Organisational boundaries completely removed in terms of discussion in and out of organisations with instant feedback including consumers, customers, partners and suppliers	Everyone can talk to everyone – social and professional networking sites – procurement conducted electronically

terms of how customers behave and define their requirements will determine how well a supplier or contractor can perform.

Procurement provides the interface and is an essential link to markets and suppliers. It has a key role in defining and managing future supply chains, how they perform and the impact they have on society and the environment. The rate of change and the wider issues that procurement professionals have to deal with means that many businesses are very sensitive to procurement activity and capabilities. Businesses and organisations that recognise this will be better placed to meet future requirements and build more sustainable and profitable enterprises.

LEARNING REVIEW

Procurement can be considered as a process that has implications upstream in relation to suppliers and contractors and downstream in relation to specifiers and end users. This process is repeated numerous times by organisations as contracts are renewed, mature and expire.

The role of procurement is to create an appropriate level of competition to manage the level of risk and value associated with that contract.

Risk and value can be quantified and understood using Kraljik's matrix where different strategies can be developed to ensure that both risk and value are properly managed.

Procurement activity has a more prominent role in relation to sourcing, which now has to consider much wider issues than price including value for money, ethics and sustainability, which if not managed properly have a huge impact on the environment and wider society.

Global businesses have complex procurement needs that have implications for how they develop procurement process, how they organise resources and the role that technology has in sharing information and data between all procurement stakeholders.

Governance and/or how, where and from whom we source are very important questions from a legal and commercial perspective but now must also stand up to public scrutiny in terms of public and consumer opinion.

Value for money provides a more informed view about how sourcing and procurement decision making is made. Price may provide a short-term benefit, perhaps at the expense of others, versus a sustainable solution based on total cost.

Procurement plays a pivotal role in terms of uniting suppliers as part of the end-to-end process from suppliers to consumers who are part of an overall supply chain.

QUESTIONS

- What are the differences between an SME business and a global business in terms of how they identify sources of supply?
- How does consumer opinion impact on sourcing decisions?
- Which environmental factors should be considered when trying to identify the total cost of procuring goods in low-cost countries.
- Are rules, like the EU Procurement Regulations, useful in certain markets and what might the different procurement issues be between the private and public sector?

- What elements of risk are there in terms of sourcing and procuring goods from a Western source versus a low-cost country source such as Vietnam?
- What type of relationship would be most appropriate with a high-risk/high-value supplier versus a low-risk/low-value supplier?
- Does value for money versus price help make a more informed procurement decision?
- What actions could Mattel take to minimise product recalls in future?
- What sustainability criteria would you include in a sourcing strategy and how would you manage and measure them in practice?
- How might technology and social networking impact on procurement activity?

NOTES

1. EU Directives 2004/17/EC and 2004/18/EC provide a European framework for the procurement of goods, works and service and utilities, which may be adopted by member states within their own legal jurisdiction. The framework includes defined financial thresholds for mandatory publication of contract notices and defined procedures for the publication, evaluation, award of and challenge to the outcome of public tender exercises.
2. *Supply Management* (2010), from Reactive Media on behalf of the Chartered Institute of Purchasing and Supply.
3. Kraljik's model appeared in the *Harvard Business Review* article, Purchasing must become Supply Management, September–October, 1983.
4. CIPS is the UK-based Institute for purchasing and supply professionals with over 65 000 members, which promotes, develops and improves the capability of members and professional standards. CIPS operates internationally.
5. ISM is a not-for-profit 40 000 member organisation representing purchasing and supply professionals based in the USA.
6. The role of category manager has emerged and evolved over the last 20 years as requirements become more complex and procurement decision making involves understanding markets and technical requirements, which can be dramatically different between different categories.
7. SAP is a German-based global provider of enterprise resource planning software and systems including tendering and procurement modules.
8. The Oracle suite of tools includes a wide range of supply chain applications and modules including advanced procurement for a wide range of sectors and businesses.
9. Office of Government Commerce (OGC) (2010) Value for money: guidance on complex procurement, www.ogc.gov.uk.
10. Emiliani, M.L., Stec, D.J. & Grasso, L.P. (2005) Unintended responses to a traditional purchasing performance metric, *Supply Chain Management: An International Journal*, 10(3), 150–156.

11. University of Pennsylvania Purchasing Services, www.purchasing.upenn.edu (accessed 10 November 2010).

12. For example the BBC *Panorama* programme produced a series of documentaries highlighting the plight of child labour in developing countries.

13. Adidas (2009) Annual Sustainability Report 2009.

14. Tim Lang, Professor of Food Policy at City University London, is credited with the phrase 'food miles'.

15. The Fife Diet is a Voluntary Association, which encourages people to eat local food and is funded by the Scottish Government.

10 Inventory Management

Chuda Basnet and Paul Childerhouse
University of Waikato, New Zealand

LEARNING OBJECTIVES

- Explain the significance of inventory in logistics and supply chain management.
- Introduce the costs involved in inventory management.
- Introduce common inventory control systems designed to reduce costs.
- Identify inventory reduction strategies including just-in-time inventory management.

INTRODUCTION

In this chapter we discuss the place of inventory in logistics and supply chain management. Both theoretical and practical aspects of inventory management are considered.

Chapter 10 comprises six core sections:

- The importance of inventory management
- The economic order quantity (EOQ) model
- Inventory control systems
- Supply chain inventory management
- Matching inventory policy with inventory type
- Inventory reduction principles

THE IMPORTANCE OF INVENTORY MANAGEMENT

The central focus in this book is on flows through supply chains. One of the flows we have been discussing is the physical flow of materials. **Inventory** is another name for

Inventory is everywhere!

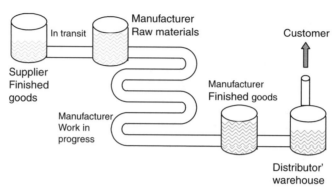

Figure 10.1 Supply chain pipeline

materials and is any material that a firm holds in order to satisfy customer demand (and these customers may be internal and/or external to the firm). Figure 10.1 shows inventory locations throughout a supply chain. This illustration should give a sense of the ubiquitous nature of inventory, and the various forms in which it is held. Supply chains hold *raw materials* in order to convert these inputs into finished products. When the raw materials are processed, but are not yet completely finished, they are called *work in progress*. Once the products are ready for shipment, they are *finished goods*. Notice also the *in transit* inventory in Figure 10.1. This is inventory being moved from one location to another.

Inventory costs money! Supply chain partners invest significant amounts of money in holding inventory in various forms. This is money that could be invested elsewhere, earning a return. Inventory ties up working capital and affects cash flow, sometimes even threatening the survival of a firm. Inventory also takes up space, and firms need to hire people to take care of inventory. Thus firms are always on the lookout for ways to reduce their inventory holding. However, inventory cannot be wiped to zero, because firms need to have raw materials, work in progress and finished goods in order to function. Without these in place, customer orders will take unduly long to fulfil. Therefore the goal in inventory management is to *minimise* inventory holding while maintaining a desired customer service level.

Inventory turnover is a concept used to measure a firm's performance in inventory management. This measure compares the annual sales a firm achieves with the amount of average inventory held throughout the year: the higher the turnover, the better a firm is doing in keeping its inventory costs down.

$$\text{Inventory turnover} = \frac{\text{Cost of all goods sold in a year}}{\text{Value of average inventory held throughout the year}}$$

Most firms achieve a turnover of about 10, while well-performing firms can achieve a turnover of 50 or more.

PROBLEM 10.1

The YouRace Company builds racing cars. In 2006, the total cost of cars sold was $3 million. Its total inventory holding changed throughout the year, but the average holding was worth $250 000. At the end of 2006, it implemented just-in-time principles to improve its inventory performance. In 2007, its sales increased and the cost of cars was $4.5 million, while the average inventory holding was $300 000. Has the performance improved?

Answer:
Inventory turnover in 2006 = 3 000 000/250 000 = 12
Inventory turnover in 2007 = 4 500 000/300 000 = 15

Thus the performance has improved, but only slightly.

Inventory can be viewed as a necessary evil. Without inventory one minor problem in the supply chain would result in a stoppage of the entire chain. Hence inventory is used as a buffer between processes along a supply chain. Table 10.1 expands on this point and highlights a range of reasons why this buffer is required. Despite managers' best efforts, supply chains never quite work to plan, therefore buffers are required to absorb the variability in demand, supply and internal processes.

An alternative view of holding inventory is based around the central theme of trade-offs. Inventory holding costs are traded-off with other economical advantages; these are also outlined in Table 10.1. It is often more economical to produce in reasonable batch sizes to minimise the downtime resulting from production line changeovers, hence inventory is built up to cover for a number of days then stored until required. This principle can also be applied to transportation where full loads are more economical than delivering single items, hence this saving is traded-off with the additional cost of holding the extra

Table 10.1   Reasons for holding inventory

Buffer against uncertainty	Economic trade-offs
Maintain customer service levels for volatile demand	Production batch size
Hedge against price and exchange rate fluctuations	Transportation batch size
Protect against delivery lead-time variability	Transportation mode
Buffer against unreliable supply sources	Order quantity size
Buffer against seasonal demand and supply	Order frequency duration
Maintain supply of scarce supply	Bulk purchase savings
Provide cover for emergencies	Supply price fluctuations

inventory. This secondary reason for holding inventory has been challenged over the past decade as just-in-time (JIT, see below) and modern information and communications technology has drastically reduced batch sizes and processing costs. A well-known example of an economic trade-off is explained in depth in the following section where the cost of placing an order is balanced against the cost of holding inventory.

THE ECONOMIC ORDER QUANTITY MODEL

The costs associated with inventory can be classified into two broad categories: one associated with procuring the inventory and the other associated with actually holding the inventory. The procurement costs can be broken into two parts: money spent to process a procurement order and the money spent to actually buy the inventory. We present some notation before considering minimisation of the total inventory costs.

Define:

D: Annual use of a particular item, in number of items per year

S: Order-processing cost, in $/order

p: Price per item, in $/unit

H: Holding cost per unit per year, in $/unit/year

Q: Number of items ordered in one purchase order, in units

T: Time periods between purchase orders in fraction of a year

SS: Safety stock, in units

L: Lead time, in fraction of a year

I: Current inventory on hand, units

TAC: Total annual cost

Figure 10.2 is an idealised depiction of inventory levels of an item over time. The graphic shows initially the inventory level of an item dropping steadily because of usage of this item.

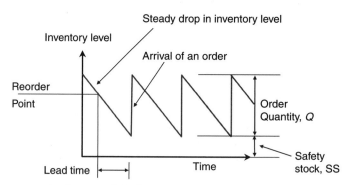

Figure 10.2   Inventory build-up and depletion

When the inventory level is at a certain level, called the **reorder point**, a purchase order is issued for this item. After the passage of a certain length of time, called the **lead time**, this order is filled and the inventory level increases by the amount of the order, Q. This cycle of inventory depletion and order fulfilment repeats itself. Note also that in the diagram the inventory level is kept above a certain amount, called the **safety stock**. Various questions arise, such as what level of safety stock should be held, what should be the reorder point, and what should the order quantity be. Let us look at the cost considerations of order quantity first.

Calculating the annual costs to buy this item is straightforward, since the usage per year is D units and the price per unit is p ($).

Purchase cost $= p \times D$

Annual holding cost is the amount of money spent in renting the space to hold the inventory, looking after it and paying for insurance. This also includes the **opportunity cost** of investing the money currently tied up in the inventory: this is the amount of money the firm would have earned if the money were invested elsewhere other than in inventory. Calculation of the annual holding cost is based on the average inventory held. From Figure 10.2, the maximum inventory held is $SS + Q$, decreasing gradually to minimum inventory level, SS. Thus the average inventory held is:

$$\text{Average inventory level} = (SS + Q + SS)/2 = SS + Q/2$$

$$\text{And the annual holding cost} = (SS + Q/2)\ H$$

Since D is the annual usage of the item, and each time an order is placed for this item the number of items purchased per order is Q, the number of orders placed over the whole year is D/Q. The annual order processing cost includes the cost of identifying the supplier, preparing a purchase order, chasing it and receiving the item. If S is the order processing cost per order, we can calculate the annual order processing cost:

$$\text{Annual order processing cost} = (D/Q)\ S$$

Adding these three costs the total annual inventory costs associated with this item are calculated below.

$$\text{Total annual cost (TAC)} = \text{Purchase cost} + \text{Holding cost} + \text{Order-processing cost}$$
$$= pAD + (SS + Q/2)\ H + (D/Q)\ S$$

How does the order quantity Q influence the total annual cost? The effect of changing the order quantity from small to large is illustrated in Figure 10.3. With a small order quantity, there is a large number of orders, but smaller average inventory holdings. When order quantity increases, fewer orders are placed, with consequent rise in average inventory holding.

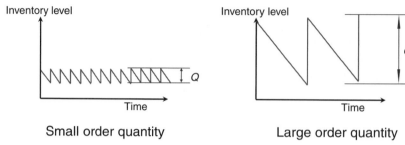

Figure 10.3 Small versus large order quantities

The variation of total annual cost with order quantity is shown in Figure 10.4. To minimise the total annual cost, there is a best order quantity, known as the **economic order quantity**, as depicted in the diagram. This represents a balance between order processing costs and inventory holding costs. With lower order quantities there are too many orders; the order processing costs are high and dominate the total costs. With higher order quantities, the average inventory holding cost is high and dominates the total costs.

The order quantity that minimises the total annual cost is known as the economic order quantity (EOQ) and is given by (see the box below for an explanation as to how the EOQ is derived):

$$EOQ = \sqrt{\frac{2DS}{H}}$$

By ordering in lots of economic order quantity, the total annual cost is the lowest it can be.

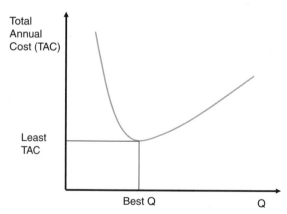

Figure 10.4 Order quantity versus total annual cost

It is straightforward to derive the EOQ formula. Differentiating the expression for TAC and setting to zero for minimisation:

$$\frac{d(TAC)}{dQ} = 0,$$

$$\Rightarrow \frac{d\left(p \times D + \left(SS + \frac{Q}{2}\right)H + \frac{D}{Q}S\right)}{dQ} = 0$$

$$\Rightarrow \frac{H}{2} - \frac{D \times S}{Q^2} = 0$$

Assuming that the purchasing cost is constant (no bulk discounts). We also assume that the safety stock remains fixed as order quantity is changed.

$$\Rightarrow Q = \sqrt{\frac{2DS}{H}}$$

To confirm that this is indeed a minimal-cost order quantity (and not the maximal-cost one), we need to check that the double derivative is positive at this quantity.

Thus, differentiating again,

$$\frac{d^2(TAC)}{dQ^2} = \frac{d\left(\frac{H}{2} - \frac{D \times S}{Q^2}\right)}{dQ} = -(-2)\frac{D \times S}{Q^3} = 2\frac{D \times S}{Q^3}$$

This quantity is always positive for $Q > 0$, and confirms that the EOQ is the order quantity with the least total annual cost.

PROBLEM 10.2

The Fine Garments Company sells fashion clothing. The forecasted annual demand for its premium leather jacket is 1200. The order processing cost per order is $25, and inventory holding cost is $50/item/year. How many leather jackets should it order in one shipment?

Answer:

$$EOQ = \sqrt{\frac{2DS}{H}}$$

$$= \sqrt{\frac{2 \times 1200 \times 25}{50}}$$

$$= 34.64$$

$$\approx 35$$

To minimise its annual inventory costs, Fine Garments should request 35 leather jackets each time it places an order with its supplier.

INVENTORY CONTROL SYSTEMS

Inventory control systems help an inventory manager decide when to order inventory and in what quantity. Inventory control systems may be set up on the basis of the economic order quantity, discussed above. There are two basic systems used in practice. These are explained below.

The reorder point inventory control system

In this system, inventory levels are continuously monitored, and orders are issued when the inventory is depleted to a predetermined level, called the reorder point (*ROP*), as shown in Figure 10.2. The order quantity is calculated on the basis of the EOQ formula, as given above.

The reorder point is set as follows. When an order is issued at the reorder point, it is gradually depleted to the safety stock (*SS*) level over the lead time *L* (see Figure 10.2). The use of inventory over the lead time *L* is $D \times L$, since the annual demand is *D*. Thus the reorder point is given by

$$ROP = D \times L + SS$$

PROBLEM 10.3

The Fine Garments Company (in Problem 10.2) wants to use a reorder point system. It has the order quantity set at 35, calculated as above. To allow for uncertainties in delivery and in customer demand, it wishes to hold 4 weeks of demand as safety stock. What should its reorder point be if the delivery lead time is 2 weeks?

Answer:
Safety stock to cover 4 weeks of demand = $1200 \times (4/52) = 92$, since 1200 is the annual demand.

$ROP = D \times L + SS = 1200 \times (2/52) + 92 = 138$

Fine Garments should reorder whenever its inventory drops below 138.

The periodic inventory control system

In this system, orders are reviewed periodically (not continuously as in the reorder point system), after the passage of a fixed time period (*T*). See Figure 10.5. At each review time, the current inventory level (*I*) is determined, and enough inventory is ordered to bring the inventory level to a target maximum level (*M*).

Often firms may decide on a weekly or a fortnightly ordering cycle, but in the absence of such a policy, the time period *T* may be calculated on the basis of the *EOQ*. If orders are

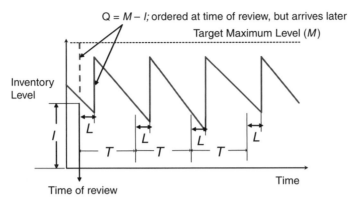

Figure 10.5   Periodic system

made in quantities of *EOQ*, each order will cover a period of *EOQ/D*. This time period may be used as the fixed time period.

$$T = EOQ/D$$

In Figure 10.5, current inventory level at the time of review is *I*; the inventory ordered now will arrive after lead time *L*, and the next order after that will arrive after a further lapse of the review period *T*. There is no inventory arrival for an elapsed period of *T + L*; thus the order at the time of review needs to cover inventory demand over the lead time (*L*) and over the next time period (*T*). The inventory should also allow for the safety stock *SS*. Thus the target maximum level is given by the following expression.

$$M = D\,(L + T) + SS$$

However, some of this requirement will be met by the current inventory level (*I*). Thus the order quantity is given by:

$$Q = M - I$$

NB: In the above formulae for *M*, demand *D* is annual demand, so *L* and *T* should also be measured in time units of years.

The reorder point system allows closer control of inventory than the periodic system, the latter only reviewing inventory at specific periodic intervals. The reorder point system is thus preferred for high-value inventory items in particular. The periodic system may be used for other inventory items because of its convenience.

PROBLEM 10.4

Design a periodic inventory control system for the Fine Garments Company (Problems 10.2 and 10.3) if it wishes to hold 5 weeks of demand as safety stock. If on a day of review, the inventory of the premium leather jacket is 102, how many leather jackets should be ordered?

Answer:

Fixed time period, *T* is given by

$$T = EOQ/D = 35/1200 = 0.029167 \text{ year} = 0.029167 \times 365 \text{ days} = 11 \text{ days}$$

The target maximum level, $M = D (L + T) + SS$

$$= 1200 \times (2/52 + 11/365) + 1200 \times (5/52)$$

$$= 198$$

A periodic review system for the Fine Garments Company should have a review period of 11 days, ordering enough inventories at the time of review to bring inventory to a maximum level of 198 leather jackets.

The order quantity for the given inventory level is, $Q = M - I = 198 - 102 = 96$. Ninety-six leather jackets should be ordered if there are 102 on hand.

Safety stock

In the discussion above, the inventory control systems allow for a safety stock, *SS*. This is the amount of inventory stocked by the system in case of unforeseen events arising. There are many events that could occur and disrupt the careful inventory planning. For example, consider late deliveries. Without safety stock, if the delivery takes longer than the average lead time *L*, some inventory demand may not be met, possibly causing serious disruptions. Consider again what happens if the inventory use is higher than that forecast; without safety stock, customer service will suffer. Other reasons for maintaining safety stock include providing a safeguard against issues such as poor quality, production problems and transportation problems. Safety stock is thus sometimes referred to as **buffer stock**.

The root reason for safety stock could be described as variation – variation of demand, variation of lead time, variation of production, etc. If there was no variation, firms would not need safety stock. Safety stock needs to be held in proportion to such variations.

Safety stock is not free! Note in the discussion above that the cost of holding safety stock is included in the total annual cost. This part of the cost is: $SS \times H$.

SUPPLY CHAIN INVENTORY MANAGEMENT

Figure 10.1 showed inventory locations across a supply chain. In a non-integrated supply chain, inventory managers in each firm along the supply chain manage their own inventory. Each location will hold its own safety stock. Consider first the inventory of the finished product from manufacturer down to the retailer (the distribution side of the supply chain).

Inventory centralisation

Manufacturers, distributors and retailers have all their own demand variations to consider. This means holding safety stock, in proportion to the variations, at each location. What if all the inventory could be centralised, say at the manufacturer's location? The manufacturer will need to consider the total demand, but the variation of the total demand will be less than the total variation of the demand considered separately. Thus less safety stock will be needed.

The first three graphs in Figure 10.6 show demand fluctuations at three distribution centres (DCs). Safety stock is maintained in each DC, in proportion to the amount of variation of demand. The bottom graph in Figure 10.6 presents an alternative scenario, where all the demand is supplied from one central location. The demand at the central location is a

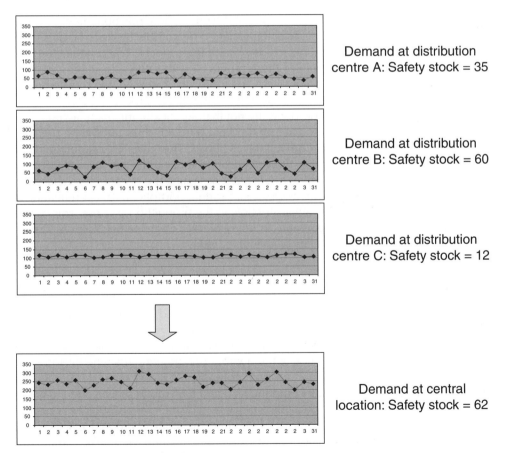

Figure 10.6 Inventory centralisation

combination of the demand at the three DCs; however, the variation of the total demand is less than the sum of variations at the three DCs. Hence the safety stock needed is less than the safety stock required for multiple locations.

With integrated supply chains, the central location could be anywhere, inventory may even be distributed at different centres (and still inventory would be saved), so long as all locations have access to inventory information and the transfers between locations can be quick. This concept is called *replacing inventory by information.*

The concept of inventory reduction by centralisation is sometimes stated as the 'square root rule'; this is an approximation and states that the inventory buffer needed is proportional to the square root of the number of locations. Thus in the above instance, the inventory buffer at the central location would be in the ratio ($\sqrt{1}:\sqrt{3} = 0.58$) of the combined buffer at the three locations, a saving of *approximately* 42%.

Delayed product differentiation

(This inventory reduction strategy makes use of the principle of postponement discussed in Chapter 4.) Another instance of reducing variation by combining demand at different points is the case of a manufacturer making multiple products. The manufacturer will need to manage inventories of each of these products, with safety stocks for each product. Now consider if each of these products has a precursor: some intermediate product from which all the (different) final products are made. If the processing steps from the intermediate product to the final products are not that significant, the manufacturer could stock the intermediate product in place of the final product, thus combining the safety stock required and gaining similar advantage as above. This gives the manufacturer the flexibility of meeting the demand of the final products, using the intermediate product, as the demand occurs. Many manufacturers are redesigning their products so that earlier stages of the products are the same across their product portfolio, and differentiating the product into distinct products as late as possible in the production process. This delayed product differentiation has the potential to not only save on inventory holding, but also gives greater flexibility and simplicity to manufacturing.

Part commonality

The concept of part commonality is similar to that of delayed product differentiation discussed above. Delayed product differentiation would use the same parts and processes in all earlier stages of manufacture, differentiating products as late as possible. However, part commonality attempts simply to reduce the number of different parts wherever possible. Figure 10.7 shows product A as built up from components B and C, while product X as made from components Y and Z. If components B and Y are quite similar, and the designers could substitute both B and Y by a third component D, then the manufacturer needs to hold a combined inventory of D in place of separate inventories for B and Y. This is often possible to do in manufacturing since engineered products often use similar components, such as simple nuts and bolts, or even complex components such as fuel injectors.

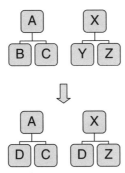

Figure 10.7   Using common parts across products

Transit inventory

When inventory moves across a supply chain, it is in transit. Regardless of whether the upstream or the downstream stage of the supply chain owns this inventory, holding costs are incurred and this cost is a cost to the supply chain. What is the magnitude of this cost? Using the same symbols as above, Q is the order quantity or the quantity that is transferred in one consignment, L is the delivery lead time or the duration when the order is in transit, and H is the inventory holding cost per item per year.

Holding cost for one order $= Q \times L \times H$, since it is held only for period L

Number of orders in a year $= D/Q$

Annual transit inventory cost $= Q \times L \times H \times (D/Q) = D \times L \times H$

The above relationship clearly demonstrates a reason to reduce lead time wherever possible, since it directly affects cost. Often in making transport mode choice decisions, a cheaper mode of transport may be chosen to lower the cost of transportation, but the cheaper mode is slower, resulting in higher transit time and thus higher transit inventory costs. Transit inventory exists in each part of the supply chain pipeline where inventory is in transit, such as from the supplier to the manufacturer and from the manufacturer to the distributor, as shown in Figure 10.1.

IN-TRANSIT INVENTORY

A key strategy of most organisations is to reduce the amount of inventory that they hold. In many instances warehouses are eliminated altogether. One consequence of this is that sometimes companies use transport as a 'mobile warehouse'. The mode of transport that they use may depend on how fast they want to get product to market. One industry professional describes this as the 'gearbox' approach to inventory management: speeding up and slowing down the flow of inventory through the supply chain by using alternative transport modes. In-transit inventory is thus an important category of inventory, and one which can sometimes account for large volumes of inventory.

PROBLEM 10.5

The Fine Garments Company (Problems 10.2, 10.3 and 10.4) has opted for the reorder point system, and it has two options for transportation: by truck and by rail. Truck transportation takes 1 week, while rail transportation takes 2 weeks of lead time. Truck transportation costs $2 per leather jacket, while by rail the transportation cost is $1 per leather jacket. It is the policy of Fine Garments to hold enough inventories to cover demand for twice the lead time. Which transportation option costs less? What is the reorder point for each option?

This decision is impacted only by the safety stock needed, transportation cost and the transit inventory cost, all other costs remaining equal.

Truck option:

Safety stock $= SS = 1200 \times (2 \times 1/52) = 46$ leather jackets

Annual cost of holding the safety stock $= SS \times H = 46 \times 50 = \$2300.00$

Annual cost of transportation $= 1200 \times 2 = \$2400.00$ (all the annual demand is transported).

Annual transit inventory cost $= D \times L \times H = 1200 \times (1/52) \times 50 = \$1153.85$

Total of the above costs $= \$5853.85$

The reorder point, $ROP = D \times L + SS = 1200 \times (1/52) + 46 = 69$

Rail option:

Safety stock $= SS = 1200 \times (2 \times 2/52) = 92$ leather jackets

Annual cost of holding the safety stock $= SS \times H = 92 \times 50 = \$4600.00$

Annual cost of transportation $= 1200 \times 1 = \$1200.00$

Annual transit inventory cost $= D \times L \times H = 1200 \times (2/52) \times 50 = \$2307.69$

Total of the above costs $= \$8107.69$

The reorder point, $ROP = D \times L + SS = 1200 \times (2/52) + 92 = 138$

The truck option is cheaper by quite a margin; even though its transportation cost alone is double that of the rail transportation.

Note that in this problem we only considered costs associated with safety stock and transport, all other costs remaining equal. Introducing other costs (for example cost implications of the reliability and security of alternative transport modes) leads us into the concept of generalised costs of transport considered in Chapter 8.

MATCHING INVENTORY POLICY WITH INVENTORY TYPE

ABC analysis

This is derived from the 'Pareto' or '80/20' rule first elaborated by the Italian economist Vilfredo Pareto in 1897. Most firms have far too many inventory items (i.e. stock-keeping units or SKUs) to manage. They often use a tool called **ABC analysis** to separate out the most important items so that more attention can be focused on those items. ABC analysis is based on the principle that out of the myriad items an inventory manager needs to handle, there are only a few that account for most of the inventory expenses. To carry out this analysis the expenses incurred annually for each individual item are collected and the items are listed in the order from the highest expense to the lowest expense. An example is presented in Table 10.2.

This is only an illustrative example! An actual table is likely to have thousands of items in practice. It can be seen that the top two items (# 373 and # 539) account for just over 65% of the expense. So from an inventory management perspective it is sensible to lavish more attention on these items. The items in the table may thus be divided into three classes (see Figure 10.8): the count of items in the 'A' class constituting only 20% of the count, but accounting for 65% of the expense; 'B' class has the next 30% of the count; and 'C' class includes the rest of the items. There is no suggestion that these percentage figures must be exactly followed – the idea is to use a classification scheme so that a few important items are given more attention than the more numerous but less important items.

ABC analysis is a focusing tool, permitting attention to be focused on the most important inventory items. For instance, different inventory control systems may be used for the different classifications: 'A' items may be controlled closely, using the reorder point system; the less demanding periodic system may be used for 'B' items; and 'C' items may be blanket purchased once or twice in a year.

Table 10.2   Expenditure on inventory items

Item	Annual Expenses	Percentage of Total	Classifications
373	46335	45.77%	A
539	19611	19.37%	A
455	8007	7.91%	B
769	6181	6.11%	B
441	5526	5.46%	B
65	5503	5.44%	B
205	3278	3.24%	C
401	3063	3.03%	C
352	2845	2.81%	C
543	603	0.60%	C
454	179	0.18%	C
432	111	0.11%	C
Total	101242	100.00%	

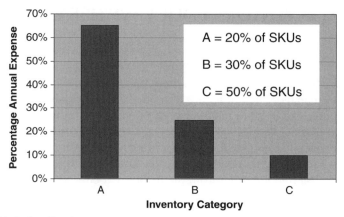

Figure 10.8 ABC classification

The ABC analysis illustrated above uses the criterion of item expense, the amount of money spent on an item (or SKU) per year; but an ABC analysis can be done with a different criterion as the need dictates. Thus a retailer may use the criterion of total sales per year. Other criteria used for ABC analysis include frequency of order picking (examining which items are picked more often than others) and frequency of customer complaints received on product items.

Inventory flow types

Gattorna and Walters[1] argue that inventory can be categorised into three flow types as illustrated in Figure 10.9. The core business products are stable and constitute the base flow inventory. The wave flow inventory is more unstable and is typified by seasonal or fashion type products. The fad products have extremely variable demand and therefore the inventory is very spiky as illustrated in the diagram (surge flow inventory).

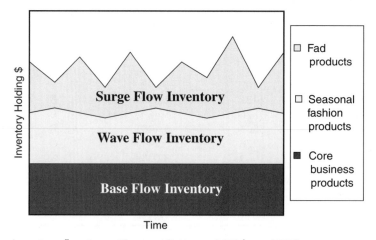

Figure 10.9 Inventory flow types (Source: Gattorna & Walters, 1996)

Table 10.3   Stockholding policies for alternative inventory flow types

Type	Characteristics	Stockholding policy
Base flow	Predictable high flow rates	Minimum stocks. Direct deliveries from suppliers
Wave flow	Slow moving flow rates. High criticality. Perishable. Peaks are relatively predictable	Minimise stockholding, building them during peak demand period. Direct delivery from supplier where possible
Surge flow (1)	High criticality. Low value. Long lead time. Small physical size	Hold high level of stock thereby allowing safety stock delivery lead time and demand fluctuations
Surge flow (2)	Low criticality. High value. Bulky physical characteristics. Peaks are relatively predictable	Minimise stockholding, building them only during peak demand period. Direct delivery from supplier where possible

The management approach for each of these inventory types needs to be tailored to the product and market characteristics. Gattorna and Walters go on to explain the most appropriate match between inventory policy and flow type as summarised in Table 10.3. Given the stability of the base flow, minimal inventory is required to maintain high service levels. Conversely the wave flow inventory is perishable and slower moving, therefore a more responsive approach is suggested where inventory is built during times of high demand. The surge flow has been further divided into two sub-categories in Table 10.3. Type 1 items have long replenishment lead times and are highly critical (e.g. maintenance parts); hence high inventory levels are required to make sure there are minimal stock-outs. The type 2 surge flow inventory is not so critical but costs more to purchase and hold. As a result it is better to minimise inventory levels and ideally to persuade suppliers to deliver directly when required.

INVENTORY REDUCTION PRINCIPLES

It has been mentioned before that reduction of inventory holding is a primary goal in supply chain management. This reduction, however, needs to be consistent with the strategic goals of customer service. Drawing from the above discussions, we outline the following principles for inventory reduction.

Pool inventory

Wherever demand for inventory can be combined, the safety stock can be lowered, while still providing the same service level. This is the case in inventory centralisation where demand from different locations is combined, or in delayed product differentiation where demand for different products is combined, or by using common components where demands for different components are combined. Inventory pooling has the added bonus of reduced inventory management.

Reduce variation

Recall that the reason for holding safety stock is variation. Variation of lead time, variation of demand, variation of supply, variation of quality, all contribute to safety stock. Wherever variation can be reduced, safety stock can be reduced too. Ironing out the wrinkles in a supply chain so that it delivers reliably the right quantity at the right time will cause safety stock holding to be reduced. A similar effect can be seen if quality is improved. With variable quality, more inventories are needed in case the inventory turns out to be defective.

Reduce lead time

Lead time directly affects inventory held. For example, the reorder point formula shows that the ROP can be reduced if the lead time can be reduced. Likewise transit inventory costs can be reduced by reducing the lead time. Consider the accuracy of the forecast of demand. It is well known that the farther into the future we forecast, the less accurate our forecast is. When the lead time is long, we need to forecast more into the future, thus the accuracy of the forecast suffers, increasing the variability of demand and consequently requiring higher safety stock.

Just-in-time inventory system (JIT)

JIT is as much a philosophy as it is a technique.[2] It was popularised by the automobile industry and largely credited with propelling Toyota[3] to the top of the automotive industry in the world. JIT has many components and principles, but at the core of JIT is the idea of making do with the minimum possible level of inventory holding. The core concepts of inventory reduction in JIT are:

- *Inventory hides problems.* Inventory holding is needed because of variation of all kinds, as pointed out above. Equipment failures, production of bad quality, all of these problems cause variations in manufacturing, and inventory is needed to cover (i.e. to *hide!*) them. JIT tackles these problems directly and goes to the root of why inventory needs to be held; by purposely removing inventory holdings, the problems the inventory was covering are surfaced, and the problems are then proactively fixed.

- *Small lot production.* The advantage of ordering in small quantities, which in turn keeps the average inventory level small, was seen above. What is the difficulty in achieving this? The problems are too many orders and the associated order processing costs. JIT seeks to reduce order processing costs so that the ideal of small quantity ordering can be accomplished. For example suppliers are located close by and the ordering protocol is simplified. In manufacturing, order processing involves setting up or reconfiguring manufacturing tools and machines. As each order arrives the machines have to be set up (or changed over) for the order. The time and effort spent in setups are the manufacturing equivalent of order processing costs. Thus manufacturing in small quantities is hindered by excessive numbers of setups and the time spent in setups. JIT seeks to facilitate small lot production by actively improving the setup process so that the time and effort in setups are reduced drastically.

LEARNING REVIEW

In this chapter we discussed the important topic of inventory management in the supply chain. Inventory is one of the most important flows in the supply chain, and how it is managed can significantly impact firm success. We saw that inventory can be found at multiple points in the supply chain, and that by measuring inventory turnover we can ascertain a measure of how effectively an organisation manages its inventory. In many instances inventory is used to buffer against uncertainty, and furthermore it can hide problems. Later in the chapter we reviewed the just-in-time inventory management approach, one of the objectives of which is to minimise inventory holding, thus highlighting any problems which need to be solved.

Trade-offs are often a feature of logistics systems, especially in the case of inventory management. We looked in detail at the EOQ model which seeks to balance two important sets of costs associated with inventory: the costs associated with ordering and receiving freight and the costs associated with actually holding the freight. Organisations also need to know when to reorder, and we looked at the two principal approaches in this regard: reordering when inventory drops to a certain level and reordering at fixed time intervals. We also looked at strategies to manage and reduce where possible inventory volumes in the supply chain, such as through centralisation, delayed product differentiation, part commonality and reduction of in-transit inventory.

Matching inventory policy with inventory type is another key concern of inventory management, and we looked at two main approaches here, namely ABC analysis and analysis of inventory flow types. We concluded the chapter by identifying four key principles that organisations can pursue to effectively manage and reduce inventory holding: pooling, reduction of variation, reduction of lead time, and following JIT principles. No matter how essential inventory is, costs are accrued by inventory holding, and supply chains and firms need to reduce such costs while keeping customer service at a satisfactory level.

QUESTIONS

- Explain how a reduction in lead time can help a supply chain reduce its inventory buffer without hurting customer service.
- Why is Amazon.com able to provide a large variety of books and music with less safety inventory than a similar bookstore chain selling through retail stores?
- Discuss the concept of replacing inventory by information.
- Why should a customer be concerned about transit inventory cost if he pays for the inventory only when the merchandise arrives at his premises?

PROBLEM

Daily demand for a product is 100 units. Design a reorder point inventory system for this product if the cost of holding the inventory is $2 per item per year, and the setup costs to manufacture this product are estimated to be $20 per setup. The replenishment lead time averages 6 days. It is desired to hold a safety stock covering twice the lead time.

Answer:
$D = 100 \times 365$ (per year)
$L = 6/365$ (year)
$H = 2$ \$/item/year
$S = 20$ \$/setup

$$EOQ = \sqrt{\frac{2DS}{H}}$$

$$= \sqrt{\frac{2 \times 100 \times 365 \times 20}{2}}$$

$$= 854.04$$

$$\approx 854$$

$SS = (100 \times 365) \times (6/365) \times 2 = 1200$
$ROP = D \times L + SS = (100 \times 365) \times (6/365) + 1200$
$\quad = 1800$

The reorder point system should have 1800 as the reorder point, and 854 units as order quantity.

PROBLEM

The annual demand for a product on periodic inventory system is 50 000 units; the replenishment lead time is 9 days. The review period has been established as 16 days. The inventory manager wants to hold enough safety stock to cover 15 days of demand. During a particular review, the on-hand inventory was 1000 units. How many units should be ordered?

Answer:
$D = 50 000$
$L = 9/365$
$T = 16/365$
$I = 1000$
$SS = 50 000 \times (15/365) = 2054.79 \approx 2055$. This is 15 days' worth of demand.
$M = D(L + T) + SS$
$\quad = 50 000 \times (9/365 + 16/365) + 2055)$
$\quad = 5479.66 \approx 5480$
$Q = M - I = 5480 - 1000 = 4480$

The inventory manager should order 4480 units now.

NOTES

1. Gattorna, J.L. & Walters, D.W. (1996) *Managing the Supply Chain*, Chapter 8, Macmillan, London.
2. Christopher, M. (2005) *Logistics and Supply Chain Management*, 3rd Edition. FT/Prentice Hall, London.
3. Petersen, P.B. (2002) The misplaced origin of just-in-time production methods, *Management Decision*, 40(1/2), 82–88.

FURTHER READING

Fisher, M.L., Raman, A. & McClelland, A.S. (2000) Rocket science retailing is almost here: are you ready? *Harvard Business Review*, 78(4), 115–124.

Lee, H.L. & Billington, C. (1992) Managing supply chain inventory: pitfalls and opportunities, *Sloan Management Review*, 33(3), 65–73.

Suzuki, Y. (2004) Structure of the Japanese production system: elusiveness and reality, *Asian Business and Management*, 3, 201–219.

Waters, D. (2003) *Logistics – An Introduction to Supply Chain Management*, Chapter 10, Palgrave Macmillan, New York.

11 Warehousing and Materials Handling

with Peter Baker
Cranfield School of Management

LEARNING OBJECTIVES

- Define the role of warehousing in contemporary global supply chains.
- Explain how material movements are planned and controlled.
- Explain materials handling processes within warehouses and distribution centres.
- Offer insights into how warehouses are managed and how work is organised.

INTRODUCTION

Chapter 10 introduced the theory and practice of inventory management. This chapter now focuses on the logistics operations that store those inventories. As well as needing to know how much inventory we have in our global supply chains, we also need to know how and where to store it. In this chapter, we will also discuss the processes, technologies and people employed in warehousing and materials handling.

Chapter 11 comprises five core sections:

- Warehousing in global supply chains
- Warehouse layout and design
- Warehouse management systems
- Materials handling and storage
- Work organisation and job design

WAREHOUSING IN GLOBAL SUPPLY CHAINS

Global supply chains commonly require multiple echelons, spread across various international locations (Figure 11.1). As well as extended in-transit inventory travelling

---

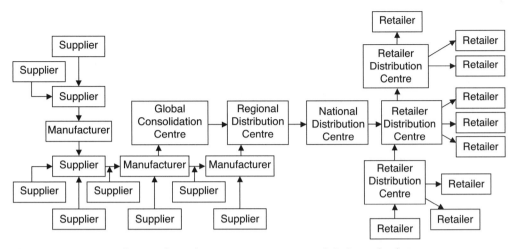

Figure 11.1   A typical map of warehousing operations in a global supply chain

between disparate locations, supply chains also have inventory stored at multiple stages in various states of manufacture or assembly. Hence warehousing and materials handling systems have become highly sophisticated to maintain the flow of freight to the end customer. At each echelon, different types of warehouse perform different functions.

Many different networks of warehouses are possible ranging from a single global distribution centre to multiple depots within a single country. These are often combined as in Figure 11.1 with, for example, manufacturers having networks that feed goods into retailer networks. It is often best to have a single inventory holding level within a supply chain, which can provide sufficient buffer stock to decouple lean production (normally based on forecasts) from an agile supply chain that serves volatile markets (based on specific customer orders). In some situations, this inventory holding level may be at a global distribution centre level (e.g. for high-value, low-volume goods, such as silicon chips) or at the local level (e.g. for low-value, high-volume goods that may be required on very short lead times, such as photocopy paper). Being able to achieve inventory holding at a single level often requires close collaboration between all parties in the supply chain involving open and rapid exchange of information.

As discussed in Chapter 10, inventory holding is a cost we would rather not have. A supply chain not only incurs the cost of the inventory itself, but also the fixed asset costs of warehouses and plant such as racks and forklifts, and the associated costs of labour and administration. Hence, the conventional view of warehousing is of it being a costly necessity of an inefficient supply chain. Whilst it is true that we must seek to minimise inventory holding and handling, the paradox is that contemporary supply chains require inventory staging posts more than ever before. Material storage and handling systems therefore have two key objectives: to minimise cost *and* to add value. That is to say that if warehouses and distribution centres are essential to global supply chains, they should complement other supply chain activities to ensure effective and efficient delivery of freight to the end customer.

Value-adding activities are those supply chain activities that enhance products to increase the customer's perceptions of those products' benefits.[1] Customer value can be added to a product by improving its quality during storage (e.g. maturing whiskey, wine, cheese or cured meats), by improving the service associated with it (e.g. delivery information availability or specialist packaging), by reducing its costs (e.g. reduced packaging or reduced administration costs) and/or by reducing its lead time (e.g. cross docking – this will be explained later). Warehousing operations can achieve each of these objectives in various ways, such as:

- Creating bulk consignments
- Breaking bulk consignments
- Combining freight
- Smoothing supply to meet demand

These material related value-adding activities are illustrated in Figure 11.2. Furthermore, warehousing plays an increasingly important role in manufacturing and logistics post-ponement (as discussed in Chapter 4). With the recognised benefits of postponing final assembly and combining freight and/or packaging, downstream distribution centres today offer much more than just storage and handling. Hence such facilities include assembly and packaging processes to ensure that order fulfilment can occur as close to the end customer as possible, postponing stock handling until the order is confirmed. In this way, the number of product lines that needs to be held only comprises those of the base components rather than all the varieties of the final goods that could be demanded. This postponement concept can therefore be used to reduce inventory significantly, where appropriate.

Increasingly, global supply chains are as concerned with information flows as they are with material flows. Hence information-related value-adding activities such as product tracking and cycle counting are also essential warehousing functions that improve supply chain performance.

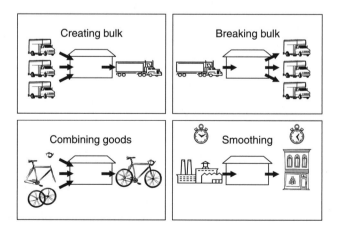

Figure 11.2   Using warehouses to add value (Source: Jessop & Morrison, 1994)[2]

This chapter will continue by explaining how modern warehouse operations are designed to not only maintain the flow of freight, but also enhance its perceived value.

> Warehouses should aim to provide value-adding services as well as minimising operating costs.

WAREHOUSE LAYOUT AND DESIGN

All activities within a warehouse can be associated with one of the four functions illustrated in Figure 11.3.

Warehouse layouts should be primarily designed to optimise the flow of freight through these four functions. However, warehouse designers should also aim to achieve optimal output, reduced costs, excellent customer service and sound working conditions.[3] At the freight receiving area, core activities include unloading, unpacking, quality control inspection and recording the receipt of freight. From here freight will follow one of two possible routes; either to 'put away' or directly to freight dispatch. This second option is referred to as 'cross-docking', which is discussed below. At 'put-away', freight is moved to a reserve storage location, either manually or via materials handling equipment (also discussed later).

When required, goods are moved from reserve storage locations to pick locations. This activity is known as replenishment, as this movement is normally triggered by the quantity at the pick locations falling below a predetermined level and therefore needing to be replenished. When orders from customers are received, a 'pick list' is created and items are 'picked' from the pick locations and 'packed' ready for 'dispatch'. During these two processes freight will be either broken down from a bulk consignment, grouped into a bulk consignment, combined with other freight, or simply held until required; thereby meeting one of the four objectives in Figure 11.3. At dispatch, freight and associated information are inspected against the original order and moved to the shipping area.

No matter what the scale of a warehouse is or its role in the supply chain, the four core functions in Figure 11.3 will be necessary. This may involve a number of processes.

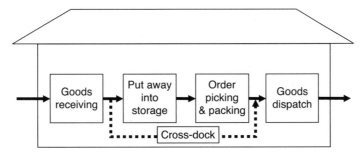

Figure 11.3   Generic warehouse functions

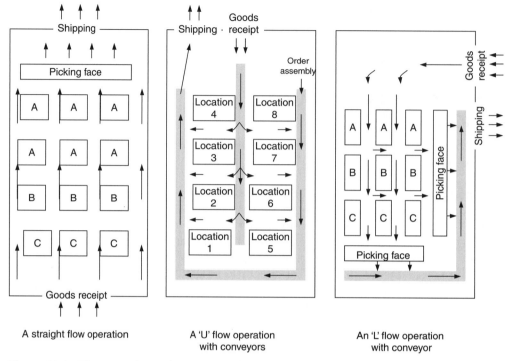

Figure 11.4 Three warehouse layout examples (Source: Warman, 1971)[4]

These processes must be designed to suit the freight and materials being handled and stored, and to minimise movements and handling. This can be achieved by minimising the distance that freight travels through the warehouse and/or through automated handling systems such as cranes, conveyors or **AGVs** (automated guided vehicles). In doing so, processes are standardised to reduce human error and therefore maintain the quality of the freight. Figure 11.4 illustrates three common warehouse layouts designed to reduce freight movement and handling.

(Note that boxes in Figure 11.4 labelled A, B or C refer to common classifications, where freight classified A is frequently ordered, B less so, and C is rarely ordered.)

Cross-docking bypasses the storage areas in warehouses and distribution centres. Storage should be avoided unless the freight requires one of the four value-adding activities in Figure 11.2, otherwise storage is costly and non-value adding. 'Creating bulk' and 'breaking bulk' are normally associated with transport economies, while 'combining goods' is part of the production postponement principle. 'Smoothing' is associated with holding buffer stock to decouple lean production from the agile supply of goods to the market. As mentioned earlier, this is often at a single inventory holding level and goods are frequently cross-docked rapidly through the supply chain down to this level and then cross-docked again after that level through to the final customer. Cross-docking reduces cost and improves customer service by accelerating the processing of freight requiring reshipment. In bypassing put away, storage, picking and packing, the associated costs and non-value-adding functions are eliminated to enhance customer service. Cross-docking is typically employed for fast-moving freight with constant demand that spends less than 24 hours on site.[5] This function is therefore a key enabler of quick response logistics as it will maintain the flow of freight and reduce lead time.

Besides the primary focus on freight flowing down the supply chain, contemporary logistics operations must also manage the reverse movement of freight in the form of defects and customer returns. The impact on warehousing is the requirement for additional processes to inspect, redirect and/or re-store such freight. Furthermore, concerns about the environmental impact of freight are driving legislation such as the European Union's Waste Electrical and Electronic Equipment (WEEE) Directive to require producers to reduce, reuse and recycle. Such developments lead to increased interest in reverse logistics. Clearly, in global supply networks, warehouses and distribution centres play an important role in managing the upstream movement of freight that has reached the end of its usable life. Whilst distribution centres located downstream will store or redirect end-of-life freight, reverse logistics warehouses may employ processes to disassemble freight, and reuse or recycle their components. Refer to Chapter 17 for a detailed discussion of reverse logistics.

AG BARR

Based in Cumbernauld, Scotland, AG Barr is a market-leading soft drinks producer and distributor. In Scotland, AG Barr's *Irn Bru* drinks outsell both *Coca-Cola* and *Pepsi*. To some extent, this can be attributed to Barr's traditional distribution network in which delivery drivers 'hawk' their wares to small retailers along well-established routes. This traditional approach to sales offers the flexibility required by small retailers due to unpredictable demand fluctuations. For example, an unseasonably hot day in March may cause an unexpected stock-out of a particular soft drink at the retailer. Drivers build up extensive knowledge of their customers and stock their trucks accordingly. However, this unpredictability does cause drivers to return to the distribution centre with approximately 26% of the freight they went out with each day. Meanwhile, AG Barr also services larger customers including wholesalers and major supermarkets. AG Barr has therefore designed its distribution centre to manage the large volume orders from large retailers, high variety orders from small retailers, and returned freight.

The Cumbernauld distribution centre holds 350 product lines, of which there are 6500 stock-keeping units (SKUs). Inventory is transported from the adjacent production plant on pallets via automated conveyors direct to an 11-storey automated high-bay storage system coordinated by a warehouse management system (WMS). A total of 32 million cases of soft drinks are shipped per year. Orders are input into the WMS and SKUs are automatically picked from the storage system and conveyed to truck loading bays. Whilst some retailers require palletised freight, others prefer wheeled totes. Totes enable retailers to wheel large batches of freight direct to the aisles in their stores. However, this creates an additional task at the distribution centre, where batches are moved from pallets onto totes and repackaged before being loaded onto trucks. Meanwhile, freight returned after a day's trading must be restocked. These items do not return to the automated storage system. Instead they are manually sorted and stored on conventional racks ready for manual repicking at a later date. Soft drinks have a shelf life, and this therefore creates a further complication in terms of stock rotation.

Hence AG Barr not only benefits from the effectiveness and efficiency of automated handling of its high-volume products, but also gains from the flexibility offered by its more conventional storage and handling methods. An important consideration in warehouse and distribution centre design is to be *fit for purpose*. The high-tech solutions are not always the most suitable solutions.

WAREHOUSE MANAGEMENT SYSTEMS

A management information system such as an enterprise resource planning (ERP) system (discussed in Chapter 12) defines the material requirements that are transmitted to the warehouse or distribution centre for a **warehouse management system** (WMS) to manage the information processes within the warehouse. As alluded to previously, product proliferation in the supply chain creates complexity in the warehouse. A warehouse system manages this complexity to trigger the right work at the right time across the operation to meet demand, as illustrated in Figure 11.5.

Information may be manually or automatically uploaded and downloaded to and from a WMS. Yet, increasingly, electronic data capture is proving to be more effective and efficient than conventional paper-based systems, particularly at the shop floor. Warehouse operatives undertaking selected information tasks in Figure 11.5 are, today, most likely to use handheld RF (radio frequency) or bar code readers, desktop and laptop computers, smartphones and tablets, label printers and pick-to-voice technologies. Each of these technologies aims to minimise human effort to reduce the time taken, errors and costs in information handling. Furthermore, processes are standardised to improve accuracy and repeatability. Meanwhile some information tasks may be fully automated within the WMS by integrating radio frequency identification (RFID) technologies. Table 11.1 lists particular technologies for selected information tasks.

Chapter 12 will discuss in more detail the role and application of information technology in the supply chain.

MATERIALS HANDLING AND STORAGE

The automation of shop-floor information tasks is a relatively recent development in warehousing, but materials handling mechanisation and automation are well established. Cranes, forklifts, reach trucks, pallet trucks, AGVs and conveyors are widely used to minimise human effort and intervention. The term **MHE – materials handling equipment –** is commonly used to describe the various types of equipment for handling freight. As in automated information tasks, automated materials handling improves and standardises

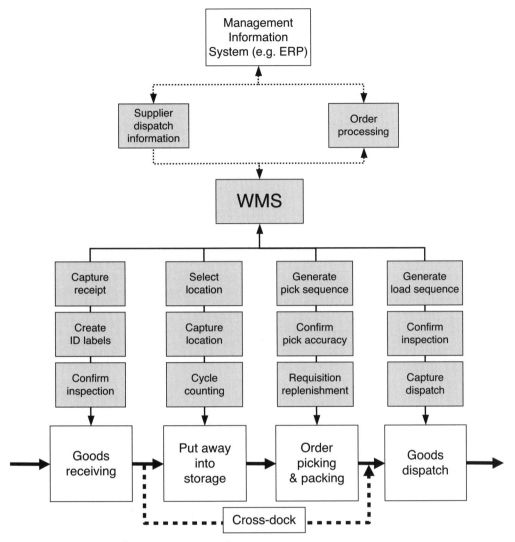

Figure 11.5 WMS information inputs and outputs

warehouse performance by minimising human intervention. A further consequence is the optimisation of warehouse space. By employing mechanical and automated handling technologies, floor space between storage locations can be minimised and the locations themselves are able to occupy multiple levels, as in the AG Barr case. AG Barr's 11-storey automated high-bay storage system is serviced via automated cranes and conveyors and requires no manual intervention other than for maintenance.

Storage solutions vary depending on the volume, variety and throughput of freight in a warehouse or distribution centre. One or more of a variety of storage and picking systems may be used.

Table 11.1   WMS data capture and transmission technologies

WMS information task	Technology used
Capture receipt	Read bar code or RFID tag (via handheld or fully automated)
Create identification labels	Print bar code label or RFID tag (via PC/handheld or fully automated) (if required)
Confirm inspection	Read bar code or RFID tag (via PC/handheld)
Select location	Normally determined by WMS
Capture location	Read bar code or RFID tag (via handheld or fully automated)
Cycle counting	Assistance provided by WMS
Generate pick sequence	Determined by WMS
Confirm pick accuracy	Read bar code, RFID tag or verbal confirm (via handheld, fully automated or pick-to-voice)
Requisition replenishment	Determined by WMS
Generate load sequence	Determined by WMS/TMS (transport management system)
Confirm inspection	Read bar code, RFID tag or verbal confirm (via handheld, fully automated or pick-to-voice)
Capture dispatch	Read bar code, RFID tag or verbal confirm (via handheld, fully automated or pick-to-voice)

Pallet storage

In the case of palletised storage, the alternatives may be classified into 'dense' storage systems and 'individual access' systems. The former are suitable where there are many pallets of a product line and where it is acceptable for any of these to be accessed. On the other hand, 'individual access' systems are suitable where there are few (i.e. one, two or three pallets per product line) or where it is important for an individual pallet to be accessed (e.g. as in the case of a master whisky blender requiring a particular cask to incorporate into blended whisky).

The simplest and cheapest form of 'dense' storage is block stacking, where boxed and palletised freight is stacked in blocks on the floor. This enables excellent use of floor space (i.e. high-density stacking), but has height restrictions based on the weight of the freight (i.e. load crushing may occur if stacked too high).

Drive-in racking offers a basic frame to support block stacking. The racking framework has horizontal flanges on which pallets can be positioned by a forklift truck. This solution prevents load crushing because palletised loads are not stacked directly on top of each other. It also enables high-density storage by enabling forklifts to drive through empty racking, putting away freight in columns.

Pushback racking also offers high-density storage by storing palletised freight in rows on each rack (normally up to about four pallets deep). Whilst being effective in storing multiple pallets, their accessibility is limited. That is to say that to reach a pallet at the back of a rack, those pallets in front of it must first be removed. Hence, it is normal for rows to be made up of the same products, and last-in-first-out (LIFO) retrieval employed (as with the previous two systems).

Pallet live storage employs racks equipped with rollers inclined at a gradient to enable palletised freight to be put away at the back of the rack and roll down towards the front where it is retrieved. This facilitates first-in-first-out (FIFO) retrieval, which is obviously preferable for lifed items, such as fresh foodstuffs.

Powered mobile racking offers racking that can be moved along tracks in the floor to offer access to specific rack locations whilst maintaining high-density storage. This is a high-cost solution that requires floor reinforcement. Although this solution offers both 'dense' storage and 'individual access', it can be slow to operate.

Adjustable pallet racking (APR) is the most common 'individual access' solution. This basic form of racking enables forklifts to load palletised and non-palletised freight onto free rack space. The racks are normally positioned back-to-back so that access can be gained from aisles on either side of the racks. It is an affordable and flexible solution but floor space utilisation is poor. To improve floor space utilisation, double-deep racking can be used (i.e. with double racks placed back-to-back). This sacrifices 'individual access' for greater density of storage and is therefore used where there are more than about four pallets per product line.

Narrow aisle racking is similar to APR and, as the name suggests, the aisles are much narrower. Specialised MHE such as narrow aisle pallet trucks and combi trucks are required and this greatly increases the equipment cost, although these trucks do have the advantage of reaching higher than conventional warehouse reach trucks. As this system provides individual access to pallets within a reasonable floor space, it is a common solution in large warehouses.

Automated storage and retrieval systems (AS/RS) are common when storing high volumes and high variety in high densities. AG Barr's 11-storey automated high-bay storage system is an example of this. They are commonly used for finished goods warehouses, particularly in regions where land values and labour costs are high.

Non-pallet storage

Although wooden pallets are the most common unit loads stored in warehouses, goods my be stored in a variety of formats, for example, in cartons, in plastic tote bins, bundled together in long loads (e.g. wooden boards), as individual items (e.g. large pieces of machinery) or as hanging garments. For small items, metal shelving is very common, arranged in aisles so that operators can access the goods easily. Mechanised solutions for small items include vertical carousels, which contain shelves that rotate vertically by means of an electric motor, and horizontal carousels, which are similar in concept but contain modules that hang from an overhead chain and are rotated horizontally.

There are also 'miniload' systems that are similar to pallet AS/RS, except that they are designed to handle plastic tote bins or cartons.

Order picking

Picking solutions also vary depending on freight volume, variety and throughput. A WMS is commonly programmed to offer different pick sequences depending on requirements.

The simplest sequence is pick-to-order, where the generated pick list will direct the picker to retrieve freight from multiple locations along a pick face or in storage in the warehouse to fulfil an order. Pick-to-order is most effective in low-volume operations and in situations where a customer may order many products that would fill a unit load, such as a roll-cage.

Batch picking is an alternative sequence whereby many orders are combined together by the WMS and the picker then retrieves all goods for those orders at the same time. This is an effective pick method but does require the subsequent sortation of goods to orders, either manually or by means of automated sorters. This sequence is suitable for large-scale operations, where there is a large product range and yet customers may only order very few product lines per order.

Pick-to-zero or pick-by-line sequences are most effective when cross-docking freight. That is to say that where an inbound shipment is deconsolidated at the receiving dock, individual product lines are moved to the dispatch dock for sorting to orders, reconfiguring and/or repacking until no freight remains at the receiving dock.

Zone picking is a method of dividing up the warehouse for picking purposes, with each zone containing the pick stock of particular groups of products, and pickers allocated to each zone. Zones may be picked at the same time and the goods brought together at packing or marshalling. Alternatively, a container (such as a tote bin on a conveyor, or a roll-cage) may be part filled in one zone and then passed to another zone for further order completion. This is referred to as 'pick-and-pass'. Zone picking is normally adopted in operations containing a wide product range and it may be combined with pick-to-order or batch picking.

Wave picking refers to how orders are released to the picking area. It is a sophisticated sequencing method suitable for the inherent complexities of warehouses storing high volumes and varieties of high-throughput freight being packed into multiple shipments (as in FMCG). Zones are picked in parallel and individual items are then sorted and packed into specific shipments. Waves of orders are released to the warehouse for picking. When a wave of picks is complete, the next wave will commence.

Besides these sequencing methods, the way in which the picking occurs can be classified as picker-to-goods, goods-to-picker or automated picking. Where the operation is small or pick density is high (i.e. a relatively high proportion of the different product lines in the pick face may be picked in a single sequence), then picker-to-goods is most effective. In its simplest form, this is where pickers go into the storage racks and retrieve the items on their pick list. Often this may be mechanised with the pickers riding on, for example, low-level order picking trucks or narrow aisle picking trucks. Goods-to-picker on the other hand delivers the freight to the picker who will select items on their pick list. Goods-to-picker solutions increase effectiveness where pick density is low. Equipment examples include vertical carousels, horizontal carousels and miniload cranes, as mentioned above. A combination of these two concepts occurs in the case of a 'dynamic pick face' where miniload equipment delivers only those product lines to a pick aisle that are needed for the next pick wave. This 'goods-to-aisle' process is then followed by a 'picker-to-goods' process for the actual picking. This may be effective where there is a very wide range of slow-moving goods. Automated picking may be employed where high variety and throughput coexist. For example, A-frame dispensers are commonly used to quickly and precisely pick and sort items such as pharmaceuticals. A further example is that of automated layer pickers that are employed to pick layers of cases from pallets. However, most picking in warehouses is undertaken manually, with the assistance of mechanisation (e.g. trucks or carousels) and information technology (e.g. radio data terminals or pick-to-light). As previously discussed, automation improves and standardises materials handling by minimising human intervention, but at an increased capital cost.

Storage and picking combinations

From this discussion it is clear that warehouse designers must select the appropriate balance between storage and picking, plus the most effective and efficient solutions depending on volume, variety and throughput of freight in a warehouse or distribution centre. Figure 11.6 summarises this from a very high-level viewpoint.

Despite the obvious benefits of automation, technologies must be fit-for-purpose. That is to say that different warehouses and distribution centres serve different purposes. As alluded to above, a warehouse storing 20-metre steel girders will require very different handling and information technologies to a supermarket national distribution centre (NDC).

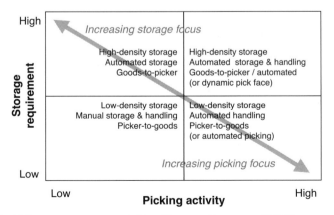

Figure 11.6   Prioritising storage versus picking (Source: Strategos, 2010)[6]

WORK ORGANISATION AND JOB DESIGN

Another important consideration in implementing warehousing technologies is the impact of those technologies on the workforce. This is the focus of **socio-technical systems (STS) theory** (Figure 11.7). The fundamental principles of STS theory are:

- Joint optimisation of the technical and social system
- Quality of work life
- Employee participation in system design
- Semi-autonomous work groups

Despite attempts in the 1980s to promote the vision of the 'lights-off factory', automated factories and warehouses remain dependent upon people. Labour remains the greatest cost in any operation, but in warehousing operators provide the dexterity, flexibility and adaptability to maintain high levels of performance. For example, it may be perceived to be more cost efficient to replace a human picker with a robot, but it is not cost effective because the robot does not have the same dexterity or the ability to think laterally and multi-task.

Addressing the four principles of STS theory, the capabilities of a social system (i.e. people) and a technical system should be balanced. There is no point in implementing high-tech solutions that operators cannot use. This also has a knock-on effect on worker's quality of work life. This will include human factors such as ergonomics. Unhappy workers are not effective workers. Indeed, this should be a key concern regarding the implementation of automation in warehousing. As discussed above, automated information systems and MHE have the potential to greatly reduce human input in warehouse operations. If STS principles are not adhered to, increased automation could result in reduced scope of work, reduced job satisfaction, demotivation and consequently reduced operational performance. The Liquor DC case below illustrates how maintaining quality of work life can result in improved performance.

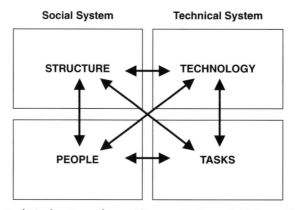

Figure 11.7   Socio-technical systems theory (Source: Bostrom & Heinen, 1977)[7]

LIQUOR DC, AUSTRALIA

A leading retailer in Australia operates two bespoke distribution centres (DCs) for the storage and supply of liquor products; one in Sydney, the other in Melbourne. Between them, these two DCs service the firm's retail outlets across Australia. Australian consumers buy liquor both in small quantities (i.e. as required) and in bulk (i.e. the monthly shopping trip). The major retail chains therefore operate two types of bespoke liquor stores: self-branded high-street outlets for the former, and larger (often drive-though) superstores for the latter. Each sell similar products, but at different price points tailored to their respective markets.

This firm's Sydney liquor DC supplies New South Wales, Queensland and the Northern Territories. Besides liquor, it also stores other products that liquor stores (i.e. bottle shops) stock, such as cigarettes. At 75% capacity, the value of the stock held is A$85 million. It is situated on the outskirts of the Sydney suburbs on an 11.2 hectare site. The floor space inside the DC is 53 000 square metres. The facility has 34 000 reserve locations and 4500 pick locations, and can handle between 1200–2000 pallets at the receiving bays per 10-hour shift, and 1600 pallets at the despatch bays. The layout is designed for straight flow, with receiving on one side of the DC, and despatch on the other. Between 300 and 400 staff are employed (depending on peak volume: Christmas, Easter) across two shifts, there are 137 manual handling machines (MHE) and 98 pick machines. The liquor DC currently holds 3500 stock-keeping units (SKUs).

The Sydney liquor DC employs a number of innovations that improve its effectiveness and efficiency. As employees enter the DC, they are greeted by a series of television screens. These provide a range of content through the day to communicate performance, achievements, health and safety information and general notices. Keeping their employees informed is a key motivator to identify with generation Y.

Humanisation and effective rotation of pick-to-voice equipment is also a significant innovation. Firstly, T5 Bluetooth (i.e. cordless) headsets were purchased, rather than T2 (corded) headsets. These make for improved ergonomics due to not having trailing cords. Secondly a bespoke storage and cleaning system is in place. Operators do not want to put on headsets that have just spent the previous eight hours in somebody else's ear. Hence used headsets are placed in a holding bay ready for cleaning. These are then cleaned with appropriate cleaning products before being recharged, stored and reissued. Not only does this improve employee satisfaction but it also engenders a sense of ownership, and has significantly reduced maintenance of the equipment at the firm's larger site from A$120 000 per quarter to less than A$4000 per quarter.

Other innovations include:

- An 'info link' system on all MHE that asks operators 12 health and safety questions before they can use that piece of equipment

- A one-way traffic system at the receiving doors to prevent collisions ('in' and 'out' doors with appropriate signage)

- Raised barriers at the pick face of gravity-fed racks for tall bottled products to prevent damage from overspills

Employee participation in system design is also important. The people who know how best to improve a process are often the people who work in it every day. Involvement encourages ownership and therefore improves motivation. Finally, ownership and motivation can also be promoted via semi-autonomous teams. Given sufficient autonomy, teams can self-manage and coordinate their work. Consequently, there is less of a burden on management through less referral of decisions.

Work organisation and structure are important considerations in contemporary warehousing. Market pressures drive down operational costs, but at the same time demand greater responsiveness, reliability and resilience. Supply chains cannot afford the time engaged in, or the cost, of the complex hierarchical management structures of the past. Flat hierarchies and devolved decision making via semi-autonomous teams goes part way to addressing this issue. Other considerations will include effective and efficient information and communication systems to facilitate improved management reporting and supply chain integration.

At the warehouse shop floor, the number and scope of individual job roles will be dependent upon the warehouse layout and design, types of products, processes and technologies employed. Nevertheless, typical job roles are focused around the four functions outlined in Figure 11.3 and include freight receipt, quality control, put away and replenishment, picking, packing, and loading. Usually there are dedicated teams in each section. However, work in warehousing is generally regarded as standardised and unskilled, requiring minimal education and training. It is therefore realistic to expect operators in selected operations to rotate around different processes or even multi-task (e.g. undertake put away, picking and packing) to maintain motivation. In the AG Barr case, shop-floor job roles encompass all tasks throughout the operation. On any given day an operative could be working on any given task, or a number of different tasks. This promotes job enlargement (i.e. multi-tasking) and enrichment to maintain motivation and therefore employee retention.

Nevertheless, as previously discussed, increased automation is reducing the amount of manual handling and increasing the amount of information processing in warehousing. Job roles are changing. Warehouse operatives today interact more with information than they do with physical materials. This evolution has socio-technical implications. Conventionally, there has not been a requirement for unskilled warehouse operatives to read and write, or indeed to be fluent in a particular language. Within the European Union for example, workers are able to migrate across national borders for work. Hence, in UK-based warehouses, it is common to find employees from a number of countries, with differing levels of education. Thus written communication of information is not always the most effective mode of communication. Technologies such as pick-to-voice therefore play an important role in communicating instructions. Operatives receive verbal picking instructions via a headset in one of many preloaded languages. Operatives respond verbally either in the same language or another language, and normally confirm that they are at the correct pick location by speaking the location check digit into the microphone. They also confirm the number of items picked. In addition, this technology may be used with bar code scanning, whereby the pickers also bar code scan the items to ensure that the correct goods have been picked. The design of technologies appropriate to the capabilities of the workforce is therefore increasingly important.

Finally, the reduction in physical handling tasks and increase in information tasks offers an opportunity for supply chains to engage their workforces in new and different tasks. With increased information, there is scope to use that information in new and innovate ways to further improve supply chain performance. Within warehouse semi-autonomous teams, opportuni-

Automation and computerisation is reducing human intervention in the physical handling of freight, and increasing information interaction. This has implications for job design.

ties will emerge for people to shift their focus from 'doing' tasks to 'thinking' tasks. Critical thinking, problem-solving and decision-making skills will therefore become important at the shop floor. Many warehouses now involve staff formally in continuous improvement programmes, for example, by displaying prominently key performance indicators, forming improvement teams and introducing improvement techniques such as six sigma.

LEARNING REVIEW

This chapter described the important role played in supply chains by warehouse operations. We discussed the need to minimise the costs of warehousing and inventory holding, whilst maximising the value added in these essential operations. At different points in a supply chain, warehouses and distribution centres will perform different functions, as detailed. Equally, different internal processes will be employed for different types of freight, as highlighted by the AG Barr case.

The role of the WMS was then discussed. The provision of such an information system enables precise management of freight through warehouses and distribution centres. We also discussed different storage and picking solutions that may be employed based on requirements. Nevertheless, the role of people should not be ignored. Hence the chapter continued with a discussion of the need to achieve equilibrium between people, processes and technology. As warehouses become more high-tech, the important roles that people play must not be neglected.

The next chapter will broaden our focus to the information flows and technologies employed along the supply chain.

QUESTIONS

- In the context of postponement, how might downstream distribution centres be viewed as value-adding?
- List the various information sources from across the supply chain that will improve order delivery and discuss how not having each would impact delivery.
- With the evolution of mobile communications (e.g. smartphones and tablet computers) and warehouse automation and MHE, consider what warehouse job roles and tasks will exist in the future. How will they differ from today?

SERVING DIFFERENT MARKET SEGMENTS AT AG BARR

Review the AG Barr case. They operate a fully automated storage system to service low-variety, high-volume, large-scale retailers, and a human-centred storage system to service high-variety, low-volume, small-scale retailers.

List the benefits of each and discuss how each system meets the demands of the two market segments they serve.

NOTES

1. Christopher, M. (2005), *Logistics and Supply Chain Management: Strategies for Reducing Cost and Improving Service*, 3rd edition, Financial Times/Pitman, London, p. 47.

2. Jessop, D. & Morrison, A. (1994) *Storage and Supply of Materials*, 6th edition, Pitman Publishing, London, p. 5.

3. Grant, D., Lambert, D., Stock, J. & Ellram, L. (2005) *Fundamentals of Logistics Management*, McGraw-Hill, London, p. 249.

4. Warman, J. (1971) *Warehouse Management*, Heinemann, London, p. 59.

5. Gümüs, M. & Bookbinder, J. (2004) Cross-docking and its implications in location-distribution systems, *Journal of Business Logistics*, 25(2), 199–227.

6. Strategos (2010) www.strategosinc.com/warehouse.htm (accessed 20 October 2010).

7. Bostrom, R. & Heinen, J. (1977) MIS problems and failures: a socio-technical perspective, *MIS Quarterly*, September, 17–31.

12 Information Flows and Technology

LEARNING OBJECTIVES

- Define the role of information in contemporary global supply chains.
- Explain the need for information visibility and transparency across the supply network and outline the barriers to achieving it.
- Define various information technologies employed in logistics and SCM.
- Discuss the use of RFID in SCM to provide real-time information visibility.
- Discuss the emerging importance of knowledge management in supply networks.

INTRODUCTION

Thus far in Part Two of the book, our focus has predominantly been on the physical flows of inventory, i.e. the movement of freight. This chapter now switches our attention to the information flows that trigger and support those physical flows. Today's market-driven global supply chains are information intensive and require adaptive information systems to manage logistics complexities. In this chapter we will learn about the information systems and technologies employed in SCM.

Chapter 12 comprises six core sections:

- The role of information in global supply chains
- Information visibility and transparency
- Information technology applications
- Radio frequency identification (RFID)
- Global standards
- Supply chain knowledge management

THE ROLE OF INFORMATION IN GLOBAL SUPPLY CHAINS

As previously discussed and illustrated in Figure 1.1, there are three key flows in any supply chain; namely material, resource and information flows. Material flows enable delivery of freight and resource flows such as finance ensure supply partners get paid.

Information flows are more complex and multifaceted. Information is the key that unlocks supply chain responsiveness to demand.

Matching supply with demand is essential to delivering freight at the right time, in the right quantity and to the customer's specification. But how do suppliers know when their freight is required, in what quantities or, indeed, what the customer's exact specification is? This is the role that demand-side information plays. Furthermore, how do downstream supply chain partners and customers know when freight will be delivered by suppliers, what quantities it will arrive in or to what specification? Supply-side information therefore plays a second essential role.

With today's global supply networks distributed across multiple, widely dispersed echelons, comes information complexity and proliferation on the supply side. On the demand side, ever more fickle consumers expect the availability of high varieties and volumes of specific consignments in shortening time frames. This creates the need for accurate high-velocity market information. So, contemporary supply chains are information intensive. *Information complexity, proliferation, diffusion, velocity* and *accuracy* are thus key drivers of developing increasingly sophisticated supply chain information technologies, as illustrated in the Gate Gourmet case at the end of Part Two of the book. In fact, as discussed in Chapter 9, managers and workers in logistics and SCM are today less connected with the physical handling of freight, but more in contact with the associated information. Hence it is not just the information itself that is important, but also how we store, retrieve and use it.

> Information complexity, proliferation, diffusion, velocity and accuracy are key drivers of developing increasingly sophisticated supply chain information technologies.

Access to timely and accurate information is fundamental to effective SCM. Information must also be useful and usable. Hence networked desktop and mobile devices such as laptops, personal digital assistants (PDAs) and smartphones are now not only the toolkit of management, but are also used at the shop floor to access real-time information from upstream and downstream in the supply chain. This information accessibility not only supports the ability to plan and control supply chain activities, but also, and arguably more importantly, provides 24/7 visibility of when things don't go to plan. For example, the availability of demand information from a range of high-street stores at a national distribution centre (NDC) will enable particular freight to be rerouted to the stores where there is demand for it. Clearly the more timely and accurate that information is, the greater the chances of meeting demand, thereby reducing the probability of overstocking some stores whilst understocking others. Imagine the benefits of having such information visibility across an entire supply network.

INFORMATION VISIBILITY AND TRANSPARENCY

The above discussion introduces the benefits of information in the supply chain, and also refers to the issue of complexity. **Information visibility** is the ability to see information at the various points across the supply chain as and when required, which can help to manage that complexity. Visibility of information is highly desirable, but is difficult to achieve. The number of supply partners alone is a major contributing factor, but is also compounded by barriers to sharing information. Effective information visibility is not only facilitated by information technologies, but also by integrated and collaborative relationships between supply chain partners. Without integrated information systems and collaborative, as opposed to competitive, relationships, information will not be shared effectively and efficiently. This was discussed in Chapter 3, which covers integration and collaboration in the supply chain, but it is noteworthy that disparity between trading partners' capabilities and information security are commonly significant barriers to an IT-enabled supply chain.[1] *Cultural barriers* between supply chain partners should therefore be addressed before embarking on the implementation of supply chain-wide information technology.

There are further barriers to gaining total visibility of information across a supply chain. The costs of implementing and maintaining supply chain-spanning information technologies can be immense. These cost implications become *financial barriers* if the aforementioned disparities between trading partners exist. For example, it would be unreasonable for a major multinational supermarket to expect their small-scale third- or fourth-tier suppliers (for example market gardeners and small dairies) to implement cutting-edge information systems. In such supply chains, the further upstream a supplier is, the tighter the profit margins; hence, the less the resources available to invest in new technologies. For example, competitiveness between supermarkets drives down store prices, which in turn drives down the prices they are willing to pay their suppliers. In March 2009, a major Australian supermarket was accused of attempting to impose a 4% trading rebate on its suppliers. This was predicted to deliver a A$500 million saving to be passed on to consumers, but would increase pressure on suppliers to cut costs.[2]

Furthermore, the various information systems at each supply chain partner should either be the same, or at least have the ability to 'talk' to each other. This issue does not end with the hardware and software. Supply chain partners must also agree on what data are required to be transmitted, when, and to whom. Hence there are myriad complex *technical barriers* to overcome before implementing information visibility solutions.[3]

FLORAHOLLAND

FloraHolland is the global market leader in cut flower and ornamental plant supply based in six locations in the Netherlands. It acts as an intermediary between growers (i.e. suppliers) and wholesale or retail buyers with 40 auctions operating simultaneously at its six sites (70% of sales), plus a direct sales (i.e. mediation) operation (30% of sales). Its large auction site alone sells approximately 20 million flowers per day. The business is a cooperative formed by Dutch growers to offer timely supply across the globe and to act as a conduit for market demand information.

Cut flowers and ornamental plants are highly seasonal and have short shelf lives. Demand fluctuations and time to market are therefore key considerations in the FloraHolland supply chain. Individual growers operate on a small scale, focusing on product variety rather than volume to remain responsive to demand. With 3500 customers who are large-scale wholesalers and major retailers demanding high volume and variety, growers operating independently would not be able to meet demand. The 5200 growers with a stake in FloraHolland therefore operate cooperatively, distributing through the auction houses and the FloraHolland direct sales system, to gain the economies of scale necessary to survive in this fast-moving market. With 4500 employees, FloraHolland not only provides auctions but also works closely with growers to develop the products and processes necessary to remain competitive, and works with buyers to improve supply chain integration.

Although buyers are not a part of the cooperative, the benefits of information integration are recognised by all supply chain partners. The traditional supply chain model was based on a series of purely transactional relationships between the auction house and the buyers. Yet with increasing market pressures such as new market entrants, FloraHolland today works closely with buyers to better meet demand and retain its business. Indeed, through integrated solutions, buyers can inform growers about consumer preferences such as a preference for four buds per stem rather than three. Of the 3500 buyers, the top 100 buyers account for 80% of turnover. Hence FloraHolland operates an account management system to maintain a sound working relationship with them. Furthermore the top 50 buyers have FloraHolland personal account managers.

e-Business is essential to this high-velocity supply network. It is in everyone's interest for buyers' information systems to be integrated with those of the auction house, direct sales and growers. However, buyers each have their own IT packages. Thus FloraHolland needs to be able to offer compatible and tailored integration solutions. Hence a dedicated IT team is employed to develop, implement and maintain supply chain integration software. The top 50 buyers' IT requirements are managed individually by a 'supply chain automation consultant'. The cost and resource implications are immense, but are offset by the business benefit gained.

Finally, *organisational barriers* to implementing supply chain-spanning technologies can inevitably exist. Divergent processes can exist within single organisations, and are commonly realigned via large-scale, resource intensive socio-technical systems (STS) or **business process reengineering (BPR)** projects. Thus to align the numerous disparate processes across multiple supply chain echelons, a highly complex programme of activities is required.

We can therefore classify the barriers to gaining information visibility and transparency as either: cultural, financial, technical or organisational. Each of these four types of barrier should be addressed to gain business benefit from supply chain-spanning information technologies.[4] Nevertheless, such substantial effort is worth while, as the benefits are substantial, and can include:[5]

- Customer-oriented operations
- Time compression
- Reduced schedule variability
- Shorter planning periods

- Consistent partnerships
- Supply chain synchronisation and coordination
- A single point of control
- Integrated information systems

Ultimately, a supply chain with information sharing, visibility and transparency can become customer focused and responsive to demand, thereby remaining competitive.

> Barriers to gaining information visibility and transparency can be classified as either cultural, financial, technical or organisational, all of which should be addressed to gain business benefit from supply chain-spanning information technologies.

INFORMATION TECHNOLOGY APPLICATIONS

As supply chains have evolved and grown, so have information flows and technologies. Information technologies (IT) such as materials requirements planning (MRP) were developed in the 1970s to meet the planning and execution needs of individual operations. As business functions have become more integrated, so have IT applications. For example, enterprise resource planning (ERP), the modern derivative of MRP, spans across organisations. Collaborative planning, forecasting and replenishment (CPFR) extends further still by spanning supply chains. CPFR is discussed below.

This section defines a selection of common core IT applications used in global logistics and supply chain management. Their application and reach are summarised in Figure 12.1.

e-Business

Before discussing particular applications, it is important to appreciate their context. e-Business is now integral to trade and commerce in the world today. Many of us purchase freight and services online. This is also true of trade between businesses across

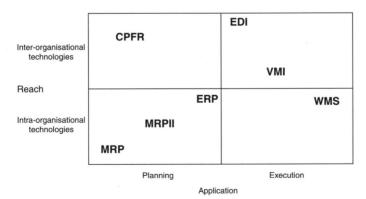

Figure 12.1   Information technologies in global logistics and supply chain management (Source: Adapted from Sherer, 2005)[6]

supply chains. Yet the term e-business encompasses more than just trading via the internet, to include all electronically mediated information exchanges across a supply chain that support the various business processes.[7] As already implied above, e-business is essential to both maintaining and improving supply chain performance.

Electronic data interchange (EDI)

Electronic data interchange (EDI) is a technology for the electronic interchange of data between two or more companies. The predominant forms of data transfer via EDI are purchase orders from customers to suppliers, invoices for payment from suppliers to customers, delivery schedule data and payment instructions. EDI can be linked to an electronic funds transfer (EFT) application that enables payment.

Data transmitted via EDI is typically automated, i.e. doesn't require human intervention. For example, when the delivery date of a particular order is reached, the supplier computer automatically sends an invoice to the appropriate customer's computer. When integrated with other IT applications across the supply chain, EDI becomes a more powerful tool. In this last example, the data is sent when the delivery date is reached, but not necessarily when the order is dispatched. When linked to an **automatic identification and data capture (AIDC)** technology such as radio frequency identification (RFID) the invoice can be sent precisely at the time the order leaves the factory gates. For example, delivery trucks pass through an RFID reader located at the factory gates. The reader automatically sends the product location data to the EDI application, which in turn transmits the invoice to the customer (see Figure 12.2 below). RFID is discussed at length below.

Enterprise resource planning (ERP)

Different products can be defined as having either **independent demand** or **dependent demand**. Products with independent demand are those that are ordered independently of any other products whereas products with dependent demand are part of an order for multiple interrelated items. This concept can be explained using the example of a distribution centre (DC) that specialises in the storage and distribution of bicycles and bicycle components. Bicycles are delivered and stored as sub-assemblies, rather than as complete bicycles so as to enable customisation to particular market requirements. The DC receives orders from wholesalers and retailers for either complete bicycles or for bicycle spares (i.e. components). When customers order bicycle pedals as spares to be sold separately, this demand is 'independent' of demand for any other items. However, when complete bicycles are ordered, pedals are required to be picked from storage and fitted to (or packed with) the bicycles before shipping. Demand for these pedals is therefore 'dependent' on demand for the complete bicycles.

Throughout a supply chain, any number and combination of various materials with either independent or dependent demand will be ordered. This creates myriad complexities for the various production plants, warehouses and distribution centres across the supply chain. The tool for planning and controlling the manufacture and assembly of orders with

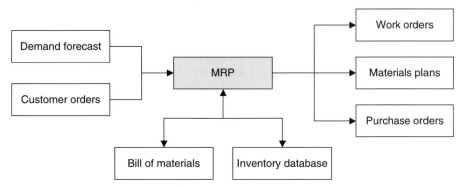

Figure 12.2   An MRP system

dependent demand is **materials requirements planning** (**MRP**). This is a software package consisting of the modules illustrated in Figure 12.2. (You will recall that in Chapter 4 we distinguished *push* and *pull* systems – MRP is more associated with *push systems* and items with *dependent* demand).

A combination of demand forecasts and customer orders are input into the *master production schedule* (MPS), which informs the shop floor of what should be manufactured and/or assembled and when. However, production cannot begin without the required materials, components and/or sub-assemblies. The MRP system therefore interrogates the *bill of materials* (i.e. list of materials and quantities required for each product) and the inventory database to generate orders for those materials as and when required. Whilst some materials will be stored in-house others will be sourced from suppliers. Up to this point no physical work has been done. The final stage is for the MRP system to generate works orders to trigger production and/or assembly, materials plans to call materials from in-house storage, and purchase orders to be sent to suppliers.

MRP forms the basis for wider business planning and control information systems, namely **MRPII (manufacturing resource planning)** and latterly **ERP (enterprise resource planning)** that integrate information from beyond the shop floor. A common misconception is that MRPII is simply an update of MRP. This is not the case. MRPII utilises the core functionality of MRP but integrates business functions beyond manufacturing and logistics to include finance, procurement, marketing, sales, etc.

ERP requires a substantial financial, resource and time investment at implementation and for maintenance and development. Hence, it is uncommon for small and medium-size enterprises (SMEs) to operate ERP systems. Instead MRPII is the application of choice. Nevertheless, scaled-down versions of ERP are now available from the major software vendors, increasing its reach and applicability. Yet ERP has one major flaw. It does not extend across the complete supply chain and therefore constrains collaborative planning and control between supply chain partners. Nevertheless, the Scala system in the Gate Gourmet case at the end of Part Two of the book represents a bespoke example of a planning and control system that is integrated with its suppliers.

Collaborative planning, forecasting and replenishment (CPFR)

CPFR was developed in the late 1990s to fill the inter-organisational gap that ERP cannot. First developed at Wal-Mart to enable collaborative scheduling with its first-tier suppliers, CPFR is more than just a software application. It is fundamentally a new collaborative method of scheduling logistics between suppliers and customers. It is, however, dependent upon timely and accurate information sharing, visibility and transparency. Hence, IT-enabled CPFR is essential in high-velocity supply chains such as those of the major supermarkets. With CPFR still in its infancy, a number of software vendors offer various solutions. However, as with any business IT, software integration is paramount. Hence, the major ERP software vendors are now offering CPFR 'bolt-ons' to their ERP solutions. However, the fundamental concept of CPFR has far-reaching supply chain benefits, and should therefore be considered a core application. As ERP superseded MRPII, a standard CPFR solution should soon supplant ERP.

CPFR is more than just another IT application. The CPFR process is illustrated in Figure 12.3.

Conceptually, CPFR should enable significant scope and depth of collaboration across a supply chain. However, scale and complexity are significant constraints. Fundamentally, it is difficult to forge close partnerships with many partners.[8] Hence some CPFR solutions will have greater scope and/or depth than others. As such, three modes of CPFR can be identified: basic CPFR, developed CPFR and advanced CPFR.[9]

Basic CPFR involves a limited number of business processes integrated between a limited number of supply chain partners (e.g. a supermarket retailer and a selected first-tier supplier). There is usually a lead partner, who selects those processes where CPFR is adopted (e.g. exchange of stock-holding data). This basic CPFR implementation is commonly the starting point of a data-sharing collaborative arrangement, which can potentially lead to developed CPFR.

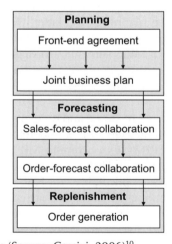

Figure 12.3 The CPFR process (Source: Cassivi, 2006)[10]

As is implied, developed CPFR has greater scope and depth than basic CPFR. This will typically involve a greater number of data exchanges between two partners, and may extend to suppliers taking responsibility for replenishment on behalf of their customer (i.e. vendor managed inventory, discussed further below).

Advanced CPFR goes beyond data exchanges to synchronise forecasting information systems and coordinate planning and replenishment processes. Hence product development, marketing plans, production planning and transport planning are seamlessly integrated with forecasts based on actual consumer demand extracted from point-of-sale data.[11] Hence, through this high level of integration and collaboration close to the consumer interface, retailers and their first-tier suppliers enable the agility to respond to ever more erratic consumer market demand fluctuations.

To make the transition to an advanced CPFR solution first requires a long-term relationship to have built up. Hence, time, complexity, scale and the substantial financial investment required are considerable constraints. Nevertheless, for large-scale multinational organisations such as the leading supermarkets and their first-tier suppliers, the benefits of CPFR outweigh the costs of the initial investment. For organisations without the same economies of scale, the development of an advanced CPFR solution is obviously considerably more difficult to achieve.

Vendor managed inventory (VMI)

As with CPFR, VMI is more than just a software application. VMI is again self-explanatory. Simply put, customers, such as high-street retailers, outsource their inventory management to their suppliers. In some cases, although suppliers are accountable for the VMI system, they may elect to outsource it to a specialist 3PL. Such collaborative arrangements are common in the fast-moving consumer goods (FMCG) sector. Dedicated VMI software solutions are available to manage the intricacies of such systems.

For VMI, a holistic view of inventory levels is taken throughout the supply chain with a single point of control for all inventory management. By enabling a vendor to manage stock replenishment at their facilities, a customer (e.g. a supermarket retailer) is effectively eliminating an echelon in the supply chain. In doing so, upstream demand visibility is improved to reduce the impact of demand fluctuations (i.e. the bullwhip effect).[12] Hence VMI can enable supply to more accurately and precisely meet demand.

Although VMI is today centred around an IT solution, the concept of a customer merely defining its requirements and the supplier being accountable for fulfilling them predates contemporary IT.[13] A simplified VMI scenario is illustrated in Figure 12.4.

By providing improved supply and demand information visibility via centralised control, VMI can specifically reduce the impact of the following sources of the bullwhip effect: price variation (e.g. three items for the price of two promotions), rationing and gaming (i.e. customers over-ordering due to stock shortages; the Houlihan effect), demand signal processing (i.e. the Forrester effect) and order batching (i.e. ordering in batches;

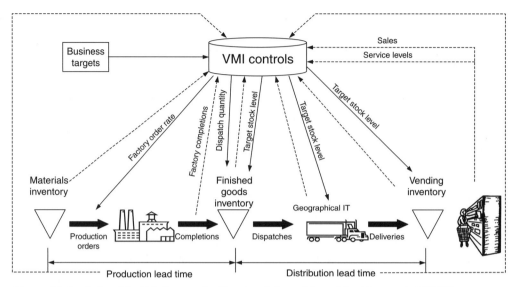

Figure 12.4　A simplified VMI scenario (Source: Adapted from Matthias *et al.*, 2005)[14]

the Burbidge effect), as discussed in Chapter 9. As with ERP, the implementation of just a software application will not derive the full benefits of VMI. By essentially eliminating an echelon, certain logistics activities and information processes will either become redundant or be redesigned. Business process reengineering (BPR) is again necessary to eliminate the non-value-adding activities created and to align the IT with the business processes. As with CPFR, significant investment in developing an appropriate collaborative relationship is a prerequisite to operating VMI.

Disney *et al.* (2007) have suggested four types of VMI as given in Table 12.1. Type I and Type II have been implemented in supply chains in various sectors, whereas Type III and Type IV are more advanced and require further research and development.

Warehouse management systems (WMS)

WMS functionality was discussed in Chapter 11. WMS applications have become essential to the management and control of warehouses and distribution centres. As with the other applications discussed, their integration with other software applications is desirable in

Table 12.1　Types of vendor managed inventory in supply chains[15]

Configuration	Description of collaborative or vendor managed functions
Type 0	Traditional supply chain
Type I	Replenishment only
Type II	Replenishment and forecasting
Type III	Replenishment, forecasting and customer inventory management
Type IV	Replenishment, forecasting, customer inventory management and distribution planning

order to integrate warehouse operations with the rest of the supply chain. For example, a customer order transmitted via EDI will trigger the ERP system to call for freight from production and/or from stock. This will then trigger the WMS to pick from stock and dispatch (refer back to Figure 11.5).

RADIO FREQUENCY IDENTIFICATION (RFID)

When applied in logistics and SCM, RFID technologies automatically identify and locate physical freight. Individual items, batches of freight or the containers in which they are held can carry an RFID transponder or 'tag' that transmits a radio frequency signal. This signal can be remotely detected by an RFID 'reader'. When connected to a materials management system, the data downloaded from the reader are used to monitor and control the movement of the freight.[16] A basic RFID application is illustrated in Figure 12.5. With RFID, line of sight is not required as is the case with traditional bar code reading systems.

The remote communication capability of RFID is what differentiates it from current traceability technologies. Existing technologies, such as printed batch cards and bar coding, require operatives to read or scan the item or batch specific data at the location of the freight. This

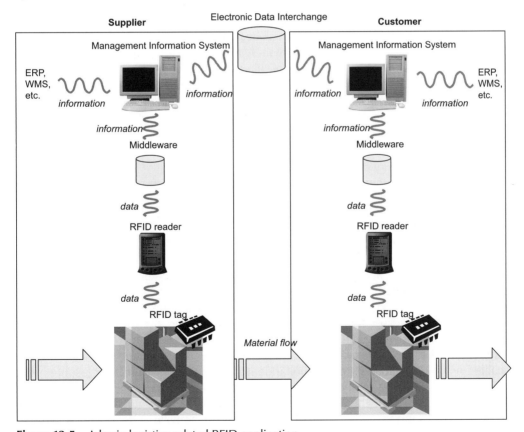

Figure 12.5   A basic logistics-related RFID application

can be time consuming, laborious and prone to inaccuracies, due to the scale and complexity of typical warehousing and distribution operations. Hence design and layout of logistics operations across the supply chain have, until now, needed to accommodate this constraint. For example, the delivery of a batch of freight via truck to the freight receiving area of a warehouse would conventionally be manually scanned using a handheld bar code reader or recorded in writing. In an RFID-enabled freight receiving area, the truck will typically pass through a reader 'gate' to automatically record the time of delivery and quantity delivered.

The advent of RFID as a supply chain traceability technology results from the drive for agility, to respond to increasing product proliferation and demand volatility. An agile, or 'quick response', supply chain is reliant on the timeliness and quality of shared information. The ability to access real-time product information anywhere along the supply chain is thus a key component of becoming truly agile. Yet existing traceability technologies cannot offer real-time information. Indeed, until the introduction of RFID, the 'Achilles heel' of supply chains has been data acquisition.[17]

> Access to real-time product information anywhere along the supply chain is a key enabler of agility.

RFID provides real-time visibility of point-of-sale data across the supply chain to trigger production and/or movement of freight for automatic replenishment. Consequently inventory holding will be minimised across the supply chain, which will lead to reduced capacity and resource requirements and in turn dramatically reduce logistics costs. This is, however, just one of the potential benefits of RFID. This new technology is multifunctional. The RFID primary applications up to point of sale can be classified under the following four headings:[18]

- Asset tracking and management
- Increased security of freight
- Improved stock management and availability
- Reduced errors in product data handling

In fact, RFID tags can be made to: resist extreme temperatures, harmful chemicals and fluids; provide the ability to scan multiple items; and be reusable. Bar codes and other existing technologies cannot. RFID can therefore achieve greater efficiencies than any other existing technology. For example, in the UK Marks & Spencer uses disposable RFID tags on high-value freight, such as suits, for in-store stock control. A typical retail store will contain hundreds of suits in various styles, colours and sizes. Conventionally, the weekly stock check was conducted manually by reading the bar code of each individual item. This was a time-consuming and laborious task. The implementation of RFID has enabled reading of multiple items simultaneously using a handheld reader (as illustrated in Figure 12.5). In doing so, the time taken is greatly reduced. Meanwhile read accuracy has also improved. Thus the suit supply network benefits by gaining more regular and accurate information to enable production of only those items in demand and delivery in smaller more frequent batches, preventing both overproduction and stock-outs.

More generically, the operational improvements from RFID include:[19]

- Shipping consolidation
- Conveyance loading
- Conveyance tracking
- Shipment and item tracking
- Verification
- Storage
- Item tracking within a manufacturing plant
- Warehouse efficiency, reach, productivity and accuracy
- Reduced retail out of stock, labour requirements, pilferage and phantom stock problems

There is also potential for consumers to benefit directly from RFID, through transaction support, increased customer interaction, improved customer monitoring and increased integration of retail partners. For example, with item-level tagging, a 'smart fridge' can read RFID-tagged products held within to offer a range of benefits, including healthcare advice.[20] Despite predicted consumer applications such as this, the omnipresent nature of RFID has led to some concern amongst consumers. RFID is a ubiquitous computing technology. As in the smart fridge example, ubiquitous computing aims to seamlessly connect the physical world with a representation of it in information systems. Hence, early RFID adopters such as Wal-Mart, Tesco, Metro and Marks & Spencer have employed strategies to 'switch off' RFID technology at point of sale to prevent consumer distrust issues. So it is likely to be several years before practical consumer benefits are seen.

With RFID still in its infancy, supply chain and logistics applications are limited. RFID is nevertheless set to transform people and processes within supply chains. As discussed, conventional traceability processes have been designed around the need for operators to be in the same physical location as the freight; more specifically, the freight must be in the operator's line of sight. With the elimination of the line-of-sight requirement, the automation offered by RFID will enable management to reconsider the design of shipping, transportation, manufacturing, warehousing and retail operations. Current predictions of future operational innovations include: [21]

- The 'store of the future': including continuous shelf inventory checking and more frequent replenishment, currently being trialled by Procter & Gamble, Phillip Morris and Metro.
- 'Future warehousing': reducing floor space requirements in warehouses, enabling them to be located closer to urban areas.
- Increased customisation in manufacturing: increased visibility of end customer requirements.

Such innovations will change the work structures and job content for workers and create new job roles across the supply chain. As discussed in Chapter 11, the reduction in manual handling and the increase in information in logistics is creating new tasks and job roles at the shop floor. In fact, the extent to which RFID will replace bar coding remains unclear. Traditionally, the diffusion of significant innovations such as the car, the refrigerator and the personal computer have led to human impacts unforeseen by the original inventors. Whilst it is recognised that RFID can significantly transform the way humans interact with freight and services, its long-term impact has not yet been fully envisaged.[22]

Meanwhile, in the short term, early adopters must bear the burden of high RFID tag costs. Typically RFID tagging can add 20–67% to the cost of distribution when implemented at pallet or case (i.e. batch) level.[23] It is anticipated, however, that widespread implementation will bring with it sufficient economies of scale. Consequently, early adopters are typically very large organisations such as Wal-Mart and Tesco. More significantly, upstream manufacturers and suppliers are concerned that the information transparency that RFID can offer will hand greater power and control to such retailers. Indeed, the success of an IT-enabled supply chain is highly dependent on all parties gaining mutual benefit. As discussed above, resistance to change, disparity between trading partners' capabilities and information security are commonly viewed by practitioners as significant barriers to an IT-enabled supply chain.[24] Hence there are several infrastructural issues to overcome before tangible wholesale benefit can be gained from RFID.

In summary, RFID has the potential to deliver real-time supply chain agility. This relatively new technology can offer accurate and precise product traceability at any point in the supply chain at any time, thereby enabling even the most complex supply networks to respond immediately to fluctuations in demand. Yet, whilst tag manufacturers and leading retailers continue research and development into cost-efficient technological solutions, substantial barriers to effective implementation remain. The benefits and limitations of RFID against more conventional technologies are summarised in Table 12.2.

FLORAHOLLAND

As alluded to in the previous caselet, FloraHolland takes supply chain information very seriously. In 2001, FloraHolland implemented RFID to manage the movement of carts across its short supply chain (growers' greenhouses are located near to each of FloraHolland's five sites). An RFID tag on each cart and readers at strategic points in the short supply chain enables them to locate and transfer these valuable assets to other locations where they are required. FloraHolland currently manages 150 000 carts across the short supply chain. The technology also reduces processing errors. Prior to 2001 track and trace was a manual operation requiring workers to input data manually into the central information system. Furthermore, labour requirements at the auction house are greatly reduced and simplified. Before RFID implementation, two operators were required for each cart: one to transport the cart and one to enter the associated data in Dutch. Now only one operator is required, and the language requirement is no longer necessary because data input is automated (see Figure 12.6). FloraHolland employs approximately 42 different nationalities.

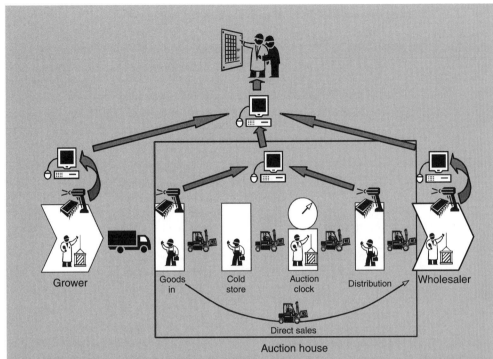

Figure 12.6   The RFID-enabled short supply chain (Source: Butcher, 2007)[25]

FloraHolland views RFID as a key enabler of further supply chain improvement. To date RFID has enabled asset management across the supply chain, internal process data accuracy and precision, and labour reduction. The next key challenge is to track and trace product batches after passing the auction clock. Up to the auction clock, each batch is associated with a cart, but afterwards the batches are split and transferred to other carts for distribution to particular wholesalers. The ability to track and trace product batches as well as assets will enable improvement of processes downstream of the auction clock to enable lead-time reduction, process rationalisation and service quality improvement. Solutions are currently being piloted, but FloraHolland has adopted an evolutionary approach to RFID technology roll-out. The corporate vision is to evolve from asset management, through track and trace, to capturing consumer market data in approximately the next 10 years.

GLOBAL STANDARDS

Throughout this chapter we have discussed the complexity, proliferation, diffusion, velocity and required accuracy of data found in today's global supply chains. Data management and synchronisation are therefore critical functions necessary to ensure the timely and accurate transmission and retrieval of a vast array of product and process data at any given time. It is therefore necessary to have global standards for data, to ensure a common data 'language' is 'spoken' between supply chain partners. For example, chocolate bars are packaged in

Table 12.2   The benefits and limitations of data capture technologies[26]

Data capture technology	Benefits	Limitations	Summary
Paper-based/ handwritten	Proven technology Minimal training for use Low cost to implement and maintain	High potential for human error Poor traceability (potential for damage/loss of data) Physical storage space required Requires literate operator Does not integrate with other information systems Time-consuming data input and extraction	A low-cost, low-tech solution
Bar coding and radio data terminals	Proven technology – robust Minimal training for use Low cost to maintain Good data traceability Virtual data storage Integration with other information systems Fast data input	Some potential for human error (e.g. mis-scans) Requires human operator in most warehouse functions Requires literate operator Some cost to implementation	A robust off-the-shelf solution
Radio frequency identification (RFID)	Automatic data capture (human operator not required) Potential to minimise human input and therefore error Real-time data input, and extraction	High cost to implement; High cost to maintain (unless tags are reusable) Early stages of adoption and therefore high risk Technologies still in development Not all solutions are robust	A solution that eliminates human error, but currently has high entry barriers

printed wrappers with bar codes at the factory in which they are manufactured. They are then shipped through supply chains to retailers. The chocolate bars must then be identified by the retailer to know which shelf to put them on, and what price to charge. The retailer's bar code scanning technology must therefore 'speak' the same 'language' as the manufacturer's bar code printing technology. Global standards are the solution.

GS1 is a global standards organisation that manages the standards for bar codes and RIFD tags for the world's leading organisations. It provides data services that ensure the proliferation of products and freight can be uniquely and accurately identified.

The GS1 Identification Keys classification system offers nine different formats of unique bar code for different types of product or freight.[27] The bar code we, as consumers, encounter most is the global trade item number (GTIN) bar code found on the products we buy. Other bar codes in other formats are available to identify anything from documents to freight containers.

With the advent of RFID, GS1 developed the EPCglobal standards system, where EPC is the acronym for electronic product code.[28] As with bar codes, different types of RFID tag are used to identify different items. Hence within EPCglobal there are different classifications for unique electronic product codes.

Another service GS1 offers is its Global Data Synchronisation Network (GDSN), which synchronises data from its various data services to provide its users with the most up-to-date and accurate data on items identified via GS1 systems such as Identification Keys and EPCglobal.[29] With the ever-increasing complexity, proliferation, diffusion, velocity and required accuracy of data across global supply chains, GDSN is another important tool in contemporary supply chain management.

SUPPLY CHAIN KNOWLEDGE MANAGEMENT

This chapter has discussed the multitude of data and information in contemporary global supply chains and how it can be managed and used. Through the synthesis and analysis of data, we gain information. For example from the interaction between an RFID reader and RFID tags, time and location data can be gained. By transmitting this to a middleware for synthesis and analysis, information about the movement of freight and delivery lead time can be generated and transmitted to a central management information system to be interrogated by other software applications such as ERP and accessed by users. Using this information and synthesising it with other business information can create knowledge. That is to say, through internalisation and understanding of information, knowledge is gained. Hence global supply chains are also filled with knowledge, some of which is *tacit* (i.e. held in the heads of employees) and some of which is made *explicit* (available to all) via knowledge repositories and information systems. Knowledge management is the term used to describe the capture, storage, use and sharing of knowledge within an organisation. The term **supply chain knowledge management** is therefore introduced here to describe those knowledge management processes that span a supply chain.

In new product development, knowledge creation has long been recognised as being fundamental to developing new and innovative products, which in turn delivers competitive advantage. This is also true of knowledge creation in other areas of a business.[30] In logistics and SCM, supply-side and demand-side knowledge is critical to managing supply chain performance. Conventionally logistics and supply chain knowledge has largely been tacit, with individual managers and workers holding the knowledge necessary to 'work around' inherent inefficiencies in logistics processes. This means that such individuals are critical to maintaining and improving supply chain performance.[31] However, this is an undesirable situation. If a particular **knowledge worker** leaves the company, their knowledge leaves with them. Hence, the ability to create knowledge, capture it and make it explicit is essential for long-term supply chain improvement.

Supply chain knowledge management is an emerging area of research. As with information, knowledge created at one point in a supply network should be accessible across that network. For example, demand-side information is essential for understanding market demand. However, knowing what to do with that information enables an effective and efficient response to demand. Furthermore, building up that knowledge over a period of time enables a supply chain to begin to *sense and respond* to actual demand. Hence the knowledge-creating supply chain is able to be first to market, gaining competitive advantage.

LEARNING REVIEW

This chapter focused on the information systems employed in contemporary supply chains. We began by discussing the role of information in the supply chain. The provision of timely and accurate information is essential for the management of both supply- and demand-side functions. Nevertheless, supply chains are typically diverse and dispersed across disparate locations. Hence, this causes issues with information visibility and transparency. Our discussion therefore addressed the barriers and solutions to achieving information visibility and transparency.

We continued by discussing common information technology applications in contemporary supply chains and their roles. These technologies are designed to manage the increasing information complexity, proliferation, diffusion, velocity and accuracy we are confronted with. One particular technology, RFID, is a key enabler of managing each of these issues, via the provision of real-time supply and demand data. This was therefore discussed at length.

Finally, it was also noted that the synthesis of the multitude of supply chain information creates knowledge. This in turn enables learning, which can be used to continually improve supply chain performance.

The next chapter will continue the journey along the supply chain and will focus on finance flows through the supply chain.

QUESTIONS

- As discussed above, information complexity, proliferation, diffusion, velocity and accuracy are key concerns in contemporary SCM. Information technologies are evolving to manage these issues, but what of the users? As discussed in Chapter 11, logistics tasks are increasingly more information intensive. Hence, how can we ensure that logistics managers and workers are able to cope with their increasingly complex information tasks?

- Discuss the four barriers to information visibility and transparency. If you were designing a new supply chain, how would you prevent each of these barriers occurring?

- A major issue for information technology adoption in SCM is the financial and resource investments required by all supply chain partners to implement state-of-the-art applications. For small-scale suppliers with low profit margins, this is difficult, if not an impossibility. How might their larger supplier partners support them?

- ERP links the operations and logistics functions with other business functions. CPFR links supply chain partner organisations. The next logical step is to link consumers with the supply chain Are there any examples of this already (e.g. supermarket loyalty cards)? What would such an application look like?

MAPPING INFORMATION FLOWS IN THE FLORAHOLLAND SUPPLY CHAIN

Review the FloraHolland case above. In particular, Figure 12.6 illustrates the application of RFID across its short supply chain. Real-time demand information flows electronically from the auctions and from direct sales. FloraHolland responds to this information, delivering the right products to the right customers within the tight time parameters set. This generates more information, which is in turn passed up the supply chain to the growers, who use it to understand actual demand and tailor their products to changing market needs.

Map the information flows across this supply chain. How many information interactions are there?

NOTES

1. Jharkharia, S. & Shankar, R. (2005) IT-enablement of supply chains: understanding the barriers, *Journal of Enterprise Information*, 18(1), 11–27.
2. Palmer, D. (2009) Coles heightens pressure on suppliers: report, www.ausfoodnews.com.au/2009/03/03/coles-heightens-pressure-on-suppliers-report.html (accessed 24 September 2010).
3. Childerhouse, P., Hermiz, R., Mason-Jones, R., Popp, A. & Towill, D. (2003) Information flow in automotive supply chains – identifying and learning to overcome barriers to change, *Industrial Management & Data Systems*, 103(7), 491–502.
4. Ibid.
5. Ibid.
6. Sherer, S. (2005) From supply-chain management to value network advocacy: implications for e-supply chains, *Supply Chain Management: An International Journal*, 10(2), 77–83.
7. Adapted from Chaffey, D. (2004) *e-Business and e-Commerce Management*, 2nd edition, FT/Prentice Hall, London, p. 10.
8. Holmström, J., Främling, K., Kaipia, R. & Saranen, J. (2002) Collaborative planning forecasting and replenishment: new solutions needed for mass collaboration, *Supply Chain Management: An International Journal*, 7(3), 136–145.

9. Skjoett-Larsen, T., Thernøe, C. & Anderson, C. (2003) Supply chain collaboration: theoretical perspectives and empirical evidence, *International Journal of Physical Distribution and Logistics Management*, 33(6), 531–549.

10. Cassivi, L. (2006) Collaboration planning in a supply chain, *Supply Chain Management: An International Journal*, 11(3), 249–258.

11. Skjoett-Larsen *et al.* (see note 9).

12. Disney, S. & Towill, D. (2003) Vendor-managed inventory and bullwhip reduction in a two level supply chain, *International Journal of Operations and Production Management*, 23(6), 625–651.

13. Ibid.

14. Matthias, H., Disney, S., Holmstrom, J. & Smaros, J. (2005) Supply chain collaboration: making sense of the strategy continuum, *European Management Journal*, 23(2), 170–181.

15. Disney, S., Farasyn, I., Lambrecht, M., Towill, D. & Van De Velde, W. (2007) Controlling bullwhip and inventory variability with the golden smoothing rule, *European Journal of Industrial Engineering*, 1(3), 241–265.

16. Wilding, R. & Delgado, T. (2004) RFID demystified: supply-chain applications, *Logistics and Transport Focus*, 6(4), 42–48.

17. McFarlane, D. & Sheffi, Y. (2003) The impact of automatic identification on supply chain operations, *International Journal of Logistics Management*, 14(1), 1–17.

18. Wilding & Delgado (see note 16).

19. McFarlane & Sheffi (see note 17).

20. Gu, H. & Wang, D. (2009) A content-aware fridge based on RFID in smart home for home-healthcare, *Proceedings of the 11th International Conference on Advanced Communication Technology*, Phonix Park, Korea, 15–18 February, pp. 987–990.

21. McFarlane & Sheffi (see note 17).

22. Sheffi, Y. (2004) RFID and the innovation cycle, *International Journal of Logistics Management*, 15(1), 1–10.

23. Twist, D. (2005) The impact of radio frequency identification on supply chain facilities, *Journal of Facilities Management*, 3(3), 226–240.

24. Jharkharia & Shankar (see note 1).

25. Butcher, T. (2007), Radio frequency identification: an enabler of agile supply chain decision making, *International Journal of Agile Systems and Management*, 2(3), 305–320.

26. Butcher, T. & Baker P. (2010) Processes and system requirements. In P. Baker (Ed.), *The Principles of Warehouse Design* (3rd edition, pp. 42–48), Chartered Institute of Logistics and Transport in the UK,.

27. www.gs1.org/barcodes/technical/id_keys (accessed 17 January 2011).

28. www.gs1.org/epcglobal (accessed 17 January 2011).

29. www.gs1.org/gdsn (accessed 17 January 2011).

30. Nonaka I. & Takeuchi, H. (1995) *The Knowledge Creating Company: How Japanese Companies Create the Dynamics of Innovation*, Oxford University Press, New York, p. 6.

31. Butcher, T. (2007) Supply chain knowledge work: should we restructure the workforce for improved agility? *International Journal of Agile Systems and Management*, 2(4), 376–392.

13 Logistics and Financial Management

Mike Tayles
The University of Hull

LEARNING OBJECTIVES

- Describe and differentiate the accounting and financial information generated within logistics companies.
- Explain the key accounting statements, their purpose and implications.
- Demonstrate the importance of cash flow to a logistics company.
- Discuss business risk for a logistics company and currency risk in the context of international logistics activities.
- Outline the taxation implications of international transfers within a logistics company.
- Understand the role played by cost and management accounting information in a logistics company.
- Identify typical components of a balanced scorecard of a logistics company.

INTRODUCTION

This chapter is concerned with the flow of financial resources through the supply chain. As we noted earlier, financial flows are the basis of trade, and logisticians need to be as competent in following the money trail as they are in following the product trail.

In this chapter we will discuss financial management and place particular emphasis on areas to which a logistics application applies. Within companies the term 'finance department' is probably the contemporary title for the department that carries out all matters concerned with accounting and financial management of the enterprise. Accounting and financial information is analysed and interpreted in different ways to meet the needs of various parties. An understanding of this is important for all managers because their fortunes, and those of their companies, are inevitably connected to financial performance in some way. Finance is the use of financial or accounting information by management at all levels to assist in planning, making decisions and controlling the activities of an enterprise. In the widest sense, this includes drawing financial information from, and communicating it to, interested parties both inside and outside the organisation.

Information traditionally presented to outsiders is usually in summary form, for the whole organisation. To insiders, the focus of information is on the part of the organisation for which they take responsibility. A consequence of this is that the finance function tends to see the organisation as consisting of vertical structures, silos, in line with the traditional organisational hierarchy. This does not fit with the process or flow mentality of providing logistics and supply chain solutions. Here management must place greater emphasis on the horizontal process; that is, the flow of product along a value chain and the support of this with appropriate finance information. If an appropriate or optimum solution to a supply chain problem requires cooperation between businesses, then this would involve creating accounting arrangements that deal with this and which perhaps share the benefits provided by the solution. Managers and accountants have to be open therefore to developments such as 'open book costing' where the parties are prepared to show each other their internal costing and profitability information, or increasing 'trust' between parties; that is, not relying on formal rules and regulations but acknowledging that all parties can, in the long term, benefit from a genuine cooperation between related parties.

As businesses develop more innovative solutions to supply chain problems it is possible that a tension may exist between accounting and supply chain managers. This offers both opportunities and problems: opportunities to do things differently, which will contribute to the development and success of a business; and problems of complying with accepted accounting principles of recording and reporting accounting information.

Accounting and financial management can be defined as the process of defining, measuring and communicating economic information about an organisation to permit informed judgements and decisions by users of the information. This definition is very broad; for example, users may be shareholders or bankers outside the organisation, and directors or managers inside it. They will receive different forms of information depending on their position and relationship with the company and they may make different use of that information. In fact accounting and financial management consists of a few different types of activities: financial accounting, management accounting and financial management. These activities are not discrete, they are interrelated as we shall see in the remainder of this chapter.

Chapter 13 comprises three core sections:

- Financial accounting
- Management accounting
- Financial management

In addition, in order to illustrate further application of material in the chapter, a case study (Deutsche Post/DHL) at the end of Part Two reviews financial data pertaining to that company.

FINANCIAL ACCOUNTING

Financial accounting is ultimately concerned with reporting to and meeting the requirements of parties outside the organisation. These include:

- *Investors:* that is, those who have subscribed to an issue of shares by the company and who are therefore part owners of the company; or *prospective investors,* people or institutions who might be thinking of buying shares in the company. Both of these parties are informed by *financial analysts* who provide investment advice or offer general commentary in the press.

- The *government,* in the form of the Registrar of Companies, or similar entity who performs a regulatory role on companies; and the *Revenue and Customs,* or similar entity, who are concerned with the taxation assessment made on companies and any duties incurred on imports, etc.

- *Business contacts,* for example *bankers* who may be approached to lend money to the company or *trade contacts,* such as *suppliers* and *customers,* who need information about the company to assess its reliability regarding a regular trading relationship. This is obviously important where a logistics solution may be provided by an external party or where external provision (outsourcing) is being considered in comparison to in-house (i.e. own account) provision of logistics.

Many other parties may also have an interest in the accounts of an organisation, for example competitors, pressure groups, employees and trades unions.

In public limited companies there is often a separation between the management of the company (including the directors), those entrusted to run it, and the owners (shareholders). The shareholders employ the directors to run the business for them. Directors may be shareholders but in most public limited companies they are not majority shareholders. Financial accounts are prepared for these public limited companies (and must be placed before the shareholders in an Annual General Meeting) and also for sole traders, partnerships and private limited companies. We, however, will focus mostly here on public limited companies.

Companies, while having a legal entity, are not human: they can't make decisions, the directors of companies do that. In recent years there has been considerable interest in *corporate governance,* that is, the way companies are directed and controlled. This involves issues such as *disclosure* – what is disclosed and when; *accountability* – the roles and duties of directors; and *fairness* – that directors do not benefit from 'inside' information. There have been various efforts by the accounting profession in the UK, for example, to address this involving the development of a Combined Code of Best Practice issued in 1998, revised in 2003. Corporate governance is an evolving phenomenon: for example, there have been dramatic and worldwide repercussions because of a small number of scandals involving large companies, such as Enron which was accused of manipulation of accounting rules and its auditors Arthur Andersen, and WorldCom, a long-distance phone company, which used fraudulent accounting methods to mask a declining accounting condition. In the USA, in response to these events, legislation was enacted to improve the oversight of accounting and reporting practices, called the **Sarbanes–Oxley Act** or **SOX** after the US Senators who sponsored the act. It established a Public Company Accounting Oversight Board to deal with overseeing, regulating, inspecting and disciplining firms.

Selected information from the financial accounts of a company is required by law to be made available to the public and deposited with the appropriate government agency. The resulting documents are referred to as the published accounts, the annual accounts or the corporate report. The law and the recommendations of financial reporting practice dictate what minimum information should be disclosed. The accounting profession recommends the style and content of the published accounts. In the UK, for example, these are known as financial reporting standards (FRS). These are not legally binding, but accountants are expected to follow them and can be disciplined if they do not do so. The Stock Exchange also has requirements which must be met by companies wishing to be quoted on it. As companies become increasingly global and in line with European and international integration, there is an increasing move to develop international reporting standards (IRS).

Financial statements in general, and published accounts in particular, perform the role of stewardship; that is, demonstrating that the directors of the company have managed the funds entrusted to them by shareholders in an appropriate manner. In other words, they have not spent unnecessarily on assets or made inappropriate decisions on the buying or selling of goods and services and making contracts with third parties. The main documents that are used as evidence in this context are the **balance sheet,** the **profit and loss account** and the **cash flow statement**. In the published accounts these are supplemented by extensive notes, a Directors' Report and a Chairman's Statement. The fact that the accounts represent a 'true and fair view' of the state of the affairs of the company has to be established by independent professional accountants in practice (known as auditors). Any interested reader could obtain a copy of a logistics company's accounts and read them in conjunction with this chapter. These may be obtained from the internet, from a library or directly from the company. An alternative would be to consult the DHL case study at the end of Part Two. The accounting documents in the published accounts are important summaries of the current financial position of the organisation, the results of the transactions of a trading or accounting period and a statement to help people to judge the current *liquid position* of the company. That is, whether the company has sufficient funds in cash or near cash to be able to pay its bills when they fall due. These documents will be examined in more detail below, but it is important to appreciate initially that:

- All the information is historical, the documents report actual past transactions. To fulfil the stewardship role only past events can be audited and reported on with any accuracy and objectivity. The fact that the company was about to sign a contact with a third party might be in the chairman's statement but would not be valued in the accounts. The information contains only those matters relating to the organisation that can be expressed in monetary terms. The ability or business acumen of the chief executive would not be reflected in the accounts or, for example, the fact that she/he had a heart condition. Only matters that can be established with objectivity are included. Values that are subjective or a matter of opinion and which cannot be verified or audited would not be included. The fact that a company had good relations with a range of suppliers or customers might influence its profitability and be important to shareholders but would not be directly incorporated in the accounts. The company or the auditors would be expected to comment if any items of a subjective or doubtful nature existed in the accounts in order to draw attention to them.

- The published accounts are prepared annually, though interim statements are often made half yearly.

Financial accounts

The *balance sheet* aims to convey the financial position of an organisation at a particular point in time. It is always dated and the information contained in it is a snapshot of the financial position of the organisation at that date, usually the end of the accounting period, typically the accounting year. It consists of a list of assets and liabilities. Assets are resources owned by the company – buildings, plant and equipment (fixed assets), stock, debtors and cash (current assets). Liabilities are obligations owed by the company to other people who may have provided funds, goods or services (for example shareholders), banks that have made loans to the company and creditors for goods or services who have not yet been paid.

Fixed assets are shown at their cost price or at some value below that, which is an adjustment to reflect their age or wearing out, called depreciation. Depreciation in accounting is how the original cost of an asset is shared out over each accounting period in which it is used. Assets may be further reduced in value if it is estimated that their market value is even lower (a concept called conservatism). Assets may be revalued upwards if they are felt to have experienced appreciation of a reasonably reliable permanent nature, though they must have been formally revalued by a professional valuer. Depreciation is an important concept in logistics due to the heavy capital-intensive nature of the sector (warehouses, vehicles, etc.). Different methods of depreciation can apply to different assets: for example a warehouse, if depreciated, may be on a straight line (equal annual sum) basis, whereas a reducing balance basis may (declining amount) apply to vehicles reflecting a greater 'front end' loading. These are acceptable methods providing they are used consistently. Some companies, not least those in logistics, may lease rather than buy some of their assets. Traditionally it was believed to be important to 'own' assets but the business imperative has moved towards simply the 'right to use' assets rather than own them. This has tended to be so popular recently that owners of valuable assets (a warehouse, for example) have been encouraged to sell the asset to a finance house and lease it back (**sale and lease back**). This can have valuable tax benefits on which the finance house is better positioned to capitalise and can make the company look more efficient, earning high revenues from an apparent lower investment in assets. Accounting rules have some approaches to deal with these situations of the difference between the 'substance over form' of a transaction in the accounts, but the readers of accounts should bear in mind that where any variations occur from very traditional ways of doing business, then what is reflected in the accounts should be read carefully.

Additionally companies in logistics may also own sophisticated systems and processes based on IT systems such as SAP and while the hardware may be owned as assets, the software may not have been 'capitalised'; rather it may have been written into the books as an expense of the profit and loss account. The skill and ability of employees to operate these systems will also be recorded as expenses. These *intangible* assets are rarely recorded in the balance sheet; in fact, current regulation discourages it. This fact could, in this event, distort the apparent state of affairs of the business and its performance as shown in various accounting measures or in its appearance to investors. Only if these intangible assets were acquired from a third party by a 'market-based' transaction would they be recorded in the accounts.

It is important to note that the balance sheet relates to the business (a legal entity), not to the shareholders. Any share capital is therefore a liability of the business because it is owed to the shareholders. Any net profit earned is also the property of the shareholders. This is paid to them either as a dividend or reinvested in the business on their behalf in which it is called a 'reserve'. A balance sheet should always balance: that is to say, assets should equal liabilities because these two aspects are looking at the same thing but from two different perspectives – what the company owns and what it owes.

The *profit and loss account* or *income statement* aims to convey to the reader the result of the trading activity of the business for a defined period of time. Profit or loss is determined by comparing revenue from sales made with expenses consumed in making and selling the products and services sold. Expenses are often subdivided into the costs of different functions of the organisation, typically manufacturing, administration, selling, research and development.

Various rules and conventions dictate how revenues and costs should be compared (called matching). It is important to appreciate that some costs incurred in one accounting period can be carried into the next accounting period, for example if they are attached to some stock which is unsold. Naturally this applies only to manufacturing costs. Non-manufacturing costs are often dealt with as an expense of the accounting period in which they are incurred, often called period costs.

From the information contained in the profit and loss account a gross profit can be determined (sales less cost of sales). The operating profit is determined by deducting other expenses, administration and selling costs, etc. from the gross profit. An item that falls within normal trading activities but is individually significant is called an exceptional item and disclosed separately. An example of a non-recurring exceptional item could be the retirement of an old fleet of aeroplanes before they were fully depreciated or the replacement of an obsolete company-wide IT system with a newer, more efficient version. Profit after deduction of tax is available to be paid to shareholders as a dividend or to be retained in the company for reinvestment, for example in new plant and machinery. An adjustment may be made to the profit after tax for any item that is derived from events outside the ordinary activities of the business, called an extraordinary item. This is sometimes referred to as an adjustment below the line.

Cash flow is sometimes called the lifeblood of the business. It is important for all businesses to trade at a profit, that is to sell their goods or services at a price that exceeds their cost. It is equally important, however, to ensure that an organisation manages the way in which cash is generated and used. That is not the same thing as ensuring profitability. A business can be profitable but short of cash and the converse can also apply. Cash can be particularly important; a company can trade at a loss for a short period providing it can pay its bills, but if it has no cash it is doomed, it is insolvent and could be bankrupt. It is useful for both management inside the company and outsiders who are appraising the company to examine how cash has been controlled in the past accounting period. The cash flow statement provides such a basis by showing *where funds have come from,* such as outside the organisation (share capital and loans), and inside the organisation (from the manufacturing trading cycle), and *where the funds go to* outside the organisation (dividends, taxation, loan interest), and inside the organisation (in the investment in fixed assets or the manufacturing trading cycle). See Figure 13.1 for the flow of funds round a traditional business.

For funds to be tied up in the business for a long time (in working capital) is wasteful and inefficient for the business; it means asking shareholders to subscribe more money than is realistically needed, and it is therefore to be discouraged. Making the amount of cash tied up as small as possible is a way to enhance performance and profit. Just-in-time manufacturers realised this a long time ago, and attempts to minimise stock and work in progress are a way to use capital and cash efficiently, providing production flow and supply can be guaranteed. Time has emerged as an important dimension of performance and logistics companies should be trying to deliver a product or service in a minimum required time, with resources committed for only a short time, thus minimising the amount of cash involved, the shortest possible cash-to-cash cycle. This is likely to result in a higher accounting performance all other things being equal.

Dell Computer Corporation, which we studied at the end of Part One, has this off to a fine art; it has a reputation for starting to assemble a computer for a customer only once the order is placed. In other words, it receives an order and within a relatively short period of time is likely to receive payment from the customer. It simultaneously sources the components and transport requirements from various suppliers, paying for them on

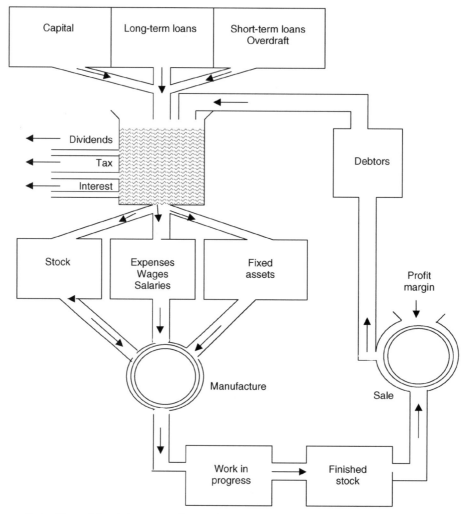

Figure 13.1 Flow of funds in a typical manufacturing business

normal credit terms (most likely anywhere between 30 and 90 days). It is quite likely that Dell has a very short cash-to-cash cycle and therefore needs to have only a very small level of working capital in its balance sheet.

FINANCIAL MANAGEMENT

Financial management is concerned with how the company manages its funds over the longer term. This involves, for example, decisions on the extent of its financing – how many shares it issues and at what price, whether it borrows money from the bank or not to supplement its financing, whether it pays a dividend from its profit to shareholders or retains this in the company. It extends to decisions as to how the company spends its finances in the acquisition of new buildings, plant and equipment and the management of its working capital – stock, debtors and cash.

Ordinary shares are the basic form of business finance. Shareholders may be a private individual, an insurance company, a unit trust, a bank, a trades union and so on. Shares are issued with a nominal value (25p for example, or in the case of Deutsche Post 1 euro, see case study), which is shown on the face of the share certificate. They may be issued by the company at any price if it is believed the investor will be willing to pay something different (a premium). This will depend on the company's prospects. Once shares are in the market they will change hands between shareholders at various prices, depending again on the company's prospects. The market price is of concern to the company but it is not incorporated into the accounts of the company in any way, other than when the shares are first issued to the public.

Ordinary shareholders carry the main investment risk of the business. They get the rewards in the form of dividend or increased share price if the company does well, but they lose some or all of their investment if it does badly. The most they can lose is the value of their shares: the principle of *limited liability* states that shareholders' liability is limited to the sum they have paid or agreed to pay for their shares.

Risk is a fundamental aspect of doing business and has taken on increasing importance recently (see Chapter 15). In any stock market, or indeed any market economy, the greater the risk incurred, the greater the reward that is expected. No one wants to take on more risk than they need to for a given level of return; likewise in competitive situations companies and investors will always select a higher rather than lower level of return for the same risk.

International business

A logistics company doing business internationally faces greater risks than one operating only nationally. It faces the higher business risk and uncertainty (market demand, delivery reliability, etc.) that may exist in the international environment and the different countries in which it does business. There may be different levels of political risk in the countries and the company may have only limited information on which to make judgements about this; naturally more information can be obtained but this is only at a cost and its validity may be suspect. A company also has to face currency risk; those trading in various international currencies must make decisions on the currency in which they will buy and sell their services. If they do not wish to operate as currency speculators, and most will not because they do not have the expertise, they will have to anticipate their currency needs and 'hedge' their risk in some way so that a trading profit is revealed rather than a currency fluctuation. It also means incorporating into the accounts of companies the 'home country' equivalent value of international transactions so they can all be accumulated in one currency for the appropriate financial reports.

Doing business, either buying or selling, in another currency, means that a company is exposed to fluctuations in that currency, called currency exposure. If the proportion of that business is considerable, it is wise for the company to obtain or develop expertise in dealing with the exposure. The accounting impacts can be various and affect both the profit and loss and balance sheet. **Transaction exposure** is related to the profit reported from a foreign transaction. For example, if a UK company is selling something in China and the contract is signed for payment to be made in the foreign currency (RMB), and between the date of the contract and the cash flow payment actually being received the currency falls in value by 4% relative to the UK currency (GBP), this will be a real loss to the company. **Translation exposure** is more of an accounting recording issue; that is, it is related to the value of assets held in China by a UK registered company which prepares consolidated accounts in the UK. The assets would be translated into the current UK balance sheet at a value relevant at the balance sheet date. This will affect the apparent value of the company on the balance sheet, but not the profitability of its trading. The same implication applies to borrowings undertaken in a foreign currency.

An international company must therefore consider its economic exposure. It may buy and sell goods and services in many parts of the world and hence the value of the stream of foreign cash flows when denominated in the 'home' currency (e.g. GBP for a UK-based company) will alter over time; this will affect the sterling value of the whole operation. It may move to favour the company or to its detriment, depending on the currency movement. Obviously it is good for, say, a UK-based company to sell to companies whose currency is likely to rise in value against GBP and to buy from those whose currency value is likely to fall, but this is clearly not always possible. One way to avoid this uncertainty is to establish all contracts in the home currency of the company and shift all risk to the trading partner. This would leave the foreign company to convert any purchase and sales to its own currency and make decisions as to the relative levels of business to undertake. Often these relative levels of economic exposure are affected by long-term and political factors affecting economic growth, taxation, etc.

Where an international company has operations in different parts of the world, *taxation* can have a significant impact on the reported financial results. This is not the same as undertaking transactions internationally, but involves operating and earning profits from activities and owning assets in different parts of the world. A fundamental point here is that the profits earned in different countries throughout the world should be taxed based on the rules existing in the country in which they were earned. This may be even though the accounts may be subsequently consolidated into a currency of the country of the holding company. It can have implications for international transactions and the transfer, say, of components between companies within the same group in different countries.

When goods or services are transferred between divisions of the same company a value is attributed to them called a **transfer price**. This is an internal price and is recorded in the books of account in order to compute the profit arising on the transaction accumulating to the profit of the two entities involved. The two parties inevitably will seek a price that makes the results in their respective accounts look best for them: that is, the highest possible selling price or the lowest possible buying price. The company as a whole may take a slightly different view when this occurs internationally. Setting a transfer price at a level to reduce the overall company tax bill may be to the financial benefit of the whole company, but this might not be what is desired by either of the businesses in their respective countries. The company would like the higher profit on the transaction to be reported in the country that has the most favourable (lowest) tax rates, or for example in the division which has accumulated losses (to act as offset), rather than a division operating in a high tax region or that already has a high level of profits. This must be acceptable to both the auditors and the taxation authorities; it must therefore reflect a reasonable price for the product or service and must not be used fraudulently. In other words, it must follow generally accepted accounting principles and appear to be a reasonable price in the circumstances, not out of line with other business by this or similar companies. Some multinational companies might move work-in-progress materials (which they would not necessarily have to move) between regions so as to use transfer pricing to minimise their overall tax charge in the accounts. An important distinction must be observed between tax avoidance, that is arranging affairs to minimise tax, and tax evasion, which is attempting to mislead and defraud the tax authorities, which is illegal.

Borrowing

An important source of finance is borrowing. Borrowing may be described variously as a loan, mortgage or debenture. Debt is often secured on the assets of the business and is basically a contract between the company and the bank for a loan of a particular term. An overdraft, which is agreed with the bank to apply over a relatively long period, may also fall into this category. Company law permits the interest paid for borrowed funds to be offset against any taxation liability and this is an important benefit for a company which engages in borrowing. In other words, the loan interest that is payable is an expense of the profit and loss account before the assessment of taxation. In contrast, dividends are paid out to shareholders out of profits after the interest and tax have been deducted. A company which has borrowed money to buy an asset, for example a warehouse, will benefit by the loan interest and the depreciation[1] being allowable against tax. This is in some contrast to sale and lease back mentioned earlier where the finance house effectively raises the loan, owns the warehouse and benefits from the tax allowance of depreciation.

The extent to which a company is financed by shares or debt is described as its *gearing*. Little or no debt is called low gearing. If a company has a large proportion of debt this is described as high gearing. In the case of high gearing much of the business risk is applied to the relatively smaller proportion of share capital and hence is a high-risk investment for any shareholder. However, if the company is successful the rewards can be proportionally greater. Naturally risk is different for different businesses and also depends on the products and markets in which the company does business.

The accounts of a company represent the results of the financial management and trading decisions made by its management. It is important for all logisticians to be able to undertake an interpretation of the accounts of a company and make judgements about the trading prospects and financial management of it. These judgements are often assisted by examining the relationship between pieces of information in the accounts called *ratios*.

To demonstrate with financial numbers from a real logistics company some of the issues discussed above, the reader is referred to the case on Deutsche Post/DHL, a leading 3PL we already mentioned briefly in Chapter 8.

MANAGEMENT ACCOUNTING

A large multi-product organisation is a complex entity and to ensure that the financial accounts and financial management of the company display a relatively stable picture is very important. That is, to show that it does not hold any surprises or shocks for the investors, because this will inevitably affect its share price. This requires detailed internal information with which to manage the development of the enterprise on a more short-term basis. This is often called **management accounting** and is undertaken to ensure that the long-term financial management of the enterprise is on track. The exact distinction between management accounting and financial management is not always clearly defined; it does not need to be, the content of this information overlaps. One thing it has in common is that information on this is internal to the company and its management; the detail and rationale does not have to be shared with the public in general, though the outcomes in the financial accounts are eventually apparent.

Inside the organisation the finance department produces information for management, which is not published because it contains details of the company's plans and its strategies for going forward. This is called *management accounting* or sometimes *cost accounting*. Management and cost accounting serves internal members of the organisation and often relates to segments of it (departments, machine groups, sales regions, individuals). It is future oriented, not governed by any legal regulation and entirely optional to the company. Its aim will be to produce the information that is most useful to management in the achievement of their organisational objectives. Internal management accounting information is not a requirement for companies, they use it only if it is seen to be helpful. But most companies make considerable use of management accounting information, rely heavily on it and it enhances their financial performance.

Cost accounting involves accumulating cost information to value stock, help with judgements on pricing and profitability analysis, decide whether a product or a contract is worth proceeding with, etc. Management accounting has a wider role, which could involve special studies relating to decision making, for example whether to make or buy a product (in-house provision or outsourcing) or whether to take a special order. It also involves the generation of financial plans and regular reporting of actual results in order to monitor the performance of departments within a company (budgetary control). Another example of a major non-recurring decision is the investment in large-scale capital projects with a time horizon of many years. Here a comparison of cost, revenue and profit is rarely sufficient and so special techniques are required. Finally, management accounting is not only inward-looking, it can also extend to the collection of valuable external information about competitors, their prices, market shares and meeting customer requirements.

Costing

Costing is concerned with the collection of costs and their relation to activities of the company, often called a cost object, which could be a product or service, a department, an operation, a machine or a sales territory. A useful and common framework within which to consider the provision of cost information is related to the major areas in which accounting information supports management. These are stock valuation and the calculation of profit, decision making and planning and control.

The calculation of a product cost requires the identification and measurement of all costs that are directly or indirectly associated with a product or any activity. Costs that can be easily and conveniently associated with a finished product are called *direct costs*. There is usually no ambiguity over the association of these costs with the item that is being 'costed', raw material or purchased components for example. All costs that are not direct are called *indirect costs,* although *overhead* tends to be a more usual term: costs of management and supervision are typical indirect labour costs. Indirect expenses are the costs incurred in providing the supporting and general facilities of the company. Rent, rates, heat and light are all examples of indirect expenses.

For a logistics company the costing may be undertaken in relation to a service, for example the delivery of the product of another company to a new location and perhaps in a different form, but the same principle applies. To an extent there may be greater complexity because costing of a service may be more difficult. Services are intangible: they are difficult to measure, for example in terms of quality, they cannot be stored (they are perishable), so if not undertaken when required they are lost for ever. In services few of the costs are often direct and many are indirect and this makes the arbitrariness more of a problem. This may be compounded in that logistics arrangements may be undertaken by more than one company working in harmony so that the total cost of a logistics operation may be the sum of various subsidiary operations carried out by different suppliers.

Many service businesses carry out costing procedures but often, given the complexity mentioned above, they either choose to (1) prepare a simplistic costing that deals very arbitrarily with the ambiguity of overhead costs, or (2) alternatively incur the higher costs of installing a sophisticated costing system to track the detail of costs along all of the supply chain. Such an arrangement is optional and entirely in the hands of the company.

The objective when dealing with indirect costs or overheads in product costing is to try to apportion them as equitably as possible to products. One principal reason for this is to arrive at a cost that will help in setting a selling price. It would be possible to add up all the overheads for a whole factory and apportion these at a single universal average rate applied in accordance with the number of each type of unit produced or relative to the number of production hours consumed by each product. However, such a single 'blanket rate' is only suited to very small operations or where only one product is manufactured; it is not very accurate. A more usual method of dealing with overheads starts with the calculation of an overhead rate for each department. Some costs can be directly identified with a department and others which are indirect can be shared between departments on an equitable basis. As a result the approximate cost of running each department is determined. A problem with this approach for modern businesses, however, is that it reinforces the department-centred or silo approach that has existed in businesses for such a long time. It runs counter to the (horizontal) cross-business culture which SCM and logistics encourage and one which managers envisage the products or services they provide actually follow.

Activity-based costing

The approach mentioned above using departmental rates has been established for many years. Recently, with the increasing use of sophisticated techniques in both manufacturing and operations management, the accuracy and value of these costing exercises has been called into question. It is suggested that it might be fruitful for organisations to examine in more detail the activities they carry out in the production and delivery of a product. They may be able to identify a number of activities which may be used to apply overheads to products more appropriately, such as number of orders processed, number of quality inspections or machine setups, deliveries, etc. Some companies have experimented with this approach, called **activity-based costing** (**ABC**, and not to be confused with the stock classification system discussed in Chapter 10, also called ABC), and have produced results that are interesting and different from the traditional method.

One useful feature of the ABC approach is that it identifies the processes and activities that a product or service incurs in a company. That is, the thinking behind it is close to the product flow or process envisaged by management and mapped out as part of a logistics operation in many companies. This was often not the case with traditional costing, which took the silo or department-centred approach mentioned earlier. The fact that it requires a more detailed analysis of activities and their costs means that the system is more expensive to operate, unless some of the data is available already, and thus often only larger companies have the resources to undertake this costing in any great detail. There is nothing to prevent smaller businesses also experimenting with the approach to determine whether it can support their decision making and control.

DHL chose to install a detailed ABC system in the 1990s because it felt that its administrative indirect (overhead) costs had grown considerably and more than some of its operations and customer service costs. The ABC system helped Dell explore the costs of some of the processes and activities it was undertaking and exactly what it was getting for these costs (i.e. did they add value?).[2] The company felt it needed to get 'a handle' on the causes of these costs and it was not happening with the information it was currently producing. Additionally, as a customer-focused company it needed an analysis of the profitability of customers and customer groups, and this was not available in any meaningful way with its present system.

It should be pointed out that having the profitability information such as this is a first step in managing costs that are incurred. Observing that the cost of a particular process is high does not alter the situation, it is up to management to respond to this by taking decisions. It might be observed that some activities are very expensive, compared with the use of competitors or external suppliers, so is outsourcing these activities an option? Alternatively, how can the company become smarter at some of these activities or processes so as reduce their cost? Does the customer value the activity (say, delivery at an agreed time), does the customer pay for this service, does it add value?

Most of the above approach to costing is carried out for the accounting year in which the company is operating. This is in line with the annual reporting that a company undertakes to shareholders. This does not have to be so. One alternative that is sometimes used is called **life-cycle costing** or **whole-life costing**. It can be applied to a product or to a resource of the company like an asset. It rejects the notion that performance can be broken down into an arbitrary annual time to suit financial reporting and instead explores costs and performance over the whole life from design to retirement or cradle to grave. It therefore gives an overview of cost performance without being distorted by showing periods of high cost at, say, introduction and relatively low cost at eventual steady-state operation. This aligns with the product life-cycle concept which management are well aware of, but which accountants have given less emphasis to, perhaps because of imperatives of periodic financial reporting that drive many company accounting systems.

As companies and business operations develop and become more sophisticated so management accounting techniques and approaches develop also. For example value chain costing has received greater prominence in recent years. This is where costing is applied to all the processes and activities along the 'value chain' of a product, where costs, benefits and investment can be compared. This might reveal where the company is particularly efficient in some parts of the value chain and less so in others. It then highlights where there is scope to improve, learn from other, collaborate, buy in expertise etc. Accountants do not make that decision but they equip management specialists with the information to make judgements. A further development in costing is termed target costing; this involves posing the question 'what will a customer pay for this product or service? and from the answer working back (by deducting a target profit) to how much it should cost the company (an allowed cost). This forms the basis of considerable management discussion and analysis in order to ensure that the product or service is delivered for this cost. This is a sophisticated and complex process of reading the market and careful engineering, operational and functional evaluation.

Management accounting information can also help management with a wider range of decisions and provide an insight into the financial consequences of a particular course of action. Ad hoc tactical decisions can vary depending on the circumstances in which the decisions are made; for example, if a business is working to full capacity it is likely to seek to establish a selling price that will cover all of its costs (assuming it is a profit seeking company). It will want the highest price it can get allowing for any issues concerned with both the wider business strategy and business ethics. If, however, a company has spare capacity it may be prepared to accept (in some cases) a price that does not cover all of its costs. That is, it may be prepared to omit any costs that in total would remain virtually unaffected by the decision to do a deal (for example rent or management salaries). It would only consider the costs that will change because of the decision, said to be the *costs at the margin* or the *marginal costs*. A special cost analysis would be necessary to identify marginal costs. A tactic such as using marginal costs must not, however, be allowed to offend regular customers who pay the full price, so such deals may need to take place in segregated markets.

One factor that is often singled out for detailed attention is the volume of output of a business; this may be influenced by manipulating price, for example. A typical decision may be to identify how many units of a particular product to make and sell at a certain price. This decision requires the identification of likely revenue, cost and profit at different levels of output, called **cost, volume, profit (CVP) analysis**. This particularly relies on the identification of variable and fixed costs. Variable costs are those that change approximately in proportion to output; fixed costs are those that in total remain unchanged despite changes in activity. In addition there are a number of mixed costs that need to be analysed as to their fixed and variable components to be incorporated into such analysis. There are no hard and fast rules governing accounting for decision making. The example just described only introduces the issues; each decision-making situation requires its own unique arrangement of costs and revenues.

Management accounting also supports managers with financial planning and control. Planning is a most important managerial function and associated with this is the need to implement plans and monitor them. Accounting can support this process using budgeting and variance analysis. The issue and use of departmental budgets is part of a system of responsibility accounting where actual results are compared with plans predicted for each department with the intention of taking action to correct any divergences. Only those costs and revenues over which a manager can exercise significant influence should be included in their responsibility report; this is a fundamental principle of controllability.

Using non-financial information

It should be noted also that control information should be in a form that is most useful and understandable to the appropriate manager. Following on from this, it is logical that some information may be of a non-financial nature. This may be provided sooner than any equivalent financial measure and would be in a form more suited to the manager's situation. Such non-financial information helps to put the financial measures into a more appropriate context and helps to ensure that wider objectives than the purely financial ones are addressed. In many companies the use of non-financial measures is not new; however, they have often been generated on a somewhat random basis without much structure as to which are the most important ones. There are various approaches or frameworks that have been put forward to help structure a meaningful set of non-financial and financial performance measures. One approach that has been used widely and quite successfully in this context is the **balanced scorecard (BSC)**, which has received considerable promotion in the literature and through consultancies (see Figure 13.2). This seeks to set performance measures from the top of the organisation; that is, those that are most important to the achievement of an organisation's strategy.

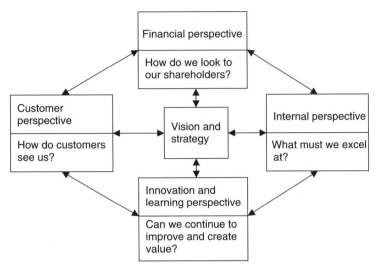

Figure 13.2   The balanced scorecard (Source: Kaplan & Norton, 1992)[3]

The original version of the BSC had four sectors: customer, finance, operations, and innovation and learning. Management would then pose the question, 'in what ways do we need to excel in these areas in order to be successful?' This would give rise to a set of measures that would be the key to the performance and adding value in the company. They would be set by, and would help set the strategy of, the company. In setting these, the company would identify appropriate objectives, measures that reflect the objectives, targets it would be expected to achieve in each measure and any initiatives to help reach the targets. The key is in having a small number of measures that reflect the strategy, not a wide range of measures over which there is no clarity. An important component is the existence of a supposed cause-and-effect relationship between the various measures.

For example, a logistics company might perceive that for them customer satisfaction was critical, in terms of delivering on schedule within the prescribed time frame. In the customer segment a *soft* measure would involve a survey of customers' scoring of their performance; a *hard* measure would be the number of times a delivery was refused. In operations, schedule adherence would be an important measure, perhaps analysed by teams, this being achieved within a target or budgeted cost. In order to achieve good operational performance, employee training may be important, so number of days on training courses may be used to encourage employee development; employee morale may also be measured. Finally, the views of shareholders may be reflected in the achievement in typical financial measures such as return on capital employed or cash flow. The cause-and-effect argument goes that better trained and motivated employees will deliver a better operational service to customers, which will result in greater customer satisfaction, more business and recommendations, and ultimately higher profit. The measures can then be cascaded down the organisation hierarchy to ensure that managers in an organisation give attention to the measures they can influence, which reflect strategic issues related to customers, innovation and operations, in addition to financial performance.

We will return to discuss other non-financial performance measures in Chapter 14.

LEARNING REVIEW

In this chapter we have seen that logistics and financial management has both internal and external perspectives. The key financial accounting documents through which a company informs existing and potential investors, governments and other business contacts have been discussed. The structure, content and importance of the profit and loss account, balance sheet and cash flow statement have been outlined. We have pointed out how expertise in logistics and supply chain activity can have a beneficial effect on cash flow.

When dealing with finance issues we have drawn attention to the distinction between shares and loans, and to the use of sale and lease back in modern finance decisions. We have discussed the implications of risk on business performance and particularly currency risk in an international logistics company. We have pointed out typical forms of internal accounting information for managers that relate to product or service costs including ABC. A wider range of management accounting information was covered with reference to cost, volume, profit analysis. Planning and control have been mentioned including the emergence of the balanced scorecard.

Chapter 14 further discusses some of the issues developed in this chapter, in particular the use of non-financial performance measures. As the concluding chapter in Part Two, the focus of which was 'doing' logistics, Chapter 14 endeavours to bring together all of the various logistics nodes, links and flows discussed in this part of the book and outlines how logistics and supply chain performance can be measured and managed.

QUESTIONS

- Briefly distinguish between financial accounting, financial management and management accounting.
- Who may be interested in the accounting information produced by a logistics company?
- In what ways might an international logistics company face currency risk?
- Differentiate between transaction and translation exposure.
- In what ways might a logistics company legally manipulate its tax bill?
- Outline typical direct and indirect costs of a logistics company known to you.
- Contrast activity based costing with traditional costing.
- Outline possible measures on a balanced scorecard of a logistics company.

NOTES

1. In taxation assessment this is called capital allowances and specific rules apply.
2. Holton, M. (1998) Implementing ABC in a service-driven business – DHL worldwide, in J. Innes (Ed.) *Handbook of Management Accounting,* Gee, London, 23A, 1–12.
3. Kaplan, R. & Norton, D. (1992) The balanced scorecard – measures that drive performance, *Harvard Business* Review, January–February, 71–79.

FURTHER READING

Drury, C. (2005) *Management Accounting for Business,* 3rd edition, Thomson, London.

McLaney, E. & Atrill, P. (2005) *Accounting: An Introduction,* 3rd edition, FT/Prentice Hall, London.

Pike, R. & Neale, B. (2003) *Corporate Finance and Investment,* 4th edition, FT/Prentice Hall, London.

Tayles, M. & Drury, C. (2001) Moving from make/buy to strategic sourcing: case study insights, *Long Range Planning,* 34, 605–622.

14 Measuring and Managing Logistics Performance

Noel McGlynn

Microsoft

LEARNING OBJECTIVES

- Understand basic forms of performance measurement used in a logistics context such as tachographs in road haulage and space utilisation in warehousing.
- Illustrate the trend towards measurement of a wider array of activities and the eight driving forces behind this trend.
- Explain why many LSPs now routinely share key performance data with customers.
- Understand the role of benchmarking in the context of logistics performance management.
- Identify how many and which key performance indicators (KPIs) to track, how they are embedded within the organisation, how they fit with wider company objectives, where the requisite data will come from, and who (at what levels within the organisation) should receive the information generated by these KPIs.
- Understand in particular warehouse/inventory metrics and total landed costs.

INTRODUCTION

The traditional practice in logistics service providers (LSPs) and related companies has been that managers in these companies do not spend substantial periods of time on measuring and managing performance. Instead, they tend to focus only on operational execution (i.e. getting the job done), and meeting only the most basic of measureable criteria. As a result they are apt not to spend much time on performance measurement, except only where deemed absolutely necessary.

This is changing, however, driven mainly by competition and especially as a result of increasing demands from customers who want to be assured of effective management of their business. This chapter is thus concerned with the measurement and management of performance in the logistics context. As such it endeavours to bring together all of the various logistics nodes, links and flows discussed in Part Two of the book and outline how logistics and supply chain performance can be measured and managed.

Chapter 14 comprises seven core sections:

- Basic measurement
- A contemporary viewpoint
- Driving forces for performance measurement

- Selecting the best measures
- Commonly used metrics
- Inventory/warehouse related metrics
- Logistics costs performance

BASIC MEASUREMENT

The performance measures that logistics companies traditionally spent some time on are those measures that were either very basic from an operational viewpoint, or imposed on them by law.

As such LSPs would have concerned themselves with ensuring that statutory requirements were met and that their financial obligations regarding preparation and filing of annual accounts and so forth were given some time and focus. For many small and larger companies alike, the main focus of this work may have been to ensure that tax affairs were in order and that the correct returns to the relevant government agencies were made. The overall profit margin of the company would also have been recorded and used as a key part of internal reviews, though little of this information would have been shared outside the company. The general exception to this would be the annual report which would have to be filed and, depending on local legislation, be publicly available.

LSPs providing transportation have, for a number of years, been required to record their transport operations. A device known as a **tachograph** is fitted to a truck and is used to record the speed of the truck, distance travelled and any breaks taken by the driver. It is an instrument used by many police forces worldwide to ensure that laws relating to the maximum hours a truck driver can work are recorded. Although there are variations among different countries, the rules are designed to limit continuous driving time and detail minimum breaks and rest periods. For vehicles over a certain payload, often defined as four tonnes or more, the tachograph is considered a legal requirement, and must be regularly tested to ensure that it is in good working order. In certain geographies the results from tachographs must be recorded and filed by the truck operator. The tachograph is still in use, though more recently instead of recording the relevant information onto a paper disk, the digital tachograph records the information onto a smart card or digital memory device.

Another area that traditionally has been a focus of measurement by LSPs has been around warehouse and other resource utilisation measures. These would typically include total number of pallet or carton spaces consumed versus total available, or simple measures of total space consumed within the warehouse. Some measure of throughput would generally also be looked at, for example the total number of shipments received. At the broader company level the key inventory measure, from a financial perspective, would be to measure inventory turnover (as already described in Chapter 10). For road transport companies, the basic operational measure could include total number of deliveries successfully completed versus **dropped deliveries** (a term sometimes used to refer to failed deliveries, i.e. the freight that could not be delivered for whatever reason).

An important point to note is that such traditional measurements would generally not have been shared with or presented to the customer. These various measurements would have been analysed internally and customers in general would not be overly concerned with them as long as their basic needs had been served.

A CONTEMPORARY VIEWPOINT

Traditional LSPs are finding that, since the 1990s, their business is either undergoing major change in order for them to hold their market position, or they are moving into niche markets. Most successful warehousing companies for example have had to invest significantly in IT, with warehouse management systems (WMS) used to record all movements within a warehouse, often controlled by a radio frequency (RF) handheld computer scanner, now seen in most modern warehouses. Traditional transport companies too have seen significant changes, with many of them moving into providing warehousing services in addition to their transportation offerings.

This physical flow of product through the supply chain is now joined by the flow of information, which records details of each transaction every time a pallet or box is touched or altered. Today's third-party logistics service providers (3PLs) not only have to display expertise in operational management, they must also keep track of each transaction and ensure that they and their customers and agents can have access to information relating to this flow as and when it is required. In fact such is the importance of monitoring this information that many 3PLs now have dedicated staff whose job it is to record data that can be used in the development of **metrics**.

Metric reviews are thus now an important part of all business reviews, not just in logistics. In the past where the management of the company would not have reviewed any performance results, now such information in the form of metrics and **key performance indicators** (KPIs)[1] are shared with staff at all levels and in all functions, with partners and agents, and most importantly with customers. Indeed most large customers now hold formal business reviews with their 3PLs where the presentation of such KPIs is a key part of the meeting's focus. Instead of providing performance data on a few select topics, logistics businesses now see measurement of the performance of all operational areas as a common requirement from their customers.

DRIVING FORCES FOR PERFORMANCE MEASUREMENT

At least eight driving forces behind the increased use of performance measurement in a logistics context can be identified.

1. Increased reliance on contract manufacturers

Outsourcing by manufacturing companies keen to focus on their core competencies has seen them outsource more supply chain activities. Many of the large electronics companies for example have long since stopped manufacturing their own products and instead for a number of years have been outsourcing their manufacturing to contract manufacturers (we discussed the distinction between contract manufacturers and OEMs in Chapter 3). Companies such as Flextronics Inc and Foxconn are now responsible for manufacturing numerous electronics items from mobile phones and electronic organisers for Apple, to computers and printers for OEM customers such as Hewlett-Packard, Dell, and games consoles for companies such as Microsoft and Sony. By outsourcing manufacturing and logistics, these companies can spend more time focusing on their key competencies such as research and development, sales and marketing, and indeed SCM. As these companies outsource more and more elements of their business including logistics, they tend to rely more on tools that can help measure the performance of their suppliers.

2. Strategic importance of LSPs to supply chain success

The strategic importance of LSPs cannot be underestimated, as it is often these companies that have a direct impact on the end customer. In an era of online purchasing and marketing through the various media channels, certain businesses do not 'touch' their customers until the point of product delivery, and this latter activity is often subcontracted to an LSP. A late delivery, or indeed a negative service encounter at point of delivery, could affect the consumer's impression of the product or the retailer. And this could be the fault not of the seller, but of its LSP.

3. Adoption of manufacturing management principles

In the recent past 3PLs were increasingly being asked by their customers to adopt more and more world-class manufacturing based principles such as just-in-time (JIT), total quality management, six sigma, and more recently lean principles among others. Quality assurance management too is often a prerequisite, with most progressive 3PLs ensuring that they have been accredited with ISO certification. Motorola, for example, works very closely with its logistics providers to implement six sigma quality throughout the supply chain. This push for mainstream LSPs to become familiar with such practices has forced them to ensure that they are better positioned to measure key areas of performance.

4. Impact on customer experience

Customer satisfaction is seen as an important business philosophy. Today's consumer is much better informed and often has much more available choice. To ensure that customers (in both the B2B and B2C contexts) are satisfied is a key requirement for any business looking to be successful in the long term. As such this requires companies to better understand performance through quality programmes, customer polls and customer service metrics.

5. Increased competition

A focus on commercial goals is never more important than in a market with high levels of competition. Today's LSPs compete not only against local competitors, but in more and more areas the presence of a multinational or global 3PL is almost always also seen. In recent years the merger of a large number of LSPs into multinational players has started to change the face of the logistics industry. For example DHL's mergers and acquisitions have allowed it to grow not only into one of the largest logistics companies globally, but also one of the largest employers in the world for any industry.

The larger 3PLs generally bring financial stability that may allow them to take certain risks in order to gain market share. Thus for all smaller competitors, it is important that they better understand and control their costs. Although the amount of work outsourced to 3PLs continues to increase, the profit margin of most companies operating in this industry is being eroded, and most now operate in a low-margin business that requires significant capital investment. Measures need to be available to give management good visibility of resource utilisation, and importantly reports should be detailed to show in what specific areas of the business profits or losses are being recorded.

6. Information technology improvements

Improvements in the IT employed both in warehouses and to control and track shipments have led to a greater availability of data. These data can now importantly be accessed and presented as useful information without significant employee input as many reports can be run from systems electronically. As these systems become more and more advanced, data are often available in real time in the form of automatic emails, via electronic data interchange (EDI) onto vendors' and customers' systems, or via web reporting tools. The information reported should also be less prone to error and so can be better used for important decision making.

7. Empowerment practices

Empowerment of lower level employees with tasks and responsibilities that were once reserved for managers has been a tool used by many successful companies to improve employee productivity. Within the logistics industry this has been used to good effect with employees allowed to make decisions quickly so as not to hold up receipt of freight or an important customer shipment. However, it is important that management is more conscious of the potential negative impact of mistakes made by those employees who are empowered with more task. As such, management needs to make better use of KPIs to monitor their employees' performance.

8. Employee motivation

Use of performance metrics as a motivation tool was initially seen in advanced manufacturing operations, but is now also common within logistics operations. In order to motivate employees to 'beat' the previous number of pallets received or orders executed, for example, some companies put more and more effort into communicating such metrics to all employees. Sometimes public recognition within the workplace for the best performing team is enough to drive the whole operation to higher levels of productivity; in other operations these metrics may need to be linked to employees' rewards to generate the same results. If metrics are used in this manner it is important to stress, however, that they must be designed to reflect employees' controllable actions.

Selecting the best measures

In the area of performance measurement a useful maxim is to 'measure results, not activities'. This is valuable advice, as it is all too easy to focus on simply assimilating data without necessarily understanding how these data may be used. When first trying to design a set of indicators, the focus should not as such be directed towards what data may be easily available, but rather towards what benefit one hopes to gain as a result of having these measures in place. For example, within a warehousing environment, one may measure the number of trucks that arrive to collect goods rather than measuring the number of pallets loaded onto trucks, the latter being a more useful result rather than simply an indication of activity occurring. In practice many metrics are developed without much thought put into what the company can do with the information collected, so as part of the process to develop the right measures one should attempt to focus on how they may impact the operation.

The majority of measures should be focused on *quantitative* results; namely measures that have their basis in numerical data. Although it is always good to add some *qualitative* measures to a set of KPIs, it is very important to stress that measures based on raw data can often be better for accurately comparing performance over time, and indeed for predicting future results. Also quantitative measures should in general be more reliable when comparing over time, as long as the data used to generate them can be replicated without error.

Benchmarking costs and other variables

When deciding on which measures to use, a company should always ensure that benchmarking against other competing companies is not made impossible by its choice of metrics. Companies should always look to emulate best in class; however, without benchmarking, it can be very difficult to do this. Some larger logistics companies use their marketing budgets to try to convince not only their potential customers that they are among the best within their industry, but also attempt to persuade their competitors that this is also the case!

The logistics industry is one that relies on referrals from not just customers, but also from competing firms, where the referring company may not have the required capacity (in terms of warehouse space, transport capacity or other capabilities) but wants to fulfil its customer's requirement. For one firm to give business to another in this manner, it is very important that some benchmarking of performance can first take place, and that both parties can see through the marketing and sales pitch put forward.

In order to benchmark against the industry, the company needs to use a similar set of measures in order to map performance against the companies being benchmarked. Thus the time to first consider benchmarking is when a company is initially putting together a set of performance measures. Benchmarking should be seen as a continuous process, and not as a one-off project. Today's logistics industry is very dynamic and benchmark levels of performance can constantly change.

Benchmarking logistics costs from one supplier to another can be a complicated task as there are almost no standard cost templates used by different firms. It also can be quite difficult for the 3PL's customers to estimate their specific business requirement at the request for quotation (RFQ) stage. As such the 3PL might quote a price against a given scope of work, only to find that, once it starts the business, the scope of work does not represent all of its customers' requirements.

Number of metrics to report

Evaluating the optimum number of measures is always a difficult task but is one that should be given some thought. Too many metrics will result in an unnecessarily large scorecard, with measures of lesser importance having the effect of adding just 'background noise' while simultaneously making it an arduous task to actually identify the critical ones. The optimum scorecard will highlight the vital indicators needed to monitor the health of the organisation's key organs.

With logistics companies being so process focused, the measures used will need to ensure that they can measure the performance of these processes. As such it will be important to tailor measures to reflect the actual work performed in the operation. Prior to putting together a set of measures, the company must first ensure that its processes and procedures are documented, as often it is only after completing this exercise that management will fully understand all of the different processes employed. If a new process is introduced, for example to meet exacting customer requirements, then a new performance measure should be developed in tandem.

Designing key performance indicators

Once a company understands the need for performance indicators, and also has an understanding of what the right measures may encompass, the design of a set of KPIs is the next step. Before KPIs are introduced, the company itself must be clear about its own aspirations (i.e. what it regards as 'success') and how performance can be measured against this.

As we noted above, globalisation of the logistics industry has been seen in recent times with the acquisition and mergers market for LSPs being increasingly busy. As some of the largest 3PLs strive to have a footprint globally to support international customers, measurement of the performance of different entities takes on an additional dimension. 3PLs now have to compare sites in completely different geographies against each other as they may be serving the same or similar customers. Geodis for example provides warehousing solutions to IBM across Europe using common metrics where possible. Such common sets of metrics between distant sites is most important, and might be required as part of contractual obligations. Indeed as companies grow into differing markets, so too is there often an increase in the distance or boundary between senior management in headquarters and the local operations. In order to close this apparent gap, management at headquarters can use the timely flow of information and performance indicators to allow them to see what is happening.

Drafting of metrics is a task that needs to be approached with some degree of patience. Typically many measures will be reported and tracked before a key set will emerge. It is important to consider at first a large range of potential measures, and not to shortlist too many until an attempt is made to trial them. Expectations of how a metric may perform often change quickly once results start to be seen. During this period of testing new metrics, it can be useful to see if a baseline, against which future performance may be measured, can be determined.

Imposing metrics on the shop floor is often not a good idea. Resistance from warehouse and transport operations can often result in incomplete or incorrect data being recorded. In the same way in which it is important to communicate the company's objectives with all employees, so too is it important to ensure that shop-floor employees are in agreement with any metrics introduced. Employees must understand the measures, take ownership of the data and also stand by the results. Instead of senior management dictating the format of metrics, employees should be asked for their own ideas of what areas need measurement. Very often the most knowledge about the operation lies with the shop floor, and management, without realising it, can often be out of touch with the reality of problems faced daily within the operation.

Sources of data

As part of the activity to develop a set of metrics, a company should look at what resource it has available to contribute to the data needed.

Information technology is an area of key investment for most logistics companies. It is also an area where companies need to first look for data that will allow them to generate metrics. A system controlling processes and managing the huge number of transactions is also a system that could potentially be able to generate automated reports. System-generated data should help reduce the possibility of errors in data collection, increase reporting time by having the ability to operate day and night, and, most importantly, limit direct employee involvement and control the costs of metric development.

Operational employees can also make a valuable contribution towards providing certain data, which is otherwise difficult to source. Logbooks for shipments and warehouse capacity reports, for example, are traditionally the type of reports that employees may measure manually, though advances in warehouse systems mean that the majority of measures no longer need to be manually derived.

COMMONLY USED METRICS

When designing a set of KPIs, the logistics company must take into account any requirements that its customers may have for specific reporting. This does not necessarily mean that the metrics should simply be what the customer demands, however, as the customer may not understand the full business offering.

Companies should appreciate that there is a need to differentiate between the measures reported to different levels within the organisation. KPIs that may be very important to the warehouse manager, for example, may not prove useful for senior management. When creating a set of metrics it is sometimes useful to split the metrics into three different categories, catering for senior management, operational management and functional operations. Figure 14.1 illustrates metrics for each of these three categories. Many of these metrics will be discussed in more detail in the next section.

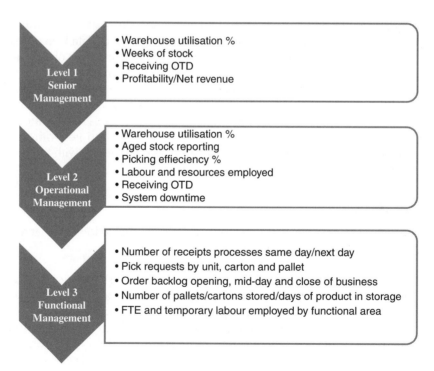

Figure 14.1   Category of metric reporting
(OTD = on-time delivery; FTE = full-time equivalent, i.e. the equivalent of one employee)

In practice, most LSPs tend to have a generic set of metrics, and also additional customer-specific metrics which would include measures relevant only to that customer. If this approach is taken, then it can result in customers thinking that they have been handed a complete set of customised metrics, while at the same time requiring the company only to add a small number of specific metrics for each customer, with the remainder being generic to the complete business (in effect this is a form of mass customisation).

In certain situations, for example where a 3PL is managing an onsite warehouse within the customer's manufacturing plant, one can find that almost all of the metrics are tailored to the operation. This in many situations is a result of the onsite operation often using the customer's IT systems rather than the warehouse management system (WMS) used in other sites operated by the 3PL.

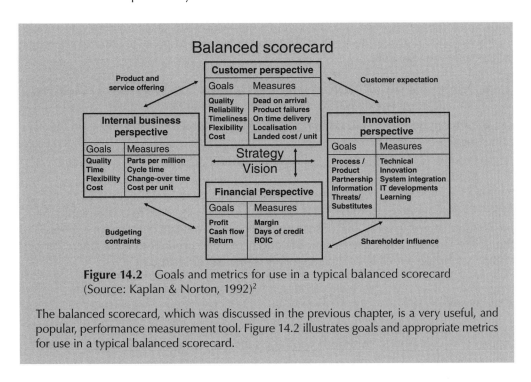

Figure 14.2   Goals and metrics for use in a typical balanced scorecard (Source: Kaplan & Norton, 1992)[2]

The balanced scorecard, which was discussed in the previous chapter, is a very useful, and popular, performance measurement tool. Figure 14.2 illustrates goals and appropriate metrics for use in a typical balanced scorecard.

INVENTORY/WAREHOUSE RELATED METRICS

External metrics for a warehousing-based operation need to be specific to the activities carried out. The following sections give a taste of the type of measures that a typical warehouse operation may employ.

Receiving

Receiving metrics are generally the first to be recorded, because receiving of product into the warehouse is often the most important transaction. If the receiving process is well thought out and implemented, then one would find that stock accuracy and product integrity should also be managed well. Indeed if product is received into the correct location, and in the correct quantity, then the subsequent picking process too has a good chance of being problem free.

Receiving time acts as a key metric in this area. Most WMSs can track the time between a shipment arriving into the warehouse through to it being formally received onto the WMS. Depending on how well developed the WMS is, advance notification of inbound shipment from the freight system can automatically initiate the inbound process prior to the shipment arriving. This **advanced shipment notification** (ASN) is used by the warehouse manager to determine workload and space requirements.

Once the shipment arrives, the receiving process will generally include a physical inspection before the formal system receipt can be completed. The specific metric can vary by facility but should always try to measure the effectiveness of receiving processes, which will include the following:

- Delivery paperwork detail is correct, ensuring exact delivery location, business unit and company delivering the product are mentioned.
- Part numbers, lot numbers and purchase order numbers match those on the paperwork and the ASN.
- Product is physically inspected with unit/carton or pallet count completed, product inspected for any signs of in-transit damage, repackaging, etc.

Adherence to the processes listed above is a basic requirement before one would measure the core metric in receiving, namely 'receiving on-time delivery'. This metric refers to the ability to receive both systematically and physically product that has been shipped to the warehouse within a set time, generally same day or next day.

Put-away

For ease of understanding we will assume that receiving and put-away are distinct tasks, though it is common to find both combined into one process and completed by the same personnel.

Put-away involves physically moving product that has just been received onto the IT system to a pallet or carton location where the product will be stored. Within some environments, product may at this stage be brought directly to the point of consumption such as a line-side kanban.

Metrics should include activity measures such as number of pallets, cartons or units put away, which in turn could be compared against the resource available to produce a productivity measure. Percentage of product put away within a stated time is another key metric. This is very important, as many warehouses might have good receiving metrics, but may end up having a lot of product sitting on the floor yet to be put away at the close of business.

Inventory accuracy

Cycle counting of product is an activity that customers usually take a keen interest in because the material being counted generally sits on their balance sheet rather than the 3PL's balance sheet. Inventory metrics really act as a measure of operational performance, and reflect the adherence to processes, rather than the performance of the inventory team who conduct the cycle counts. For example, if the receiving team make mistakes and put product into the incorrect aisle or stocking location, this may only be noticed during cycle counts.

System-generated cycle counts, often completed by the inventory team using a hand-held radio frequency (RF) terminal or alternatively a printed stock report, are used as the starting point for compiling inventory metrics. More advanced WMSs have the capability to generate cycle counts automatically, often taking into account any product classification (such as 'ABC' classification), which may exist to determine when products of a certain value should be counted. In order to ensure that accurate counting is maintained it is important that count sheets, or counts using the RF terminals, do not give visibility of the system quantity to the counter.

Cycle counts can be completed where a complete rack or segment of the warehouse is checked in sequential order. Random counts will require the cycle counter to count all inventory held in certain pallet locations across the warehouse. Part counts may exist to count all locations where a particular product is stored, and empty cycle counts should direct a counter to locations where the system does not show any stock as stored on the assumption that if the counter finds anything then it indicates an inventory accuracy problem.

Inventory accuracy may also need to be compared against that stated on the 3PL's WMS and the customer's own system. From a financial auditing perspective, there can only be one system of record, but in many environments dual systems without real-time EDI linkage are seen. In some warehouses, dual keying of stock transactions onto two systems can be seen, though every effort should be made to avoid such a system solution, and in these environments more stringent inventory control metrics need to be designed and monitored.

- 'Unadjusted inventory accuracy': inventory metrics should show 'first count results', i.e. the initial count results before the inventory team carry out any stock reconciliation.
- 'Adjusted inventory accuracy': once any required adjustments have been carried out, the inventory should be recounted and the results published.
- 'Net variance': this is the metric used to compare the total quantity of units for all part numbers on the system versus that counted.
- 'Absolute variance': takes into account the complete variance, i.e. it is arrived at by adding any positive and negative stock discrepancies. If reported absolute variance was high, but net variance was low, it would signal that stock was out of position.

It is important to remember that inventory metrics can often highlight a particular problem within warehouse processes. In order to improve inventory accuracy, improvements need to be made in either the design or execution of the warehouse transactions. Although most inventory metrics will be quantitative in nature, there should be some effort to also record some qualitative measures such as 'housekeeping' or 'completion of cycle counts'.

Measures may exist to determine the length of time that inventory is sitting in the warehouse. An aged stock report, detailing by part number the number of weeks that product is in stock, is the easiest of these metrics to report. Alternatively an overall view of stock movements within the warehouse can be given with a report outlining the number of inventory turns (as we saw in Chapter 10 this is the number of times on average the complete stock in the warehouse moves in and out).

LOGISTICS COSTS PERFORMANCE

Total landed costs

Financial measures are obviously key metrics for 3PLs, and indeed ones that their shareholders will place ultimate importance on. The customers of 3PLs too are also becoming more focused on analysing their overall logistics costs, and comparing them across different regions and product lines. They are demanding more and more information to allow them to better understand the cost of their logistics activities.

We discussed earlier in the book the growth that has taken place in recent years in both outsourcing and offshoring. Once the various strategic issues concerning whether or not to outsource and so forth have been resolved, companies need a tool which will enable them to compare alternative sources while taking account of all of the various costs that will be incurred. This is the concept of **total landed costs** and takes into account the following costs:

- Vendor (i.e. material) and packaging costs
- Transportation charges
- Working capital employed/opportunity costs
- Costs associated with risk migration
- Broker fees
- Insurance costs
- Taxes and duties
- Management costs
- Reverse logistics costs

The concept of landed costs allows managers to make better decisions regarding raw material sourcing, and rather than just going with the lowest possible product cost, companies can compare the overall financial impact from using different potential suppliers in different markets. Software tools are available that allow importers to compare landed costs. OOCL Logistics (www.oocllogistics.com) for example has launched a software tool called 'Landed Cost' which allows such calculations to be made.

Costing materials on an 'ex works' basis is not adequate to make a purchasing decision and so it is important that all related costs are considered, and compared. For example:

- *Freight*. The further from the intended destination that raw materials are sourced, the greater the freight costs. Even if freight is planned to be moved via ocean, the greater distance will result in longer lead times, and the chance of moving at least some product via air (at up to 10 times the cost) will increase.

- *Carrying costs*. Longer transit time will often lead to higher inventory in the supply chain, which in turn will increase the working capital employed and the risk of obsolescence, damage and shrinkage.

- *Duty*. Local sourcing is often the only way to minimise potential import duty of raw materials. Although some countries offer certain duty avoidance measures for materials bought overseas, the risk of paying higher rates of duty and inbound taxes, along with charges for more complicated clearance processes, increases.

- *Packaging*. The longer a product is in transit, the better the packaging needs to be. Also the potential for using re-useable packaging decreases.

- *Warehousing*. Longer lead time for products may increase buffer inventory storage locally.

- *Localisation*. Converting product for a local country may be cost prohibitive.

As freight costs can change dramatically over the short term, due to changing fuel and security surcharges and differing demand patterns for cargo along with changing air and ocean timetables, it is important that companies continually review their landed product costs by having metrics to measure these costs on an ongoing basis.

Unit-based costing, which often has its basis in management accounting principles such as 'activity-based costing' (ABC), is another important measure. Manufacturing and distribution companies need to understand the entire logistics costs on a per SKU (stock-keeping unit) basis because small changes in product specification or packaging can have a dramatic effect on the overall logistics costs. Nokia have for example tried to standardise its mobile phone packaging, so that different models use packing that is the same size and differs only by print. This has given the company an advantage over competitors who appear to have different packaging for each model.

3PL cost models

In the highly competitive logistics market, 3PLs are often placed under significant pressure to ensure that their response to requests for quotations (RFQs) are the most competitive, while at the same time ensuring that they do not engage in business that may run losses during the duration of the contract. In order to manage these pressures, many 3PLs use a number of different cost models.

(i) Cost plus margin

Cost plus margin is often the preferred model for 3PLs engaging in a new business where the statement of work is not detailed, or where the customer demands complete transparency of all costs.

This model is based upon a general assumption that space will be charged at a fixed cost per square or cubic metre, and staff costs will generally be presented as a loaded cost to include base wages and related employer costs including contribution to social taxes, health insurance, pensions and so forth. Material handling equipment (MHE) such as forklift trucks, racking and any other equipment used would generally be charged as a depreciated annual charge. IT charges would usually be the next item to be listed in a schedule of charges and may be split between user licences, IT support and development, in addition to depreciation for equipment used including warehouse management systems and office servers and computers.

When all charges are identified, the 3PL will generally then try to negotiate a mark up to cover corporate allocation or management overhead. Finally the required profit margin will be added.

The main advantages with this type of model are:

- It provides complete transparency for all parties involved.
- Risk is reduced for both parties – the customer should be better able to budget and the 3PL will also live in the certainty that its costs should be covered.

The main disadvantages are:

- There may often be reluctance for the 3PL to drive continuous improvement in order to reduce cost as the 3PL's profit margin increases as the total cost increases.
- Resources may be fixed at a level that meets the peak season demand, thus resulting in excess cost during quieter periods. Also resources employed may not be adequate to meet business requirements.
- From the 3PL's perspective there is little opportunity to make high profits as it will be very difficult to negotiate a margin higher than that quoted by competitors.

(ii) Transactional pricing

Transactional pricing would generally see a 3PL use all its available resources across multiple customers and quote a unit rate for standard warehouse activities:

- Receiving charged per carton or per pallet.
- Storage charged per carton or pallet on a weekly or monthly basis.
- Picking and handling out at unit, carton or pallet level.

These typical charges would be fully inclusive and include all staffing, space and equipment. IT setup charges would likely be charged as part of the original account project setup costs.

The main advantages of this type of model are:

- Resources are generally not fixed by the customer. Thus during the off-peak period, the customer does not have to pay for space or labour for which it does not have a requirement.
- The 3PL will be highly motivated to drive efficiency at all stages of the process as any savings made will result in higher profits. An efficient warehouse operation running to capacity should make it possible for the 3PL to make a larger potential profit with transactional pricing in place with its customers.

The main disadvantages are:

- The customer may not always get the customer service that is required unless it separately pays for fixed office resource.
- The 3PL needs to ensure that special requests are charged separately as the base rates should in general over cover a minimum level of service.
- The customer does not have transparency to resources employed supporting its business.

(iii) Alternative pricing models

As the service offered by 3PLs can involve a range of services, some cost models can be highly complex and may include an element of fixed and variable costs that may be billed on cost plus or transactional basis, or indeed any combination of each. Often it is critical for customers to have certain resources within the 3PL dedicated to them while still ensuring that other resources are only employed as required. For example the customer may decide to pay for a dedicated account manager, but may only pay space on a pallet or carton basis.

SERVICE LEVEL AGREEMENTS (SLA)

As well as negotiating and managing LSPs or other supplier costs, companies need to also ensure that a mutually agreed and understood agreement is in place between both the company buying the service and the company providing the service. The document that covers this area is commonly known as an SLA – a service level agreement. It is typically within the SLA that the selected performance metrics are detailed and elaborated. Typically SLAs will include details of:

- Roll-out and duration of the service or process being purchased
- Scope of services
- Areas of responsibility
- Performance metrics

LEARNING REVIEW

In this chapter we looked at basic forms of measurement in use in logistics systems, the trend towards measurement of a wider array of activities and the driving forces behind this trend. Customers in particular may attempt to dictate what metrics are used. It is important to remember that although customers may have specific requirements, which should be met, they may be out of touch with the day-to-day operation, and so may not be best positioned to decide how the complete metric set should look. Once the metric set has been decided, we saw that the current practice has evolved to such an extent that metrics are routinely shared with customers.

We realised that metrics are never set in stone, and they can and indeed should change as processes alter and the company's commercial focus changes. Before implementing a set of measures, we must first understand why this task is important, and, to determine what type of measures should be implemented, it is important to get a good understanding of what the driving force behind the overall activity is.

Metric development is a complicated activity, but collection of data should nevertheless not be allowed to take too much time. Operational resources must be first prioritised to ensure that operational tasks are completed before data collection and related metrics generation are started. We examined where metric data should come from, which and how many KPIs to track, and importantly who in the organisation should receive the data and reports generated.

We also looked in this chapter at benchmarking of logistics costs and other variables. Commonly used metrics were also reviewed, in particular warehouse/inventory metrics and total landed costs. The various costs associated with using LSPs were also reviewed and the framework for service level agreements outlined.

This chapter concludes our series of chapters (Part Two of the book) dealing with how to 'do' logistics and emphasising the key flows in supply chains. The next, final part of the book now moves on to deal with strategic issues, for example how to design effective and efficient supply chains and how to deal with important issues such as risk and sustainability.

QUESTIONS

- What are the various driving forces leading to greater use of KPIs in the logistics environment?
- In your view should all metrics be routinely shared with customers?
- Where do the data for metrics come from, and who within the organisation should receive KPI reports?
- Describe the various warehouse/inventory metrics currently in use.
- Why are service level agreements needed in the logistics sector?

PURCHASING 3PL SERVICES

Chapter 8 introduced the whole area of logistics service provision and the role played by 3PLs. In this chapter we looked at how those who purchase the services of 3PLs can manage their performance, and how the 3PLs themselves can manage their own performance.

The 3PL sector, as you will have observed, is now a global business with global players who in turn typically have large, global contracts with leading companies. Search for examples of any large, high-profile, global 3PL contracts and endeavour to see what metrics they employ within these contracts (sometimes new contracts are reported in the media with headlines that the new 3PL partner will reduce costs or increase performance in some specific area – metrics will be put in place to track this).

NOTES

1. The terms 'metric' and 'KPI' are usually used interchangeably; in a literal sense, while there may be many metrics, some will be more important than others and more accurate measures of important areas of performance, and would thus be more correctly labelled as 'key performance indicators'.

2. The reference for the balanced scorecard is: Kaplan, R. & Norton, D. (1992) The balanced scorecard – measures that drive performance, *Harvard Business Review*, January–February. For further insights and applications to the balanced scorecard, see also Kaplan's and Norton's various subsequent writings.

FURTHER READING

For a comprehensive series of readings on different aspects of business performance management by various contributors see: Neely, A. (2002) *Business Performance Measurement: Theory and Practice*, Cambridge University Press, Cambridge.

PART TWO CASE STUDIES

John Lewis Partnership: Semi Automated National Distribution Centre

Peter Baker

Cranfield School of Management

BACKGROUND

John Lewis Partnership is one of the UK's top 10 retail businesses and has a distinctive ownership structure, being the country's largest employee cooperative. All 70 000 permanent staff are partners in the business and own 28 John Lewis department stores, 2 John Lewis At Home stores, 234 Waitrose supermarkets and various other businesses, with a total turnover of £7.4 billion in 2009/10. The partners share in the benefits and profits of the business.

The John Lewis department stores sell high-quality goods under a slogan of 'never knowingly undersold' – which the company has used for over 75 years. The stores typically stock more than 350 000 product lines, ranging from fashion to furnishings and household goods.

The company has had strong sales even through the recession of 2008/10 and plans to open more stores in the UK in the coming years. The John Lewis stores have been supplied from six distribution centres (DCs), each handling distinct groups of products, identified either by size (e.g. small and medium-size item DCs) or by category (e.g. jewellery/garments, outdoor/lighting, white goods and furniture DCs). In addition, there is a central returns centre. The DCs deliver goods either directly to the stores or to service centres, which tend to act as stockrooms and home delivery points for individual stores or for groups of stores.

The Partnership's growth necessitated further warehousing capacity and it was decided that the best way to complement the existing distribution infrastructure was to introduce a new Semi-Automated National Distribution Centre (SANDC) to handle small-sized items, employing the latest technology so as to improve efficiency and accuracy. The SANDC is located at Magna Park in Milton Keynes, near the centre of the UK, and commenced operations in 2009.

The SANDC is a £46 million capital investment. It is 60 393 square metres in floor area with a height of 15 metres. There are 33 receiving docks and 46 despatch docks. The SANDC is designed to operate two shifts per day after ramp-up with potential to increase to three shifts per day at peak in future years. It is planned to hold 87 000 SKUs.

The SANDC is designed to enable item-level picking and thus reduce the need for back-of-store facilities. In addition, the SANDC can assemble goods in the planogram (i.e. layout sequence) of each individual store so that items can easily be placed on the store shelves. The business case is thus based on substantial store economies, as well as warehouse operational economies.

The warehouse is designed to be environmentally friendly with such features as:

- Solar panels
- Storm water collection
- 15% roof lights
- Automated lighting control systems

RECEIVING

Most goods are received packed in cartons on pallets. These are moved by reach truck onto a lift which raises each pallet to the appropriate handling height so that the goods can be extracted, checked and placed into plastic tote bins. There are a total of 52 decant workstations on raised platforms. Any new product lines are weighed, scanned for their cubic measurements and photographed at this stage. The tote bins are then normally transported by conveyor directly to the 'Miniload' Automated Storage and Retrieval System (AS/RS) or Order Storage and Retrieval (OSR) storage areas (see below). In total, there are over 10 kilometres of conveyor connecting the different operations.

Some goods are received in tote bins, in the correct quantities, and pre-advised electronically by the supplier using an Advance Shipping Notification (ASN). The pallets containing the tote bins are moved by a powered pallet truck (PPT) to depalletising robots which unload the pallets and place the tote bins onto a conveyor, for transport to the AS/RS or OSR.

Goods that are not required for picking in the immediate future are moved on pallets (or tote bins placed on pallets first) and transported by reach truck to the narrow-aisle storage area. Any pallets that have not been given a Licence Plate Number (LPN) by the supplier are provided with one at goods receiving for subsequent identification. All receiving operations are conducted with the aid of radio data terminals.

STORAGE

The narrow-aisle storage area comprises 26 × 1.75 m aisles, operated by wire-guided narrow-aisle turret trucks. 'Bus-bars' are fitted to some aisles for battery recharging so that the trucks can operate continuously over multi-shifts. There are a total of 22 500 pallet locations. When the goods are required for replenishment to the tote bin storage areas, they are moved to the tote bin filling platform (or directly to the bin storage area if they are already in tote bins). This narrow-aisle bulk storage area is thus used for replenishing the tote bins storage areas described below. There is also a separate hazardous narrow-aisle area with mesh protection.

The AS/RS is used to store tote bins of fast- and slow-moving lines. There are 13 cranes (one per aisle) capable of moving two bins at a time. The storage system is double-deep. The throughput rate of the cranes is 125 bins per crane per hour (both in and out). The tote bins are then placed onto a conveyor for movement to the picking operation.

Medium-moving lines are placed in the OSR storage area, which has 20 aisles. This area is similar to the AS/RS store, except that there is a shuttle car at each of the 16 levels of single-deep racking in every aisle. These remove tote bins, one at a time, to an automated lift at the end of the aisle, which then transfers them to a conveyor. These bins can be put away at a rate of 265 bins per aisle per hour (plus the same for retrieval), thus offering a greater throughput rate per aisle than the AS/RS. The OSR storage area is used for medium-moving lines as these require greater movements than the fast-moving lines (which are normally depleted in one picking movement) or the slow-moving lines (which are not required very often).

The AS/RS and OSR areas can store a total of 240 000 tote bins.

ORDER PICKING

The tote bins are moved by conveyor to the bin-to-bin picking area. There are 33 picking stations in this area. Each picking station comprises 12 tote bins on a lower level conveyor, representing the stores that need to be picked. On a higher level conveyor the tote bins are brought to two locations in front of the picker. Instructions are given to the picker by a pick-to-light system. The total number of items to be removed from an upper bin is displayed next to that bin. At the same time, the requirements for each of the lower bins (representing the stores) are also displayed. The picker completes each requirement for that product line and then presses a button next to each display to indicate that the task has been completed. The upper level bin is then returned to the

AS/RS or OSR storage area, and the picker starts to pick from the second upper bin. By the time this pick is complete, a further bin will have been moved into the upper position vacated by the first bin. Rates in excess of 650 picks-and-puts are achieved per picker per hour with this system. When picking to the store bins is complete, these bins are moved away by the conveyor system.

DESPATCH

The picked bins are transported by conveyor to an OSR despatch buffer store and then called forward as required to automated dolly loading machines, which place 10 tote bins on each dolly (i.e. wheeled platform for transit). The dollies are assembled in groups of three by the machine, ready for movement to marshalling (or directly onto the vehicle) by a PPT. The vehicles then transport the bins either directly to the stores or to the service centres that serve the stores.

DIRECT TO CUSTOMER

The direct delivery operation holds its own inventory so that it can control stock availability via the website, and call centre, to customers. Deliveries may be directly to customers' homes or to the retail stores for collection (known as 'click and collect' service). This operation is located in a specific area of the warehouse and has its own OSR storage and picking system. Additional goods may be brought from the narrow-aisle racking, from other sites, and occasionally (if needed) from the retail store AS/RS and OSR storage systems. There are 48 packing stations so that products are delivered in John Lewis[1] own packages.

GIFT LISTS

John Lewis operates a service to their customers known as Gift Lists. The most common use of this service is for customers to place a wedding list on the John Lewis website or in store. Previously, goods were taken from store shelves and held at stores (or the nearby service centres) until the day of the wedding. This reduced on-shelf availability, led to inaccurate store stock levels and took up valuable space. All Gift Lists are now assembled at the SANDC. Required products are reserved on the system until time for picking and are then packed into Gift List presentation cartons. Gift Lists are then loaded into roll cage pallets for transport to the Service Centre on the due day, ready for delivery.

WAREHOUSE MANAGEMENT SYSTEM

It was decided to use the warehouse management system (WMS) of the main materials handling supplier (i.e. Knapp's KiSoft) so as to have clear responsibility for the total warehouse software system. This software manages all warehouse movements and locations, as well as Knapp's OSR and other manufacturers' automated equipment, and controls all warehouse processes, including, for example, narrow-aisle put-away and retrieval by on-board radio data terminals.

There is a team of maintenance engineers on site throughout the operational hours, monitoring the automated equipment, via visual diagnostic computer screens and CCTV.

STAFFING CONSIDERATIONS

The operation has been designed to be an appropriate mix of manual and automated operations. Ergonomic considerations include a clean and bright environment, an automated control of maximum tote weight of 25 kg, pallet height adjustment in the tote filling area to avoid bending, waist height picking, staff rotation and other features.

THE FUTURE

The company is continuing to expand but in different directions to that originally anticipated. The SANDC was designed for 2013 store volumes but growth is now being generated increasingly by the home shopping and small store channels.

Research[1] has shown that there is very often a service level dip at the start of major automated warehouse operations. The SANDC implementation was planned in detail and allowed sufficient time for testing the equipment and information technology, resolving equipment and software issues and ramping up to full operation. However, this case study shows that even after a successful implementation, there are still continual challenges to be faced to maintain an effective 'business-as-usual' operation to serve constantly changing markets.

QUESTIONS

- With the changing demand patterns, fewer full bins are being required and a greater proportion of goods need to be picked at the picking stations. What alternatives may be considered to accommodate this?
- Should home shopping continue to have its own dedicated area within the SANDC, with its own inventory and OSR equipment? How flexible is a SANDC to such changes in demand patterns, and what are likely to be the key implementation issues for any future operational change?
- Continuous improvement is being sought in all operations. How can the present SANDC operation be improved still further in terms of efficiency, service levels, ergonomics and sustainability? What areas may be worthy of examination?

NOTES

1. Baker, P. & Halim, Z. (2007) An exploration of warehouse automation implementations: cost, service and flexibility issues, *Supply Chain Management: An International Journal*, 12(2), 129–138.
2. This case was written by Peter Baker, Centre for Logistics and Supply Chain Management, Cranfield School of Management. It is intended to be used as a basis for class discussion rather than to illustrate either effective or ineffective handling of a management situation. This case was made possible by the cooperation of John Lewis Partnership. Copyright © 2010 Peter Baker, Cranfield University.

Deutsche Post/DHL

Mike Tayles

The University of Hull

DHL (the letters stand for Dalsey, Hillblom and Lynn, the surnames of the three company founders) started life in 1969. In fact it was one of the first air courier companies in that its original product was the delivery by air of ships' papers from San Francisco to Honolulu (allowing customs clearance of a ship in Honolulu before the ship actually arrived, thus dramatically reducing waiting time in the harbour). Today the company is 100% owned by Deutsche Post World Net, a global organisation with a workforce of over 500 000 employees present in more than 220 countries and territories. Along the way it has acquired a number of logistics companies including Danzas and Exel, making DHL today one of the world's largest logistics companies. The Chairman of the Board of Management declared in the latest annual report 'we are both the market leader and a pioneer in our industry, always a step ahead of the competition. Our next mission is not just to be the biggest logistics company in the world but also the best.' Deutsche Post's accounts are denominated in euros. A brief summary and interpretation of their accounts follows to illustrate issues contained within Chapter 13.

Deutsche Post consists of five business segments, which are shown in the Deutsche Post Revenue by Segment table. In order to examine in an approximate way the accounts of the logistics aspects of the group, certain adjustments have been made to the published accounts in the 2006 annual report. This adjustment particularly removes the implications of the company's activity in financial services (Postbank), which would otherwise distort any appreciation of the accounts of a typical logistics company. Postbank offers financial services facilities to customers in Germany and the nature and content of some aspects of financial reporting in banks would distort the appreciation of what would be the content of the accounts of a typical trading company. It should be stressed that these adjustments are approximate and would be improved with greater access to the companies' accounts; it cannot be claimed therefore that these adapted accounts are detailed and authoritative. The published accounts of Deutsche Post can be located at http://www.dpwn.de. It can be observed that a number of the statistics quoted within the 170 pages of their published accounts are similar to the results presented here.

Deutsche Post Revenue by Segment

	Percentage
Logistics	34.0
Express	25.7
Mail	19.9
Financial Services	14.3
Services	6.1

Deutsche Post Balance Sheet as at 31.12.2006

Assets	Euros (millions)	Euros (millions)
Intangible Assets	14652	
Property, Plant, etc.	9510	
Financial Assets	994	
Other Non-current Assets	918	
Total Fixed Assets		26074
Inventories	324	
Receivables	9587	
Financial Services	7164	
Cash and Equivalent	2391	
Total Current Assets		19466
Total Assets		45540
Equity and Liabilities		
Issued Capital[1]	1202	
Reserves and Retained Earnings	10018	
Equity of DP Shareholders	11220	
Minority Interest	2732	
		13952
Non-current Provisions	12340	
Non-current Liabilities	5285	
Total Non-current Liabilities		17625
Current Provisions	1893	
Financial Services Liabilities	1945	
Trade Payables	5069	
Other Current Liabilities	5056	
Current Liabilities		13963
Total Equity and Liabilities		45540

The current market price per share of the company at the year end was 22.84 euros.

---

[1]This represents 1202 million 'one euro' shares in the company in this case.

Deutsche Post Income Statement – Year to 31.12.2006

	Euros (millions)	Euros (millions)
Revenue		63 366
Material Expenses	34 349	
Staff Costs	18 616	
Depreciation etc.	1 771	
Other Operating Expenses	4 758	
Less Total Operating Expenses		59 494
Net Income		3 872
Less Net Finance Costs		1 030
Profit Before Tax		2 842
Less Taxation		560
Net Profit		2 282
Attributable to DP Shareholders		1 916
Attributable to Minority Interest[2]		366

[2]The entry in the accounts of a minority interest indicates that Deutsche Post has a majority interest in some companies but does not own them entirely. As a consequence the companies' accounts are incorporated into the results of Deutsche Post (DP), but their total results are not the property of DP shareholders. The minority interest is the sum owed to others outside the company, but because of its majority status DP has to take responsibility in accounting for and reporting this.

INVESTOR RATIOS

A common ratio of which investors and analysts take notice is the *earnings per share* (EPS). This is based on the annual total profit after tax divided by the number of shares in issue. A trend of this figure over a number of years is a good indicator of the overall success or otherwise of the company.

$$\frac{\text{Earnings for shareholders (€ million) 1916}}{\text{Number of shares (million) 1202}} = 1.60 \text{ euros per share}$$

Another overall value that may be of interest to an outsider is the *market capitalisation* of the company, that is the value the market places on the company as a whole in its present state as a going concern, the number of shares multiplied by its current market price. For Deutsche Post this is:

$$1\ 202 \text{ million} \times 22.84 = 27\ 454 \text{ million euros}$$

This figure can be contrasted with the value shown in the balance sheet, where for example the equity (shareholders' investment) is valued at €11 220 million. This suggests that in addition to their tangible assets the stock market perceives the company has considerable intangibles, for example management ability, good reputation, a brand, etc. This is in addition to intangibles already mentioned in the balance sheet. The balance sheet shows that shares and accumulated profit invested in the company is €11 billion approximately, yet if sold today it would raise €27 billion.

Another externally quoted statistic which is used is a *price earnings (PE) ratio,* a relationship between the current market price per share and the EPS quoted above. In this case the calculation is:

$$\frac{\text{Market price } (\text{€})}{\text{EPS}(\text{€})} \quad \frac{22.84}{1.60} = 14.3 \text{ times}$$

This reflects the fact that the stock market values the company at over 14 times its current reported earnings. In other words it would take over 14 years to recover the share price based on its current earnings and is a statement about the confidence in the company's ability to continue its earning and future potential. If a PE ratio was about 2 this would be a very low estimate of the potential of the company and the quality of its earnings. In a reasonably healthy mature economy it could be said that a PE of 14 is representative of an upper quartile performance. It needs careful interpretation, however, in that the ratio compares an estimate of future performance (market price) with a past measure (last year's profit).

MANAGEMENT RATIOS

Some of the investor ratios featured above are reflected inside the company by measures that relate key components of the profit and loss account or the balance sheet. For example *return on equity* compares the annual net profit with the balance sheet value of shareholder funds, thus:

$$\frac{\text{Net profit after tax (attributable to shareholders)}}{\text{Shareholders'equity}} \quad \frac{1916 \times 100}{11220} = 17.1\%$$

The above figure is after tax but it may be given greater relevance to management by being computed before tax; after all, management cannot easily influence the tax burden of the company. If a profit figure before tax and interest charges is used it should be related to investment in the company by both shareholders and lenders, in other words it is a broader measure of financial performance:

$$\frac{\text{Net profit before interest and tax}}{\text{Capital employed (shares and loans)}} \quad \frac{3872 \times 100}{13952 + 17625} = \frac{3872 \times 100}{31577} = 12.3\%$$

A useful indicator of overall profitability of sales is the relationship of net profit to total sales value. It is a key profitability ratio and indicates the average net profit margin being earned on all business undertaken. For Deutsche Post this is:

$$\frac{\text{Net profit before interest and tax}}{\text{Total sales revenue}} \quad \frac{3872 \times 100}{63366} = 6.1\%$$

While profitability is important, the absolute scale of the business is also significant: that is, the rate at which this profit is being earned (how busy is the company, is it working its people and its tangible assets hard, is it 'sweating' the assets?). A ratio that displays this aspect is the *turnover of capital employed:*

$$\frac{\text{Total sales revenue}}{\text{Capital employed}} \quad \frac{63366 \times 100}{31.577} = 2 \text{ times approx.}$$

Note that the turnover of capital employed when multiplied by the net profit ratio is equivalent to the return on capital employed ($2 \times 6.1\% = 12.3\%$ approx.).

It should be noted that the above illustrates the ratios for the whole company, but they can be broken down by major business segments if this information is available. For example, within Deutsche Post they could produce this for the business segments mentioned above. However, they are not obligated to provide all this detail to outsiders; furthermore some of the analysis may require an arbitrary split of costs, revenues and assets to do it. Some overview of performance by segment is required to be reported to investors and the public so some insight can be obtained for this.

CAPITAL STRUCTURE AND LIQUIDITY

It is important for any reader of accounts to realise that a company can raise funds from both shareholders, who have an ownership interest in the company, and lenders who look only for a reward of regular and contractually agreed interest payments. The balance between these two represents the *gearing* of the company and can have implications for the risk the stock market perceives the company is bearing. There are many alternative formulae for gearing but a common one is the relationship of debt to debt plus equity. Thus for Deutsche Post:

$$\frac{\text{Debt}}{\text{Debt} + \text{Equity}} \quad \frac{17625 \times 100}{17625 + 13952} = 56\%$$

Deutsche Post is funded by 56% of loans and other fixed liability funding, which is perhaps an average level of gearing.

Finally it is important to examine whether the company is likely to be able to pay its way in the future. Does it have sufficient *liquidity?* That is, does it have the funds to meet its bills when they fall due? These bills can be for general trading activities or one-off bills such as taxation, dividend, etc. A financial measure used for this purpose is the *current ratio,* a comparison of current assets and current liabilities, thus:

$$\frac{\text{Current assets}}{\text{Current liabilities}} \quad \frac{19466}{13963} = 1.4 \text{ times.}$$

The fact that current assets exceed current liabilities is reassuring. For some manufacturing businesses a ratio as high as two times is suggested to be appropriate; however, this varies with different types of company. In this case, Deutsche Post is not in manufacturing: it holds very little inventory of its own, often it is other people's inventory, the balance sheet shows a very small inventory, so a figure well below two times is acceptable. It is not advisable for a company to carry a high level of current assets because it has to finance this by raising money from shareholders.

It should be noted that the accounts shown here may be distorted by some current assets which relate particularly to the financial services business of Deutsche Post. If these are removed a lower current ratio emerges, indicating prudent use of resources.

$$\frac{\text{Current assets}}{\text{Current liabilities}} \quad \frac{19466 - 7164}{13,963 - 1945} = 0.9 \text{ times.}$$

Gate Gourmet: Success Means Getting to the Plane on Time*

M. Day

Headquartered at Zurich Airport, Switzerland, and Reston, VA, USA, Gate Gourmet is the world's second largest airline catering company, providing catering services to many of the world's major airlines, such as British Airways, Swissair, United Airlines, Delta Airlines, Virgin Atlantic and Cathay Pacific to name just a few. In a very competitive and low-margin industry, the company manages to provide more than half a million meals a day worldwide, on average 195 million every year. It has 115 flight kitchens in 30 different countries, in locations as diverse as Hawaii, Los Angeles, Buenos Aires, New York, Madrid, London, Bangkok, Sydney and Tokyo. However, it is far more than a food preparation operation; most of its activities involve organising all on-board services, equipment, food and drinks, newspapers, towels, earphones and so on. And that's not all. Gate Gourmet also unloads from the aircraft, disposes of waste, cleans the cutlery, trays, and trolleys, stores all these customer-specific accessories for each airline, and makes everything ready for the next time it's needed at the required location. In sum it is, essentially, a specialist logistics operation for the aviation industry.

Gate Gourmet places considerable emphasis on working in unison with cleaning staff, baggage handlers and maintenance crews to ensure that the aircraft are prepared quickly for departure. Normally, no more than 40 minutes are allowed for all these activities in the tight confines of an aircraft cabin and hold, so complete preparation and a well-ordered sequence of working are essential. Eric van den Berg, Director of Business Applications at Gate Gourmet, gives a practical example of the complexity that is involved

---

*Marc Day (2006) Gate Gourmet: Success Means Getting to the Plane on Time, Henley Management College, © Marc Day. Reproduced by permission of Marc Day.

in servicing an aircraft in a tight schedule: 'For example, a long-haul flight from Asia may stop at Zurich Airport for only two to three hours before it returns. In this time slot, beside un-boarding and re-boarding passengers plus cabin cleaning, we are scheduled to unload the plane of used cutlery and rubbish, and prepare and load about 5 tons of new food, drinks and equipment for the return flight.' He goes on to say: 'The process is further complicated by the fact that last-minute passengers can show up shortly before departure and also would like a meal according to the airline's specification. Then there are the passengers that require special meals (e.g. a kosher meal or a low-fat meal) and at the same time we try to avoid producing and loading more meals than actual passengers (so-called "over-catering") as this is a loss for the airline and us. People often talk about "just-in-time" delivery, but for us, just-in-time delivery is literally down to minutes.'

These requirements for speed and total dependability would be difficult enough to achieve in a stable environment, but as Eric explained there are wide-ranging uncertainties that have to be managed. Although Gate Gourmet is advised of the likely numbers of passengers for each flight, the actual number of passengers for each flight is only fixed 6 hours before take-off (although numbers can still be increased after this, due to late sales). The agreed menus are normally fixed for six months, but the actual requirements for each flight depend on the destination, the type of aircraft and the mix of passengers by ticket class. Finally, flight arrivals are sometimes delayed, putting pressure on everyone to reduce the turnaround time, and upsetting work schedules.

BUSINESS-CRITICAL PROCESSES

Gate Gourmet has chosen to use information technology to assist in the scheduling of food and ancillary goods. The system, called Scala, covers almost all business processes for the company's catering operation. Food cannot be easily produced too far in advance as most of it has to be freshly prepared. Preparation and production for a flight usually starts 12–24 hours before departure, at a time when passenger numbers for this flight often still change both up and down.

The focus for Scala is to make sure that all the meals and all their accessories are delivered at the right time, at the right place and in the right quantities. The flight kitchen's control area monitors all flight operations and responds to any last-minute changes. This is vital, too: every delay, every cancellation, every rebooking and every aircraft reassignment will have a direct and immediate impact on the catering process. Minutes can often be crucial; and Gate Gourmet's dedicated teams need to respond with the utmost flexibility. This is why close contacts are constantly maintained between the purchasing, kitchen and logistics units.

Eric explains more about how Gate Gourmet uses Scala in practice for its internal processes: 'The service contracts we have with the airlines include flight schedules and meal specifications (bill of material), which are pre-set into Scala,' he says. In the days leading up to a flight, the company is kept updated with the latest passenger numbers by the airline. These numbers are either entered or electronically uploaded into Scala where, in conjunction with the flight schedule and bill of material, the daily demand for meals is calculated, and a timetable for production is worked out. Through Scala and additional fax software, the chefs in the kitchen can directly send daily purchase orders for, for example, vegetables to the suppliers. 'You will find Scala terminals everywhere on the shop floor in our flight kitchens.'

When food for a flight is ready to be boarded, a last quality check is made and trolley labels and delivery notes are printed from Scala. Once shipped and confirmed in Scala, invoices are printed either on paper or in electronic form and sent to the airline.

Scala relies on vast databases that store thousands of detailed recipes to ensure consistent ingredients, presentation and taste, even on the largest of scales and stowing modules in which the layout for each aircraft is captured.

HAND-CRAFTED FOOD MANUFACTURING

Yet despite these high-tech inroads into the cooking world, the majority of the food preparation work is still done by hand. The vast range of products for snacks, tasters, starters, main courses, desserts and in-between meals for over 250 airline customers has to be processed and prepared every single day. No conveyor-belt production is possible here: every day, Gate Gourmet prepares over 570 000 hot and cold meals in repetitive batch processes that use a small range of cooking techniques that preserve the quality of the ingredients. On top of this, the group produces a large quantity of special meals, which are also changed daily. All these products need to pay due and full regard to the cultural and culinary features of each specific destination.

Needless to say, the strictest hygiene standards are applied at all Gate Gourmet's production premises, which are regularly inspected by the relevant authorities. One hundred per cent cleanliness is constantly maintained; and the correct handling of foodstuffs is an uncompromising imperative. Gate Gourmet's in-house laboratories and hygiene specialists are a further guarantee of the group's full compliance at all times with the highest quality and hygiene standards.

THE WIDER SUPPLY CHAIN

Gate Gourmet has also invested a great deal of time and money in integrating its supply base into the systems that provide real-time data into the Scala system. Under the banner of 'e-gate-matrix', a series of web-enabled systems capture schedule data from Gate Gourmet's airline customers, using it to schedule meal deliveries, procure and synchronise deliveries from suppliers, and finally close the purchase-to-pay loop by managing supplier and airline invoicing.

One of the most testing times for Gate Gourmet and the e-gatematrix system came during the weeks and months following September 11, 2001, when there was an endless stream of changes regarding in-flight services that needed to be communicated and implemented. A number of Gate Gourmet's customers needed to communicate changes about:

- Flight schedules
  - Over 10% of the flights were eliminated
- Meal services
  - The number of flights with meal service was reduced by over 40%
  - Meal service levels were changed on the remaining flights
- In-flight equipment
  - Regulations required that certain equipment could no longer be used during the flight (i.e. knives)
- Supply chain issues
  - Equipment and perishable inventory re-balancing in the network.

The workload involved service scheduling, galley planning and menu specifications. Using e-gatematrix's integrated technology systems, the e-gatematrix team created all the changes necessary to maintain accurate communications to the upstream supply chain about the current in-flight service specifications. Additionally, technology interfaces with the airline's legacy systems allowed Gate Gourmet to communicate new demand expectations to the supply chain by publishing accurate passenger load forecasts and service level demand forecasts, reducing production volumes throughout the supply chain.

As a result Gate Gourmet and its airline partners were able to successfully communicate thousands of individual changes regarding in-flight services to the airlines' in-flight supply chain. The changes were created and managed using the e-gatematrix technology systems, providing the supply chain with real-time communication of those changes. Communications were made to the service providers and suppliers who serviced over 140 worldwide stations and encompassed hundreds of flight schedule changes and many more service level, meal and equipment changes. The ultimate result of quickly implementing all of these changes was Gate Gourmet's airline customers realised significant savings and cost avoidances, quickly adapting to the changes in the industry's economic environment.

QUESTIONS

- What supply chain challenges does Gate Gourmet face when dealing with demand fluctuations from airlines? Comment on how its supply chain investments support its overall customer service and resource utilisation objectives.

- What prerequisites are important for the operation of the lean systems that Gate Gourmet has in place?

Supplier Evaluation at EADS*

Roger Moser

European Business School

On 8 March, 2004, John Summers, head of the supply management strategy at EADS, a company based in Europe, got the assignment from the Procurement Directors Board (PDB) to make suggestions for improving the company's supplier evaluation system. The proposal was to be presented at the PDB meeting the following month.

EADS AND THE AEROSPACE INDUSTRY

EADS was one of the largest players in the aerospace industry. There were only a few other companies in the market and therefore the competition was characterised by oligopolistic structures.

EADS had a sales volume of approximately €30 billion while its biggest competitor sold airplanes and other products for the aerospace industry worth around €40 billion, followed by some other competitors with sales volumes of €10–20 billion. Due to its strong sales position in North America and Europe, but some weaknesses in Asia and South America, EADS was looking for new ways to improve its competitive position on the last-named continents.

EADS's main customers were airlines from all over the world which were using their increasing purchasing power to get price reductions and flexible contracts. Since EADS and its competitors had a degree of value added of only 25–35%, the suppliers were an important source of competitive advantage and a potential leverage for cost reductions, revenue enhancements and risk reduction.

*This case was written by Roger Moser, Supply Management Institute (SMI), European Business School. It is intended to be used as the basis for class discussion rather than to illustrate either effective or ineffective handling of a management situation. The case was made possible by the cooperation of European Aeronautic Defence and Space Company (EADS).

THE SUPPLY SITUATION IN THE AEROSPACE INDUSTRY

Due to long development cycles and extremely long product lives in the aerospace industry, the supplier situation in this industry was determined by some special requirements. The suppliers had to be able to guarantee the durability and quality of their products in a high-tech environment and under extreme conditions. EADS and its suppliers had to fulfil the needs of its global customers on the one hand and very demanding requirements from official bodies, such as the Federal Aviation Administration (FAA) of the United States of America, on the other. Therefore, every supplier for critical parts had to go through a tough and costly quality audit process and had to prove regularly that their products meet the certification requirements.

Due to the outstanding product complexity, EADS and its competitors could not handle all the requirements and necessary activities of airplane manufacturing on their own. Interdependent relationships occurred between EADS and its most important suppliers in terms of innovation and efficiency management. As a consequence, EADS had to buy most of its crucial manufacturing parts from single source suppliers.

THE SUPPLY ORGANISATION OF EADS

The final decision-making body for all supply management issues of EADS was the Procurement Directors Board. The PDB consisted of the procurement directors of the eight business units of EADS. On the second level, the corporate supply organisation was divided into PDB subgroups that were responsible for different tasks such as the management of the specific lead-buyers within the organisation, the e-procurement processes or the supply management strategy for which John Summers was responsible. On the third level, there were the different sourcing organisations of EADS's business units with about 1800 buyers.

THE SUPPLY STRATEGY OF EADS

The supply vision of EADS was to achieve competitive advantage by winning, integrating and developing the world's best suppliers. Therefore, EADS had a supply strategy that aimed at getting the best suppliers possible in order to fulfil the following objectives:

- Procurement marketing: the supply activities of EADS needed to support its sales department because selling airplanes to certain countries required that the airplanes are produced in line with local content requirements.
- Risk and opportunity management: suppliers had to share the risks and opportunities of the aerospace industry with EADS.

THE SUPPLIER EVALUATION SYSTEM OF EADS

When John Summers and his team analysed the supplier evaluation system at EADS they found five common criteria for evaluation:

1. Commercial performance (product cost, delivery cost, quality cost, etc.)
2. Logistics performance (reliability, delivery precision, etc.)
3. Customer support (geographical distribution of plants and service stations,etc.)
4. Quality performance (quality level, quality reliability, etc.)
5. Technical performance (product design and development, process development, etc.).

EADS had implemented a system that measured the different evaluation ratings for each supplier on the basis of the delivered commodities on business unit and corporate level (see Figure C9.1). The supplier value was determined on the aggregated performance and future contracts were given to high scoring suppliers. However, the rating measures sometimes bore little relationship to the supply strategy requirements.

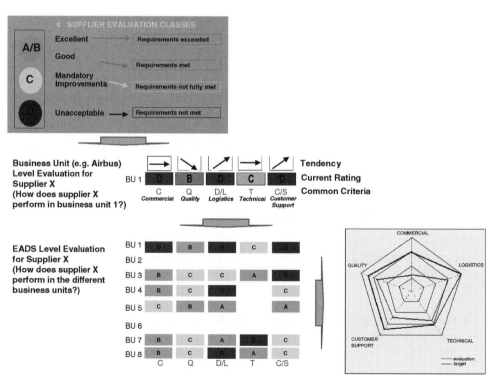

Figure C9.1 The supplier evaluation system at EADS.

THE SUPPLIER STRUCTURE OF EADS

In 2003, EADS had approximately 24 000 suppliers in total. However, it bought almost 65% of its supply volume from only about 250 suppliers. It sourced more than two-thirds of the products and services in Europe and only a quarter in North America. The supply volumes in Asia or South America were almost negligible. Therefore, the supply volume of EADS was even more unequally distributed than its sales volume.

JOHN'S SUGGESTIONS FOR IMPROVEMENT

John knew that the current supplier evaluation system had worked smoothly for more than four years and was well implemented. However, he was not sure whether EADS was really measuring all important dimensions of the supplier value in order to achieve new competitive advantages in the relevant markets.

QUESTIONS

- If you were in the position of John Summers, what problems and weaknesses could you identify?
- Suppose you were John Summers and you had prepared a list of suggested improvements for discussion at the PDB meeting. Discussion of other agenda items at the meeting however took longer than expected, with the result that John now only has 10 minutes (and not 30 minutes) to present his ideas. Given this time constraint what three steps would you prioritise for discussion at the meeting?

Part Three

Supply Chain Designs

15 Supply Chain Vulnerability, Risk, Robustness and Resilience

Helen Peck

Cranfield University

LEARNING OBJECTIVES

- Provide working definitions for key concepts.
- Explain why supply chain risk, robustness and resilience have emerged as important themes in supply chain management.
- Address the problems surrounding interpretations and the treatment of 'risk' in management.
- Highlight the need for a holistic approach to managing supply chain vulnerabilities.
- Provide a structured framework for the identification and management of supply chain risk and resilience.

INTRODUCTION

In the mid-1990s the subject of supply chain risk or vulnerability would have been of little interest to anyone but professional logisticians and supply chain managers. Even then they would likely have interpreted risk as simply the financial or competitive disadvantage resulting from a failure to implement 'best practice' SCM concepts. But times have changed. It is no longer unacceptable to acknowledge that bad practice may still flourish elsewhere in the network or that even well-managed operations can, and occasionally do, fail. This chapter provides an introduction to the complex, but fascinating subject of supply chain risk, and the related concepts of vulnerability, robustness and resilience.

Chapter 15 comprises five core sections:

- Some working definitions
- Changing times and an uncertain world
- The shortcomings of risk management
- The need for holistic approaches
- A simple framework for a wicked problem

SOME WORKING DEFINITIONS

Chapter 1 of this book highlighted an enduring problem in logistics and supply chain management – confusion over key terms, even amongst specialists and academics. Things become doubly difficult when we begin to look at matters of supply chain risk, robustness and resilience.

Risk

The main problem stems from multiple meanings of the term 'risk'. In decision theory it is a probability or a measure of the range of possible outcomes from a single totally rational decision and their values, in terms of upside gains and downside losses. The concept tends to be illustrated by examples from gambling. Alternatively, 'risk' is sometimes used to refer to a particular type of hazard or threat, for example technological risk or political risk. Finally, 'risk' may describe the downside-only consequences of a rational decision in terms of the resulting financial losses or number of casualties. The latter can be traced back to risk management disciplines, notably the safety and engineering literature.[1] The reasoning behind each of these interpretations and why they matter in a logistics or SCM context will be visited later in this chapter.

Supply chain vulnerability

In the meantime we will use the term 'risk' as it relates to **vulnerability** as our point of embarkation; that is, *'at risk:* vulnerable; likely to be lost or damaged'. In Chapter 1 of this book we adopted a definition of a supply chain as 'the network of organisations that are involved through upstream and downstream linkages in the different processes and activities that produce value in the form of products and services in the hands of the ultimate customer'.[2] Given that supply chains comprise many different elements and that SCM embraces many different functions, it is perhaps useful to ask the question 'What is it that is vulnerable, in other words *at risk?'* Is it a product or service, the performance of a process or specific activities, the well-being of an organisation, a trading relationship or the wider networks as a whole? Or is it the vulnerability of one or more of these to some external malevolent force that should be the focus of our consideration? In fact, supply chain vulnerability takes in all of these.

Ideally we should strive to identify and manage known vulnerabilities by asking questions such as:

- What has disrupted operations in the past?
- What known weaknesses do we have?
- What 'near misses' have we experienced?

Recording near misses is something that all organisations should do. Unfortunately, it does not always happen. Sometimes no one was aware that a near miss took place, and often they go unreported because people feel that the incident might reflect badly on them or their department. The willingness to report events of this kind is often dependent on the culture of the department or wider organisation. Forward-thinking organisations recognise that near misses are often warnings of worse to come.

Taking a more proactive stance, a good supply chain manager should also be asking 'effects' based questions, such as:

- What would be the effect of a shortage of a key material?
- What would be the effect of the loss of our distribution site?
- What would be the effect of the loss of a key supplier or customer?

Robust SCM

Whilst individual managers might focus on the effects of a range of eventualities, some argue that everyday SCM strategy also plays a part. In Chapter 4 reference was made to the work of Christopher Tang,[3] who identifies key elements of a **robust** SCM strategy. The dictionary definition of 'robust' is 'strong in constitution, hardy, or vigorous'.[4] Tang suggests that a robust strategy should enable a firm to manage regular fluctuations in demand efficiently under normal circumstances regardless of the occurrence of a major disruption. It might be supposed that any organisation would actively seek to ensure such a position. However, as Tang points out, for a variety of reasons, this is not always the case. What is more, even if your own organisation has implemented the tenets of best practice SCM, does this mean that your supply chain will not fail? Have other organisations in the supply chain all done the same? Even if they have, will that be enough to ensure operations continue? Research by Cranfield University into the UK food and drink industry suggests that there are instances when they will not.[5] A robust strategy has much to commend it, but does not in itself make a resilient supply chain.

Resilience

The term **resilience** is used to mean 'the ability of a system to return to its original (or desired) state after being disturbed'. Based on a dictionary definition borrowed from the science of ecosystems,[6] this definition has been adopted in much of the work by Cranfield University into supply chain vulnerability, risk and resilience[7,8] for three reasons:

- It encourages a whole system perspective
- It explicitly accepts that disturbances happen
- It implies adaptability to changing circumstances

If we are really to embrace the notion of global inter-organisational supply chains within a complex and dynamic environment, then this whole system-wide perspective is the position we should adopt when considering matters of supply chain risk or vulnerability.

CHANGING TIMES AND AN UNCERTAIN WORLD

In a complex inter-organisational supply chain it would of course be difficult if not impossible for anyone to identify every possible hazard or point of vulnerability. Moreover, it must be remembered that 'known' problems are only part of the picture.

Known unknowns, knowable unknowns and unknowable unknowns

To illustrate the point, we will look at some of the high profile events that have propelled supply chain vulnerability, risk and resilience onto the political and corporate agendas. First, though, we turn to the words of former US Secretary for Defense Donald Rumsfeld,[9] whose famous and much derided quote[10,11] brought to wider public attention the idea of 'known unknowns', 'knowable unknowns' and 'unknowable unknowns'. These are useful touchstones to bear in mind when considering the wider subject of supply chain vulnerability, risk and resilience.

> Reports that say that something hasn't happened are always interesting to me, because as we know, there are known knowns; there are things we know we know. We also know there are known unknowns; that is to say we know there are some things we do not know. But there are also unknown unknowns – the ones we don't know we don't know. And if one looks throughout the history of our country and other free countries, it is the latter category that tends to be the difficult ones (Donald Rumsfeld, 12 February 2002)

Contrary to popular belief, Rumsfeld did not invent the concepts himself in an off-the-cuff attempt to justify the case for US military action against Iraq. He was in fact drawing directly on concepts used by researchers such as Chris Demchak, who drew on high reliability organisations[12] and complex systems theory when working in the field of military logistics.[13] Demchak investigated the underlying thinking behind the technology-driven idea of a 'managed battle space' in which all battlefield weapons systems are synchronised in real time with just-in-time logistics and supply. She concluded that this optimistic vision tends to ignore organisational implications and the uncertainties of the battlefield environment.

Y2K: the millennium bug

Y2K highlighted how dependent the societies of the developed world had become on information and communications technologies. In the UK, the government launched a public information campaign to encourage businesses to take the necessary measures to prevent systems crashes as dates rolled over to the year 2000, and to engage in business continuity planning[14] just in case systems failures arose. Y2K was a 'known known', a discrete, known threat, within engineered systems. Once identified, the 'millennium bug' could be controlled and eliminated. As a result, the widely anticipated disruptions to supply chains never occurred. The government was delighted, believing that business continuity planning had saved the country from disaster, but the non-event left many managers sceptical as to whether the costly preventative measures had really been necessary.

Y2K highlights one of the intractable problems about proactive measures to improve organisational and supply chain resilience: if successful, preventative measures mean that nothing happens, which inevitably leads to questions of value or cost/benefits justification. Moreover, managers are highly unlikely to be promoted for spending money to prevent a non-event!

> It is very difficult to make a business case for proactive 'just-in-case' measures to improve resilience.

Creeping crises

Having survived Y2K with minimal problems, the UK economy fared less well in September 2000, when a small number of protestors blockaded some of the country's oil refineries, causing chaos at the petrol pumps. The protests were an outpouring of simmering resentment among farmers and transport operators over rising fuel costs, driven in part by the government's 'fuel price escalator'. The escalator increased prices annually by 6% over and above the general rate of inflation. Within days the fuel crises escalated, resulting in serious disruptions to the operations of countless companies and to the national economy as a whole. The outbreak of foot and mouth disease in British livestock herds in February 2001 again resulted in damage to whole sectors of the economy.

What made these events so memorable was that even those who were aware of threats did not anticipate the scale of their impact across the UK economy. A survey undertaken by Cranfield University[15] in 2002, involving 137 senior managers from both public and private sector companies, found that 82% of the organisations represented had been affected by the fuel protests, with 49% experiencing some impact from foot and mouth. Both these events could arguably be said to have been caused by 'knowable unknowns'. There were clear warnings that farmers and transport companies were aggrieved over fuel duties and that some form of protest was a real possibility. Foot and mouth was a known threat to livestock, albeit one that had not been seen in the UK for a generation.

The impact of livestock diseases is something that might reasonably be expected to be included in the supplier monitoring activities of companies engaged in the production and distribution of food. But what about car manufacturers or high fashion apparel companies? The shortage of high-quality leather following the foot and mouth outbreak affected automotive manufacturers and fashion houses across Europe. It also had a catastrophic effect on the British tourism industry.

The scale and extent of the disruptions prompted the UK government to seek a better understanding of what are now sometimes referred to in emergency planning circles as

creeping crises. During the fuel protests and the foot and mouth outbreak it was industry and government – not the usual 'blue light' emergency services – that found themselves in the unfamiliar role of 'first responders'. These 'creeping crises' were remarkable in one other respect – they represented *systemic supply chain disruptions*.

Creeping crises illustrate the fact that supply chains are more than value-adding mechanisms underlying competitive business models. Supply chains link organisations, industries and economies. They are part of the fabric of society. Back in 1958, Jay Forrester, a Professor at Massachusetts Institute of Technology, predicted that 'there will come a general recognition of the advantage enjoyed by the pioneering management who have been the first to improve their understanding of the interrelationships between separate company functions and between the company and its markets, its industry and the national economy'.[16] Forrester is widely regarded as one of the founding fathers of SCM and of the study of industrial dynamics. SCM has made some progress towards Forrester's vision, but the creeping crises of recent years suggest there is still work to be done.

Few realise that it was the creeping crises of 2000–2001, together with the outbreak of bovine spongiform encephalopathy (mad cow disease) in the 1990s, and increased incidences of flooding (not the threat of international terrorism) that prompted the most extensive review of UK national emergency planning policy since World War II. The inability of civil authorities to overcome the collapse of vital supply chains providing food, water, medicine, money, transport and communications to the citizens of New Orleans following Hurricane Katrina in 2005 is a clear example of why such work is necessary.

Post-9/11 security matters

More than any other event, the 9/11 terrorist attacks on New York and Washington marked the beginning of a change in attitude towards the whole notion of supply chain vulnerability. The events of 9/11 were so far outside the risk managers' field of reference that they can arguably be classed as 'unknowable unknowns'. It is widely recognised that the terrorist attacks did not themselves cause any significant disruption to global supply chains or even North American industry. But the reaction of the US authorities did.[17] The closure of US borders and the grounding of transatlantic flights dislocated international supply chains making supply chain vulnerability front page news.

After 9/11, new security measures were hurriedly introduced at US border posts, ports and airports, affecting inbound freight to the USA, including the **Container Security Initiative (CSI)** and customs-trade partnership (C-TPAT). CSI looked to new technology to pre-screen 'high-risk' containers (those where declared cargoes deviated from usual profiles) before they arrived at US ports. C-TPAT is a 'known shipper' programme, which allows cargoes from companies certified by US Customs to clear customs quickly with minimum inspection. Around the world national or supranational customs authorities adopted similar mindsets and soon tabled rafts of similar measures. The European Union's Approved Economic Operator scheme is an example. Chapter 7, which deals with security in the transport chain, discusses some of these initiatives further.

Corporate scandals, operational risk and business continuity

Societies around the globe reeled from the shock of 9/11, but within a few months, supply chain risk was once more synonymous with the perils of poor performance. However, in the world of corporate risk management, events were unfolding that would push 'operational risk' (i.e. internal threats to organisational well-being) to the very top of the corporate agenda.

The Enron Corporation, once held up as a model of best practice corporate risk management, collapsed in late 2001. Inadequate internal management controls were blamed. Another North American giant, WorldCom, quickly followed. In Europe, Dutch retailer Royal Ahold and Italian dairy conglomerate Parmalat Finanziara did the same. In a bid to protect shareholders and ultimately the well-being of the financial markets, regulators hurried to bring in their own more rigorous reporting requirements. The international banking community had faced the same stark realities only a few years earlier, when the unchecked activities of Singapore-based 'rogue trader' Nick Leeson led to the collapse of London-based Barings Bank, threatening irreparable damage to Singapore's reputation as a financial centre.

These financial scandals highlighted the need for more diligent corporate governance in general. They also increased the appetite for measures to monitor, manage and control operational risk. The Basel Accords in International Banking (1998, 2004), and the introduction of new stock-market regulations formalised the requirements.

Among the wave of new regulations, the *Sarbanes–Oxley Act 2002* (SOX) (which you may recall we discussed in Chapter 13 is particularly noteworthy. Applied to all US quoted companies in 2002, and a year later to their overseas suppliers, SOX requires full disclosure of all potential risks to corporate well-being within the business. Importantly it also requires disclosure of potential vulnerabilities that might once have been considered to be beyond the legal boundaries of the firm. Among its many requirements is an obligation to declare all 'material off-balance sheet transactions' including 'contingent obligations' and 'interests transferred to an unconsolidated entity'. These encompass some inter-organisational risk sharing and risk transfer activities, including fixed volume shipping service contracts, vendor managed inventory (VMI), and outsourcing agreements.

SOX also demands that providers of outsourced services (including LSPs) must be able to demonstrate the existence of appropriate internal process controls. Finally, it requires consideration to be given to other possible externally induced disruptions. Externally induced disruptions include disruptions to transport and communications. Failure to identify and disclose any of the above may result in a jail sentence for the company's chief executive. As a result, board members have became much more interested in identifying 'knowable unknowns' and have turned to risk management and to *business continuity management* (BCM) to help them prove that they have acted with 'due diligence'.

BCM efforts tend to start with the preparation of a **business continuity plan (BCP).** A business continuity plan is defined as 'a documented collection of procedures and information that is developed, compiled and maintained in readiness for use in an incident to enable an organisation to continue to deliver its critical products and services'.[18] Continuity planning is part of the wider BCM discipline which overlaps SCM, operational risk management, corporate governance and other associated concerns. Current best practice BCM would include an ongoing programme of training, rehearsals and reviews of the initial plans to cope with various eventualities as well as careful consideration to the management of an after-the-event recovery phase.

BCM is rooted in IT disaster recovery, but its remit has expanded greatly. In the months before Y2K it focused on protecting 'mission critical computer data'. In more recent years it has moved on to encompass the protection of all 'mission critical corporate assets'. These assets include: data and information; high-value physical items; people and their experience; knowledge; commercial contracts; and, ultimately, corporate reputation. More recently still, best practice BCM has looked beyond traditional tangible asset-based approaches to risk management, to focus on maintaining 'mission critical activities'. This is particularly so for service sectors such as retailing, banking and other financial services. Financial services is also the sector where many of the 'classical' approaches to risk management have been developed over the last century. It is also the area where they have recently failed so badly, triggering arguably the biggest and most far-reaching creeping crisis to date. The risk management approaches used by banks to satisfy the requirements of the Basel Accords failed catastrophically in 2008, when the collapse of US-based investment bank Lehman Brothers triggered a global financial crisis. Only direct interventions by governments prevented the total collapse of the global financial system, though the shock-waves will be felt across economies for years to come.

THE SHORTCOMINGS OF RISK MANAGEMENT

Earlier in this chapter we mentioned that the term risk has several different meanings. All are used, often indiscriminately in the context of SCM. This is not simply a shortcoming of managers working in SCM. Scholars have been grappling with the nature of risk for centuries, but risk management is a far from mature discipline, with significant disagreements raging over some of its basic tenets.

Decision theory and managerial tendencies

The starting point for many discussions of risk is as it is presented in the gambling-dominated thinking of classical decision theory.[19] Some years ago, researchers James March and Zur Shapira defined risk – from a financial decision theory perspective – as 'variation in the distribution of possible outcomes, their likelihoods and their subjective values'.[20] In their seminal paper on managerial perceptions of risk and risk taking, the same writers observed that even in financial management circles this much cited interpretation had actually been under attack for many years. Their own research showed that the rational assumptions of classical decision theory do not reflect how managers see risk, nor do they reflect managers' behaviours or the social norms that influence them. March and Shapira cited findings that showed that managers adopt and apply only selected elements of the total risk equation. The managers concerned paid little attention to uncertainty surrounding positive outcomes, viewing risk in terms of dangers or hazards with potentially negative outcomes. Moreover it was the scale of the likely losses associated with *plausible* outcomes, rather than the range of *possible* outcomes, that tended to qualify for consideration.

Furthermore, March and Shapira observed that individual managers' risk-taking behaviour changed with circumstances. 'Attention factors' such as performance targets and questions of survival are likely to have the greatest impact. In comfortable circumstances managers are likely to be risk-averse, but when staring failure in the face – in terms of shortfalls in performance targets – research shows that this tendency reverses and they become risk-prone. Of course when a person is faced with a proposition with upside incentives for him or her and no downside consequences (known or otherwise), then there is no risk for the decision maker. It becomes a 'one-way bet'. The same decision can become problematic when the downside exposure is borne by someone else, either in the same organisation or across the wider network.

This leads us into the question of risk appetites in organisations. There is often an assumption that an organisation has a single definable risk appetite and risk strategy, yet more recent research suggests that risk strategies can and do vary between functions within the same business.[21] For example, a propensity for risk taking was found to be acceptable in the areas of core competencies, but much less tolerated in non-core activities within the same firm.

In the real world, where managers routinely deal with imperfect information, these behavioural characteristics may not be as irrational as it might first seem. That is because managers are for the most part making decisions under uncertainty. *Risk* and *uncertainty* are terms that in practice are often used interchangeably, but back in the 1920s Knight made a helpful distinction: 'If you don't know for sure what will happen (e.g. when throwing dice) but you know the odds, that's risk and if you don't even know the odds, that's uncertainty'.[22] Uncertainty is, according to Knight, 'the realm of judgement'.

- Managers focus on the possible losses associated with plausible outcomes
- Decisions involving risk are heavily influenced by their impact on the manager's own performance targets
- There is unlikely to be a single unified attitude to risk taking within a large organisation

Objective risk and perceived risk

Despite the wisdom of Knight, the words of Rumsfeld, and the canon of research to date, the dominant paradigm in risk management remains that of the cold logic of 'objective risk'. Objective risk reflects a view of risk set out by the engineers and physicists of The Royal Society in a report published in London in 1983.[23] The report stated that risk was 'the probability that a particular (known) adverse event occurs during a stated period of time, or results from a particular challenge. As a probability in the sense of statistical theory, risk obeys all formal laws of combining probabilities'.

Furthermore, the report made a clear distinction between *objective risk* as determined by experts applying quantitative scientific means, and *perceived risk* – the imprecise and unreliable perceptions of ordinary people. This 'objective' position, combined with the Royal Society's definition of 'detriment' as 'the numerical measure of harm or loss associated with an adverse event' reflects the compound measure of risk widely encountered within the engineering, health and safety literature, and frequently within SCM. It is a position supported by the work of other prestigious institutions such as the National Academy of Sciences and the National Academy of Engineering in the USA in the 1980s and 1990s.[24]

However, it is also a position that has been vehemently contested by social scientists. Social scientists contend that, where people were involved, objective and perceived risk become inseparable. They argue that risk is not a discrete or objective phenomenon, but an interactive culturally determined one, that is inherently resistant to objective measurement. The essential problem is, as distinguished writers such as John Adams point out, that people modify their behaviour and thereby their likely exposure to risk in response to subjective perceptions of that risk, subtly balancing perceived costs and benefits.[25]

Nevertheless proponents of 'objective risk' continue to champion the view that we *should* promote the scientific management ideal, of a rational, predictable world, populated by rational predictable people. As a result Adams observed that 'virtually all the formal treatments of risk and uncertainty in game theory, operations research, economics and management science require that the odds be known, that numbers be attachable to the probabilities and magnitudes of possible outcomes.' In these disciplines, risk management still strives to identify, quantify, control and where possible eliminate specific narrowly defined known threats. The same disciplines continue to underpin much of SCM theory and best practice.

Many of the commonly used tools, techniques and concepts used to identify, evaluate and estimate risk remain rooted in the 'divide and conquer' thinking of engineering and scientific management. Consequently it has been argued that they fail to consider that failures and accidents may be 'emergent properties'; that is, unexpected and often undesirable effects, arising within the wider system as a whole.[26] In this instance the systems we are talking about are the multi-organisational networks that characterise contemporary supply chains.

Even in enterprise risk management, it is clear to some that risk management models have failed to keep pace with the realities of our networked world. They have been slow to account for operational interdependencies between firms brought about by the trend to outsourcing. Consequently they underestimate the range and severity of risks faced by a company.[27] The Sarbanes–Oxley Act has helped to highlight this shortcoming.

Why this all matters from a practical supply chain risk management perspective is that if supply chains are only seen from a business process engineering and control perspective, then the selective (downside only) engineering-derived views of objective risk sit quite well. However, if we also accept that supply chains

> It is important to recognise that 'objective risk' and 'perceived risk' both have places in logistics and SCM.

involve relationships that link organisations, populated by people, then there is an equally persuasive argument for perceived risk, with supply chains viewed as open *interactive societal systems*. If we also accept that these may be global supply chains, then those culturally determined perceptions of risk could vary greatly from one region to another. Along the way the forces of nature can demonstrate just how far removed from the controlled environment of the casino this all might be.

THE NEED FOR HOLISTIC APPROACHES

Chapter 1 underlined the fact that SCM is integrative and interdisciplinary, and that logistics is just one of several established sub-disciplines that fall under the SCM umbrella. It is therefore important to recognise that managers from many interacting disciplines as well as from different organisations will have interests in supply chain risk management. Each will likely be viewing risk management decisions in relation to their own performance measures, sometimes using quite different assumptions and interpretations of risk as points of reference. The result is that in practice supply chain risk management is likely to be a patchwork of sometimes complementary, but often conflicting or competing efforts. This means that supply chain risk management can be expected to display all the characteristics of a 'wicked problem'.

Wicked problems

A 'wicked problem' is a technical term first coined back in the early 1970s by Horst Rittel and Melvin Webber, two professors from Berkeley, who produced a paper on 'Dilemmas in a General Theory of Planning'.[28] Rittel and Webber's contribution was to produce a lucid explanation of why societal problems are inherently different from the problems that scientists and some engineers tackle in their daily work.

Scientists and engineers deal with discrete identifiable problems (Y2K is a good example), where the desired outcome is known, providing clarity of mission and an easily recognisable desired end state.

Wicked problems are different, because they involve multiple stakeholders, each with slightly different interests and value sets. As a result, there is no single common definitive goal, no clarity of mission and no universal solution. Rittel and Webber observed that, 'with "wicked problems" . . . any solution, after being implemented, will generate waves of consequences over an extended – virtually an unbounded – period of time. The next day's consequences of the solution may yield utterly undesirable repercussions . . . If the problem is attacked on too low a level, then successful resolution may result in making things worse, because it may become difficult to deal with the higher problems.'

Therefore to understand a wicked problem you must understand the wider context. To that end Rittel and Webber recommend that problems should be considered within 'valuative' frameworks, where multiple and differing perceptions are retained. Such frameworks recognise problems as the links tying open systems into large and interconnected networks of systems, and that the outputs from one become the inputs from another.

A SIMPLE FRAMEWORK FOR A WICKED PROBLEM

Taking Rittel and Webber's advice, Figure 15.1 shows a supply chain broken down into its component parts, hopefully without losing the sense of dynamic interaction. Looking at supply chains in this way enables the inclusion of many different functional and hierarchical perspectives, their respective interpretations of risk, as well as an opportunity to position some of the management tools and techniques currently available.

Level 1 – process engineering and inventory management

Level 1 in the figure concentrates on a process engineering or inventory management perspective. It focuses on what is being carried – work, cash and information

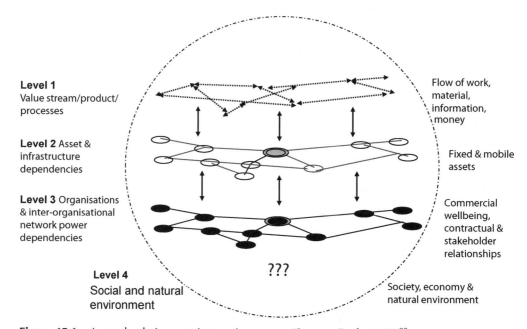

Figure 15.1 A supply chain as an interactive system (Source: Peck, 2005)[29]

flows – and process design *within and between* organisations. This perspective underlies lean manufacturing and the 'end-to-end' view required for the 'agile' supply chain concept. Risk management is largely about improved visibility (of demand and inventory), velocity (to reduce the likelihood of obsolescence and optimise asset utilisation) and control. If processes are tightly monitored and controlled, then nonconformance to plan can be quickly detected. Risk reduction tools are often borrowed from total quality management. Related process improvement and control methodologies such as 'six sigma' are also favoured by some, as are automated event management systems, which readily alert managers to deviations from plan and minimise human intervention.

In the ideal world of scientific management, mastery of process control methodologies would facilitate the identification, management and elimination of risk. Unfortunately we do not live in an ideal world, so levels 2, 3 and 4 of the model bring in a host of other factors that often intervene.

Level 2 – assets and infrastructure dependencies

Level 2 considers the fixed and mobile assets used to source, produce or carry the goods and information flows addressed at level 1. When viewed at this level, nodes in the networks may be farms, factories, distribution centres, commercial retail outlets, or public service delivery points such as schools or hospitals. Alternatively they may be facilities housing IT servers and call centres. Links in the network are the transport and communications infrastructure; that is, roads, railways, flight paths and sea lanes, pipelines and grids, plus mobile assets – boats, trains, trucks and planes. The transport and communications networks have their own nodes in the form of ports, airports and satellites.

Well-known asset-based approaches to risk management, developed in insurance for tangible assets or other insurable interests (e.g. a building, a life or a vehicle), are appropriate and commonly used in this context. These actuarial approaches draw on plentiful historical data to provide some indication of for example the likelihood of fire, flood and many other eventualities affecting the insured asset. They tend to define risk along the lines of the *Probability* (likelihood of a given event) × *Severity* (negative impact should it occur) within a given timeframe. In a wider vein it is helpful to explore the impact on operations of the loss of links or nodes in the production/distribution and infrastructure networks, through network modelling.

Mitigating the impacts of potential disruptions to nodes and links is where business continuity planning (BCP) also has a place. As often as not level 2 disruptions are not the result of catastrophic failures caused by the phenomena that have exercised generations of actuaries. The disruptions are just as likely to be the results of poorly managed IT upgrades or physical network reconfigurations. Planned site closures and relocations are often to blame. Nevertheless it is perhaps worth noting that cross-sector surveys suggest that loss of key skills is actually a more frequently encountered problem than either loss of site or IT systems.[30]

Level 2 is of course the territory of unglamorous 'trucks and sheds' logistics – an early candidate for outsourcing (along with IT support) in most manufacturing and retail organisations. The increase in global sourcing and supply that we discussed earlier in the book means that, for much of the developed world, the transport element of SCM and the associated resource requirements are increasing. It also means that more shipments are travelling further than ever before, increasing the possibility that assets (and their goods) may be damaged, stolen or simply mislaid along the way. To reduce the likelihood of this happening RFID is sometimes used in asset and consignment tracking.

Naturally, technological solutions, or any other aspect of operations at this level, need appropriately trained personnel, though this simple fact is often overlooked. The case below provides a real example of why consignment tracking matters and why staff training is so vitally important.

RFID AND THE COST OF LOSING TRACK

Hundreds of thousands of people met violent and untimely deaths in Iraq in the years following the invasion in 2003. Few of these individual tragedies have been so well investigated as the death of a British soldier, Sgt Stephen Roberts, who died in action after being hit in the chest by a wayward bullet. A shortage of essential body armour meant that he had been required to hand his over to a fellow serviceman who was judged to be more 'at risk'. The tragedy of this incident was that an investigation by the UK National Audit Office would later reveal that 200 000 components of body armour had been purchased by the Ministry of Defence, but misplaced somewhere within the logistics system. The scandal made an indisputable case for the extension of RFID within the UK defence logistics system.

RFID was used to track consignments by US forces and to a limited extent by UK forces during the 2003 invasion of Iraq. However, even tagged consignments appeared to be going missing. The root cause was a training failure. Back at base, enthusiastic logisticians were aware of the potential benefits of RFID technology and its operating requirements. Unfortunately neither US nor UK forces fully recognised the need to inform their frontline troops, who had no idea what the tags were, or what should be done with them when they reached their destination. As a result many were simply unclipped and thrown into buckets when the containers were unloaded. Some were shot off the containers by US troops believing them to be improvised explosive devices.

Level 3 – organisations and inter-organisational networks

Level 3 looks at supply chain risk at the strategic level of organisations and inter-organisational networks. These are the organisations that own or manage the assets and infrastructure, that create or carry the freight, information or cash flows. At this level, risk is likely to be perceived as the financial consequences of an event or decision for an organisation – particularly its impact on budget or shareholders. This is where strategic management concerns, corporate governance requirements and conflicts of interest in risk management become most evident.

From a purely SCM perspective, risk at this level is the downside financial consequences of a specific event. The loss of a sole supplier or customer is the most obvious danger here. The trading relationships that link organisations and power dependencies between them should also be watched carefully.

Low margins are likely to encourage consolidation within industry. Consolidation can change the balance of power between organisations in a supply chain, reversing dependencies, changing service priorities, negotiating positions and risk profiles. Post-takeover or merger, once compliant suppliers may no longer be willing to dance to a customer's tune. They may wish to concentrate on other bigger customers, or have completely different strategic priorities. Consolidation also heralds network reconfigurations and the associated disruptions described at level two.

Partnering, dual sourcing and outsourcing are likely to be put forward as risk management solutions, backed up by contractual obligations. However, anecdotal evidence abounds to suggest that in times of shortage contractual guarantees become unreliable, with suppliers diverting scarce resources to their largest customers, regardless of contractual requirements. Software is available that allows companies to divert supplies automatically to service their most valuable accounts.

Best practice strategic management and corporate governance tend to see risk differently from SCM. Here risk retains the upside as well as downside connotations of decision theory. Strategic management is likely to encourage managers to take 'big bets' to maintain competitive advantage in core competencies. The high-risk big bets are offset by a requirement for lower risk taking in non-core activities. This line of logic encourages strategists and corporate risk managers (few of whom have operational SCM experience) to attempt to transfer risks associated with non-core activities off balance sheets to suppliers. One pitfall associated with this reasoning is that the definition of what is and is not a core capability may be too narrowly drawn, with key elements of SCM falling by the wayside. Outsourcing and contractual means are nevertheless seen as legitimate methods employed to reduce exposure to financial risk. The option is even more tempting if short-term cost savings can be realised. However, when liability for risk management is transferred in this way, the operational consequences of failure remain.

The industrial relations battle between Swiss-based, North American-owned airline catering company Gate Gourmet (you will recall we also studied the operations and logistics processes in this company in the case study at the end of Part Two) and its UK workforce in the summer of 2005 illustrates the point. The Gate Gourmet dispute was a landmark case in that it marked the return of secondary industrial action, not seen in the UK for decades.[31] It also illustrates why supply chains should also be viewed as interactive societal systems.

GATE GOURMET

Gate Gourmet was sole supplier of in-flight catering services to British Airways (BA). Many of the staff had been BA workers until a cost reduction programme prompted the airline to outsource the activity in 1997 to Swiss-owned company Gate Gourmet. The move had been financially beneficial to BA, which, in a competitive environment, had continued to pursue further cost reductions through its supply chain. The pressure to continually cut costs was in turn cited by some as the root cause of the Gate Gourmet dispute.

In the post-9/11 climate of fear, demand for transatlantic air travel dropped and oil prices rose. These were hard times for the airline industry and its suppliers. The catering business went into loss. In 2002 Gate Gourmet was sold on to US-based private equity firm Texas Pacific Group (TPG). At this point BA exercised an option within the original outsourcing agreement to renegotiate the contract for more favourable terms. The new owners improved productivity and increased management pay, but continued to lose money on the BA contract. In 2005 the new owners sought to cut its costs with redundancies amongst catering staff, and by imposing less generous terms and conditions on those who remained. At the same time the company took on 130 seasonal workers on lower rates of pay. The resulting dispute and 670 sackings – involving mostly women drawn from the local Asian community – did not on the face of it represent a significant threat to BA. The airline could operate its core business without in-flight meals. However, when about 1000 BA ground staff – many of them with family ties to the sacked catering workers – decided to walk out in sympathy, the consequences for BA were unavoidable. The four-day strike halted BA flights out of its Heathrow hub, damaging the airline's reputation, and costing BA (and its shareholders) an estimated £40 million in cancelled flights and the cost of food and accommodation for 70 000 stranded passengers.

With bankers threatening to move against TPG and TPG threatening to take Gate Gourmet into administration, BA was forced to intervene. The airline agreed to renegotiate its catering contract, and to donate about £7 million towards the cost of enhanced redundancy packages, but did so on the condition that Gate Gourmet settled its own labour dispute. On 27 September 2005 an agreement was reached between the trade unions and Gate Gourmet. About 700 catering staff volunteered to accept the new redundancy offer, slightly over the number required. In March 2007, TPG sold its holding in Gate Gourmet to bankers Merill Lynch.

Level 4 – the macro-environment

The fourth and final level of analysis is the macro-environment, within which the assets and infrastructure are positioned and organisations do business. The 'PEST' (political, economic, social and technological) analysis of environmental changes, used in strategic management, is appropriate here. Sometimes 'green' environmental and legal/regulatory changes are included in the basic analysis or given separate treatment. Socio-political factors, such as action by pressure groups (e.g. environmentalists or fuel protestors) can be identified by routine 'horizon scanning' using specialist or general media sources, allowing measures to be put in place to mitigate the impact. Geo-political factors, such as war, often take time to build, but the extent to which they can influence demand for all manner of goods and services should not be underestimated. For example, the 2003 invasion of Iraq coincided with a drop in business confidence, leading to a fall in advertising, and a marked reduction in demand for high-quality paper. The war had the reverse impact on the demand for oil as fears of oil shortages swept the world, and on oil prices, which are critical for the global economy.

Beyond a controlled 'casino' or even factory environment, there are the forces of nature – meteorological, geological and pathological – to contend with. Most are likely to be far beyond the control of supply chain managers, so risk avoidance or contingency planning are appropriate courses of action. Meteorological events include the effects of extreme weather. Geological disturbances can involve the devastation to communities and dislocation to supply chains caused by earthquakes, tsunamis or volcanic activitiy. The widespread closure of areas of European airspace due to the ash cloud during the 2010 eruptions of the Icelandic volcano Eyjafjallajökull is an example, as is the similar such event in 2011. However, one category – pathogens – such as contaminants and diseases – is worth particular attention here. Whether it is foot and mouth, a human pandemic, the computer viruses that mimic them, or even 'toxic assets' in the banking system, what makes pathological factors so dangerous is that they are *mobile*. They have the ability to hitch a ride with the flows of products and information (and people) that logisticians and supply chain managers work so hard to speed around the globe. Once inside the system, they have the potential to bring it down from within. With more goods, information and money travelling further and faster than ever before the potential for this to happen cannot be ignored.

The creeping crises referred to earlier in this chapter could all be regarded as level 4 disruptions, but it would be wrong to regard them only as *external* threats to the supply chain. Their potency as disruptive challenges is a reflection of our interconnected, interdependent societies and the efficiency of our supply chains.

LEARNING REVIEW

This chapter has provided an introduction to the complex, but fascinating subject of supply chain risk, and the related concepts of vulnerability, robustness and resilience. It has tackled some of the competing concepts of risk, the shortcomings of risk management and their relevance to a logistics and SCM context. The chapter draws on earlier writings in open systems theory to explain why supply chains should be viewed as open societal systems as well as engineered processes. How, when and why the different concepts of risk fit with some elements of supply chains but not others were explained. Throughout, the chapter has endeavoured to provide a holistic overview of supply chain vulnerability, providing a multi-level framework, based on a simple exploded model of a supply chain. Within this framework appropriate supply chain risk management tools are positioned.

QUESTIONS

- What is meant by supply chain vulnerability?
- Why is a robust supply chain not necessarily a resilient supply chain?
- Distinguish objective and perceived risk.
- Discuss the relevance of the Sarbanes–Oxley Act 2002 (SOX) to logistics.
- Outline how risk might be dealt with in levels 1, 2 and 3 of Peck's model of the supply chain.

THE IMPACTS OF CREEPING CRISES

We discussed above the role of creeping crises in today's uncertain and changing world. Can you think of other creeping crises in addition to the ones mentioned in this chapter?

Taking either your own examples or the ones described in this chapter, outline the impacts these crises had on economies and societies.

NOTES

1. For an explanation of the origins of orthodoxies in risk management see: Adams, J. (1995) *Risk*, Routledge, Abingdon.
2. Christopher, M. (1998) *Logistics and Supply Chain Management* (2nd edition), Financial Times/Pitman Publishing, London.
3. Tang, C. (2006) Robust strategies for mitigating supply chain disruptions, *International Journal of Logistics Research and Applications*, 9(1), 33–45.
4. *Collins English Dictionary* (2000) Harper Collins, Glasgow.
5. Peck, H. (2006) *Resilience in the Food Chain: A Study of Business Continuity in the Food and Drinks Industry*, Department for Environment, Food and Rural Affairs, London.
6. *Collins English Dictionary.*
7. Peck, H. (2003) *Supply Chain Resilience*, Department for Transport, London.
8. Peck, H. (2005) Drivers of supply chain vulnerability: an integrated framework, *International Journal of Physical Distribution and Logistics Management*, 35(4), 210–232.
9. Rumsfeld, D., www.defenselink.mil/transcripts/transcript.aspx?transcriptid=2636.
10. Matthews, R. (2004) QED: science and philosophy, *The Daily Telegraph*, www .telegraph.co. uk/connected/main.jhtml?xml=/connected/2004/07/07/ ecrqed07.xml.
11. BBC News, Rum remark wins Rumsfeld an award, 2 December 2003.
12. For an introduction to the concept of high reliability organisations see: La Porte, T.R. & Consolini, P. (1991) Working in practice, but not in theory: theoretical challenges for

'high reliability' organizations, *Journal of Public Administration Research and Theory,* 1(1), 19–47.

13. Demchak, D. (1996) Tailored precision armies in fully networked battlespace: high reliability organizational dilemmas in the 'information age', *Journal of Contingencies and Crisis Management,* 4(2), 93–103.

14. For an introduction to business continuity planning and its place within the wider discipline of business continuity management see: Hiles, A. & Barnes B. (1999) *The Definitive Handbook of Business Continuity Management,* John Wiley & Sons, Chichester.

15. Peck, H. & Jüttner, U. (2002) Risk management in the supply chain, *Logistics and Transport Focus,* 4(11), 17–22.

16. Forrester, J.W. (1958) Industrial dynamics: a major breakthrough for decision makers, *Harvard Business Review,* 38, July–August, 37–66.

17. Sheffi, Y. (2001) Supply chain management under threat of international terrorism, *International Journal of Logistics Management,* 12(2), 1–11.

18. British Standard 25999 Business Continuity, British Standards Institute (2006) www.bsi-global.com/en/Assessment-and-certification-services/management-systems/Standards-and-Schemes/BS-25999.

19. Borge, D. (2001) *The Book of Risk,* John Wiley & Sons, New York.

20. March, J.G. & Shapira, Z. (1987) Managerial perspectives on risk and risk taking, *Management Science,* 33(11), 1404–1418.

21. Noy, E. & Ellis, S. (2002) Corporate risk strategy: is it a unified whole or does it vary across business activities? Unpublished paper, Tel Aviv University.

22. Knight, F. (1921, 1965) *Risk, Uncertainty and Profit,* Harper and Row, New York.

23. Royal Society for the Prevention of Accidents (1983) *Risk Assessment: A Study Group Report,* Royal Society, London.

24. National Research Council (1983) *Risk Assessment in the Federal Government: Managing the Process,* National Academy Press, Washington DC.

25. Adams, J. (1996) *Risk,* Routledge, London.

26. White, D. (1995) Applications of systems thinking to risk management: a review of the literature, *Management Decision,* 33(10), 35–45.

27. Martha, J. & Subbakrishna, S. (2002) Targeting a just-in-case supply chain for the inevitable next disaster, *Supply Chain Management Review,* September/October, 18–24.

28. Rittel, H.W.J. & Webber, M.M. (1973) Dilemmas in a general theory of planning, *Policy Sciences,* 4, 155–169.

29. Peck (2005) (see note 8).

30. Peck & Jüttner (see note 15).

31. Arrowsmith, J. (2005) British Airways Heathrow flights grounded by dispute at Gate Gourmet. European Industrial Relations Observatory online (Eironline), 20 September, www.eurofound.europa.eu/eiro/2005/09/feature/uk0509106f.html.

16 Sustainable Logistics and Supply Chain Systems

LEARNING OBJECTIVES

- Understand what sustainability involves in the context of logistics and SCM.
- Understand key terms such as carbon footprints, food miles, reverse logistics, etc.
- Illustrate best practice examples of attempts to reduce environmental footprints.
- Understand the link that exists between growth in logistics and concomitant growth in the demand for transport.
- Examine the different aspects of the two key dimensions used in logistics to reduce environmental impacts, namely scale and efficiency.

'You turn over an iPod and there are six words that are a metaphor for the global economy: 'designed in California, made in China' (Professor Gary Hamel, London Business School)

INTRODUCTION

The above quote comes from one of the world's most respected management thinkers and aptly sums up the way the world's economy increasingly works today. We already looked in depth in Part One of the book at globalisation and international trade, and how both shape today's logistics systems. We also saw that in particular increased outsourcing and offshoring to lower cost locations have generated huge flows of international freight. Many of the preceding chapters in this book have given various insights into how effective and efficient logistics and SCM can influence the success of organisations. Success, however, has different interpretations which go past consideration of only economic success. The purpose of this chapter is to look beyond how logistics and SCM can influence organisational success and to consider the issue of sustainability as it applies to logistics and SCM.

Often, people regard sustainability as just referring to 'green' issues. This, however, is just one (albeit very important) dimension and in this chapter we will also consider the issue of economic sustainability, i.e. how can the firm itself survive and grow in a sustainable manner without having adverse impacts on future generations, and specifically what is the role of logistics and SCM in this context. The important, and growing, area of reverse logistics (both in terms of return of end-of-life products and packaging, as well as return of

> Sustainable logistics is concerned with reducing the environmental and other disbenefits associated with the movement of freight. Sustainability seeks to ensure that decisions made today do not have an adverse impact upon future generations. Sustainable supply chains seek to reduce these disbenefits by *inter alia* redesigning sourcing and distribution systems so as to eliminate any inefficiencies and unnecessary freight movements.

defective and unwanted products) is also covered in this chapter. Kleindorfer *et al.*,[1] for example, use the term sustainability to include 'environmental management, closed-loop supply chains and a broad perspective on triple-bottom-line (3BL) thinking, integrating profit, people and the planet into the culture, strategy and operations of companies.'

Later in the chapter we consider two caselets which describe the significant increases in scale that have occurred in global container shipping. The facts in the caselets go to the heart of the sustainability debate: some argue that by enjoying such scale as is evidenced in the examples cited is the only way to ensure that global trade can continue by helping to further reduce unit transport costs; others argue that scale is not the solution and that the answer must lie in local sourcing and production.

It is important to also note that the movement of freight is not responsible for all of the environmental disbenefits associated with transportation (we use the term 'externalities' to refer to these disbenefits): the movement of people also creates disbenefits and some logisticians argue that freight takes an unfair share of the blame!

In our discussion in this chapter we will draw upon examples from maritime transport, air transport and road haulage to highlight issues of sustainability.

Chapter 16 comprises four core sections:

- The 'green revolution' and supply chain redesign
- The link between economic growth and transport growth
- The role of 'scale' in logistics and SCM
- Efficiency solutions

THE 'GREEN REVOLUTION' AND SUPPLY CHAIN REDESIGN

Recent years have seen a dramatic increase in what have come to be known as 'green' issues, which can generally be regarded as encompassing respect for the world's natural environment (including its atmosphere) so as to ensure that actions taken today do not hinder future generations. Figure 16.1 summarises the key drivers behind the increased emphasis on green issues.

A key concern centres in particular around the use of fossil fuels for power generation and the resultant carbon emissions. The international Kyoto Protocol has called for a 60% reduction in carbon emissions by 2050. This is a steep target with many commentators pessimistic it will ever be achieved (the Deutsche Post World Net case at the end of the chapter conveys, however, a less pessimistic view). 'Emissions trading' has now come into fashion whereby companies and countries engage in environmentally positive activities (for example planting trees) in order to offset the deleterious effects of carbon emissions.

The term **carbon footprint** has come into use to describe the environmental disbenefits associated with economic activities such as the movement of freight. Consumers are becoming increasingly aware of the impact of purchasing goods which may have been sourced over long distances. It may generally appear to be the case that such goods have a larger carbon footprint, although we would caution that this view is overly simplistic. For example if locally produced goods are manufactured and distributed in an environmentally damaging manner, then this may be worse than procuring goods from overseas which are manufactured and distributed in an environmentally sustainable manner.

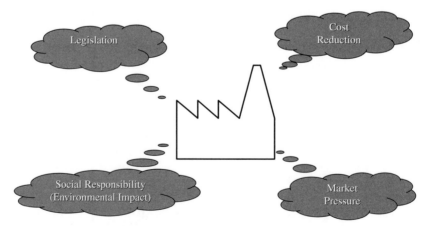

Figure 16.1   The drivers behind the increased emphasis on green issues
(Source: Kevin Ord, Scarborough Campus, The University of Hull)

MEASURING THE CARBON FOOTPRINT

Greenhouse gas (GHG) emissions are those that contribute to climate change, with most (approximately 95%) being in the form of carbon dioxide (CO_2), which results from, among other activities, the burning of fossil fuels. Various entities have developed guides on how to measure and report GHG emissions.

In the UK for example, Defra (the UK government department responsible for the environment, food and rural affairs) has produced a guide for measuring and reporting GHG emissions from freight transport (www.defra.gov.uk/environment/business/reporting/). Detailed guidelines and look-up tables are available online but in essence the calculation comprises:

(Fuel used) $\times$ (The appropriate emission factor for the type of fuel used) $=$ kgCO$_2$eq

Note: eq refers to 'equivalent' as this also captures other gases such as methane and nitrous oxide.

Moving beyond transport, the challenge is to conduct carbon auditing of supply chains at the product level. Research led by Professor Alan McKinnon (one of the world's leading experts in the areas of logistics, transport and the environment) of Edinburgh's Heriot-Watt University has concluded, however, that product-level carbon auditing and labelling is a 'wasteful distraction' and that it would be better to devote management time and resources to other decarbonisation initiatives.[2]

Another term that has come to be increasingly used is **food miles**: this refers to the distance over which the various components of a particular food item have to travel before final consumption. In time it may be the case that ingredients labels on foodstuffs will also include such food miles data.

It is difficult to know exactly how *green* a supply chain actually is, and there is no industry standard to measure it. What is accepted, however, is that greening a supply chain is largely about forward planning, with some commentators noting that over 80% of carbon savings are only achievable at the supply chain design stage.[3] While various initiatives such as, for example, switching to hybrid fuel vehicles are obviously welcome, and generate publicity benefits for companies, it is the (often unnoticed in the public eye) *supply chain design* decisions, such as deciding where to locate warehouses and distribution centres and which transport modes to use, that have the greatest impact. In Europe, for example, there is something of a *renaissance* in short sea shipping, where goods are increasingly moved over short sea routes (a more environmentally friendly mode of transport) rather than along congested (and environmentally more harmful) roads.

Other examples of sustainable supply chain redesigns include reconfiguring distribution networks so as replace small deliveries direct to all end customers with centralised deliveries to a hub from where end customers retrieve their goods. London's Heathrow Airport for example has developed a retail consolidation centre adjacent to the airport which receives deliveries on behalf of the various retailers within the airport. Deliveries from different suppliers for these retailers can then be grouped together and delivered to the retailers. The key principle at play here is that it is, other things being equal, more environmentally sustainable when freight moves *in bulk* as far downstream as possible; conversely we can envisage a delivery truck with a small consignment going to a single customer as having relatively high environmental costs. It is important to add that other benefits can also accrue with such an initiative; for example in the airport environment freight could be security checked and rendered safe to be delivered 'airside' once it passes through the hub, thus cutting down on the need for other security checks. Another example is DHL's PACKSTATION initiative illustrated in the Deutsche Post World Net case at the end of the chapter.

As was noted in the chapter outline section above, a possibly more environmentally friendly scenario is local sourcing. One should not, however, underestimate the role of the various factors we discussed with regard to outsourcing and offshoring (such as cheaper labour and materials costs), combined with the fact that many companies have made substantial investments in overseas lower cost locations, which they will want to recoup. These factors can thus still render locally sourced goods more expensive. The key then is to ensure that if goods are sourced overseas, that this is done in an environmentally sustainable manner. Furthermore, as many businesses have profit as their primary objective, the key is to ensure that they see the business benefits of environmentally sustainable activities, which may include for example reduced energy bills and enhanced consumer loyalty (although we know that there is a limit to how much more customers will be willing to pay for goods with a low carbon footprint).

We can conclude at this juncture that there are in effect three ways in which to improve the sustainability of logistics and supply chain systems (Figure 16.2):

- Redesigning supply chains
- Using *scale* to reduce the negative environmental effects of logistics activities (i.e. by moving freight in larger single loads, thus cutting down on both unit costs and disbenefits)
- Similarly promoting various *efficiency* solutions (by transporting and handling freight more effectively)

It is important to note that these three solutions are not mutually exclusive: a smart, environmentally sensitive supply chain will combine all three.

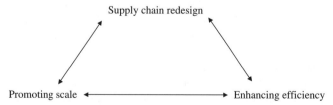

Figure 16.2   Sustainable logistics and SCM

We have already considered supply chain redesign, in the following sections we will look at the role of scale and efficiency in the context of sustainable logistics and SCM, but first we will look at the link between economic growth and transport.

THE LINK BETWEEN ECONOMIC GROWTH AND TRANSPORT GROWTH

It can generally be shown that there is an inexorable link between economic growth (as measured usually by GDP) and transport, i.e. as economies grow, more transport is required to move the freight that economic growth inevitably generates. A core issue for policy makers is to endeavour to *decouple* economic growth and transport growth, i.e. to find ways of allowing economic growth without comparable growth in transport (see the caselet: Decoupling road freight transport and economic growth). There are numerous factors behind such decoupling, as the analysis in the caselet illustrates.

> Economic growth and growth in transport are closely linked.

DECOUPLING ROAD FREIGHT TRANSPORT AND ECONOMIC GROWTH

In the UK, research by Professor Alan McKinnon at Heriot-Watt University in Edinburgh has shown a partial decoupling between road haulage growth and economic growth.[4] On the surface this looks like a very positive outcome. However, as Professor McKinnon's research shows, the reasons behind this decoupling are varied. Between 1997 and 2004, GDP in the UK increased by one-fifth, while the volume of road freight movement remained stable. His analysis showed that around two-thirds of the decoupling is due to three factors, which can be quantified: more non-UK hauliers operating in the domestic market (the relevant UK road haulage statistics just capture the freight tonne-kilometres of UK-based hauliers); a decline in road transport's share of the freight market (i.e. freight is shifting from road to other more environmentally friendly modes such as rail and coastal shipping, which obviously is a positive development); and real increases in road freight rates.

Professor McKinnon cites several other factors as having a significant effect, though these cannot be measured on the basis of available statistics. These factors include the relative growth of the service sector (i.e. an increased share of non-manufactured products in economic growth), the diminishing rate of centralisation and the offshoring of manufacturing. Professor McKinnon concludes that, while the decoupling is in the right direction from a public policy standpoint, the net environmental benefits are likely to be modest.

The world economy is likely to continue to grow in the medium term, and a feature of such economic growth will be increased demand for transport and distribution. It will be essential that logisticians seek to reduce as much as possible the environmental disbenefits associated with such growth. We already saw that one way they can do this is by reconfiguring supply chains; we will now look in turn at two other approaches, namely *scale* and *efficiency*.

THE ROLE OF 'SCALE' IN LOGISTICS AND SCM

THE *EMMA MAERSK*: 'SANTA'S SHIP'

In Chapter 8 we introduced the global shipping and logistics company A.P. Moller – Maersk. Established in Denmark in 1904, today the group employs more than 110 000 people in over 125 countries. The group's shipping subsidiaries operate some of the world's largest container vessels. Maersk Line's flagship, the *Emma Maersk*, which won the title of ship of the year at the 2007 Lloyd's List awards in London, is one of the world's largest container vessels with an operating capacity of some 11 000 TEUs (twenty-foot-equivalent units). She is one of five sister vessels.

Emma Maersk received widespread media interest during her inaugural visit to the UK port of Felixstowe.[5] Media reports noted that the ship is a quarter of a mile long, 200 feet high and as wide as a motorway. And it can be operated by a crew of just 13. The welcome for the vessel was not, however, universal with the Green Party Member of the European Parliament for South East England, Dr Caroline Lucas MEP, suggesting that the environmental costs of long-distance trade need to be properly taken into account. She was quoted as saying that 'we must manage international trade in a way which is socially and environmentally sustainable, working towards global agreement on a raft of measures such as taxation on fuel and import tariffs designed to support home-grown businesses'[6]

More recently, Maersk has ordered new vessels with a capacity of up to 18000 TEU (see the dedicated website on this initiative: www.worldslargestship.com). They are labelled 'Triple-E' (the three Es being: energy efficiency, economy of scale and the environment) and Maersk states that these giants will reduce CO_2 emissions by more than 50% per container moved and will be the world's largest and most efficient container vessels.

According to the global shipping and logistics company A.P. Moller – Maersk:[7]

- If all the containers in the world were lined up, it would create a container wall with a length of 108 000 kilometres: a third of the way to the moon!
- The volume of freight that can be held in one standard 40 foot container is quite significant: 200 dishwashers, 350 bicycles or 5000 pairs of jeans.
- The shipping cost per unit is thus quite low: Maersk estimates, for freight coming from Asia to Europe, it costs £9 per dishwasher, £5 per bicycle and just £0.35 per pair of jeans.

Only certain ports can handle such ultra large vessels like the *Emma Maersk*, however, and many container vessels in routine operation are much smaller than this. With fewer ports able to handle larger vessels, there is growing traffic concentration at certain ports. Increasingly, many mid-sized ports are playing a feeder role to the very large ports as hub and spoke networks have emerged. In these networks the larger vessels ply between the major transhipment hubs, with the result that the prosperity of the smaller ports is increasingly dependent on the route strategies of the major shipping lines. This then is the impact of increasing scale on global shipping and port operations. Regardless of the impact of these developments on ports and shipping, important as they are, the question we need to address is: are these patterns of trade sustainable going forward?

Given the increasingly integrated nature of the global economy, some commentators argue that such developments are both inevitable and necessary. Others argue that the frequent movement of low-value products around the world is unnecessary, deleterious to the environment, and not sustainable in the long term (especially in the context for example of some of the risks that were outlined in Chapter 15). A cursory analysis of the Moller – Maersk figures quoted above, however, shows that container shipping costs are only a fraction of end-product value; unless there is a dramatic rebalancing between regions of other costs in the global economy (such as raw materials and labour costs) it is likely that these patterns of trade are set to continue. If they are, our concern from a logistics standpoint must be how to facilitate them while reducing as much as possible their negative consequences on the environment.

Oglethorpe and Heron[8] note that many commentators believe the solution to environmental sustainability and social responsibility issues lies in the 'downscaling, decentralising and deconsolidating of supply chains and logistics systems'. However, they challenge this and, using research on the food supply chain, suggest that 'environmental burden actually decreases across increasing logistical scale and supply chain sophistication'.

EFFICIENCY SOLUTIONS

IKEA PROVES ITS GREEN CREDENTIALS[9,10]

In Christmas 2006, the Swedish retailer Ikea gave its 9000 employees a free bicycle as a Christmas present. They also offered staff a 15% subsidy on public transport. Ikea has long been regarded as a very environmentally conscious company and these initiatives were part of many wider efforts to evidence the company's commitment to sustainability and which are detailed in its 'Social and Environmental Responsibility' report. One example is where Ikea worked with a supplier to reduce by 1 cm a package containing a sofa from 91 cm wide to 90 cm. As a result, four extra sofas could now be fitted onto each trailer, with obvious cost and environmental benefits.

As well as looking to increased scale, many logistics operators are also seeking efficiencies with how they move and store freight so as to reduce the environmental impact of their activities. The caselet on 'Port-centric logistics' gives insights into how for example logistics companies are seeking to reduce unnecessary road haulage movements for imported maritime freight, and in turn reducing the carbon footprint of such freight movements. Table 16.1 lists some of the many ways in which logistics efficiencies can be generated, and simultaneous environmental penalties reduced, in the case of road haulage. You will recall that we also looked at the efficiency of transport services and asset utilisation in Chapter 6. We noted then that the issue of supply chain strategy can impact the efficiency of the transport services demanded, with JIT strategies for example leading to inefficient transport utilisation with frequent small loads. Whether JIT systems are sustainable from an environmental perspective going forward is an important question.

PORT-CENTRIC LOGISTICS: ONE POSSIBLE SOLUTION?

Some ports are actively encouraging companies to locate distribution centres at ports rather than in their traditional locations, which tend to be in geographically central, inland locations. These ports argue that current patterns of (inland) distribution centre location ignore the fact that most of the freight that passes through these distribution centres first transits through a port. Therefore they argue that it is logical (and often easier in terms of land cost, lack of congestion, etc.) to site such distribution centres at ports. The term **port centric** is sometimes used to refer to this approach.[11]

One advantage of port-centric logistics is that it cuts down on the number of empty (return) containers on roads by 'stripping' (i.e. emptying) imported containers at the port. This also allows faster repositioning of containers to another port where they are required (we saw in Chapter 2 the significant directional imbalances that exist on global shipping corridors, consequently shipping lines endeavour to reposition empty containers to where they are next needed as quickly as possible).

In the port of Felixstowe in the UK for example, the BAP Group operates half a million square feet of on-port warehousing and is a major logistics provider for the retailer Sainsbury's. They cite a variety of examples where port-centric logistics has been effectively employed:[12]

- Sainsbury's previously took imported containers to an inland RDC, but now the containers are stripped at the port, eliminating a return leg of empty containers. They estimate that this saves 700 000 road miles for every 5000 TEUs handled.

- Many imported containers are not completely full because of weight restrictions on UK roads. However, if the containers are to be emptied at the port, and not travel on the roads, then the containers can be filled to capacity, which they estimate can in some instances be up to 40% more.

In transportation, it is not just the road haulage sector that is seeking to reduce its environmental footprint. With the growth of air travel, spurred on in particular by rapid growth in the so-called low fares category of air travel, many commentators

Table 16.1   Improving road haulage logistics efficiency and reducing environmental penalties[13]

- Reducing empty running, pooling and sharing capacity, obtaining 'backhaul' loads (a number of websites have been developed which match carriers who have available capacity with shippers seeking capacity – see the caselet on electronic logistics markets)
- Increasing vehicle payload capacity (by weight and/or by cubic volume) – double deck and higher trailers, single tractor unit and multiple trailer combinations, etc.
- Improved vehicle routeing using GPS and other systems
- More efficient use of packaging and loading of containers
- Improved vehicle driving (in-cab computer monitoring of driving style, even examining the benefits of air conditioning versus open windows!)
- Enhancing vehicle operating efficiency (for example using hybrid fuels, ensuring correct wheel alignment and enhanced aerodynamic styling of trucks)

are looking towards the air transport sector to reduce its impact on the environment. The European low-fare airline easyJet for example recently unveiled its 'easyJet ecoJet' concept (i.e. a next-generation aircraft design which it believes aircraft manufacturers should be seeking to create). The chief executive of easyJet is quoted as saying that 'the aviation industry has an excellent record in reducing the environmental footprint of aircraft . . . . Today's aircraft are typically 70% cleaner and 75% quieter than their 1960s' counterparts'.[14]

In logistics, efficiency solutions are not just restricted to transportation. The area of green warehouse design is also growing in popularity. Many warehouses are vast structures and their environmental footprints can be reduced by for example more efficient lighting and heating/refrigeration systems.

ELECTRONIC LOGISTICS MARKETS[15]

As we noted in Table 16.1 a number of websites have been developed that match LSPs who have available capacity with shippers seeking capacity. These electronic logistics market-places (ELMs) provide opportunities both for the LSPs and for those companies using them: the LSP can offer excess capacity within its fleet to a greater potential client base, thus maximising its loaded miles and leading to an ability to reduce freight charges; for shippers, ELMs enable them to increase the number of LSPs, and their concomitant services, that they can reach. Various ELMs provide services ranging from matching of one-off backhaul loads through to managing complex tendering processes for consignors.

DEUTSCHE POST WORLD NET AND SUSTAINABILITY[16]

Deutsche Post World Net, one of the world's largest logistics companies, comprises three core divisions: Deutsche Post, Postbank and, its most well-known division, DHL. According to the company's chairman: 'during the last few years we have become the global leader in our industry. This leadership entails great responsibilities toward society, the environment and our employees, as well as with respect to our continued sound financial performance.'[17]

In its first sustainability report, Deutsche Post outlines some of the company's initiatives, including: a partnership with the UN in the area of disaster management, reducing the amount of paper used in air waybills (with a potential annual saving of 207 tonnes of paper, and other savings such as reduced fuel consumption from the transportation of lighter air waybills; in addition the company has long been regarded as a pioneer in the use of electronic air waybills), and its PACKSTATION initiative whereby parcels are sent to a central collection point where consignees can retrieve them from an automated storage unit using an emailed password.

LEARNING REVIEW

The chapter sought to investigate the important, and rapidly growing, area of sustainable logistics and supply chain systems. We first looked at the growth of interest in environmental and sustainability issues, the so-called 'green revolution'. We also saw that there is a link between economic growth and increased demand for transport, although policy makers are endeavouring to weaken this link so that economic growth does not always have to be accompanied by concomitant growth in the demand for transport. Some commentators argue that the solution to reduce the environmental impact of current logistics systems is to source more freight locally, as opposed to overseas, but we saw that the issues surrounding this are more complex than they first appear. We also touched upon the impact of prevalent JIT systems and whether these are sustainable from an environmental perspective going forward.

We then reviewed the three key (and not mutually exclusive ways) in which the environmental footprint of logistics and SCM can be reduced: by redesigning supply chains, by exploiting the benefits of scale (for example using larger ships), and by seeking out efficiencies in terms of how we move freight. Having studied the critically important area of sustainability, the next chapter focuses on the important area of reverse logistics where, among other considerations, significant environmental benefits can also be realised.

QUESTIONS

- What are the pertinent sustainability issues in the context of logistics and SCM?
- What are the different ways by which the environmental footprint of logistics and SCM can be reduced?
- What is meant by the term 'port-centric logistics'?
- How might we 'decouple' economic growth and transport growth?
- Why might JIT inventory management approaches not be sustainable from an environmental perspective?
- What is meant by the term 'carbon footprint'?

LOCAL VERSUS OVERSEAS SOURCING?

Some commentators argue that the solution to reduce the environmental impact of current logistics systems is to source more products locally, as opposed to overseas.

In your view what factors militate against this? It may be helpful to consider specific products and markets, and to consider the *price elasticity* of demand for those products (i.e. how will demand for the product change as the market price for the product changes?).

NOTES

1. Kleindorfer, P., Singhal, K. & Wassenhove, L. (2005) Sustainable operations management, *Production and Operations Management*, 14(4), 482–492.

2. McKinnon, A. (2010) Product-level carbon auditing of supply chains: environmental imperative or wasteful distraction? *International Journal of Physical Distribution and Logistics Management*, 40(1/2), 42–60.

3. French, E. (2007) Green by design, *CILT Focus*, June, gives an excellent insight into the issues discussed in this paragraph.

4. McKinnon, A. (2007) Decoupling of road freight transport and economic growth trends in the UK: an exploratory analysis, *Transport Reviews*, January, 27(1), 37–64.

5. Giant Christmas goods ship docks, *BBC News Online*, 5 November 2006.

6. Ibid.

7. www.maerskline.com.

8. Oglethorpe, D. & Heron, G. (2010) Sensible operational choices for the climate change agenda, *International Journal of Logistics Management,* 21(3), 538–577.

9. Ikea gives staff a chance to get on their bikes, *The Independent,* 20 June 2007.

10. IKEA 'Social and Environmental Responsibility Report', available at www.ikea.com.

11. Falkner, J. (2006) A better place to do logistics? *Logistics Manager*, May.

12. Port-centric logistics, *Ship2Shore* (customer magazine of Hutchinson Ports UK), Issue 1, June 2007.

13. Many of the ideas in this table have been elicited from www.freightbestpractice.org.uk.

14. www.easyjet.com.

15. See, for example, Wang, Y., Potter, A.T. & Naim, M.M. (2007) Evaluating the reasons for using electronic logistics marketplaces within supply chains, *Proceedings of the Logistics Research Network Conference*, Hull, 5–7 September, pp. 137–142.

16. Facing the challenges of global logistics, DHL Sustainability Report 2006, available from www.dhl.com.

17. Ibid.

17
Reverse Logistics

Shams Rahman
RMIT University, Australia

INTRODUCTION

Unlike other chapters, which concentrate on the forward movement and transformation of materials from suppliers to end customers, this chapter focuses on the management of the reverse flow of materials from end customers to the original suppliers, either for reprocessing or disposal. On the one hand, environmental-related legislation is forcing companies to be responsible for their waste, on the other hand, waste disposal costs are increasing rapidly. As a result of depleted landfill and incineration capacities, the cost of landfill activities has increased incrementally and is still on the rise. In this evolving business environment, many world-class companies have realised that reverse logistics practices can be used to gain competitive advantage. Companies such as Xerox, Hewlett-Packard, Eastman Kodak, Sears and many others have successfully implemented reverse logistics practices. These initiatives not only have reduced waste and its adverse effect on the environment, but have also lowered operating costs and improved profitability and the public image of these companies.

Chapter 17 comprises six core sections:

- Definition of reverse logistics
- Motivations for reverse logistics
- Recovery options in reverse logistics
- Characteristics of the remanufacturing environment in reverse logistics
- Factors for successful reverse logistics implementation
- Performance measures of reverse logistics

DEFINITION OF REVERSE LOGISTICS

Concern over resource consumption and other environmental issues has led to the creation of an international sustainable development initiative. This initiative aims to achieve economic growth for the current generation without depleting resources for future generations. One method for achieving sustainable growth is to increase the amount of product materials recovered from the world's waste stream by using **reverse logistics**.

Logistics management focuses primarily on the movement of material from the point of origin to the point of consumption, whereas reverse logistics concentrates on the flow of material from the point of consumption towards the point of origin. Using this notion Rogers and Tibben-Lembke[1] (p.2) defined reverse logistics as:

> The process of planning, implementing, and controlling the efficient, cost effective flow of raw materials, in-process inventory, finished goods, and related information from the point of consumption to the point of origin for the purpose of recapturing or creating value or proper disposal.

Hence, reverse logistics is a process in which a manufacturer systematically accepts previously shipped products or parts from the point of consumption for possible reuse, remanufacturing, recycling or disposal (with and without energy recovery). A generic reverse logistics process with various recovery options is shown in Figure 17.1.

The following section discusses several factors that motivate firms to implement reverse logistics activities.

MOTIVATIONS FOR REVERSE LOGISTICS

One of the fastest growing waste categories is electronic waste (e-waste, i.e. discarded computers and electronic goods). A report by the Australian Bureau of Statistics (ABS)[2] shows e-waste is growing three times faster than regular waste. Australia, a nation of just

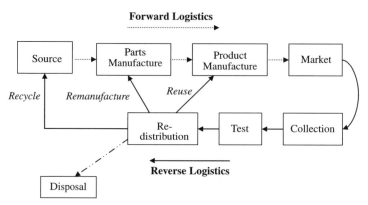

Figure 17.1 A generic reverse logistics system with recovery options

over 20.6 million people, had discarded or stockpiled a total of 8.7 million computers at the end of 2006. This report predicted that by the end of 2008, 1.6 million computers would have been sent to landfill rubbish dumps, while a further 1.8 million would join the 5.3 million old computers already in storage.

Many organisations that previously did not devote resources to the understanding and management of return flows have begun to allocate time and energy to reverse logistics. Many high-profile global companies have considered the management of return flows as part of their strategic agenda. Several factors motivate this development. The following factors are important.

Government policy and legislation

Several countries, especially in Europe, have enhanced legislation and policy, forcing manufacturers to take back their products after use. This legislation generally concerns collection, transportation, recovery and disposal of used products. In the Netherlands, for instance, from January 1999 manufacturers and importers of white-and-brown goods have to take back and recover their products after use. Similar legislation was adopted for the car industry, with an obligation to take back and recover used cars. Germany introduced a Packaging Ordinance, under which companies must collect all sales packaging materials. The German Recycling and Waste Control Act requires manufacturers to actively seek techniques and technologies that avoid waste and to promote the recovery processes of unavoidable waste materials. Some of the other countries of the European Union have followed the German initiative.[3] A benchmark was created in 1998 when the European Union adopted a directive on Waste Electrical and Electronic Equipment (WEEE) to increase recycling, reduce hazardous substances and to properly dispose of leftover waste.[4]

Take-back programmes are not prevalent in the USA, although, some are developing. The state of Maryland passed legislation requiring manufacturers and retailers to take back mercury oxide batteries after use. At least 15 states have laws requiring retailers to take back vehicle batteries. The Japanese manufacturers of electrical devices have been required to recycle their own products since 2000.

Economic considerations

Along with rapid depletion of landfill space, the landfill usage cost has increased heavily. The national average tipping fee (a standard cost charged to dispose a ton of waste) in the USA increased from $8 to $31.50 between 1985 and 1996, an increase of about 300%.[5] As disposal costs increased so rapidly, recoverable manufacturing systems became more profitable. The profitability through reverse logistics recovery processes has been reported for a number of products such as automobile parts, copier machines, computers, tyres and aviation equipment.

Environmental considerations

Manufacturers can no longer ignore public concern about sustainable development. Successful design and implementation of reverse logistics can have two effects. One, it can help companies to adhere to environmental legislation. Two, it can create an opportunity to project themselves as 'green' companies, increasingly an important marketing element.

Shift towards buying sets of services

Instead of buying physical products, consumers are gradually moving towards buying a set of services along with their products. This may include maintenance contracts covering repairs and parts deliveries. Such contracts facilitate the take back of end-of-life products.

RECOVERY OPTIONS IN REVERSE LOGISTICS

A reverse logistics system incorporates a logistics system designed to manage the flow of products and parts destined for reuse, recycling, remanufacturing or disposal with or without energy recovery. The recovery options in reverse logistics such as reuse, recycling and remanufacturing (see Figure 17.1) are discussed below. The 'test' phase shown in Figure 17.1 helps to identify at which phase a particular recovery option enters the forward logistics chain.

Reuse

Reuse refers to a process in which the recovered product is used again for a purpose similar to the one for which it was originally designed. This is a common practice for many manufacturers as an alternative to new parts and products. Reusable packages and products are recovered for direct reuse, after some simple operations such as inspection and cleaning. Examples of reusable items include bottles, pallets, containers and furniture.

Remanufacturing

Remanufacturing involves a process of reducing a product into its constituent parts. It requires more extensive work, often complete disassembly of the product. These parts can be reused in the assembly of new products. Some examples of remanufacturing products are copiers, printers, computers and car engines. Remanufacturing seeks to bring products to an 'as good as new' quality state. Thus, remanufacturing focuses on value-added recovery, rather than just materials recovery, e.g. recycling. In some cases, the remanufactured product can actually exceed the original product in quality. This is due to the fact that during the remanufacturing process, the design of the replaced components may have been improved since the original product was manufactured.

The reverse logistics system for remanufacturing consists of three main recovery processes: dismantling, in which products are disassembled to a certain level; preparation, in which critical parts are inspected and, if required, replaced; and reassembly, where new and repaired components are reassembled into new products. The remanufacturing option of recovery provides customers with an opportunity to acquire products that meet the original product standards at a lower price than a new product. The remanufacturing process is not only environmentally sound but also economically profitable.

Recycling

Recycling is the process of collecting and disassembling used products, components and materials, and separating them into categories of like materials, such as plastic and glass, and then processing them into recycled materials. Sending cartons back to a paper mill or metal scraps to a foundry are examples of recycling. The variety of industries involved in the recycling option of recovery is wide and includes the consumer electronics, carpet, plastics, automotive, metals and paper industries. Approximately 4 billion pounds of carpet are disposed of in the USA each year.[6] In Western Europe the amount is estimated to be 1.6 million tons per year.[7] Recycling is considered as the least value-added recovery process of the three options since it does not retain the functionality of used parts or products. However, increasingly restrictive environmental regulations and a potential economic benefit have encouraged firms and municipalities to recycle. The success of recycling depends on:[8]

1. whether or not there is a market for the recycled materials; and
2. the quality of the recycled materials.

The hierarchy of recovery options shown in Figure 17.2 is in accordance with the value-adding concept. A firm should attempt to maximise value from the recovery options and thus first concentrate on the option that will provide maximum value. Resource reduction, which refers to the 'minimisation of materials used in products and minimisation of waste and energy achieved through the design of more environmentally efficient products',[10] should be the main objective of any supply chain. Development and utilisation of the resource reduction option would help firms minimise flows of materials both

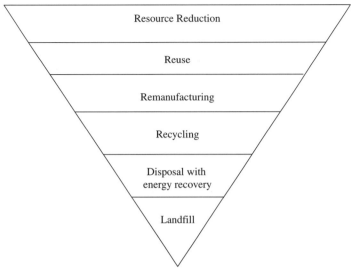

Figure 17.2   A recovery options hierarchy (Source: Carter & Ellram, 1998)[9]

in the forward and reverse direction of supply chains. The next option to be considered in the hierarchy is reuse, followed by remanufacturing and recycling. Remanufacturing focuses on higher value-added recovery, compared with recycling, which concentrates just on materials recovery. Disposal, with and without energy recovery, should be the last option to be considered. The recovery options must be considered within the context of total supply chain cost and are not mutually exclusive.

A reverse logistics network may occur in either a closed- or open-loop system. In a closed-loop reverse logistics system, origins (sources) and destinations (sinks) coincide so that flows cycle in the system. Companies adopting this system collect their used products and either refurbish and resell or remanufacture them or they recycle them. A typical closed-loop logistics system is shown in Figure 17.3.

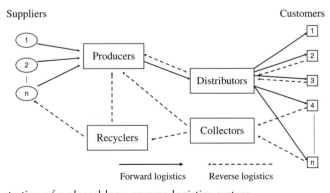

Figure 17.3   Illustration of a closed-loop reverse logistics system

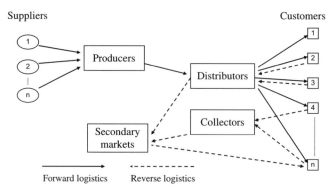

Figure 17.4   Illustration of an open-loop reverse logistics system

In an open-loop system, on the other hand, flows enter at one point of the logistics system and leave at another. Companies using this system might assume responsibility for collecting and finding markets for their products, but do not use the recovered materials for themselves. Figure 17.4 illustrates an open-loop reverse logistics system. Examples of closed- and open-loop reverse logistics systems from the real-world business context are discussed below.

Recorded case studies in reverse logistics are summarised in Table 17.1. Within each reverse logistics type, the case studies were compared in terms of product material and type of network. For instance, the oldest study, by Kroon and Vrijens,[11] is the first in the relevant literature that provides an example of a closed-loop deposit-based logistics network. It was for reusable containers in the Netherlands and utilised the reuse recovery option. Within this system, the reusable containers move from the distribution depot to sender, sender to receiver, receiver back to the collection depot, collection depot to distribution depot. There are five groups of actors involved in the system: a central agency owning a pool of reusable plastic containers; senders and recipients of full containers; a logistics service provider, responsible for storing, delivering and collecting the empty containers; new senders filling the containers; and then carriers, transporting full containers from sender to recipient.

The study by Louwers et al.[28] is an example of recycling carpet by using an open-loop reverse logistics network system. A key limiting factor to recycling carpet is the lack of an efficient system to collect and process this material, so recyclable carpet was considered an untapped resource. This study involved activities such as collection and sorting of waste carpet from various sources (such as households, office buildings, carpet retailers), shredding and palletising and transportation to chemical companies for further processing. The pre-processing activities are carried out in regional recovery facilities. The aim of the study was to identify appropriate locations and capacities for these regional facilities.

The remanufacturing option of reverse logistics focuses on value-added recovery, rather than just materials recovery. An estimate from the turn of the century indicates

Table 17.1   Reverse logistics network type[12]

Recovery option	Source	Material	Network type	
			Open-loop	Closed-loop
Reuse	Kroon & Vrigens (1994)[13]	Reusable container		X
	Jayaraman et al. (2003)[14]	Retail products		X
	French & LaForge (2006)[15]	Food, chemical etc.		X
	Tan & Kumar (2008)[16]	Computer		X
	Aras et al. (2008)[17]	Generic product		X
Recycle	Barros et al. (1998)[18]	Sand	X	
	Louwers et al. (1999)[19]	Carpet	X	
	Realff et al. (1999)[20]	Carpet	X	
	Spengler et al. (1997)[21]	Demolition waste	X	
	Listes & Dekker (2005)[22]	Sand	X	
Remanufacture	Jayaraman et al. (1999)[23]	Mobile phone		X
	Krikke et al. (1999)[24]	Photocopier		X
	Inderfurth (2005)[25]	Generic product		X
	Teunter et al. (2008)[26]	Auto parts		X
	Zuidwijk & Krikke (2008)[27]	Consumer electronics		X

that there were over 73 000 firms engaged in remanufacturing in the USA alone[29]. The study by Krikke et al.[30] is an example of a closed-loop remanufacturing recovery process. They considered the design of a multi-echelon logistics network for a certain type of photocopy machine. In this case the reverse logistics system consisted of three main recovery processes: dismantling; preparation and, if required, replacement; and reassembly. While the locations of dismantling processes were fixed, the objective of the study was to identify the optimal location of preparation and reassembly facilities.

The following section identifies the unique characteristics of the remanufacturing environment in reverse logistics and compares them with the characteristics of the manufacturing environment in the forward logistics environment.

CHARACTERISTICS OF THE REMANUFACTURING ENVIRONMENT IN REVERSE LOGISTICS

The operational characteristics of reverse logistics are more complex to manage than forward logistics activities. The unique characteristics of reverse logistics are discussed in this section. Table 17.2 shows the differences between the recoverable (includes both forward and backward flows of materials) and traditional (includes only forward flows

Table 17.2   A comparison of recoverable and traditional manufacturing environments[31,32]

Factors	Traditional manufacturing environment	Recoverable manufacturing environment
Environmental focus	Focus on preproduction, environmentally conscious design and manufacturing Pollution prevention and remediation	Seeks to prevent post-production waste
Forecasting	Forecasting relatively straightforward Forecast only end products No parts forecasting needed	Forecasting is more difficult Forecast both core (returned product) availability and end-product demand Must forecast part requirements because materials recovery rates are uncertain
Purchasing	Material requirements deterministic Raw materials, new parts and components	Highly uncertain material requirements due to variable recovery rates Cores (returned product) and parts and components, replacement parts, components
Inventory control and management	Inventory management is consistent Types of inventory: raw materials, work-in-progress, finished goods Must track and provide accounting for work-in-progress and finished goods	Inventory management is not consistent Types of inventory: cores (returned product), remanufactured parts, new parts, new and remanufactured substitute parts, original equipment manufacturer parts Must track and provide accounting for all part types
Production planning and control	Product quality uniform No need to balance demands with returns Certainty in planning materials Fixed routeings and more stable processing times Manufacturing system has two major components: fabrication and assembly	Product quality not uniform Need to balance demands with returns Material recovery uncertainty Stochastic routeings and processing time Manufacturing system has three major components: disassembly, remanufacturing, and reassembly
Logistics/transportation	Open forward flow No returns Demand-driven flows Visibility of process more transparent	Forward and reverse flows Uncertainty in timing and quantity of returns Supply-driven flows Visibility of process less transparent

of materials) manufacturing environments. The comparison is made using the following six aspects:

1. Environmental focus
2. Forecasting
3. Purchasing
4. Inventory control and management
5. Production planning and control
6. Logistics

Some of the unique characteristics of the remanufacturing environment in terms of supply–demand balance, accumulation and shortage of parts, logistics network and transportation are discussed below.

Supply–demand balance

One of the most difficult variables to predict in a remanufacturing environment is the distribution of returns of end-of-life products. This is in large part a function of a product's expected life and the rate of technical innovation. The mismatch between demand and returns leads to excess stocks of unwanted parts and components and shortages of those that are required. This makes inventory management and purchasing complex and difficult to plan and control.

Accumulation and shortage of parts

There are two main reasons why there can be accumulations of certain kinds of parts and shortage of others in a remanufacturing environment.

Uncertainty in timing and quantity of returns: a number of factors influence the return of used products. These may include lifecycle stage of a product and the rate of technological innovation. Uncertainty in the timing and quantity of returns affects inventory control decisions. Early in the lifecycle, when few units are in the field, one can expect a low return rate. As the product matures, a higher rate of return can be expected. Since recovered products might be damaged during servicing or while disassembling or customers may fail to return the products, the recovery rate of cores (items which will be used to repair and remanufacture) will never be 100% of sales of product. The uncertainty in the timing and quantity of returns makes materials requirement planning difficult.

Stochastic routeings and processing times: firms involved in remanufacturing need to assess the condition of parts disassembled from return products and this means scheduling work stations. Also, because the parts recovered for disassembly vary from unit to unit, processing times vary and thus routeings vary. These additional forms of uncertainty make production planning and control and inventory control more difficult than in a traditional manufacturing environment.

Logistical network

A recoverable manufacturing system has three major components (disassembly, remanufacturing and reassembly) compared to two major components (fabrication of the parts and subsequent assembly of the product) in a traditional manufacturing environment. Reverse logistics networks typically have a convergent structure, whereas forward logistics networks most often assume a divergent structure.

Transportation

Plant location decisions are generally driven by the transportation cost of raw materials. In a recoverable manufacturing system locational decisions will be influenced by locational cost of assembly, disassembly and remanufacturing plants.

FACTORS FOR SUCCESSFUL REVERSE LOGISTICS IMPLEMENTATION

In this section the key factors for successful reverse logistics implementation are discussed. There are at least eight factors which play a significant role in the implementation of reverse logistics.[33] They can be grouped into external factors and internal factors.

External factors:

1. Legislation
2. Customer demand
3. Incentive

Internal factors:

1. Environmental concerns
2. Strategic cost/benefits
3. Volume and quality of returns
4. Resource
5. Integration and coordination

A brief discussion on each of these factors is given below.

Legislation

Legislation is considered one of the main drivers for a firm's environmental efforts. Legislation refers to regulations or Acts passed by government agencies to ensure firms take back and reuse the products they produce. The major aims of these legislative initiatives are to protect the environment, avoid landfill and to prevent contamination of water. Experts suggest that a trade-off view between ecology and economy is wrong.[34] Environmental regulations can be seen as a motivator to innovate and reduce environmental impact at low cost, rather than be a cause for litigation.

Customer demand

There is an increasing customer demand for green products and for organisations to engage in environmental supply chain practices.[35] The stakeholders of large firms have become more concerned about customer attitudes and are also more conscious of environmental issues. They want to ensure their company is seen as socially responsible itself. The impact of customer demand is felt fairly equally by manufacturing and retail businesses. For example, nowadays vehicle manufacturers are competing on environmentally responsible features. In turn, manufacturers are forcing their strategic suppliers to obtain environmental accreditation. Similarly, big retailers are pressuring their suppliers to be more environmentally responsible as consumers become vocal about 'food miles' and 'carbon footprints'.

Incentive

There is no doubt that an appropriate level of incentive for the end users will enhance return rates and change the behaviour of the reseller. Also, a firm could benefit if it is able to relate incentive to product obsolescence. To benefit from remanufacturing it is vital that manufacturers align incentives with proper access to used products. However, for streamlining the collection process, a firm has to decide whether it, as the manufacturer, or the retailer should collect returned products and whether this should be under a monopoly or competitive situation.

Environmental concerns

Environmental concerns and green issues are also drivers of reverse logistics. A study of leading-edge ISO 14001 certified companies in South East Asia suggests that sustainable logistics practices lead to firm competitiveness and higher economic performance.[36] Gradually, managers are considering environmental factors in their decision-making process and it is becoming increasingly mandatory to do so.

Strategic cost/benefit

Strategic costs are non-recurring costs incurred for the design and implementation of a reverse logistics system. These may include costs associated with the acquisition of additional machinery and equipment to remanufacture and refurbish products, acquisition costs for additional warehousing, and costs associated with hiring additional skilled managers and workers. However, such investment must be planned, controlled and minimised for effective reverse logistics implementation. Firms engaged in reverse logistics are in the process of investment recovery and certainly would receive direct (input materials, cost reduction, value-added recovery) and indirect benefits (meeting requirements of impeding legislation, market position protection, a favourable green image and improvement in customer/supplier relations). A study in the USA revealed that US$700 million of perfectly operating computer network equipment that could be recovered was destroyed.[37] Another study showed that returns of Hewlett-Packard's products could cost around 2% of its total outbound sales and only half of them were being recovered.[38] These examples indicate that if additional resources, as part of the strategic costs, are planned and controlled effectively, companies will be financially benefited in the long run by implementing reverse logistics.

Volume and quality

When it comes to economic feasibility, volume of returns and quality of products are important. When compared with forward logistics, product quality is not uniform in reverse logistics. The returned product quality could fall into categories such as faulty, damaged or unwanted by customers. Good quality product requires fewer processes to reuse it. The quality of returns has significant impact on reverse logistics operations. Effective gate keeping will avoid the additional logistics cost of unnecessary transportation and storage of scrap.[39]

Resource

The overall success of reverse logistics systems depends on the effective use of available resources. The available resources are referred to as facilities, personnel, manufacturing/material handling and processes capabilities. If a firm uses its resources properly, they would become assets and generate sound reverse logistics decisions. Effective utilisation of resources could minimise the strategic cost involved in reverse logistics systems. Use of existing resources for reverse logistics operations depends on the compatibility of remanufactured product and the overall product strategy of the firm. A reverse logistics system could rely on available resources to effectively cope with the stochastic nature of supply and demand and to obtain a yield from a remanufacturing process.[40]

Integration and coordination

The role of coordination and the importance of communication in both speedy and early disposition of returned products, and in remanufacturing planning, have been discussed extensively. Efficient information systems are needed to individually track and trace product returns, to forecast return product and for inventory management. A slow reverse supply chain that takes 10 weeks to put returned products back on the market can translate to a loss of 10% of the total value in that product.[41] In some instances, for example with consumer electronics, this far exceeds profit margins. So a computer manufacturer is well advised to develop competencies in fast recovery systems. Not only that, without integration and coordination transportation and supplier delay in processing, returns may significantly impact the viability of an entire reverse logistics process.

PERFORMANCE MEASURES IN REVERSE LOGISTICS

A performance measure, or a set of measures, is used to ascertain the efficiency or effectiveness of logistics systems. Traditional measures are typically concerned with:

Table 17.3   Performance metrics for reverse logistics systems[42]

Product recovery option	Performance metrics
Reuse, remanufacturing and recycling	Time required for product recovery
	Per cent recyclable/reusable materials available at the end of product life
	Per cent product volume or weight recovered and reused
	Purity of recycled materials recovered
	Per cent recycled materials used as input to remanufacturing
	Per cent product disposed
	Fraction of packaging or containers recycled
	Core (return product) return rate
	Ratio of virgin to recycled resources
	Ratio of materials recycled to materials potentially recyclable
	Per cent product (weight or volume) disposed in landfills

1. Customer satisfaction
2. Service level
3. Responsiveness
4. Cost
5. Quality

These measures, or a combination of these measures, are discussed in Chapter 14. Although these measures are appropriate for traditional logistics systems, they are inadequate in capturing the reverse logistics objectives of environmental protection. The relevant performance metrics in reverse logistics are shown in Table 17.3.

In order to achieve efficiency and effectiveness for reverse logistics systems, firms must develop procedures that focus on continuous improvement of the metrics shown in Table 17.3. However, not every firm will employ all the metrics. For example, Fuji Xerox Australia uses per cent product disposed in landfills as one of its key performance metrics.

AN AUSTRALIAN CASE: COMPANY ABC LTD[43]

Company ABC Ltd is a recycler of various products in Australia. The company has received a number of awards for best practice and quality management practices. The company started its business in the mid-1980s. Its recycling operations started in 1988, in the form of precious metal recovery from computer mainframe equipment. Currently, with over 40 employees and operations in Sydney and Melbourne, ABC Ltd has become a leader in e-waste solutions. The company is an ISO 14001 and Environmental Protection Authority,

Victoria (EPA) accredited recycler. The company entered into strategic alliances with Dell and Toshiba, two original equipment manufacturers committed to reducing e-waste by implementing reverse logistics processes for end-of-life computers.

Every year ABC Ltd collects up to 60 000 CRT monitors, 100 000 central processing units (CPUs), 400 tonnes of batteries, 200 tonnes of computer casings, 50 tonnes of LCD screens and 500 tonnes of other peripherals. By applying innovative methods of disassembly and carefully managing resulting waste streams, ABC Ltd reclaims precious metals for reuse and diverts up to 98% of product (by weight) from landfill.

LEARNING REVIEW

This chapter focused on the management of the reverse flow of materials from end customers towards the original suppliers, either for reprocessing or disposal. There are many ways to minimise the environmental costs of business activities, but the prevention of waste products through reverse logistics activities such as reuse, remanufacturing and recycling avoids many environmental costs. In this chapter we discussed what motivates a firm to initiate reverse logistics activities. We next discussed different recovery processes and highlighted the unique characteristics of the remanufacturing recovery option and compared these characteristics with the forward manufacture environment.

Many world-class companies have realised that reverse logistics has important environmental dimensions, as well as dimensions relating to value reclamation. Companies such as Xerox, Hewlett-Packard, Eastman Kodak, Sears and many others have successfully implemented reverse logistics practices. In this chapter we identified and discussed key factors for successful implementation of reverse logistics. Finally, we discussed the performance metrics relevant to reverse logistics systems.

The next chapter continues to focus on supply chain designs and will focus on services supply chains.

QUESTIONS

- This chapter identified six different manufacturing aspects. Use these aspects to compare the characteristics of remanufacturing with the traditional manufacturing environment.
- If you were designing and implementing a reverse logistics process for your firm, what are the key factors you would consider for implementation, and why?
- Identify a few performance metrics for reverse logistics. Why are traditional performance metrics inadequate in capturing the reverse logistics objectives?

NOTES

1. Rogers, D.S. & Tibben-Lembke, R.S. (1999) *Going Backwards: Reverse Logistics Trends and Practices*, Reverse Logistics Executive Council, Pittsburg, PA.

2. Australian Bureau of Statistics (ABS) (2006) *Environment Snapshot: Recycling up, but e-waste a Looming Issue*, ABS, Canberra.

3. Rembert T.C. (1997) Package deal: the European war on waste, *Environmental Magazine*, 8, 38.

4. Rogers & Tibben-Lembke (see note 1).

5. Ibid.

6. Realff, M.J., Ammons, J.C. & Newton, D. (1999) Carpet recycling: determining the reverse production system design, *Polymer-Plastics Technology and Engineering*, 38, 547–567.

7. Bohnhoff, A. (1996) Recycling of textile floor coverings. In *Proceedings of Globec'96/Recycle'96*, Davos.

8. Beamon, B.M. (1999) Designing the green supply chain, *Logistics Information Management*, 12(4), 332–342.

9. Carter, C.R. & Ellram, L.M. (1998) Reverse logistics: a review of the literature and framework for future investigation, *Journal of Business Logistics*, 19(1), 85–102.

10. Ibid.

11. Kroon, L. & Vrijens, G. (1994) Returnable containers: an example of reverse logistics. *International Journal of Physical Distribution & Logistics Management*, 25, 56–68.

12. Rahman, S. (2003) Reverse logistics: an overview and a causal model. In Hensher & Button, *Handbook of Transport and the Environment*, Elsevier, Oxford.

13. Kroon & Vrijens (see note 11).

14. Jayaraman, V., Patterson, R.A. & Rolland, E. (2003) The design of reverse distribution networks: models and solution procedures, *European Journal of Operational Research* 150, 128–149.

15. French, M. & LaForge, R.L. (2006) Closed-loop supply chains in process industries: an empirical study of producer re-use issues, *Journal of Operations Management*, 24, 271–286.

16. Tan, A. & Kumar, A. (2008) A decision-making model to maximise the value of reverse logistics in the computer industry, *International Journal of Logistics Systems and Management*, 4(3), 297–312.

17. Aras, N., Aksen, D. & Tanugur, A.G. (2008) Locating collection centers for incentive-dependent returns under a pick-up policy with capacitated vehicles, *European Journal of Operational Research*, 191, 1223–1240.

18. Barros, A.I., Dekker, R., & Scholten, V. (1998). A two-level network for recycling sand: a case study, *European Journal of Operational Research*, 110, 199–214.

19. Louwers, D., Kip, B.J., Peters, E., Souren, F. & Flapper, S.D.P. (1999) A facility location-allocation model for reusing carpet materials, *Computers & Industrial Engineering*, 36, 855–869.

20. Realff, Ammons & Newton (see note 6).

21. Spengler, T., Puchert, H., Penkuhn, P. & Rents, O. (1997) Environmental integrated production and recycling management, *European Journal of Operational Research*, 97, 308–326.

22. Listes, O. & Dekker, R. (2005) A stochastic approach to a case study for product recovery network design, *European Journal of Operational Research*, 160, 268–287.

23. Jayaraman, V., Guide, V.D.R. & Srivastava, R. (1999) A closed-loop logistics model for remanufacturing, *Journal of the Operational Research Society*, 50, 497–508.

24. Krikke, H.R., von Harten, A. & Schuur, P.C. (1999). Business case Oce: Reverse logistics network-design for copiers, *OR Spektrum*, 21, 381–409.

25. Inderfurth, K. (2005) Impact of uncertainties on recovery behaviour in a remanufacturing environment: a numerical analysis, *International Journal of Physical Distribution & Logistics Management*, 35(5), 318–336.

26. Teunter, R., Kaparis, K. & Tang, O. (2008) Multi-product economic lot scheduling problem with separate production lines for manufacturing and remanufacturing, *European Journal of Operational Research*, 191, 1241–1253.

27. Zuidwijk, R. & Krikke, H. (2008) Strategic response to EEE returns: product eco-design or new recovery processes? *European Journal of Operational Research,* 191, 1206–1222.

28. Louwers *et al.* (see note 19).

29. Lund, R. (1998) Remanufacturing: an American resource. *Proceedings of the Fifth International Congress on Environmentally Conscious Design and Manufacturing*, 16–17 June, Rochester Institute of Technology, Rochester, NY.

30. Krikke *et al.* (see note 24).

31. Guide, V.D.R. Jr., Jayaraman, V., Srivastava, R. & Benton, W.C. (2000). Supply chain management for recoverable manufacturing systems, *Interfaces*, 30, 125–142.

32. Rogers, D.S. & Tibben-Lembke, R.S. (2002) Difference between forward and reverse logistics in a retail environment, *Supply Chain Management: An International Journal*, 7(5), 271–282.

33. Rahman, S. & Subramanian, N. (2010), Factors for implementing end-of-life computer recycling operations in reverse logistics, Unpublished manuscript, School of Business IT & Logistics, RMIT University.

34. Porter, M.E. & Van de Linde, C. (1995) Green and competitive, *Harvard Business Review*, September–October, 120–134.

35. New, S., Green, K. & Morton, B. (2000) Buying the environment: the multiple meanings of green supply. In S. Fineman (Ed.), *The Business of Greening* (pp. 33–53). Routledge, London.

36. Rao, P. & Holt, D. (2005) Do green supply chains lead to competitiveness and economic performance? *International Journal of Operations and Production Management*, 25(9), 898–916.

37. Guide, V.D.R. Jr. & Van Wassenhove, L.N. (2009) The evolution of closed-loop supply chain research. *Operations Research*, 57 (1), 10–18.

38. Guide, V.D.R. Jr., Souza, G., Van Wassenhove, L.N. & Blackburn, J.D. (2006) Time value of commercial product returns, *Management Science*, 52(8), 1200–1214.

39. Tan, A. & Kumar, A. (2006) A decision-making model for reverse logistics in the computer industry, *International Journal of Logistics Management*, 17(3), 331–354.

40. Pokharel. S. & Mutha, A. (2009) Perspectives in reverse logistics: a review, *Resources, Conservation and Recycling*, 53, 175–182.

41. Guide & Van Wassenhove (see note 37).

42. Beamon (see note 8).

43. Rahman & Subramanian (see note 33).

18 Service Supply Chains

LEARNING OBJECTIVES

- To highlight the increasing importance of service supply chains in the global economy.
- To define service, service science and service supply chains.
- To distinguish service supply chains from conventional manufacturing supply chains.
- To conceptualise service supply chain models.

INTRODUCTION

Throughout this book we have largely focused on supply chains in the manufacturing context. That is to say that most of our discussion has centred on those logistics operations and supply chains that deliver freight. There is, however, a relatively new body of research that recognises that different operations and supply chain management practices are required for the delivery of services. Hence in this chapter we now focus on **service supply chains** to identify their importance, their distinctions, their contexts and their future.

Chapter 18 comprises four core sections:

- The transition to service economies
- Service science
- Service supply chains versus manufacturing supply chains
- Service supply chain models

THE TRANSITION TO SERVICE ECONOMIES

The rapid development of the world's leading economies during the 20th century resulted from the Industrial Revolution of the 18th and 19th centuries. This key event in history saw countries such as the UK, USA and Germany shift from predominantly agricultural economies to manufacturing economies. People moved off the land and into the mass production systems that would sustain those countries' burgeoning populations. This period can be termed as 'post-agricultural'.[1]

In the second half of the 20th century, another macroeconomic shift could be observed; the transition of those (then) advanced economies from manufacturing to services. This 'post-manufacturing'[2] world has emerged from the demand for value-added services by those countries' populations. Simply put, people migrated from rural to urban areas to work in factories to earn far more than they could on the land. In so doing, they increased their personal wealth and leisure time. Consequently those workers demanded more and better services to complement their lives, such as healthcare, retail and tourism. Hence, businesses and organisations have developed to provide such services.

This increasing consumption of services is evidenced in Table 18.1. From the data in this table we can see that the economies listed have transitioned to become dominated by service-oriented employment. For example, the percentage of the United States' employment in the service sector increased from 59.5% to 78.6% between 1965 and 2005. As discussed in Part One of this book, globalisation has enabled these economies to offshore their manufacturing capabilities to lower cost economies. Hence, the current macroeconomic climate is often perceived as one of 'factories in the East and markets in the West'. As the data in Table 18.1 show, this dynamic is also changing. Even though China's and India's newfound prosperity can be attributed to their provision of low-cost manufacturing for the world, they too are becoming service economies, as wealth creation within those countries increases. Indeed it is interesting to observe that in developing countries such as China, a growing share of their manufactured output is being consumed domestically, thus lessening the dependence on exports for economic growth.[3] The transition to service economies is a global trend as illustrated in Table 18.1. In 1999, services accounted for 58% of global gross domestic product (GDP). This trend will continue, and economies will become more dependent on service organisations for continued national prosperity.[4]

The data in Table 18.1 emphasise the increasing importance of service organisations to national economies. At the microeconomic level, organisations are refocusing their strategies and operations to define themselves as service-centric rather than manufacturing-centric.

Table 18.1 Share of total employment in manufacturing and services sectors, 1965 and 2005[6]

Country	1965		2005	
	Services (%)[5]	Manufacturing (%)	Services (%)	Manufacturing (%)
United States	59.5	27	78.6	
United Kingdom	51.3	35	77	13.3
Netherlands	52.5	28.6	76.5	13.9
Sweden	46.5	32.6	76.4	15.3
Canada	57.3	23.8	76	13.6
Australia	54.6	26.1	75.8	10.8
France	43.9	27.5	74.8	15.5

Major enterprises such as General Electric (GE) and IBM were founded on their manufacturing excellence. Today, however, they have reshaped their organisations to focus more on the provision of value-added services. For example, IBM's main source of revenue is currently derived from its Global Business Services unit, which offers business consulting services to other enterprises. This now major component of IBM's global footprint did not exist before the 1990s.[7] Business services accounted for $54 billion of IBM's $99 billion total revenue in 2007.[8]

SERVICE SCIENCE

Early in the 21st century, researchers recognised the need to address the service sector differently from the manufacturing sector. A definitive definition of service was sought to provide a foundation for this emerging body of knowledge. To a service scientist, the term service is defined as 'the application of competences (knowledge, resources) for the benefit of another'.[9] We explore this definition further in the supply chain context to distinguish it from the delivery of manufactured goods in a later section.

Based on the above definition of service, the term service science was coined to capture and consolidate research into the various business functions that combine to provide a service. Service science is 'the study of the application of the resources of one or more systems for the benefit of another system in economic exchange'.[10] In so doing, this unifying term brings together researchers from related but often previously disparate disciplines, such as operations management, economics and computer science. Supply chain management researchers who focus explicitly on service supply chains can thus also be said to be service scientists.

What informs service science research is the need to create value in the provision of a service. Hence much of the research in this field is focused on service innovation. Service innovation is what is driving the expansion of the service sector. As discussed above, our personal wealth and leisure time are increasing so we are able to afford to consume a greater diversity of services. As a consequence we will

> Service science is the study of the application of the resources of one or more systems for the benefit of another system in economic exchange.

also expect greater value from those services. Hence organisations must perpetually innovate to at least meet, if not exceed, our expectations. For example, as a student, you might work out at the university gym, which offers basic equipment. When you graduate, your income will increase and your work–life balance will change; you may therefore join a gym that offers a wider variety of resources such as a swimming pool, sauna and a personal trainer. These are all value-added services. Organisations such as Virgin Active and Fitness First are examples of such gyms and in fact brand themselves as 'health clubs' as opposed to gyms. Membership of such clubs aims to offer greater value than that offered by your university gym. Both organisations recognised the market opportunity and developed innovative service solutions to offer value-added propositions.

THIRD-PARTY LOGISTICS SERVICE INNOVATION

An excellent example of service innovation in the supply chain context is online package tracking. When we order items from a retailer, they are often shipped by a 3PL service provider from a regional distribution centre. There is a lead time of days for that service, and the 3PL may transit the items through staging posts (e.g. from the RDC via heavy goods vehicle to a local DC, and on to their final destination via light goods vehicle) before we receive them. We, the customers, are provided with a unique order tracking number and a link to the 3PL's order tracking web service when the order is confirmed. We can then use this to track our order. This transparency adds value to the 3PL service by assuring us of where our package is and when it will be delivered. We, the consumers, become part of the supply chain. Transparency is often a key driver for service innovation.[11]

SERVICE SUPPLY CHAINS VERSUS MANUFACTURING SUPPLY CHAINS

As a key component of service operations, service-specific supply chains are now also recognised as being distinct from manufacturing supply chains. A service supply chain is the network of suppliers, service providers, consumers and other supporting units that performs the functions of transaction of resources required to produce services; transformation of these resources into supporting and core services; and the delivery of these services to customers. This is the definition accepted by the Global Supply Chain Forum.[12] This helps us to distinguish service supply chains from manufacturing supply chains. Furthermore, the distinction is clarified in Table 18.2 in terms of intangibility, heterogeneity, perishability and inseparability (i.e. simultaneity). This table illustrates that services portray very different characteristics and cannot therefore be managed along a supply chain in the same way as manufactured goods (i.e. freight). Services are less tangible, more heterogeneous, more perishable (i.e. can't be stored), and inseparable from the point of consumption (i.e. the customer is directly and simultaneously involved in the service).

> A service supply chain is the network of suppliers, service providers, consumers and other supporting units that performs the functions of transaction of resources required to produce services; transformation of these resources into supporting and core services; and the delivery of these services to customers.

The distinct characteristics of services compared with manufactured products dictate that their supply chain must be managed differently. Generically, the emphasis of a service supply chain is predominantly on the creation of value through labour and knowledge, whereas a manufacturing supply chain will create value through the provision of standardised, repeatable processes that ensure the delivery of freight to the end customer in a timely fashion. Standardisation and repeatability are less easy to achieve in a service setting because customers require more variety and in some cases bespoke

Table 18.2   Characteristics of freight versus services[13]

Service attribute	Impact of attribute on purchasing	Freight	Services
Intangibility	Expectations	Specifications are precise	Vague service level agreements
	Predictability of demand	Dependent on the accuracy of forecasts for final customer demand	Vary with project scope
	Problem resolution	Formal processes, clear responsibilities	Lack of set processes, more subjectivity
	Cost	Pre-negotiated, per unit, easy to determine in advance	Dependent on changing scope and requirements, situation specific, often is re-negotiated or changes with scope
	Payment	Match receipts with purchase orders, verifiable	Bills submitted without tangible evidence, pay-as-you-go
	Verification of contract completion	Physical evidence in shipment	Internal sign off
Heterogeneity	Quality	Measureable, pre-specified	Subjective, user dependent
	Consistency of output	Clear specifications, tight quality control	Services vary with the provider. Broader specifications with range-acceptable outcomes
Perishability	Interface between providers	Planning and inventory allow for easier transitions	Requires more communication, can't store services
	Inventory policies	Buffer demand fluctuations with inventory	Buffer demand fluctuations with capacity
Inseparability	Points of contact	Few points of contact, usually purchasing or project manager. Limited to no customer contact	Increases the interactions both from a B2B perspective and a B2C perspective
	Physical separation of host firm and provider facilities	Physical distance between buyer and seller	Service is created at point of use, tight coupling
	Security of information/data	High due to physical separation	More difficult to control due to low physical proximity

solutions. That is to say that in Apple's iPhone supply chain its manufacturers and logistics providers use standard, repeatable processes to make and deliver the millions of iPhones sold globally every day to the high standards we expect. However, the service we gain from the cellular network provider or retailer when we purchase our iPhone will be tailored to our needs (e.g. they will offer various pre-paid and post-paid call and data plans that meet a variety of customer needs). Although we all have the same iPhone, the network service attached to it will vary depending on our usage and other personal requirements. Hence the labour and knowledge input into a service offer adaptability to a given situation or customer requirement, which is not commonly found in manufacturing supply chains.[14] The challenge for service providers is to structure and automate where possible their processes in such a way that they can gain economies similar to those enjoyed by manufacturers.

Having said that, some similar functions exist in both service supply chain management and manufacturing supply chain management. For example, demand management, customer relationship management and supplier relationship management are required in both sectors, and will be practised in very similar ways.[15] Hence some basic principles of supply chain management are transferable across sectors in those management functions.

As is the case in the manufacturing sector, the operational performance of a service supply chain is improved by increased information sharing, and financial performance is improved by focusing strategically on the distribution network. And as is increasingly so in the manufacturing sector due to ever more fluctuating demand patterns, service supply chain operational performance is also improved through increased customisation.[16] In other words, quick response logistics and supply chain operations are fundamental enablers of value-added service provision. It is therefore important to involve supply chain professionals in procuring and delivering the inputs into a service organisation. Whilst the service provision professionals (e.g. lawyers, surgeons, call centre managers, sales staff) have a comprehensive understanding of how to provide their particular service, they are not necessarily best placed to source the resources they require. Their knowledge should therefore be supported by the procurement and logistics expertise of supply chain professionals to optimise service delivery. Table 18.3 shows how the two skill sets can complement each other. This point is further illustrated in the healthcare inventory management and procurement caselet below.

HEALTHCARE INVENTORY MANAGEMENT AND PROCUREMENT

Supply chain costs are today widely recognised as the second highest costs, after labour costs, to healthcare providers such as hospitals. To provide effective healthcare services requires the input of various resources. From surgical supplies for operating theatres to drugs and wound care supplies on wards, and from cleaning supplies to laundry services, there is a multitude of inventory that healthcare providers must replenish on a regular basis. By adopting inventory management and procurement principles and practices commonly found in manufacturing and retail supply chains, healthcare providers have gained significant cost savings and service improvements.

Today it is not unusual to find hospital wards, for example, with local storage organised and managed as might be found in factories or supermarkets. Regular replenishment of inventory can be achieved by ward staff scanning the bar codes of storage bins with a handheld RF reader when they remove items. Capturing that data informs the inventory management module of the hospital's ERP system that particular items require replenishment. This, in turn, informs the purchasing module of the system to place orders with the necessary suppliers. The system will be preset to determine the safety stock levels, reorder quantities and delivery lead times to: (a) minimise stock-outs at the ward, and (b) not burden ward staff with inventory management tasks so that they can focus on their core activities of servicing patients. In some cases, vendor managed inventory (VMI) might also be employed to further streamline replenishment.

Table 18.3   Relative expertise of supply chain and service provision professionals[17]

	Supply chain professionals' expertise	Service provision professionals' expertise
Providing a comprehensive, competitive process for managing selection	Bring discipline to process Consistency in analysis methods	Deep understanding of true needs
Identifying opportunities and sourcing	Identify multiple qualified sources to consider Source/qualify supplier Educate management/team on importance of choosing right supplier as well as ongoing analysis	Knowledge of some key suppliers and past performance issues Articulate needs, including timing, duration and specific skills
Aiding the selection of sources	Run competitive process Market analysis Qualitative and quantitative issues Understand true cost picture/total cost of ownership	Provide major input into supplier selection criteria Major voice in selecting supplier
Developing and negotiating contracts and ordering	Commercial skills Negotiate relationship breadth/services/performance Contract process/management Gain sharing arrangements	Provide specifications for contract terms related to service performance
Receipt and payment	Specify in the contract the payment terms Work with accounts and service provision professionals to set up payment system that conforms to contract, with proper controls	Supervise/benefit from the work performed Ensure that work is performed to contract before approving payment
Identifying potential relationship issues and ongoing monitoring/management	Set up measurement process and systems Identify potential benefits and risks Train service provision professionals to identify issues and manage the supplier Manage supplier relations if major issues arise Manage strategic risks Support 're-sourcing' relationship if needed	Manage ongoing relationship Provide supplier performance feedback Manage the operating risks communicated to the supplier Manage day-to-day supplier relations

SERVICE SUPPLY CHAIN MODELS

Referring back to Chapter 1, we discuss a simplified representation of a supply chain. This is replicated here in Figure 18.1(a) and is distinguished as a manufacturing supply chain where materials such as raw materials, components or finished goods flow along the chain. In a service setting it is knowledge and resources that flow along the chain instead. This is represented in Figure 18.1(b) as a simplified model of a service supply chain.

Referring back to Table 18.2, it is important here to pick up on the inseparability (i.e. simultaneity) attribute listed above. The customer (who is also normally the consumer) is directly and simultaneously involved in the service. Hence the service provision usually occurs when the service provider is in direct contact with the consumer. For example, consider when you the consumer go to a restaurant for a meal. You must be present at the time it is cooked and brought to your table to consume the food and drink. What Figure 18.1(b) also illustrates is that the service provider is supplied with resources (and in some cases knowledge) prior to service provision. In the case of a restaurant, the chef will order the ingredients for your meal to be ready to cook it. The restaurant manager will also coordinate the setting up of the restaurant before 'service' begins. This will likely include having tablecloths, etc. laundered by a specialist supplier.

However, Figure 18.1(b) is an oversimplification. Whilst service supply chains receive inputs from suppliers to provide outputs to customers, they very often also receive inputs from the customers. This may be in the form of knowledge (e.g. advising a doctor of my symptoms before he/she can diagnose), but may also be resources (e.g. taking my bicycle (the resource) to a bike shop mechanic for 'servicing' and repair). Hence there exists a bi-directional duality between the supplier and customer (i.e. knowledge and or/ resources flowing in both directions), where the customer supplies inputs to the service provision and receives outputs from it.

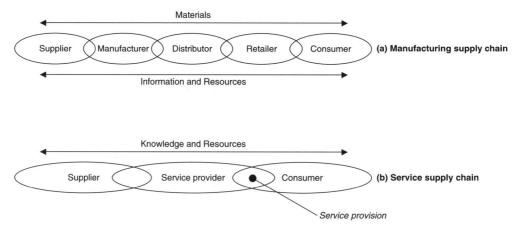

Figure 18.1   The manufacturing supply chain model versus the service supply chain model

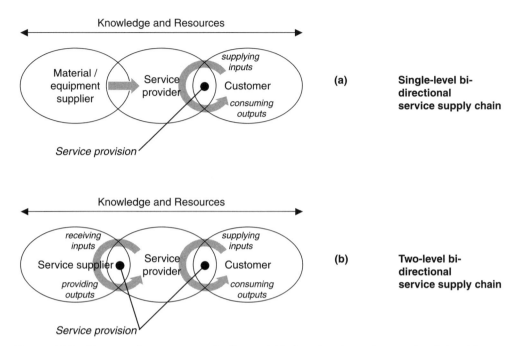

Figure 18.2   The supplier–customer duality and bi-directional service supply chains (Source: Sampson, 2000)[18]

In some cases, the bi-directional duality may be single level or two level. In the former, the duality exists only at the interface between the service provider and the customer (see Figure 18.2(a)). There may also be some resources received by the service provider as inputs from a supplier. In the example above where I visited the doctor, I input my knowledge (a description of my symptoms) and resources (my body for examination). To treat me, my doctor will have a small inventory of drugs and wound care resources delivered prior to the service provision by a third-party supplier.

In the case of a two-level bi-directional duality, a duality will not only exist between the service provider and customer, but also between the supplier and service provider (see Figure 18.2(b)). Hence knowledge and/or resources are input from the customer to the service provider, *and* from the service provider to the supplier. They in turn supply the outputs necessary to complete the original service provision. In the case of taking my bicycle to a bike shop mechanic, I provide one input, the bicycle. When the mechanic examines the bike, he might find that it requires the replacement of a component that is no longer manufactured due to the bike's age. He must therefore have a replacement component manufactured by a specialist engineering company. To do so, he must provide them with the broken original component and any knowledge he has about its dimensions, materials, function or how it may have broke. This represents a two-level bi-directional duality. Thus service supply chains vary in their complexity depending on where they receive their inputs.

LEARNING REVIEW

This chapter discussed the growing importance of services. Many of the world's economies are increasingly dependent on services for wealth creation, more so than agriculture and manufacturing. Hence researchers and practitioners alike are focusing on service innovation to develop the sophistication of the services we consumers receive. Service science is a new and burgeoning academic discipline that brings together scholars from related fields of study to address service sector-specific issues. This includes service supply chains.

We find that service supply chains cannot be managed in the same way as manufacturing supply chains. While some similar functions exist, there are attributes of services that dictate that their supply chains must be managed differently. The models we present in Figures 18.1 and 18.2 illustrate this.

The next chapter will advance our thinking about such supply chain models and innovations to discuss emerging supply chain designs.

QUESTIONS

- With the global transition of developed and developing countries to service economies, consider the implications for manufacturing supply chains. How will the world look 100 years from now if this trend continues?

- Consider how many services you have encountered today (e.g. your mail being delivered, the café where you bought your morning coffee, the lunch queue at the university cafeteria, the shop where you bought groceries, the call centre you called to query your mobile phone bill). List them, reflect on how the service provider performed and score them out of 10 for speed, quality and cost. Evaluate their scores and suggest how they might improve.

- Consider the role technology plays in both of this chapter's caselets. How do you think advances in technology (e.g. mobile communications, cloud computing, social media) will influence the service sector? Consider potential technology-based service innovations.

- Referring to Figures 18.2(a) and (b), list five single-level bi-directional service supply chain examples and five two-level bi-directional service supply chain examples. Compare and contrast these examples. What are the factors that distinguish a single-level bi-directional service supply chain from a two-level one?

THIRD-PARTY LOGISTICS SERVICE INNOVATION

Review the 3PL service innovation caselet above and our previous discussions in this book on outsourcing logistics activities to third parties. As an outsourcee, a 3PL offers a value proposition that reflects its specialist knowledge and resources (i.e. services) being superior to those of the outsourcer's for those activities (refer to Chapter 3). For the outsourcee to offer improved service and for it to maintain competitive advantage against other 3PLs, it must innovate to extend its value proposition.

List the core activities a 3PL undertakes to move freight through a supply chain. Review the websites of the major 3PLs (e.g. FedEx, UPS, TNT/Ceva) and list the value-added service innovations they offer that complement those core activities. Evaluate those service innovations and consider what else they could do to add value to their customers and maintain their competitive position.

NOTES

1. Chesborough, H. & Spohrer, J. (2006) A research manifesto for services science, *Communications of the ACM*, 49(7), 33–40.

2. Ibid.

3. Horn, J., Singer, V. & Woetzel, J. (2010) A truer picture of China's export machine, *McKinsey Quarterly*, September.

4. Baltacioglu, T., Ada, E., Kaplan, M., Yurt, O. & Kaplan, C. (2007) A new framework for service supply chains, *The Service Industries Journal*, 27(2), 105–124.

5. Employment shares shown do not represent the total economy, because employment in agriculture, mining and construction is excluded; therefore, the shares for each country do not sum to 100%.

6. Bureau of Labor Statistics (2008), www.bls.gov/spotlight/2008/around_the_world/data.htm#chart_08 (accessed 9 November 2010).

7. Chesborough & Spohrer (see note 1).

8. Spohrer, J. & Maglio, P. (2008) The emergence of service science: toward systematic service innovations to accelerate co-creation of value, *Production and Operations Management*, 17(3), 238–246.

9. Spohrer, J., Anderson, L., Pass, N., Ager, T. & Gruhl, D. (2008) Service science, *Journal of Grid Computing*, 6, 313–324.

10. Ibid.

11. Chesborough & Spohrer (see note 1).

12. Lambert, D.M., Cooper, M.C. & Pagh, J.D. (1998) Supply chain management: implementation issues and research opportunities, *International Journal of Logistics Management*, 9(2), 1–19. Cited by Baltacioglu *et al.* (see note 1).

13. Ellram, L., Tate, W. & Billington, C. (2007) Services supply management: the next frontier for improved organizational performance, *California Management Review*, 49(4), 44–66.

14. Sengupta, K., Heiser, D. & Cook, L. (2006) Manufacturing and service supply chain performance: a comparative analysis, *Journal of Supply Chain Management*, Fall, 4–15.

15. Ibid.

16. Ibid.

17. Ellram *et al.* (see note 13).

18. Sampson, S. (2000) Customer–supplier duality and bidirectional supply chains in service organisations, *International Journal of Service Industry Management*, 11(4), 348–364.

19 Emerging Supply Chain Designs

LEARNING OBJECTIVES

- Review the many strategies and practices employed in logistics and SCM today.
- Appreciate the emerging and changing context within which logistics and SCM exists.
- Understand the need to synchronise the design of supply chains with the design of products.
- Understand the disparate costs that exist across supply chains.
- See how modelling approaches can assist in supply chain design.
- Detail the skills and knowledge areas required of logistics and supply chain managers in the future.

INTRODUCTION

This concluding chapter of the book endeavours to bring together many of the key issues discussed in the preceding 18 chapters. The particular focus of this chapter is to elaborate how various trends are shaping logistics and SCM, and in turn how supply chains can be best designed to meet these challenges. As we noted in Chapter 4, and reiterated throughout the book, increasingly it is supply chains that compete more so than individual firms and products. A company can have the best and most sophisticated product in the world, but if it doesn't have a good supply chain behind it then it will likely not be able to compete, especially in terms of cost and speed, and indeed many other attributes also. The design of appropriate supply chains is thus a critically important factor for many organisations today.

Chapter 19 comprises six core sections:

- Strategies and practices in SCM
- The ever changing context
- Synchronising product design and supply chain design
- Determining supply chain costs and value
- Modelling supply chain designs
- The supply chain manager of the future

STRATEGIES AND PRACTICES IN SCM

In Chapter 4 we discussed the wide and important area of strategy, and in particular the role of logistics/supply chain strategy, and we noted the current focus on adopting strategies based around lean and agile principles, and various combinations of both. A particular focus in this regard was on choosing strategies appropriate to various demand and lead-time characteristics. In Chapter 4 we also elaborated some key principles in supply chain planning: that a 'one-size-fits-all approach' doesn't always work, to again quote Gattorna[1] that companies need to use a process of 'dynamic alignment' to match changing customer needs and desires with different supply chain strategies; the need to focus on processes and flows, rather than getting stuck in a functional/silo mentality; the need to focus on high-level objectives; and the importance of people in SCM, a topic we will discuss further below.

We have described a variety of different strategies and practices throughout the book. These are all detailed in the glossary. The common strategies and practices that logistics and supply chain managers usually need to consider are summarised in Table 19.1.

Table 19.1   Common logistics/supply chain strategies and practices

- Pursuit of strategies based around lean and agile principles, and varying combinations of both
- Mass customisation/postponement
- Time compression – faster order to delivery cycles and elimination of non-value-adding time
- Developing value-adding activities
- Managing reverse logistics flows
- Operating in a more sustainable fashion, especially by exploiting scale and seeking out greater efficiencies
- Operating 'own-account' transport versus using LSPs – and with regard to the latter identifying and selecting LSPs, and determining whether or not to employ a 4PL approach
- Coordinating and managing transport flows and directional imbalances; selecting modes and routes
- Use of electronic logistics markets
- Integration of systems, business processes, etc.
- Collaboration with supply chain partners, use of strategies such as CPFR and VMI
- Managing distribution centres and cross-docking facilities
- Application of factory gate pricing and consolidation
- Managing outsource and offshore activities
- Procurement (sourcing and purchasing)
- Supplier rationalisation and development
- Determining how much inventory to hold, in what location(s) to hold it, and what inventory control system to use
- Increasing visibility and information enrichment in supply chains
- Determining costs – activity-based costs, generalised costs, landed costs and whole-life costs
- Selecting tracking and materials handling technologies
- Use of WMS, MRP, MRP II and ERP systems
- Identifying and tracking appropriate metrics, ensuring compliance with SLAs
- Coordinating and managing upstream and downstream materials flows
- Business continuity planning
- Maximising capacity utilisation and efficiency
- Assessing risks and complying with security, customs, food safety and other requirements

The extensive list illustrates the diverse and multifaceted areas of activity logistics and supply chain managers need to be concerned with. This in turn requires a particular skills mix, as noted above something we will discuss further later in the chapter.

Another way of thinking about logistics and SCM is to consider how it can contribute across different industry sectors. DHL, for example, lists the following industry sectors where it can offer specialist expertise and services:

- Aerospace
- Automotive
- Chemical
- Consumer
- Fashion
- Life sciences and healthcare
- Industrial, engineering and manufacturing
- Renewable energy
- Retail
- Technology

Best practice logistics and SCM can of course contribute across all of these sectors. Throughout the book we have illustrated examples (such as Zara in the fashion sector) where logistics and supply chain-led developments can lead to a shift in how companies within the sector operate and compete.

THE EVER CHANGING CONTEXT

The plethora of strategies and practices listed in Table 19.1 make the logistics/supply chain manager's job complex and wide ranging. Added to this is the rapidly changing context within which these managers, and their organisations, have to operate. Professor Martin Christopher[2] from Cranfield University has identified seven major business transformations that must be undertaken for competitive success in tomorrow's marketplace and these are detailed in Table 19.2.

The seven transformations in the table provide a good insight into the new and emerging context within which logistics and supply chain managers increasingly have to operate. Professor John Gattorna from the University of Wollongong lists 13 strategic issues likely to have an impact on supply chains in the future: these can be summarised as:[3]

- Sustainability
- The impact of oil prices on cost-to-serve
- Outsourcing
- The adoption of supply chain principles by service organisations

Table 19.2   Christopher's key business transformations

Business transformation:	Leading to:
From supplier-centric to customer-centric	The design of customer-driven supply chains
From push to pull	Higher levels of agility and flexibility
From inventory to information	Capturing and sharing information on real demand
From transactions to relationships	Focus on service and responsiveness as the basis for customer retention
From 'trucks and sheds' to end-to end pipeline management	A wider definition of supply chain cost
From functions to processes	The creation of cross-functional teams focused on value creation
From standalone competition to network rivalry	More collaborative working with supply chain partners

- Vulnerability of supply chains; designs with embedded resilience
- The rise of genuine collaboration in supply chains
- Increased use of talent
- Learning to design and manage multiple organisation formats
- Increased geographical spread of supply chain networks
- Adopting whole-of-enterprise mindset in managing supply chain operations
- Collaborating with the enemy
- Innovation, product design and product life cycles
- Learning to manage inherent complexity in supply chains

Again, the ever changing and challenging context within which logistics and supply chain managers have to operate is evidenced from this wide-ranging list of issues.

An important area to consider with regard to how future supply chains will be structured concerns changes in global transport routes. The map at the start of the book illustrates the current picture of international shipping routes. The shape of these routes, and the distribution of traffic across them, can change over time. Two drivers for this might include the impact of current engineering works to widen the Panama Canal (allowing it to handle larger vessels) and the impact of climate change leading to the opening up of the Northern Sea routes.

Another area that drives the shape and structure of supply chains concerns product movements for reasons other than to satisfy demand. For example some products move in order to exploit transfer pricing benefits (Chapter 13); similarly many multinationals move more product towards end of quarter in order to boost quarterly sales figures and in turn stock-market perceptions of their firm's performance. Trends such as these can significantly impact supply chain designs.

SYNCHRONISING PRODUCT DESIGN AND SUPPLY CHAIN DESIGN

The concept of **design for manufacture** (**DFM**) was introduced in Chapter 3. Simchi-Levi *et al.* (2003) note that a similar transformation has begun in SCM, whereby managers have started to realise that 'by taking supply chain concerns into account in the product and process design phase, it becomes possible to operate a much more efficient supply chain'.[4] Mass customisation for example can be enabled by designing postponement into the production process – this can be something straightforward such as delayed product differentiation enabled by downstream supply chain partners.

Notwithstanding all of this, it is of course important to note that no matter how well designed a supply chain is, it cannot overly compensate for poor products. You will recall that in Chapter 4, in the context of our discussion on supply chain strategy, we quoted Christopher *et al.* who state that 'responsive supply chains . . . cannot overcome poor design and buying decisions which fail to introduce attractive products in the first place'.[5]

Synchronising product design and supply chain design is, as we saw in chapter 16, also important from a sustainability perspective. We noted then that greening a supply chain is largely about forward planning, with some commentators noting that over 80% of carbon savings are only achievable at the supply chain design stage.[6] We also noted that while various initiatives, such as for example switching to hybrid fuel vehicles, are obviously welcome, and generate publicity benefits for companies, it is the (often unnoticed in the public eye) *supply chain design* decisions, such as deciding where to locate warehouses and distribution centres and deciding which transport modes to use, that have the greatest impact.

From a societal perspective, supply chain design is not just concerned with sustainability issues, important as they are. Sustainability is one part of the wider framework of corporate social responsibility (CSR). Increasingly, ethical shareholders, regulators and customers are using their power to ensure organisations act responsibly, and the implications of this need to be considered at the supply chain design stage.

It is often the case that supply chains are not, as it were, designed *ab initio*; often an extant supply chain is already in place, but may need for a variety of reasons to be modified or redesigned. A good example of this is in many countries the supply chain for blood transfusion products, which needed to be redesigned following on from some very significant concerns in terms of product traceability and integrity (many countries have witnessed in recent years awful scandals around the issue of contaminated blood products infecting already ill people). Indeed more generally the area of pharmaceutical SCM has undergone significant transformation in recent years and this area, together with what has become known as good distribution practice (GDP), is detailed in the case study on 'Patient safety and the pharmaceutical supply chain' that follows this chapter.

DETERMINING SUPPLY CHAIN COSTS AND VALUE

In designing or modifying any supply chain, one of the key considerations is to know what costs are incurred, where they are incurred and how can they be managed. Conversely, we need to understand where cost can be minimised and where value can be maximised. We met the various categories of costs in different parts of the book, and it is worthwhile to summarise them here.

Generalised costs (Chapter 8)

The concept of generalised costs is often used in transport and includes all of the disparate costs that form the overall *opportunity costs* of a trip. Thus, in addition to the actual rate charged by the LSP, other costs are also taken into account such as packaging costs, insurance costs, and costs associated with transit time (the longer the trip takes, the longer the value of the freight is 'tied' up in transit).

Total landed costs (Chapter 14) and Total cost of outsourcing (Chapter 3)

Total landed costs incorporate the various costs associated with sourcing from different suppliers in different places (actual material costs, generalised transport costs, import duties, etc.). The total cost of outsourcing extends this to also incorporate the costs associated with identifying and managing suppliers.

Inventory costs (Chapter 10)

Chapter 10 described in detail the various costs associated with inventory and how inventory can be both controlled and minimised. We saw, for example, that inventory can be *hidden* at multiple points in the supply chain and that as well as the costs associated with carrying inventory, there are also costs associated with ordering and receiving inventory.

Financial accounting, financial management, management accounting (Chapter 13)

A wide variety of financial issues pertinent to supply chain design were discussed in Chapter 13. These included issues such as ensuring sufficient cash flow for the business to survive, financial risk and exposure to currency fluctuations, how much debt to carry, whether to employ transfer pricing, and how to cost various activities (for example activity based costing on a per SKU basis, which was also discussed in Chapter 14, and wholelife costing). Ensuring the supply chain is designed to accord with whatever financial objectives are to be prioritised is obviously a primary objective of supply chain design.

Once the various costs are understood, the issue of monitoring performance, discussed in detail in Chapter 14, needs to be considered and supply chains need to be designed with cognisance of such performance measurement requirements.

MODELLING SUPPLY CHAIN DESIGNS

In order to assess if a supply chain configuration accurately reflects the intended design, modelling techniques can be used.[7] These tools can generally be divided into two categories: optimisation techniques and simulation techniques.[8] Simulation techniques are discussed extensively in Chapter 5.

Optimisation techniques can be used to determine the supply chain networks that will produce minimum total transport cost solutions. In applications where the data on transport costs are not available, these techniques can be used to determine minimum total tonne kilometres solutions. Optimisation techniques used for modelling network designs are *static* and model only a given set of origins and destinations. The optimal solution consists of which supplier should supply to which distribution centre/warehouse to achieve minimum total cost for a single product. If new suppliers/warehouses are added in the network, the model needs to be rerun with a new formulation and a new data set.

One of the frequently used optimisation techniques is the 'transportation model' discussed in Chapter 6. Transportation models used for allocation of suppliers to distribution centres or warehouses can also assist in determining the optimal number of distribution centres/consolidation centres needed for a total minimum cost solution for a distributor.[9] These models are used with a route planning software to include actual travelling distance between an origin and a destination. A popular software package is 'CAST-dpm' developed by Radical Ltd (www.radical.co.uk/cast/), which can be used with transport route planning software such as 'Paragon' developed by Paragon Software Systems plc (www.paragonrouting.com). Transportation models use linear programming for problem formulation and numerical methods for finding the optimal solution.

One of the other optimising techniques used for network design applications is integer programming. Integer programming formulation uses binary variables and is considered as suitable for applications in network design where a variable can take only one of the two states such as 'yes' or 'no'. Integer programming has been used for design of production, distribution and vendor network supply chains.[10]

THE SUPPLY CHAIN MANAGER OF THE FUTURE

In Chapter 1 we noted that the supply chain encompasses three flows – material, information and resources – and we considered different aspects of them in this book. To again note what was pointed out in Chapter 1, no single flow is more important, and all are interdependent. The challenge then for the logistics/supply chain manager is to operate within such complexity and competing demands.

Christopher added requisite skills for each of the seven business transformations outlined in Table 19.2 and these are detailed in Table 19.3. As the table illustrates, the skills required are wide ranging and challenging.

As we noted in Chapter 4, the aim of SCM is to take a cross-functional, process perspective as distinct to a functional or silo-based perspective. The implication of this

Table 19.3   Christopher's key business transformations and the implications for management skills[11]

Business transformation:	Leading to:	Skills required:
From supplier-centric to customer-centric	The design of customer-driven supply chains	Market understanding; customer insight
From push to pull	Higher levels of agility and flexibility	Management of complexity and change
From inventory to information	Capturing and sharing information on real demand	Information systems and information technology expertise
From transactions to relationships	Focus on service and responsiveness as the basis for customer retention	Ability to define, measure and manage service requirements by market segment
From 'trucks and sheds' to end-to end pipeline management	A wider definition of supply chain cost	Understanding of the 'cost-to-serve' and time-based performance indicators
From functions to processes	The creation of cross-functional teams focused on value creation	Specific functional excellence with cross-functional understanding Team working capabilities
From standalone competition to network rivalry	More collaborative working with supply chain partners	Relationship management and win–win orientation

re-orientation is that the supply chain manager of the future will require a 'T-shaped' skills profile (see Figure 19.1).

The idea is that as well as bringing specific logistics management skills to the job (the vertical bar) supply chain managers need to have a wide understanding of related areas such as business process engineering, asset management and activity-based costing (the horizontal bar). Research into the development of future logistics and supply chain managers identified the pertinent knowledge areas and competencies/skills illustrated in Table 19.4.

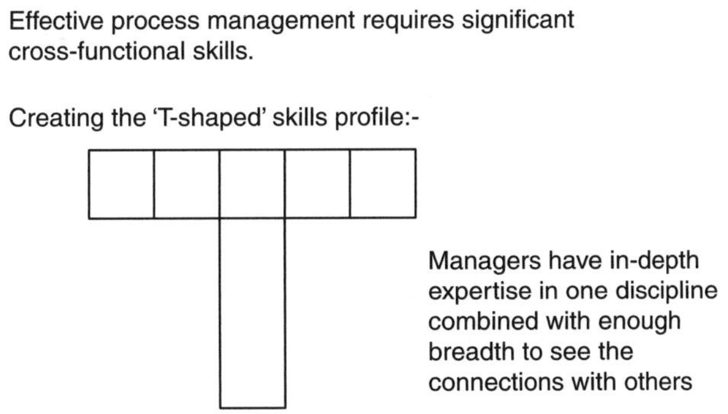

Effective process management requires significant cross-functional skills.

Creating the 'T-shaped' skills profile:-

Managers have in-depth expertise in one discipline combined with enough breadth to see the connections with others

Figure 19.1   Skills profile (Source: Mangan & Christopher, 2005)[12]

Table 19.4   Key knowledge areas and competencies/skills required by logistics and supply chain managers[13]

Knowledge areas	
– General	Finance
– Logistics/SCM specific	IT
	Management/Strategy
	Operations/SCM
	Focus on processes/flows
	Legal, security and international trade
	Multimodal logistics
	Logistics in emerging markets
Competencies/skills	Analytical
	Interpersonal
	Leadership
	Change management
	Project management

People, with the right skills and knowledge, are thus critical to effective SCM. As Professor John Gattorna has noted 'it is people who drive the supply chain, both inside and outside your business, not hard assets or technology'.[14] We also note the views of James Quinn who stated that to achieve any measure of supply chain success, three critical elements (people, process and technology) need to be kept in balance.[15] He added that there is no single answer as to which of these three is the most important to supply chain success, although in his view 'you can't do *anything* without the right people'.

This is an appropriate topic on which to conclude the book; essentially supply chains are all about people. As a student of this fascinating subject, by equipping yourself with the appropriate knowledge and skills, an engrossing and rewarding career hopefully awaits you. We hope this book will be of help to you on your journey.

SO WHO HAS THE BEST SUPPLY CHAIN?

Gartner (www.gartner.com) each year produces a list of the top 25 supply chains, which is generated from an analysis that uses various input metrics. The top 25 for 2010 were:

1. Apple
2. Procter & Gamble
3. Cisco Systems
4. Wal-Mart Stores
5. Dell
6. PepsiCo
7. Samsung

   8. IBM
   9. Research in Motion
  10. Amazon.com
  11. McDonald's
  12. Microsoft
  13. The Coca-Cola Company
  14. Johnson & Johnson
  15. Hewlett-Packard
  16. Nike
  17. Colgate-Palmolive
  18. Intel
  19. Nokia
  20. Tesco
  21. Unilever
  22. Lockheed Martin
  23. Inditex*
  24. Best Buy
  25. Schlumberger

  _____
  * Inditex is Zara's parent company.

LEARNING REVIEW

This chapter served to bring together the material developed in the preceding 18 chapters. The many strategies and practices employed in logistics and SCM today were detailed and illustrated the wide-ranging demands on logistics and supply chain managers. We also identified appropriate trends and the changing context within which logistics and SCM exists.

The point was developed that it is important, when designing supply chains, to endeavour to synchronise the design of supply chains with the design of products. We also reviewed the disparate costs that exist across supply chains (cost and value being key criteria in the context of supply chain design) and saw how modelling approaches (in particular optimisation and simulation) can assist in supply chain design.

The chapter concluded with a discussion on the skills and knowledge areas required of logistics and supply chain managers in the future. Logistics and SCM are ever changing and demanding disciplines, but provide attractive and rewarding opportunities to people who wish to work in these areas. The purpose of this book has been to equip you, the reader, to do this.

QUESTIONS

- Table 19.1 listed a wide-ranging number of common logistics/supply chain strategies and practices. In your view are all of these undertaken regularly by all organisations, or are some of them specific to certain types of organisations?
- Why is it important to synchronise product design and supply chain design? What are the implications of this from an environmental perspective?
- Summarise the various costs incurred in a typical supply chain.
- How might a supply chain be redesigned to allow for transfer pricing?
- Describe the various approaches for modelling supply chains.
- To what extent do you believe a supply chain can be redesigned to compensate for poor product design or poor product quality?
- Why do you think logistics and supply chain managers require a 'T-shaped' skills profile?

THE EVER CHANGING CONTEXT AND SKILLS REQUIRED OF LOGISTICS AND SUPPLY CHAIN MANAGERS

Look at the general business literature and try to identify various pertinent trends (in addition to those detailed in this chapter) which you believe are shaping the areas of logistics and SCM today.

What are the implications of these trends in terms of skills requirements?

You could, for example, review online and other job advertisements for the logistics and related sectors and try to identify skills requirements. If you can look at past advertisements you will be able to identify various trends such as an increased requirement for skilled logisticians; in addition it should be apparent that logistics and supply chain managers are being appointed at higher levels within organisations.

NOTES

1. Gattorna, J. (2006), *Living Supply Chains*, FT Prentice Hall, London.
2. Christopher, M. (2005) *Logistics and Supply Chain Management* (3rd Edition), FT/ Prentice Hall, London.
3. Gattorna (see note 1).
4. Simchi-Levi, D., Kaminsky, P. & Simchi-Levi, E. (2003) *Designing and Managing the Supply Chain* (2nd Edition, p. 214), McGraw-Hill, New York.
5. Christopher, M., Peck, H. & Towill, D. (2006) A taxonomy for selecting global supply chain strategies, *International Journal of Logistics Management*, 17(2), 277–287.
6. French, E. (2007) Green by design, *CILT Focus*, June.
7. Mason, R. & Lalwani, C. (2006) Transport integration tools for supply chain management, *International Journal of Logistics: Research & Applications*, 9(1), 57–74.

8. See, for example, Schary, P. & Skjott-Larsen, T. (2001) *Managing the Global Supply Chain*, Copenhagen Business School Press.

9. Potter A., Mason, R. & Lalwani, C. (2007) Analysis of factory gate pricing in the UK grocery supply chain, *International Journal of Retail and Distribution Management*, 35(10), 821–834

10. Simchi-Levi *et al.* (see note 4).

11. Christopher, p. 291 (see note 2).

12. Mangan, J. & Christopher, M. (2005) Management development and the supply chain manager of the future, *International Journal of Logistics Management*, 16(2), 178–191.

13. Ibid.

14. Gattorna, p. xiii (see note 1).

15. Quinn, F. (2004) People, process, technology, *Supply Chain Management Review*, January/February, 3.

Part Three Case Studies

Patient Safety and the Pharmaceutical Supply Chain

Ciarán M. Brady

PLS Pharma Logistics

The import of fake medicines across EU borders has grown in the last year with 11.4 million counterfeit items seized in 2009, a 28% increase on 2008. Fake medicines were the third biggest category of seized goods.

In Switzerland alone, in the first six months of 2010, reports of 992 suspicious, potentially illegal imports of medicinal products were reported by the Federal Customs authorities. Most were prescription-only drugs. This is 75% increase on the same period in 2009.[1]

The pharmaceutical industry has a vital role, and responsibility, to ensure that the products it manufactures, distributes and delivers are fit for purpose and safe for the patient. Counterfeit medicines are a growing concern with the resilience of the pharmaceutical supply chain under constant pressure as economic conditions continue to pose significant challenges for business and consumers globally.

Assuring supply chain integrity and patient safety is today more important than ever, as all of us depend on safe medicines at various times in our lives. Recently in Africa a young child died because of the medicine he had taken which, when later analysed, was found to be a counterfeit. It had been administered by a doctor and delivered through what was thought a safe, secure supply chain.

The pharmaceutical supply chain is somewhat unique in that compliance at every point along the supply chain is essential. In the pharmaceutical industry a manufacturer's responsibility begins at sourcing materials from approved suppliers, continues through manufacturing under **good manufacturing practice (GMP)** and on to delivery/distribution of the finished product to the final customer under **good distribution practice (GDP)**. The entire supply chain and the distribution network are focused on supplying a quality product that complies at every point with regulatory requirements. It is approved and registered with regulators to ensure it is suitable and safe for use. Any failings within the pharmaceutical supply chain can seriously compromise the quality of the product and patient safety.

The pharmaceutical supply chain extends well beyond the vehicles used to move bulk pharmaceutical materials, ingredients and components to the manufacturing facility and finished products from manufacturing facility to distributors/wholesalers worldwide. It also must ensure compliant delivery to hospitals, pharmacies and even supermarkets where the consumer can now purchase medicines. As patients we would like to be guaranteed that the excellent quality under which medicines are produced, in the manufacturing facility, extends all along the legitimate distribution chain.

> Good manufacturing practice (GMP) ensures that products are manufactured batch upon batch, year upon year, to the appropriate and consistent quality standards and in accordance with regulatory requirements.

Driving higher standards and compliance in the distribution chain is essential for continued success. As mergers within the pharmaceutical industry continue at a pace, and more blockbuster drugs come off patent, there is continued pressure on the industry, governments and patients worldwide. As a greater number of new products require cold chain distribution, temperature-controlled transportation will be the standard required throughout the supply chain for the majority of pharmaceutical products in the future.

Product traceability continues to be a challenge and there are many new developments in technology and labelling. This is a great step forward in driving improvements and helping protect patients; especially in the case of a recall when full traceability is essential.

Good distribution practice remains an essential aspect of compliance for all pharmaceutical companies as products are stored, transported and delivered on a global and local basis.

WHAT IS GOOD DISTRIBUTION PRACTICE (GDP)

GDP can be defined as the part of quality assurance that ensures the quality of a pharmaceutical product is maintained, through adequate controls throughout the numerous stages of the distribution process. This definition could reasonably be extended to include sourcing, receipt, storage and transportation. This would encompass the full supply chain

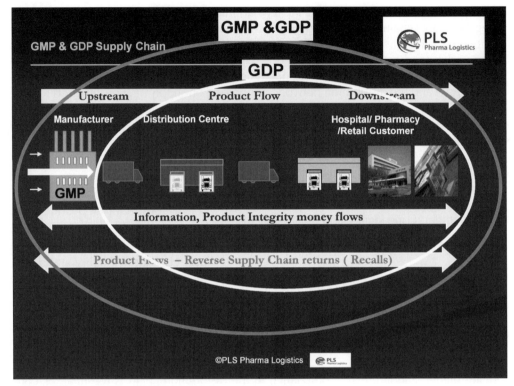

Figure C10.1   GMP and GDP in the pharma supply chain

that is necessary to make and sell pharmaceutical products (see Figure C10.1). The critical need is to establish controls, and manage risks at all points along the supply chain, so that all partners handling and transporting pharmaceuticals do so within compliance.

The importance of GDP is elaborated in the EU Guidance on Distribution Practice. Although hugely paraphrased, the following summary of that Principle does reliably reflect its observations:

> The Community pharmaceutical industry operates at a high level of quality assurance . . . . . and this level of quality should be maintained throughout the distribution network so that authorised medicinal products are distributed to retail pharmacists and other persons entitled to sell medicinal products to the general public without any alteration of their properties.
>
> To maintain the quality of the products Directive 92/25/EEC provides that wholesalers must comply with the principles and guidelines of good distribution practice published by the Commission of the European Communities.[2]

The World Health Organisation (WHO) publications under Good Distribution Practice for Pharmaceutical Products states that 'distribution forms an important activity of the integrated supply chain management of pharmaceutical products. Various persons and entities are often responsible for the handling, storage and distribution of such products.'[3]

The WHO is looking for total ownership for all the steps in the distribution process and the entire distribution/supply chain.

The US Food and Drug Administration documents the requirement for 'storage of drug products under appropriate conditions of temperature, humidity and light so that the identity, strength, quality and purity of the drug products are not affected'.[4]

DEFICIENCIES FOUND IN PHARMACEUTICAL SUPPLY CHAINS

European regulators continue to see deficiencies in pharmaceutical supply chains. Some of the key deficiencies found included:

- Inadequate temperature management for warehouses/vehicles and temperature excursions in storage and transportation of products both cold chain and ambient/room temperature products.
- Cold chain packaging and transport vehicles not properly approved to guarantee products remain within their approved temperature ranges for the duration of the delivery.
- Training of key staff especially in GDP was inadequate.
- Bona fides of suppliers and customers were not established and maintained.
- Unauthorised activities taking place.
- Duties and responsibilities of staff not defined and/or not carried out in compliance with licence conditions.
- Quality systems not adequate.
- Drivers handling pharmaceutical products not trained in GDP.
- Risk and due diligence in the supply chain not carried out.
- Counterfeit awareness, procedures and processes not in place or inadequate.

COUNTERFEITING

The US based Center for Medicines in the Public Interest predicted that counterfeit drug sales were valued in the region of US$75 billion globally in 2010, an increase of more than 90% from 2005.[5]

In some countries counterfeiting is a rare occurrence and in others it is an everyday reality. The WHO website suggests that counterfeits account for around 1% of sales in developed countries to over 10% in developing countries. One of the biggest challenges for the industry and one of the main reasons why good supply chain management is critical is the growth of counterfeit medicines on a global basis.

(Source: © Pfizer; see also note 8 with regard to www.realdanger.co.uk)

WHAT ARE COUNTERFEIT OR SUBSTANDARD MEDICINES?

Counterfeit medicines are part of the broader phenomenon of substandard pharmaceuticals. 'They are fraudulently and may be deliberately mislabelled with respect to identity and/or source. Counterfeiting can apply to both branded and generic products and counterfeit medicines may include products with the correct ingredients but fake packaging, with the wrong ingredients, without active ingredients or with insufficient active ingredients.'[6]

Substandard medicines are products whose composition and ingredients do not meet the correct scientific specifications and which are consequently ineffective and often dangerous to the patient. Substandard products may occur as a result of negligence, human error, insufficient human and financial resources or counterfeiting.

Untrained, unsuspecting consumers are vulnerable to the potentially lethal outcomes of buying medicines online. Increasing numbers of consumers are choosing to source their medicines this way, having stated cost, convenience and privacy as some of the key reasons they chose to purchase online. A global marketplace exists for counterfeiters who know where the maximum profits can be made through illegal websites.

'The Counterfeiting Superhighway', produced by the European Alliance for Access to Safe Medicines (EAASM), reveals the scope and repercussions of this dangerous practice:[7]

- 62% of medicines purchased online are fake or substandard (including medicines indicated to treat serious conditions such as cardiovascular and respiratory disease, neurological disorders, and mental health conditions).
- 95.6% of online pharmacies researched are operating illegally.
- 94% of websites do not have a named, verifiable pharmacist.

A recent campaign in the UK to heighten awareness of the risks of buying counterfeit medicines using the internet, 'Get real get a prescription',[8] is helping to educate consumers to the real dangers of buying counterfeit medicines online and that such a transaction could end in death.

A recent example[9] of counterfeit medicines reported from the Medicines and Healthcare products Regulatory Agency (MHRA) are slimming pills. Counterfeits of two prescription-only anti-obesity pills were found in the basement of a central London house, revealing the booming market in counterfeit slimming pills seen in the UK. The drugs were found simply wrapped in newspapers alongside piles of 'patient instructions' ready to be supplied to unsuspecting internet consumers. One of the counterfeit slimming pills found has been withdrawn from legal sale in Europe over possibilities it could increase the risk of heart attacks in those with cardiovascular disease.

Mike Deats, head of enforcement with the MHRA in 2010 said 'There is no such thing as a good counterfeit medicine. These have been made in substandard conditions, they contain impurities we don't even know about. Just because they contain some active ingredient doesn't mean that they're good.'[10]

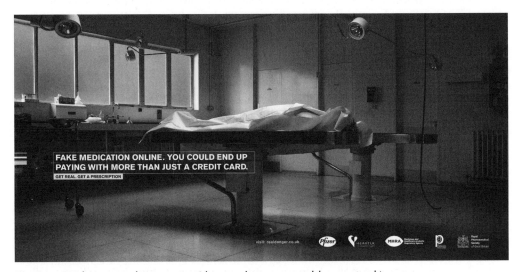

FAKE MEDICATION ONLINE. YOU COULD END UP PAYING WITH MORE THAN JUST A CREDIT CARD.
GET REAL. GET A PRESCRIPTION

(Source: © Pfizer; see also note 8 with regard to www.realdanger.co.uk)

World Customs Organization (WCO) Secretary General Kunio Mikuriya signed a declaration in June 2010 pledging the 176 member customs administrations to combat the counterfeit pharmaceutical industry. 'Countries across the globe, in particular those in Africa, suffer the scourge of being flooded with fake and sub-standard medicine.'[11]

Good supply chain management coupled with best in class good distribution practice is a minimum requirement in helping to stem the flow of counterfeit products into legitimate distribution channels and pharmaceutical supply chains.

CONCLUSION – THE WAY FORWARD

If we are to deliver patient safety there is a need for all stakeholders in the pharmaceutical industry to work in partnership to ensure supply chain integrity and compliance. Regulators across the world are working with manufacturers, distributors and all involved in pharmaceutical supply chains to embrace and drive compliance standards. The EU Commission is working to update Directive 2001/83/EC and the Pharma Package with regard to the specific amendment that aims to prevent falsified medicine from entering into the legal supply chain. Preparations are also underway to publish shortly a new set of EU Good Distribution Guidelines. The many advances in technology will help but unfortunately the great majority of reported defective medicinal products has resulted from human error or carelessness, not from failures in technology.

The critical need to establish controls, review real risks in complex supply chains and understand where individual responsibilities start and finish is essential. Legislation and good practices oblige pharmaceutical manufacturers and distributors to exercise control over the distribution chain and ensure that the quality of medicines is maintained. Critical in this regard is control of the environmental conditions under which medicines are stored and transported. As global temperatures increase, the need to carefully transport all pharmaceutical products within their specific temperature ranges will remain a significant challenge.

Optimising the pharmaceutical supply chain is a competitive necessity but delivering patient safety should never be put at risk. Suppliers, manufacturers, distributors and partners who transport and distribute products must ensure that the high level of product quality achieved by observing good manufacturing practice is maintained throughout the distribution network as products are transported and delivered on a global and local basis.

Whilst the regulators are doing all they can to heighten awareness, everyone working in this area must ensure they act as part of the team delivering best practice and patient safety all along the supply chain. Now, more than ever, education, training and awareness are essential to maintain and continuously improve quality and supply chain standards. Operating without supply chain integrity and product authenticity will not deliver patient safety.

NOTES

1. The Counterfeiting Superhighway, published by European Alliance for Access to Safe Medicines (EAASM), 2008, Surrey, UK.
2. Ibid.
3. Good Distribution Practice for Pharmaceutical Products, World Health Organisation, Geneva.
4. Food and Drug Administration (FDA) of the United States, Code of Federal Regulations Title 21, 21 CFR 211.142, 2010.
5. Center for Medicines in the Public Interest, 2010, New York.
6. MHRA Rules and Guidance for Pharmaceutical Manufacturers and Distributors, 2007, London.
7. The Counterfeiting Superhighway (see note 1).
8. www.realdanger.co.uk, supported by Pfizer, MHRA, RSPGB, HEART UK and The Patients Association.
9. www.bbc.co.uk/news/10258849 (accessed 7 July 2010).
10. Ibid.
11. www.medicalnewstoday.com/articles/193089.php (accessed 28 June 2010).

Contamination in the Bulk Agri-Commodity Logistics Chain

Elizabeth Jackson

Newcastle University

TRADING RELATIONS BETWEEN WESTERN AUSTRALIA AND JAPAN

Japan imports 5–6 million tonnes of bulk wheat each year to manufacture products such as Udon noodles, bread, cake, Chinese noodles, white salted noodles, spaghetti, instant noodles and beer. Each year Western Australia ships nearly 1.5 million tonnes of bulk grain to Japan, with the income from wheat for noodle production alone estimated to have a value of A$150 million to the local economy. While Japan buys a significant amount of wheat from Western Australia, it is also the largest market for other bulk agri-commodities, such as barley, oats, canola and cereal hay, thereby indicating the importance of the trade relationship between the two nations. The Japanese market for Australian wheat is relatively stable although Australia only supplies Japan with about a fifth of its demand (Figure C11.1), so market competition with suppliers such as Canada and the USA is a key concern for Australia. As a consequence, a great deal of care is needed for managing and maintaining this high-value commodity supply chain. To add to this, market relations in the Japanese context are largely based on trust, honour and long-term relationships between supply chain actors, which makes establishing and maintaining markets a delicate and complex task.

AN OVERVIEW OF THE WESTERN AUSTRALIAN EXPORT GRAIN INDUSTRY

From 1933 to the beginning of the new millennium, Western Australian's grain export industry, which accounts for 95% of the state's annual harvest, was highly regulated with each sector of the supply chain operating as a government statutory authority. The

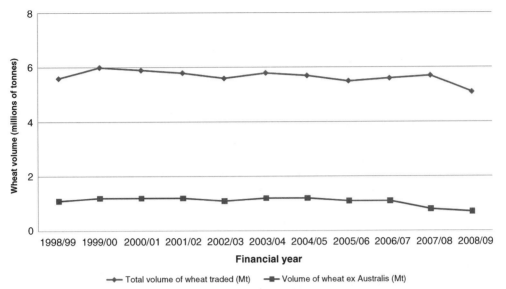

Figure C11.1 Annual wheat trading activity – Japan 1998/99–2008/09 (Source: ABS, various publications)

ports, railways, quarantine services, grain traders and grain handlers all operated as statutory monopolies with specific charters to service one another's needs. Information was exchanged freely between the firms and all collaborated with a unified mission: to optimise market returns for grain producers by selling and transporting export grain at peak efficiencies. Most of the time, the exporting of bulk grain from Western Australia's ports at Geraldton, Fremantle, Albany and Esperance was very successful. To this day, the logistics and quality control systems for moving grain from country storages to ports, onto ships and then to the destination port are highly efficient but, on two occasions in March 2002, this world-class system failed and cost the industry approximately A$5 million, with untold damage to the collaborative relationships in the international wheat supply chain.

OBJECTIONABLE CONTAMINANTS IN EXPORT GRAIN

The problem started when loading a vessel of barley destined for Saudi Arabia from the port at Fremantle. For this shipment, all quality control checks had been undertaken[1] and showed that all standards for shipping barley to Saudi Arabia had been met, including a particular additive to the cargo: namely, carmoisine. Carmoisine is a red food dye that is often used in the red meat industry to certify carcass grading. The Saudi Arabian market demands that about 1% of all imported grain is coloured with carmoisine in an attempt to minimise black market grain trading. The colouring process is carried out at the time of loading bulk grain onto the ship destined for Saudi Arabia. The liquid food dye is slowly dripped onto the conveyor belt that is loading the grain onto the ship.

After the shipment of barley left for Saudi Arabia, the next ship to be loaded at the port of Fremantle was high-value noodle wheat bound for Japan. As per standard practice, all quality checks were undertaken, the vessel was loaded and set sail. Once the vessel reached its destination in Japan in early March 2002, unloading commenced and local authorities began their stringent import checks during which they identified an 'objectionable contaminant' in the cargo – this is one of the most serious claims that can be made about a cargo of food. Western Australia's most important Japanese customers were horrified by this finding and contacted the grain marketing agent immediately to express their outrage about the unacceptable condition of the cargo. Upon rigorous testing of the grain samples, it was found that the objectionable contaminant was traces of grain that had been treated with carmoisine. Unloading the vessel was ceased and the ship was to be berthed until the problem was resolved.

The allegation of the carmoisine-contaminated cargo had the Western Australia grain industry in turmoil: valuable customers had been disappointed, an entire cargo of premium-quality wheat was split between the ship and port storage, the Japanese port had ceased operations thereby preventing other vessels from berthing, extraordinary demurrage costs were being incurred from the ship being left idle and there was a threat of the customers demanding monetary compensation for loss of earnings. Western Australian grain marketers found it perplexing that their Japanese customers should find miniscule traces of a food dye so unacceptable; particularly because it is an additive that another customer (Saudi Arabia) demands as a standard treatment. After identifying the immediate problem, substantial cracks started to appear in the seemingly robust supply chain.

OBJECTIONABLE CONTAMINANT: CARMOISINE

Objectionable contaminants in bulk grain commodities are usually traces of poisonous or dangerous substances such as pesticides, traces of herbicides used in crop management, traces of fertiliser from previous handling equipment, rust or paint flakes from inside the hold of a vessel, small pieces of metal from handling machinery, bird or rodent droppings from unclean storage facilities, poisonous gases from antiquated storage facilities or fungal mycotoxins produced during growth or storage of wheat crops. International food standards specify a nil tolerance of generic objectionable contaminants (such as those listed above) but individual markets also specify particular substances as objectionable. In Japan, Canada, the USA, Norway and Sweden, carmoisine is banned[2] based on evidence that it is linked to hyperactivity in children[3] and hence is regarded as an objectionable contaminant in food importing.

The confirmation that the objectionable contaminant found in the wheat cargo was carmoisine resulted in the entire cargo being rejected by Japan. This left the cargo of high-quality grain split between the port and the vessel, and also without an owner. The grain marketer eventually found a new buyer for the cargo at an enormous financial cost but the most significant operational cost was finding a way to return the part-unloaded cargo onto the ship. Japan is principally an importing nation so its port infrastructure has world-class facilities for unloading ships but very few, if any, facilities for loading ships.

So reloading a bulk commodity onto a bulk vessel proved extremely costly in terms of emergency engineering and demurrage expenses. The reverse is true for Western Australia's bulk commodity ports which are principally for exporting goods so returning the cargo to its home port was out of the question; hence the need for the grain marketer to make a quick sale of the redundant cargo.

When the matter was closed, the grain marketer responsible for selling the wheat and the bulk handler responsible for assembling and loading the cargo realised how dependent they were on one another to work collaboratively in protecting Japan as a valued customer. Relations between the two firms had been pushed to the limit with both blaming each other for the losses suffered: the grain marketer being blamed for not clearly communicating the fine detail of the exporting contract and the bulk handler being blamed for being so careless with assembling and loading the cargo (essentially not ensuring that all traces of carmoisine had been cleaned from the port's conveyor systems). Nevertheless, the relationship was recovered for the benefit of maintaining the important trade between Western Australia and its Japanese customer. The relationship with the Japanese customers had also been severely tested over this incident and the Japanese still had a sceptical view of Western Australia even after relations had appeared to be mended. However, this situation was to worsen. The media was informed on 22 March 2002 that a 20 000 Mt cargo of noodle wheat had been rejected by Japan due to contamination with carmoisine. This was the second cargo to be rejected within a month for the same reason. This second incident was almost too much for the Japanese to bear. They were furious that the promises that had been made regarding ship and handling hygiene were not taken seriously. They considered that trust had been abused and that they had been dishonoured. As a consequence, two vital aspects of conducting business with Japan had been neglected – twice. At this point, grain producer lobbying groups had become involved with concerns about the breakdown of relations with Japan as a major buyer of their wheat.

Fortunately, the Japanese were savvy enough to have not unloaded the second cargo before testing it for traces of carmoisine so the operational losses experienced when the first cargo was rejected were not experienced to the same extent. Nevertheless, significant demurrage costs were incurred while a new buyer was sought for the second contaminated cargo.

IMPORT REFUSALS AROUND THE WORLD

Incidents of import refusals, like those cargoes rejected by the Japanese noodle wheat market, are costly in terms of financial (tangible) losses and damaged supply chain relationships (intangible losses); Figure C11.2 illustrates the tangible and intangible losses experienced at each tier of the supply chain as a result of an import refusal.

Published research on the frequency of cargo rejections from Australia and elsewhere[4] is extremely sparse as data of this kind can be commercially sensitive and are often only collected internally by marketing and handling organisations. This type of data is also very difficult to collect, simply based on how to define a cargo rejection or import refusal. It is rare for a cargo to be rejected outright, like this Japanese noodle wheat cargo; it is much

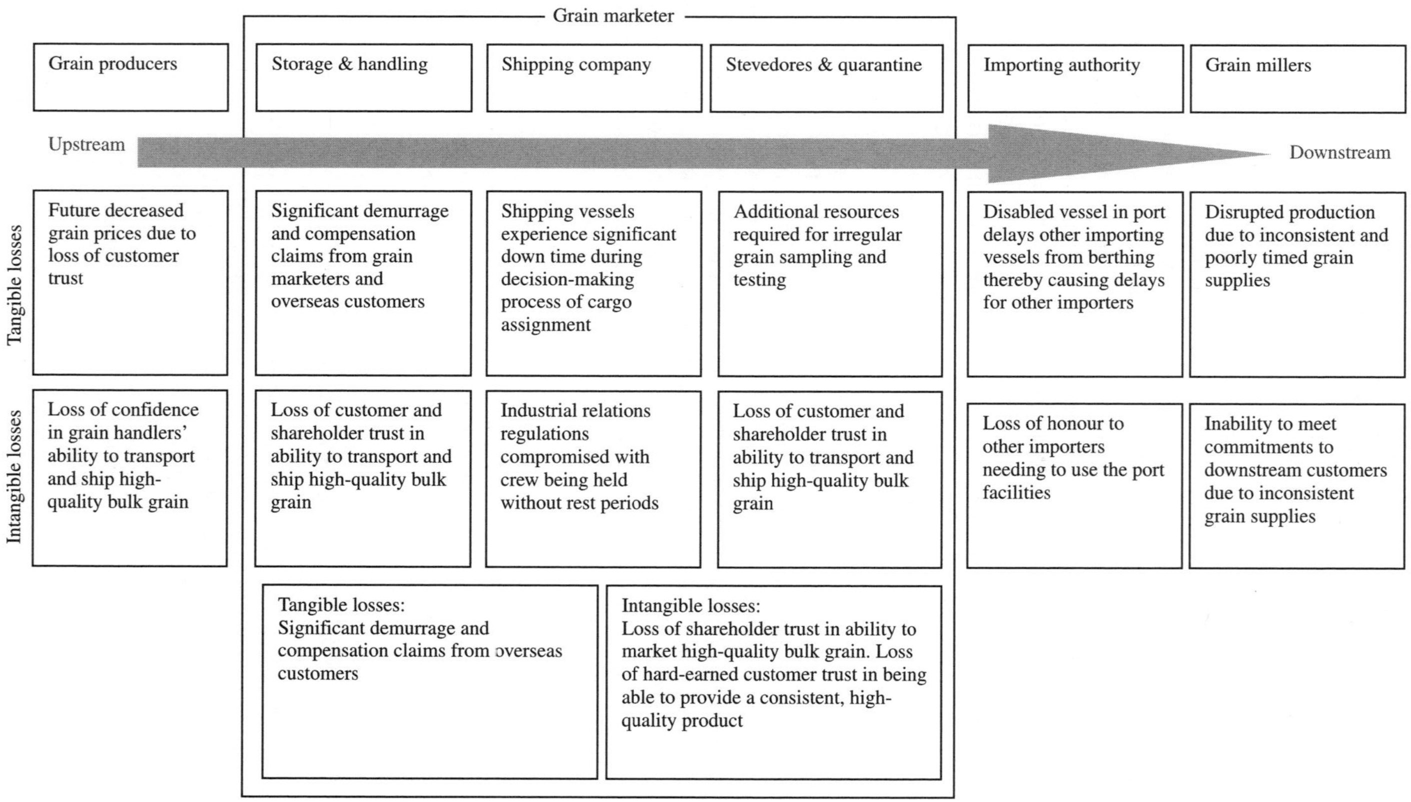

Figure C11.2 Tangible and intangible losses in the Australian wheat supply chain from an import refusal

more common for 'near misses' to occur. This is when a mistake is corrected before any operational losses are incurred or financial losses are experienced (as a result of compensation claims from cargoes that are accepted but fall short of some quality standard).

Despite the difficulty of measuring shipping rejections, the USA's Food and Drug Administration has been collecting high-quality data on food import refusals for over 10 years. While their data shows that USA import refusals of whole grain, milled grain products and starch are extremely low (1.4% of refusals between 1998 and 2004), researchers who have analysed the data agree that refusals of any imported goods have a negative impact on trade relations.[5] In the case of Japan's refusal of contaminated Western Australian noodle wheat, the trade ramifications were significant. The trusted relationship between Australia's largest grain- producing state and a long-term, high-value customer was damaged; not to mention the animosity caused between the various members of the grain supply chain within Western Australia. Essentially, the harmony within a long-established supply chain was temporarily destroyed.

CONCLUDING COMMENTS

In March 2002, the Western Australian grain supply chain suffered a desperate shock to its system with two consecutive cargoes of noodle wheat being rejected from Japan due to contamination by the food dye carmoisine. Relationships between actors in the supply chain were stretched to the limit. The Japanese demanded answers about the quality of the cargoes and supply chain actors were looking for compensation for the loss of income they experienced. At the same time further upstream, grain producers were worried about losing a valuable downstream customer. It was not only relationships that were tested; this case also provides an interesting insight into how sophisticated port infrastructures have become rigid in terms of optimising efficiency whereby irregular occurrences, such as this, turn out to be unmanageable. The outcomes of these incidents were that the Western Australian grain industry had suffered a substantial economic loss and relations between numerous members of the grain supply chain and some of its customers had been severely damaged; damage that only hard, collaborative work could repair.

This case has shed light on the importance of port efficiencies and has also demonstrated that, despite the complexity of the global grain supply chain, relations between supply chain actors are at the pinnacle of importance in managing such chains. The fact remains that the trade of agricultural commodities fluctuates as a consequence of numerous factors such as global seasonal conditions, erratic currency markets and changes to government import/export regulations. Japan's Ministry of Agriculture, Forestry and Fisheries has a highly regulated method of buying wheat for the nation's milling industry which facilitates competition between suppliers. So while Figure C11.1 suggests that the Japanese market is reasonably stable, it does not reflect the ill-will Japanese grain buyers had for Western Australia; nor does it show the colossal effort the Western Australia grain industry had to put into re-establishing the trust of one of its key customers.

QUESTIONS

- Using the actors illustrated in Figure C11.2, what factors led to the breakdown of relationships between members of the noodle wheat supply chain?
- What supply chain management processes could have been put in place to ensure the second contamination of carmoisine did not occur?
- Discuss the importance of collaboration in the development and maintenance of an international agri-food market.
- Provide justification for the idea that the Western Australian export grain supply chain, as described in this case study, had robust qualities.

NOTES

1. For a more complete description of this process, see www.wea.gov.au/Publications/FactSheets/090520_Costtoindustryvessels3.pdf.

2. CBC News (2008) Food additives, *CBC News in Depth: Food Safety*, available at: www.cbc.ca/news/background/foodsafety/additives.html (accessed 19 March 2010).

3. McCann, D., Barrett, A., Cooper, A., Crumpler, D., Dalen, L., Grimshaw, K., *et al.* (2007) Food additives and hyperactive behaviour in 3-year-old and 8/9-year-old children in the community: a randomised double-blinded, placebo-controlled trial, *The Lancet*, 370(9598), 1560–1567.

4. Baylis, K., Martens, A. & Nogueira, L. (2009) What drives import refusals? *American Journal of Agricultural Economics*, 91(5), 1477–1483.

5. Baylis *et al.,* ibid. Buzby, J.C., Unnevehr, L.J. & Roberts, D. (2008) *Food Safety and Imports: An Analysis of FDA Food-Related Import Refusal Reports*, ERS Economic Information Bulletin No. 39, September, US Department of Agriculture, Washington, DC.

Why Supply Chains should be Involved in Product Design

Anne Nagle

Nagle Business Solutions

Seamus O'Reilly

University College Cork

INTRODUCTION

Poor choices of material or supplier in the design process can have a significant impact on a company's performance. The case study below illustrates a scenario where both of these factors were simultaneously at play.

Supply chain considerations in design need to include inventory, logistics, transportation efficiencies, customs and duties, customer responsiveness and flexibility. The challenge for many organisations is that those involved in design tend to have little involvement once a product is launched, so they may not get to experience that supply chain in action or indeed live with the consequences of their decisions. Bringing that supply chain execution experience to the design table provides organisations with a great opportunity to design out potential inefficiencies and design in customer responsiveness. The term DFx (design for x, where x can mean a variety of things such as C = cost, M = manufacturability) is sometimes used as an all-encompassing term to flag the need for multiple perspectives in the design process.

CASE STUDY

Background to the design chain

The case company (TechCo) is a high-tech electronics manufacturer supplying products to original equipment manufacturers (OEMs), who bundle these products with other products and services for end-customer supply. Given the structure of this industry there are very few, very large OEMs. We typically refer to this type of supplier (TechCo) as a tier 1 supplier.

TechCo had a significant engineering team who were responsible for product design. Engineering worked closely with these OEM customers in product design and qualification and also with tier 2 and tier 3 suppliers upstream who manufactured various components or parts and sub-assemblies that made up the product. Initial prototypes were made in the engineering laboratories with materials procured by Engineering. The next stage was small-scale production managed by a new product introduction (NPI) group within Operations. There were a number of resources in this NPI team – mainly Project Management and Buying. The NPI group was responsible for ensuring the product could be produced in volume and produced initial volumes for OEM customers. The process of getting information from Engineering was difficult – one of those scenarios where the 'paperwork' lagged behind the activity of design and supply. Different information systems used by each team did not help since Engineering used 'Agile' as their system of record; this held detailed specifications, but Operations needed the information on their Oracle Enterprise Resource Planning (ERP) system in order to drive demand through the supply chain.

Thus product design (i.e. new product development – NPD) was largely the remit of Engineering and product launch (i.e. NPI) was largely the remit of the NPI team in Operations. Operations had established an Advanced Manufacturing Operations (AMO) to introduce new products. This unit had a capacity to assemble about 50 units/day. Once customer demand ramped-up, manufacture was then transferred to the large-scale production organisation (capacity to assemble 100s of units/day).

Background to the supply chain

TechCo employed a mix of own-production and contract manufacturing in supplying the products to its customers. Parts or components were supplied by what could be considered as tier 3 suppliers. Some of these parts went to tier 2 suppliers for sub-assembly – either printed circuit board assembly (PCBA) or mechanical sub-assembly – and others directly to TechCo for finished goods assembly. Hence a problem with one part would have a domino impact throughout a rather interdependent and thus complicated supply chain. A simplified schematic of TechCo's supply chain is presented in Figure C12.1.

New part, supplier, technology and problems

In 2006, TechCo discovered the importance of supply chain involvement in product design when a problem arose that significantly threatened current and future revenues

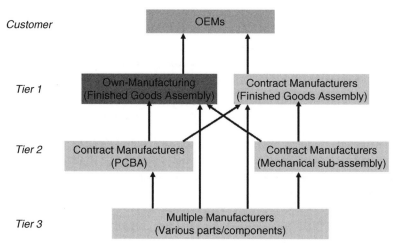

Figure C12.1   Simplified supply chain

for the company. The design of a $3 part from a tier 3 supplier (supplying mechanical sub-assembly contract manufacturer) using new technology (thixomoulding) went somewhat unnoticed in the product design process. The difficulty of getting a high volume of parts became apparent when problems arose with the initial supplier and the product volumes began to ramp from Engineering to Production volumes (i.e. from producing about 50 units/day to 100s/day). This $3 part, in a product sold for $2000 upwards, limited sales revenue for the company for a four-month period. More significantly, there was a huge risk that customers identified for the product would move to a competitor's technology and the product would fail in the market. This was avoided only by massive management attention on recovering the situation.

The designers of the part were looking for a material with greater hardness and that would have less vibration than current designs. They sourced injection moulded magnesium (known as 'thixomoulded') parts from a supplier to the automotive industry. The design of the part was more detailed than parts produced in this process for automotive applications, but this was not considered further once initial parts were produced to meet specification. Through all these stages there was no SCM involvement – just design engineers making the best design decisions for product performance in the lab.

SCM became involved as the product moved from Engineering to Production stage in the product management process. Initial involvement was in determining the commercial aspects of supply since the tooling and initial parts had already been approved by Engineering. Shortly after this transition, the supplier went into liquidation and this galvanised numerous activities to secure future supply at this critical stage in the product lifecycle. As this part was customised for TechCo the tooling used to manufacture it also needed to be customised. This customised tool was owned by TechCo.

Once it was determined that the current supplier would not be a viable option for the future, the identification of alternative suppliers began and so too did the SCM function's learning curve on the detailed technology used in the production of this part. Choices of alternative sources were limited to three in the whole of North America. Initial repair of the tool by the new supplier suggested that the previous supplier had not maintained the tool correctly. Subsequently it was discovered that the design of the part made it difficult to produce using this technology and one of the side effects was a build up of material on the tool leading to significant down time for cleaning and high potential for tool damage.

The planned production of new tools to support higher volumes was slowed down through this learning period since it was unclear if further changes to tooling should be made to address the issues arising in production. After two months at a new supplier it became obvious that the output expected from each tool for the part was much lower than initial expectations. TechCo had to increase its plan for five customised tools to eight tools within the first six months of product life.

QUESTIONS

- Identify and discuss the fundamental issues that this case highlights.
- What actions would you take to address these issues? Consider both short-term actions and long-term learning and reconfiguration of product design and supply processes.

From Terrestrial to Extraterrestrial Supply Chain Networks

Louis Brennan[1]

Trinity College Dublin

The space industry traces its origins to the middle of the twentieth century as an exclusively government/military domain involving the United States and the former Soviet Union. It has evolved to one which is increasingly commercialised and internationalised involving a host of activities and countries. Today the OECD defines the space economy as encompassing all public and private actors involved in developing and providing space-enabled products and services. It includes research and development; manufacturers of space hardware such as launch vehicles, satellites, ground stations; providers of space-enabled products such as navigation equipment and satellite phones; and providers of services to final users such as satellite-based meteorological services and direct-to-home video services.

As the space industry evolves from one dominated by governments and their military establishments to one which is undergoing rapid commercialisation across a wide number of areas, there is a need for a business perspective on the industry which can help to address many of the managerial and operations issues that face the industry players. As the business of space expands to incorporate space tourism and extraterrestrial mining, manufacturing and energy generation, logistics infrastructures and supply chain networks will need to be designed and implemented to support these areas of endeavour.

As the impact of climate change makes terrestrial survival for the human species increasingly problematic, the imperative to develop the means of evacuating planet Earth and sustaining extraterrestrial human existence becomes critical. However, the challenges around sustaining extraterrestrial human existence, aka the humanising of space, are immense. In this respect the development and sustaining of a robust supply chain network capacity linking Earth and extraterrestrial nodes will be crucial. In designing such a network, there are many issues to be addressed – some that already pertain to terrestrial supply networks but some that arise solely in this unique context.

QUESTION

- What are the key decisions facing the designers of supply chain networks if the humanising of space is to become a reality?

NOTE

1. Louis Brennan is the co-author of *The Business of Space: The Next Frontier of International Competition*, Brennan and Vecchi, published by Palgrave Macmillan, 2011.

Glossary

Chapter	Term	Definition
10	ABC – stock classification system	An inventory management system that separates out the most important inventory items so that more attention can be focused on those items
13	Activity-based costing (ABC)	Where organisations examine in detail the activities they carry out in the production and delivery of a product, and subsequently identify a number of activities (for example number of orders processed, number of quality inspections or machine setups, and number of deliveries) which may be used to apply overhead to products more appropriately
14	Advanced shipment notification (ASN)	Advance notification to a WMS of an arriving shipment
3	Aggregated procurement	A method for selecting suppliers based on their capabilities rather than individual suppliers tendering for particular orders
4	Agile	Ability to cope with volatility in demand
8	Air trucking	Moving freight, which will be carried by air at some stage on its journey, by road (often air freight rates will be applied for the *full* journey)
7	Authorised Economic Operator (AEO)	an EU voluntary security initiative which is designed to reflect the US C-TPAT security initiative
11	Automated guided vehicle (AGV)	A mobile robot used to move materials between locations in a warehouse or factory
12	Automatic identification and data capture (AIDC)	Technologies that automatically identify assets and freight, capturing specific data to enable traceability and security amongst other benefits
3	Backshoring	Where a company abandons offshoring and moves the activities back to the original home market.
13	Balance sheet	A snapshot of the financial position of the organisation at that date and consisting of a list of assets and liabilities

13	Balanced scorecard (BSC)	A tool which seeks to include other factors, and not just financial factors, in measuring organisation performance
8	Bill of lading	A document that contains all of the key information in relation to a consignment being transported (referred to as an air waybill in air transport)
10	Buffer stock	Also known as safety stock, it is inventory held in the event that unforeseen issues lead to insufficient inventory being available to meet demand
4	Bullwhip effect	The distortion of orders along the supply chain, where small fluctuations in end customer demand result in amplification of demand upstream
15	Business continuity plan (BCP)	A documented collection of procedures and information that is developed, compiled and maintained in readiness for use in an incident to enable an organisation to continue to deliver its critical products and services
12	Business process reengineering (BPR)	A management technique commonly used to realign business processes with new technology implementations such as ERP
16	Carbon footprint	A term that has come into use to describe the environmental disbenefits associated with economic activities such as the movement of freight
13	Cash flow statement	Illustrates for an organisation where funds have come from and where the funds go to
9	Category managers	Category managers manage a portfolio of contracts or category of spend with similar characteristics that can be grouped and considered in strategic terms in relationship to supplying across different business units or parts of an organisation
8	CFR	Cost and freight
8	CIF	Cost, insurance and freight
8	CIP	Carriage and insurance paid
3	Collaboration	A relationship between supply chain partners developed over a period of time
8	Consignee	Recipient of a consignment
1	Consignment	A shipment of freight which is passed on, usually to some type of logistics service provider, from a manufacturer or other source
8	Consignor	Originator of a consignment
8	Consolidated shipment	Where smaller shipments from various consignees are grouped into one single, full load

15	Container Security Initiative (CSI)	The use of IT to pre-screen high-risk containers prior to their arrival at the destination port
5	Continuous simulation	A type of simulation where state variables change continuously with respect to time and therefore observations are collected continuously
3	Contract manufacturer	First tier suppliers who manufacture products for OEMs
3	Corporate social responsibility (CSR)	A term used to refer to a multitude of activities and issues, and in essence concerns how 'ethical' a company's activities are
14	Cost plus margin	A charging mechanism used by 3PLs which incorporates actual incurred costs plus an agreed margin
13	Cost, volume, profit (CVP) analysis	Identification of likely revenue, cost and profit at different levels of output
8	CPT	Carriage paid to
15	Creeping crises	Systemic supply chain disruptions that arise usually from unexpected sources and with widespread consequences
11	Cross-docking	Transfer of inventory between two vehicles without the inventory going into storage
7	Customs-Trade Partnership Against Terrorism (C-TPAT)	A voluntary government–business initiative to build cooperative relationships that strengthen and improve overall international supply chain and US border security
8	DAT	Delivered at terminal
8	DAP	Delivered at place
8	DDP	Delivered duty paid
4	Decoupling point	The point in the production process at which the base product is customised to become the end product
4	Demand amplification	The amplification of demand upstream in the supply chain, where downstream activities create fluctuations in demand, causing suppliers to overproduce
12	Dependent demand	Products with dependent demand are part of an order for multiple interrelated items
1	Deregulation	Reduction/removal of various government-imposed barriers that hinder competition in markets
6	Derived demand	The fact that people or freight do not travel for the sake of making a journey, they travel for some other reason

3	Design for manufacture (DFM)	Designing products that can be assembled or manufactured cheaply and efficiently
5	Deterministic models	Simulation models that have no random input variables
2	Directional imbalances	Mismatches in the volumes or types of freight moving in opposite directions in a freight market (leading to different freight rates being charged in opposite directions)
5	Discrete event simulation	A type of simulation where state changes occur at discrete points in time as triggered by events; observations are then gathered at these points in time when changes occur
6	Distribution centre (DC)/regional distribution centre (RDC)/national distribution centre (NDC)/consolidation centre (CC)	Terms used to describe different types of warehouses depending upon their particular role and geographic coverage
1	Downstream	Customer end of the supply chain
14	Dropped delivery	A consignment that is not delivered for any of a variety of reasons (e.g. insufficient address details or consignee not present)
5	Dynamic models	Simulation models that include the passage of time and represent systems as they change over time
10	Economic order quantity (EOQ)	That order quantity which seeks to balance two important sets of costs associated with inventory: the costs associated with ordering and receiving freight, and the costs associated with actually holding the freight
12	Electronic data interchange (EDI)	Intercompany, computer-to-computer transmission of business data in a standard format
4	Electronic point of sale (EPOS) data	Electronically available data that capture, usually real time, sales to customers
12	Enterprise resource planning (ERP)	An enterprise-wide planning and control software package, which plans and controls all resources required from receipt of an order to delivery of freight
3	Environmental separation index (ESI)	An index that measures the difference between the working environments of outsourcer and outsourcee companies
2	Ethnocentricity	Thinking only in terms of the home country environment
3	External integration	Integration of business processes across more than one organisation in the supply chain
8	EXW	Ex-works

6	Factory gate pricing (FGP)	The use of an ex-works price for a product plus the organisation and optimisation of transport by the purchaser to the point of delivery
8	FAS	Free alongside ship
8	FCA	Free carrier
6	FCL	Full container load
13	Financial accounting	Using the balance sheet, the profit and loss account and the cash flow statement, largely for reporting to and meeting the requirements of parties outside of the organisation
8	FOB	Free on board
16	Food miles	Term used to refer to the distance over which the various components of a particular food item have to travel before final consumption
2	Foreign direct investment (FDI)	Financial flows from a company in one country to invest (e.g. in a factory) in another country
8	Fourth-party logistics (4PL®)	Invented and trademarked by Accenture in 1996, who originally defined it 'as a supply chain integrator that assembles and manages the resources, capabilities and technology of its own organisation, with those of complementary service providers, to deliver a comprehensive supply chain solution'
6	Freight tonne kilometre (FTK)	Volume of freight measured in tonnes multiplied by the distance the freight travels measured in kilometres
8	Generalised costs	A single, usually monetary, measure combining, generally in linear form, most of the important but disparate costs which form the overall opportunity costs of a trip
2	Geocentricity	Acting completely independent of geography and adopting a global perspective
2	Globalisation	An umbrella term for a complex series of economic, social, technological, cultural and political changes which continue to take place throughout the world
2	Glocalisation	Thinking on a *global*, world market scale, but adapting to *local* wants as appropriate
8	Groupage	The provision of freight transport using consolidated shipments
3	Horizontal collaboration	Collaboration between suppliers who would conventionally be viewed as competitors
3	Humanitarian logistics	Logistics to deliver humanitarian aid
8	Incoterms	Abbreviation for international commercial terms that are now commonly accepted standards in global trade

12	Independent demand	Products with independent demand are those that are ordered independently of any other products
12	Information visibility	The ability to see information at the various points across the supply chain as and when required
6	Intermodal transport	Where freight moves within a loading unit (known as an ITU – intermodal transport unit), this unit may move upon a number of different transport modes, but the freight remains within the unit at all times
3	Internal integration	Integration between business functions within a single organisation
1	Intersectionist view	Suggests that there is overlap between parts of both logistics and SCM, but also that each has parts that are separate and distinct
10	Inventory	Any material that a firm holds in order to satisfy customer demand (and these customers may be internal and/or external to the firm)
10	Inventory turnover	A measure of a firm's performance in inventory management, which compares the annual sales a firm achieves with the amount of average inventory held throughout the year
7	ISPS Code	The ISPS Code is a mandatory security initiative which came into force on 1 July 2004 and applies to all countries that are members of the International Maritime Organisation
4	Just-in-time (JIT) inventory management	A production philosophy and set of techniques which has many components and principles, but at its core is the idea of making do with the minimum possible level of inventory holding. Inventory is thus kept to a minimum and replenished only as it is used
14	Key performance indicators (KPIs)	Specific metrics used to monitor performance on an ongoing basis
12	Knowledge worker	A knowledge worker is defined by Peter Drucker as someone who knows more than anyone else about their job role
9	Kraljik matrix	A simple but powerful tool to understand and quantify relative value and procurement risk issues for any business or organisation
6	LCL	Less than full container load
10	Lead time	The time between placing an order and receiving inventory
4	Leagile supply chain	A supply chain that combines both lean and agile logistics philosophies; sometimes referred to as a 'hybrid strategy'

4	Lean	Elimination of waste and 'doing more with less'
13	Life-cycle costing/ whole-life costing	Determining the costs associated with a product or service over its entire life
1	Logistics	The process of planning, implementing, and controlling procedures for the efficient and effective transportation and storage of goods including services, and related information from the point of origin to the point of consumption for the purpose of conforming to customer requirements
8	Logistics service providers (LSPs)	The various types of companies (hauliers, freight forwarders, etc.) that provide logistics services
4	Make-to-order (MTO)	Producing product only to meet actual customer demand
4	Make-to-stock (MTS)	Producing product which is subsequently put into storage
13	Management accounting	The use of detailed internal information with which to manage the development of the enterprise on a more short-term basis, undertaken to ensure that the long-term financial management of the enterprise is on track
12	Manufacturing resource planning (MRPII)	A planning and control software package, which plans and controls all manufacturing resources required to source, manufacture and deliver products
4	Mass customisation	Customisation into various different finished products of what are often largely mass produced products
1	Material substitution	Replacement of physical product by virtual product
11	Materials handling equipment (MHE)	A term used to describe the various types of equipment for handling inventory
12	Materials requirements planning (MRP)	A planning and control software package, which plans and controls the manufacture and assembly of products
14	Metric	A measurement of an activity; specific important metrics are usually referred to as 'key performance indicators' (KPIs)
2	Multinational companies (MNCs)	Companies with operations in areas beyond their home country
3	Nearshoring	Where companies move their offshored activities to countries closer to their home market as a result of the potential risks and delays associated with moving products from a distant location
8	Non-vessel-owning common carrier (NVOCC)	Refers to companies who consolidate smaller shipments from various consignees into full container loads which the NVOCC then takes responsibility for
2	Offshoring	Offshoring is the transfer of specific processes to lower cost locations in other countries

10	Opportunity cost	In the case of inventory management this is the amount of money the firm would have earned if the money were invested elsewhere other than in inventory
3	Order qualifiers	Those criteria and/or performance expectations that a company must meet for a customer to even consider it as a possible supplier
3	Order winners	One or more criteria that lead to the selection of a particular outsourcee by an outsourcing company
3	Order-losing sensitive qualifiers	Order qualifiers that are more critical than other order qualifiers in terms of the outsourcer's requirements
3	Original equipment manufacturer (OEM)	Companies that produce final, branded products (with the components often produced by CMs)
3	Outsourcing	Outsourcing involves the transfer to a third party of the management and delivery of a process previously performed by the company itself
8	Own-account transportation	Where a company does not use an LSP to transport its freight, but instead transports the freight using its own vehicles
2	Polycentricity	Adopting the host country perspective
16	Port centric	The co-location of various logistics activities at a sea port rather than at inland locations
4	Postponement	The reconfiguration of product and process design so as to allow postponement of final product customisation as far downstream as possible. Other names for this approach are simply 'delayed product configuration', 'delayed product differentiation', and 'late stage customisation'
9	Procurement	Procurement includes sourcing and purchasing and covers all of the activities from identifying potential suppliers through to delivery from supplier to the customer
13	Profit and loss account	An account of the trading activity of the business for a defined period of time
4	Pull philosophy	Materials are only produced and moved when they are required
4	Push philosophy	Materials are produced according to a planned forecast (which may or may not be accurate) and moved to the next stage of the supply chain
2	Regional trade agreements	Agreements between neighbouring countries that allow free trade between those countries
1	Re-labelling view	Contends that logistics has been re-labelled by the more recent term SCM
10	Reorder point	The inventory level at which an order for more inventory is placed

15	Resilience	The ability of a system to return to its original (or desired) state after being disturbed
17	Reverse logistics	The process in which a manufacturer systematically accepts previously shipped products or parts from the point of consumption for possible reuse, remanufacturing, recycling or disposal (with and without energy recovery)
15	Robust	Used in a supply chain context to imply a strong or vigorous capability to for example manage regular fluctuations in demand
10	Safety stock	See buffer stock
13	Sale and lease back	The sale, usually for tax and other reasons, of valuable assets to financial intermediaries from whom the assets are subsequently leased back
13	Sarbanes–Oxley Act 2002 (SOX)	Legislation enacted in the USA to improve the oversight of accounting and reporting practices
18	Service supply chain	The network of suppliers, service providers, consumers and other supporting units that performs the functions of transaction of resources required to produce services; transformation of these resources into supporting and core services; and the delivery of these services to customers
4	Silo	A term used to describe teams or business functions operating in isolation to others
5	Simulation	The process of building a model and experimenting with it in order to develop insight into a system's behaviour based on a specific set of inputs and assist in decision-making processes
11	Socio-technical systems (STS)	A management philosophy that promotes: joint optimisation of the technical and social system; quality of work life; employee participation in system design; and semi-autonomous work groups
5	Static models	Simulation models that do not include the passage of time and represent the system at a particular point of time
5	Stochastic models	Simulation models that have at least one input variable that is random
4	Stock-keeping unit (SKU)	A unique version in terms of size, packaging, etc. of a particular product type
3	Supplier development	Activities led by buyers which seek to assist their suppliers in improving the services or products which their suppliers provide to them
3	Supply base rationalisation	The process of reducing or rationalising the number of suppliers in a supply network, typically to reduce complexity and therefore cost

1	Supply chain	The supply chain is the network of organisations that are involved, through upstream and downstream linkages, in the different processes and activities that produce value in the form of products and services in the hands of the ultimate consumer
3	Supply chain Integration	The alignment and interlinking of business processes
12	Supply chain knowledge management	A term used to describe those knowledge management processes that span a supply chain
14	Tachograph	A device typically fitted to a truck and used to record the speed of the truck, distance travelled and any breaks taken by the driver
8	Third-party logistics companies (3PLs)	LSPs that provide multiple logistics services, often in an integrated fashion
14	Total landed costs	The total costs associated with sourcing and receiving products from another location
4	Toyota Production System (TPS)	A production system designed by Toyota to eliminate waste in seven key areas
1	Traditionalist view	Regards SCM as a subset of logistics, as if it were an add-on to logistics
13	Transaction exposure	Exposure to potential financial loss as a result of trading in another currency
13	Transfer price	The value attributed to goods or services when they are transferred between divisions of the same company
13	Translation exposure	Variation in asset value arising from currency fluctuations
2	Transnational corporations (TNCs)	Companies that trade across many borders, with operations in multiple countries
1	Transport cost sensitivity	The relationship of transport costs to freight value: high sensitivity implies minor changes in transport rates will have a major impact on transport choice decisions
6	Transportation model	A model used to work out a minimum total transport cost solution for the number of units of a single commodity that should be transported from given suppliers to a number of destinations
1	Unionist view	Logistics is seen as part of a wider entity, SCM
1	Upstream	Supplier end of the supply chain
11	Value-adding activities	Supply chain activities that enhance products to increase the customer's perceptions of those products' benefits
3	Vertical collaboration	Collaboration between suppliers and customers along the supply chain

1	Vertical integration	Ownership, or at least control, of upstream suppliers and downstream customers
3	Virtual organisations	Companies which outsource most, if not all, major functions
6	Volumetric charging	Charging for freight based on the dimensions of the consignment
15	Vulnerability	The likelihood of a supply chain or logistics system being exposed to damage, disruption or failure
11	Warehouse management system (WMS)	Software that manages materials and freight movement throughout the warehouse. This may interact directly with automated handling equipment or provide work instructions for operatives

Index

3PLs (third-party logistics) companies 156–8
  'asset unencumbered' 3PLs 164
  competition levels 270
  considerations when selecting 161
  cost models 279–81
  offering 4PL solutions 158–9
  purchasing services of 283
  service innovation 358, 364–5
4PL (fourth party logistics) 158–9
80/20 (Pareto) rule 203
9/11 attacks, security concerns 142, 312

ABC (activity-based costing) 260
ABC analysis, inventory management
    system 203–4
access control measures 150
accounting
  financial 249–54
  management 258–64
activity-based costing (ABC) 260
actuarial approaches 319
Adams, J. 316
Adidas 182–3
advanced shipment notification (ASN) 276, 285
AEOs (authorised economic operators) 149
aerospace industry
  supplier evaluation 300–3
  supply chain redesign 53–5
AG Barr 215–16
aggregated procurement 52–3, 170–1
agile supply chains 66–9
  and RFID technology 237–41
AGVs (automated guided vehicles) 214
AIDC (automatic identification and data
    capture) 232
air transport sector
  airline catering case study 295–8
  freight documentation 159
  reducing environmental footprint 334–5
  security issues 149, 151
air trucking 162
airport security 149, 151
airwaybills (AWBs) 159, 336
A.P. Moller-Maersk 158, 332, 333
Apple 359–60
Asia, offshoring/outsourcing to 37–8
ASN (advanced shipment
    notification) 276, 285
'asset unencumbered' 3PLs 164
assets 251–2, 294
Australia
  contaminants in export grain 386–91
  liquor DCs 223
  recycling case study 351–2
Authorised Economic Operators
    (AEOs) 149
automated guided vehicles (AGVs) 214
automatic identification and data capture
    (AIDC) 232
  see also radio frequency identification
automation
  and changing job roles 224–5
  John Lewis case study 284–8
  materials handling 216–17
  order picking 220–1
  and RFID technology 218, 237–41
  storage & retrieval systems 219
  and STS principles 222
  see also information technology
automotive industry
  collaborative planning case
    study 112–20
  external integration 48
  JIT inventory system 206
  lean production 63–5
  mass customisation 67–8

backshoring 42
balance sheet 250, 251
balanced scorecard (BSC) 262–3, 275
barcodes 150
   benefits & limitations 242
   biometric ID cards 150–1
   global standards for 242–3
   and WMS data capture 218
base product 67, 71
batch picking 220
BCM (business continuity
      management) 313–14
BCP see business continuity plans
benchmarking 26–7, 271–2
bill of lading 159
bill of material (BoM) 179, 233, 296–7
biometrics 150–1
Booz Allen Hamilton 143
borrowing 257–8
BPR (business process
      reengineering) 230, 236
buffer stock 198
building to order, Dell 96–7
'bullwhip effect' 75, 235–6
Burbidge effect 75
business continuity plans (BCP) 313–14
   and the millennium bug 310–11
   mitigating disruptions to nodes/links 319
business-humanitarian partnerships 103–4
business process reengineering
      (BPR) 230, 236
business transformations 368–9
   management skills for 372–3
Button, K. 163
buyer motivation 167–8
buyers, role of 173
BX Shoes 56–7

C-TPAT (customs-trade partnership against
      terrorism) 147, 312
carbon footprint 328–9
cargo rejections, case study 386–92
carmoisine contamination in cargo 387–9
cash flow 253
cash flow statement 250
category managers 175–6
centralisation of inventory 199–200
child labour 182
China 25, 32, 37, 178, 179, 356
   collaborative planning case study 112–20

Christopher, M. 10–11, 12, 66, 69, 71,
      73–4
   key business transformations 368–9,
      372–3
collaboration 49–51
   Mediaware 108–9
   methods of 51–3
collaborative planning, forecasting and
      replenishment (CPFR) 234–5
   China auto parts case study 112–20
combined logistics strategies 69–72
company structure, changes in 7–8
confidence interval estimation 87–8
consignee 153
consignments 7–8
consignors 153
consolidated shipment 155
consolidation centres (CCs) 127
Container Security Initiative (CSI) 147–8, 312
container shipping 332–3
containerisation 6
containers 20–2
continuous simulation 80
contract manufacturers 40
   increased reliance on 269
coordination
   humanitarian supply chains 100–1
   and reverse logistics 350
   see also collaboration
corporate governance 249–50, 313
corporate scandals 250, 313
corporate social responsibility (CSR) 44, 370
cost accounting 258–62
cost-benefit analysis 139–40
   reverse logistics 349–50
cost plus margin 280
cost, volume, profit (CVP) analysis 262
costs 371
   3PL cost models 279–81
   benchmarking 271–2
   of container shipping 332, 333
   generalised costs 162, 163
   indirect 259–60
   inventory-related 192–5, 201–2
   procurement 177–8
   total landed costs 278–9
   transportation 126, 134–6
   versus price 177, 179–80
counterfeit medicines 378–84
couriers 155, 157–8, 290–4

CPFR (collaborative planning, forecasting and
    replenishment) 234–5
creeping crises 311–12, 323, 324
cross docking 214–15
currency exposure 255–6
current ratio 294
customisation 66–9, 96–7
customs-trade partnership against terrorism
    (C-TPAT) 147, 312
CVP (cost, volume, profit) analysis 262
cycle counting, inventory 277

data, global standards for 241–3
DCs (distribution centres) 127
debt 257–8, 294
decoupling point 67, 71
delayed product differentiation 200
Dell 95–7, 253–4
demand amplification 75
Demchak, C. 310
Deming, W.E. 63
dependent demand 232–3
depreciation of assets 251–2
deregulation of transport 5–6
derived demand 137
design for manufacture (DFM) 40, 370
design process, role of supply chains 370,
    393–6
detection systems, security 151
deterministic models 80
Deutsche Post World Net 335–6
DHL 157–8, 290–4
digital printing technology 107–11
directional imbalances, freight 31–2
disaster relief see humanitarian logistics
discrete event simulation (DES) 80, 89–91
distribution centres (DCs) 127
    Australia liquor DC 223
    John Lewis case study 284–8
    see also warehousing
downstream 10–11
dropped deliveries 268
Drucker, P. 7
dummy plant/DC 136
duty 279
dynamic models 80

e-Business 230, 231–2
e-seals, containers 22
e-waste (electronic waste)

growth of 339–40
    recycling of 351–2
    strategic cost/benefit 349–50
EADS case study 300–3
earnings per share (EPS) 292–3
'easyJet ecoJet' 335
eAuctions 176
economic growth, link to transport
    growth 331
economic order quantity model 192–5
EDI (electronic data interchange) 232
efficiency
    sustainability issues 333–6
    transport infrastructure 138–9
    transport services 131–2
electronic data capture 216, 218, 232, 242
electronic data interchange (EDI) 232
electronic logistics market-places (ELMs) 335
electronic point of sale (EPOS) 70
electronic waste (e-waste) 339–40, 351–2
emergency supply chains 99–105
Emma Maersk (container vessel) 332
employee motivation 223–4, 271
empowerment of employees 270–1
Enron collapse 250, 313
enterprise resource planning (ERP)
    systems 176, 232–3
environmental issues see sustainability issues
environmental separation index (ESI) 44–5
EPOS (electronic point of sale) 70
ERP (enterprise resource planning) 232–3
ESI (environmental separation index) 44–5
ethical issues 182
    corporate social responsibility
        (CSR) 44, 370
    ethical sourcing 181–2
ethnocentricity 29
expertise of professionals 360, 361
exports 24–5
    contamination in 386–9
    and import refusals 389–91
external integration 48
extraterrestrial supply chains 397–8

factory gate pricing (FGP) 127–31
failed deliveries 268
fake medicines 378–84
FCL (full container loads) 132
FedEx 6, 157
FGP (factory gate pricing) 127–31

financial accounting 249–54
financial measures 278–81
financial scandals 250, 313
Fisher, M. 69
FloraHolland 229–30, 240–1, 245
food miles 183, 329
foot and mouth disease 311–12
Ford 39, 62–3
forecasting 234–5, 346
foreign direct investment (FDI) flows 29
Forrester effect 75
Forrester, J. 4, 75, 312
fourth party logistics (4PL) 158–9
freight
    containerisation 6, 20–2, 332
    costing 278–9
    cross docking of 214–15
    deregulation of transport 5–6
    directional imbalances 31–2
    equipment for handling 216–17
    growth in, and economic growth 331
    logistics service providers 153–62
    picking solutions 220–1
    reducing transport cost sensitivity of 4–5
    RFID technology 237–42
    security measures 312
    storage 218–20
    terminology 7–8
    transport of 123–32
    versus services 359
freight forwarders 154–5
freight tonne kilometres (FTKs) 127
fuel protests 311–12
full container loads (FCL) 132
funds, flow of 254

game theory 49–50
gaming 75
Gate Gourmet, case study 295–8
Gattorna, J. 69, 73, 204–5, 368–9, 374
gearing 257, 294
generalised costs 162, 163
geocentricity 29
Global Data Synchronisation Network
    (GDSN) 243
global logistics performance index
    (LPI) 26
global perspective 15
globalisation 27–31
    impact on manufacturing 37–8

glocalisation 28
good distribution practice (GDP) 379–81
good manufacturing practice (GMP) 379, 380
goods-to-picker solutions 221
green products, customer demand for 349
'green revolution' 328–31
greenhouse gas (GHG) emissions 329
groupage 155
GS1, global standards organisation 242–3

hauliers 154, 331
healthcare sector 14
    inefficiency of waiting 64
    inventory management 360–1
    triage 14–15
hierarchy of needs, freight purchasing 162–3
hierarchy of recovery options 342–3
holding costs, inventory 193
holistic approaches, risk management 317–18
holistic view of logistics and SCM
    strategy 61
horizontal collaboration 50, 51, 52
Houlihan effect 75
hub and spoke model 157, 332–3
humanitarian logistics 51, 52, 99–100
    business-humanitarian partnerships 103–4
    importance of coordination in 100–1
    problems encountered in practice 102–3
    reducing uncertainty in 101
    role of human resources in 102
hybrid strategy 71

IBM 357
IKEA 14, 333
import refusals case study 386–92
incoterms 159, 160
independent demand 232
India 37, 38, 40, 56–7, 178
indirect costs 259–60
information, role of 227–8
information sharing 48, 49, 114–16,
    176, 360
information technology
    applications 231–7
    and data reporting 270
    and data sourcing 273
    disaster recovery 314
    enabling supply chain integration 47–8
    Gate Gourmet case study 295–8
    Mediaware case study 107–11

millennium bug 310–11
procurement systems 176–7
RFID technologies 237–41, 242, 320
standards for data 241–3
and transport security 150–1
information transfer 114–16
information visibility 228–9
barriers to gaining 230–1
infrastructure dependencies 319–20
intangible assets 252
integration
and reverse logistics 350
of supply chains 47–8
integrators 155
intermodal transport 124
internal integration 48
international commercial terms
(incoterms) 159, 160
International Maritime Organisation (IMO),
security initiative 144–7
International Ship and Port Facility Security
(ISPS) Code 144–7
International Standards Organisation
(ISO) 20
ISO 17712, container seals 22
ISO 28000, supply chain security 149–50
international trade
directional imbalances 31–2
financial aspects 255–7
and globalisation 27–31
growth in 24–5, 37–8
logistics performance measurement 26–7
'international' vs. 'global' 15
intersectionist view 13
in-transit inventory 202
inventory 189–90
centralisation of 199–200
control systems 196–8
costs associated with 192–5, 201–2
flow types 204–5
metrics 277–8
reasons for holding 191–2
inventory management 189–92
ABC analysis tool 203–4
economic order quantity model 192–5
in hospitals 360–1
inventory control systems 196–8
inventory flow types 204–5
and risk management 318–19
in the supply chain 198–202

inventory reduction 6–7
by centralisation 200
delayed product differentiation 200
just-in-time (JIT) system 206
and part commonality 200–1
by pooling 205
principles of 205–6
inventory turn/turnover 118–19, 190–1
investor ratios 292–3
iPhone, Apple 359–60
ISO 28000, supply chain security 149–50
ISPS Code, transport security 144–7
Italian outsourcee case study 56–7

Japan
import refusal 386–9, 391
keiretsu supply chain structure 48
lean production 63–5
job design 222–5
John Lewis Partnership case study 284–9
Jones, D. 65
just-in-time (JIT) inventory system 63, 206,
334

keiretsu supply chain structure 48
key performance indicators (KPIs) 268–9
categories of 274–5
data sources for 273–4
designing 272–3
driving forces behind 269–71
financial measures 278–81
selection of best 271–2
warehouse-related 275–8
'knowable unknowns' 310, 311, 313
knowledge management 243–4
expertise of professionals 360, 361
knowledge areas for SCM 374
knowledge workers 243
'known unknowns' 310
Kraljik matrix 171–2
Kuehne + Nagel, logistics company 158

landed costs 278–9
landfill usage cost 341
layout of warehouses 213–16
LCL (less than full container load) 132
lead time, definition 193
lead time reduction 206
leagile supply chain 71
lean consumption 65

lean production and logistics 63–5
  combining with agile 69–71
legislation
  environmental 215, 338, 341, 348
  financial accounting 250, 313
  pharmaceutical distribution 384
  reverse logistics 340–1, 348
  transport security 142
Lehman Brothers, collapse of 314
less than full container loads (LCL) 132
Levitt, T. 28
liabilities 251, 252
lifecycle costing 261
limited liability 255
liner shipping connectivity index (LSCI) 26–7
liquidity 294
liquor DC, Australia 223
livestock diseases, impact of 311, 312
loans 257
local sourcing 330, 337
logistics 8–10
  applications of 13–15
  evolution of 4–8
  role in national economies 8
  versus SCM 12–13
  see also reverse logistics
logistics service providers (LSPs) 154–6
  fourth party logistics (4PL) 158–9
  responsibilities of carriers 159
  selection of 159–63
  see also 3PLs
long range acoustic device (LRAD) 144
low-cost country sourcing 178–9

macro-environment 322–3
make-to-order (MTO) 64
make-to-stock (MTS) 64
management accounting 258
  activity-based costing 260–2
  costing 259–60
  using non-financial information 262–4
management information systems 216, 232–7
management ratios 293–4
management skills 372–4, 376
manufacturing
  Dell's strategy 95–7
  globalisation of 37–8
  lean production 63–5
  mass customisation 66–9
  mass production 62–3
  remanufacturing 342, 345–8

traditional vs. recoverable 346
  vs. service supply chains 358–61
manufacturing resource planning (MRPII) 233
maritime transport 6, 127
  piracy as threat to 143–4
  security initiatives 144–8
Marks & Spencer 238, 239
mass customisation 66–9, 95–7
material substitution 5
materials handling equipment (MHE) 216–17,
    223, 280
materials (inventory) 189–90
materials requirements planning
    (MRP) 231, 233
Mattel 179
McKinnon, A. 331
McLean, M. 6, 20
measurement see performance measurement
Mediaware case study 107–11
medical devices case study 98
medical triage 14–15
medicines, counterfeit 378–84
metrics see performance measurement
MHE (materials handling equipment) 216–17,
    223, 280
Microsoft 109–10
military logistics 9, 310
millennium bug 310–11
modelling techniques 372
Moller-Maersk Group 158, 332–3
motivation
  of buyers and sellers 167–8
  employee 223–4, 271
  for reverse logistics 339–41
MRP (materials requirements planning) 231,
    233
MRPII (manufacturing resource planning) 233
multinational companies (MNCs) 29, 37
  and procurement 169–70

national distribution centres (NDCs) 127
national emergency planning and creeping
    crises 311–12
natural disasters 323
  and humanitarian supply chains 99–105
NDCs (national distribution centres) 127
nearshoring 42
networks 12
  and factory gate pricing 129–31
  Global Data Synchronisation Network
    (GDSN) 243

hub and spoke 157, 332–3
inter-organisational 320–1
and procurement 185
reverse logistics 343–5, 348
of warehouses 211
newspaper vendor simulation problem 84–9
Nigeria, public procurement
    regulations 168–9
non-financial information 262–4
non-vessel-owning common carrier
    (NVOCC) 155

objective risk 315–17
OEM (original equipment manufacturer) 40
offshoring 31, 37–8, 41–2
operational risk 313, 314
opportunity cost 163, 193
optimisation techniques 372
order batching 75
order-losing sensitive qualifiers 44
order picking 220–1, 286–7
order qualifiers 39, 44
order winners 39, 45
ordinary shares 255
original equipment manufacturers (OEMs) 40
  China case study 112–20
outsourcing 38–41, 158, 269
    evaluating oursourcees 44–5
    failures in 42–3
    of inventory management 235
    legislation 313
    relationships 45–7
    and risk management 321
    to Asia 37–8, 56–7
    of transportation 154
    see also 3PLs
overheads 259–60
own account transportation 154

packaging solutions 107–11
pallet storage 218–19
Pareto rule 203
Pareto, V. 203
part commonality 200–1
'Penn Purchasing Services', top-down
    procurement approach 180–1
perceived risk 315–17
performance measurement 266–7
  benchmarking costs 271–2
  commonly used metrics 274–5
  contemporary 268–9

driving forces for 269–71
inventory accuracy 277–8
key performance indicators 272–3
logistics 26–7
logistics costs 278–81
optimum number of metrics 272
for procurement 179–81
reverse logistics 350–2
selecting best measures 271
sources of data 274–5
traditional 267–8
warehouse related 275–6
periodic inventory control system 196–8
pharmaceutical supply chains 378–84
picking solutions 220–1
pipeline transport 126
piracy 143–4
POD (print on demand) 107–11
polycentricity 29
port centric logistics 334
Port Facility Security Assessment
    (PFSA) 146
port security 144–8, 151
portfolios of spend, managing 171–3
postponement 66–7, 70, 71, 96, 200, 212
PPV (purchase price variance) 179–80
price/pricing 5, 177
  factor gate pricing 127–31
  price variation 75
  transactional pricing 280–1
  transfer pricing 256–7
principle of postponement 66–7, 96
print on demand (POD) technology 107–11
prisoner's dilemma, game theory 49
probability 315–16
process engineering 318–19
procurement 166–88
  costs 192
  ethical sourcing 181–2
  and markets 169–71
  performance 179–81
  private vs. public sector 168–9
  process/lifecycle 173–9
  risk management 171–3
  role of the buyer 173
  and supply chain management 183–4
  sustainability 182–3
product costing 259–60
product design
  involvement of supply chains 393–6
  synchronising with supply chain design 370

productivity improvements 6
profit and loss account 250
pull philosophy 63, 65
purchase price variance (PPV) 179–80
push philosophy 63, 65, 233
pushback racking 218–19
put-away metrics 276

Quinn, F. 73, 374

radio frequency identification (RFID) 150,
    232, 237–40
  benefits & limitations 242
  biometric security systems 150–1
  FloraHolland case study 240–1
  military consignments 320
rail transport 126
  cost calculations 201–2
random number generation 82–3
random variate generation 83–4
rationing 75
ratios 258
  investor 292–3
  management 293–4
RDCs (regional distribution centres) 127
re-labelling view 13
receiving metrics, warehousing 275–6
recovery options 341–5
recycling 342–5
regional distribution centres (RDCs) 127
regional trade agreements 24
regulations
  environmental 342, 348
  financial 313
  procurement 168–9
  see also legislation
relationship strategies 184, 185
remanufacturing 342
  characteristics of 345–8
reorder point (ROP) 193
  inventory control system 196
replications, simulation 91–2
resilience 309
  proactive measures to improve 311
resource reduction 342–3
resource utilisation, reverse logistics 350
resources, flow of 11
return on equity 293
reuse 341, 343, 344, 345
reverse logistics 215, 338–9

motivations for 339–41
performance measures 350–2
recovery options 341–5
remanufacturing 345–8
success factors 248–50
RFID see radio frequency identification
risk 255, 308
  objective and perceived 315–17
risk management 314, 319
  and procurement 171–3
  shortcomings of 314–17
  and wicked problems 317–23
Rittel, H.W.J. 317–18
road transport 331
  improving efficiency of 334
  performance measures 267–8
robust SCM 73, 309
Roos, D. 65
Rumsfeld, D. 310

safety stock 193, 198
sale and lease back 252
Sarbanes-Oxley Act 2002 (SOX) 250, 313
Scala software system 296–7
scale, role of 332–3
Seabourn Spirit (cruise ship) 144
security
  post 9/11 attacks 312
  transport 142–51
Semi-Automated National Distribution Centre
    (SANDC) 285, 288
service, definition of 357
service innovation 357–8, 364–5
service level agreements (SLAs) 39, 281
service science 357–8
service sector 355–8
  lean thinking applied to 65
  logistics applied to 14–15
  transition to service economies 355–7
service supply chains 355
  models 362–3
  versus manufacturing 358–61
services
  characteristics of 359
  costing of 259
shares 254–5
shipping, meaning of 155
shipping sector
  containers 6, 20–2, 332
  costs 332, 333

directional imbalances 31–2
import refusals 386–92
Moller-Maersk Group 158, 332–3
performance measures 26–7
piracy problem 143–4
security initiatives 144–8
silos 61, 73
simulation 78–9
    discrete event 89–91
    methodology 82–9
    models 79–81
    process 81–2
    replications 91–2
    supply chain management 92
Singapore 28
Sirius Star (hijack of) 144
SLAs (service level agreements) 39, 281
social networking 185
socio-technical systems (STS) theory 222
sourcing strategies 170–1
    ethical sourcing 181–2
    and food miles 183
    local sourcing 330, 337
    low-cost country sourcing 178–9
SOX (Sarbanes-Oxley Act 2002) 250, 313
space industry 397–8
spreadsheets, simulation models 81,
        88–9
square root rule 200
standard cost 179
standard deviation 87
standard normal distribution 94
standardisation 66–7, 96–7
standards
    for data 241–3
    financial reporting 250
    for security 149–50
static models 80
stochastic models 80
stock classification systems 203–4
stock keeping units (SKUs) 68
storage
    John Lewis warehouse 286
    non-pallet storage 219–20
    pallet storage 218–19
    and picking 221
strategies 59–62
    'bullwhip effect' 75
    combining lean and agile 69–72
    guidelines for managers 72–4

lean production 63–5
    manufacturing 62–3
    mass customisation 66–9
    sourcing 170–1
Student t table 94
substandard medicines 382–4
supplier development 39, 52–3, 54
supplier evaluation systems 300–3
supplier motivation 167–8
suppliers
    tier-one suppliers, case study 112–20
supply base rationalisation 52
supply chain collaboration 49–55
supply chain integration 47–8
supply chain inventory
        management 198–202
supply chain knowledge management 243
supply chain management (SCM) 10–12
    7 principles of 72
    applications of 13–15
    evolution of 4–8
    versus logistics 12–13
supply chain planning *see* strategies
supply chain relationships 36–7
    collaboration 49–55
    integration 47–8
    and international trade 37–8
    offshoring 41–2
    see also outsourcing
SupplyAero Holdings Ltd 53–5
sustainability issues 327
    efficiency solutions 333–6
    green issues 328–9
    in procurement activity 173, 182–3
    and reverse logistics 349
    role of scale 332–3
    and supply chain redesign 329–31

'T-shaped' skills profile, logistics
        managers 373
tachographs 267–8
take-back programmes 340–1
Tang, C. 73, 309
target costing 261
taxation 256–7
TechCo case study 394–6
technology
    advances in medical 14
    improving productivity 6
    socio-technical systems theory 222

technology (*continued*)
   training, importance of 320
   transport security 150–1
   see also information technology
terrorism, security concerns 142,
   147, 312
Texas Pacific Group (TPG) 322
third party logistics (3PL) companies
   see 3PLs
tiers of suppliers 40
   tier-one suppliers, case study 112–20
TNT-WFP partnership 104
total cost of outsourcing 45
total landed costs 278–9
Toyota Production System
   (TPS) 63–5
traceability technologies 237–41
trade *see* international trade
traditionalist view 13
training, importance of 320
transaction exposure 256
transactional pricing 280–1
transfer price 256–7
transit inventory 201–2
translation exposure 256
transnational corporations
   (TNCs) 29–31
transport 123–4
   deregulation of 5–6
   different modes of 124–7
   efficiency of 131–2, 137–40
   and factory gate pricing (FGP) 127–31
   growth of, link to economic
      growth 331
   infrastructure planning 137–40
   lean thinking 64
   security initiatives 144–50
transport cost sensitivity 5
transportation model 129,
   134–6, 372
triage 14–15
turnover of capital employed 293–4

uncertainty 310
   in a remanufacturing environment 347
   in humanitarian supply chains 101
   reason for inventory 191
   use of simulation to model 83, 92
   versus risk 315

unionist view 13
unit-based costing 279
University of Pennsylvannia Purchasing
   Services 180–1
'unknowable unknowns' 310, 312
upstream 10–11

value for money (VfM) 137, 177–8
value-added recovery 342, 343,
   344–5
value-added services 356, 357
value-adding activities, warehouses 212
value chain costing 261
value, managing 171–3
variation
   in demand 67, 199–200
   price 75
   reduction of 206
   and safety stock 198
vendor managed inventory
   (VMI) 235–6
vertical collaboration 50, 51
vertical integration 7
virtual organisations 39
VMI (vendor managed inventory) 235–6
volumetric charging 124
Volvo Trucks India 38
vulnerability of supply chains 308–9

Wal-Mart 8
warehouse management systems (WMS) 216,
   217, 236–7
   data capture and transmission
      technologies 218
   John Lewis case study 287–8
   metrics relating to 275–6
warehousing 210–12
   layout and design 213–16
   metrics 275–6
   workforce issues 222–5
   see also warehouse management systems
waste
   disposal costs 341
   increase in electronic 339–40
   legislation 340–1
   recycling of 342–5
Waste Electrical and Electronic Equipment
   (WEEE) Directive 215, 340
waterways 126

wave picking 220
Webber, M.M. 317–18
WFP-TNT partnership 104
whole life costing 261
whole lifecycle costs, procurement 177–8
wicked problems 317–18
    simple framework for 318–23
Womack, D. 65
work organisation 222–5
World Bank
    logistics performance tool 26
    public transport infrastructure 137–40
World Health Organisation (WHO) 380–1

Xerox 108

Y2K, millennium bug 310–11

Zara 70, 71–2
zone picking 220